Fundamentals of Site Remediation

For Metal and Hydrocarbon-Contaminated Soils

Second Edition

John Pichtel

Government Institutes
An imprint of
The Scarecrow Press, Inc.
Lanham, Maryland • Toronto • Plymouth, UK
2007

**Government
Institutes**

Published in the United States of America
by Government Institutes, an imprint of The Scarecrow Press, Inc.
A wholly owned subsidiary of
The Rowman & Littlefield Publishing Group, Inc.
4501 Forbes Boulevard, Suite 200
Lanham, Maryland 20706
http://www.govinstpress.com/

Estover Road
Plymouth PL6 7PY
United Kingdom

British Library Cataloguing in Publication Information Available

Library of Congress Cataloging-in-Publication Data
Pichtel, John, 1957–
  Fundamentals of site remediation for metal and hydrocarbon-contaminated
soils / John Pichtel. — 2nd ed.
    p. cm.
  Includes bibliographical references and index.
  ISBN-13: 978-0-86587-154-0 (pbk. : alk. paper)
  ISBN-10: 0-86587-154-X (pbk. : alk. paper)
  1. Hazardous waste site remediation. 2. Metals—Environmental aspects.
  3. Hydrocarbons—Environmental aspects. I. Title.
  TD1052.P53 2007
  628.5'5—dc22   2007005099

∞™ The paper used in this publication meets the minimum requirements of
American National Standard for Information Sciences—Permanence of Paper
for Printed Library Materials, ANSI/NISO Z39.48-1992.
Manufactured in the United States of America.

DEDICATION

To my parents:

Rose Gonzalez
Ed Gonzalez
Stan Pichtel

Contents

Figure and Table Titles

FIGURES

TABLES

Acknowledgments

Many individuals have contributed in various ways to bringing this work to fruition.

Thanks to Holly Chaille, Eamonn Ertel, Chris Higginbotham, Lucas Marshall, Sarah Matheny, and Connie Ronald for compiling historical data relating to contamination episodes.

Sincere gratitude is expressed to Jason Higgs and Valerie Morris for their expert preparation of the figures, and to Joann Woy for her editing of the manuscript.

Special thanks to all those who provided their support during the formulation of this work: my parents Rose Gonzalez, Stan Pichtel, and Ed Gonzalez; my wife Theresa, my children Yozef and Leah; and my respected colleague Joseph Timko.

Many thanks to Werner Erhard, who assisted me in discovering so many avenues for growth.

Finally, much gratitude to my students: your eagerness to question, to argue, and ultimately to discover provided me with the motivation to pursue this project.

Preface

Since earliest recorded times, humans have manipulated their surroundings in order to extract and exploit resources. In the modern era, resource extraction, processing, and utilization have soared. There has been a concurrent production of wastes, many of which are now classified as hazardous. As an unanticipated side effect of industrial development, nations are experiencing events of soil, groundwater, and surface water contamination on an unprecedented scale; many of these contaminants pose an immediate threat to public health and the environment.

In the United States, the urgency of addressing the land contamination issue is made evident in recent legislation. For example, Section 121(b) of the Comprehensive Environment Response, Compensation, and Liability Act (CERCLA) mandates the U.S. Environmental Protection Agency (EPA) to encourage the use of remedies for site cleanup that "utilize permanent solutions and alternative technologies or resource recovery technologies to the maximum extent practicable" and to encourage the use of remedial actions in which treatment "permanently and significantly reduces the volume, toxicity, or mobility of hazardous substances, pollutants and contaminants as a principal element." Additionally, the EPA is directed to "avoid off-site transport and disposal of untreated hazardous substances or contaminated materials when practicable treatment technologies exist." Emphasis is placed on treatment and destruction of the contaminants affecting a site; gone are the days when contaminated soils or other media are simply abandoned, covered over, or excavated and transferred to a new location.

Unfortunately, there is no standard set of "cookbook" instructions that can be applied toward the remediation of a contaminated site, because each situation is unique and, typically, rather complex. Each site possesses its own distinct range of soil, geologic, and groundwater conditions, which will influence the migration behavior of a contaminant plume. Additionally, each contamination situation has experienced unique release characteristics (for example, a large single spill versus deliberate dumping over many years) and composition of contaminants, which will vary in terms of toxicity, volatility, mobility, and so on. Based on these considerations, a substantial body of data is required in order to fully understand contaminant behavior, and how to remove the contaminant plume efficiently while minimizing damage to the site and its environs.

Few references in environmental contamination and site restoration provide a satisfactory discussion of the underlying chemical processes inherent during a contamination episode; likewise, chemical processes during the remedial phase of activities are often incomplete. This book is intended to serve as an introductory manual for environmental site restoration practices as mandated by CERCLA and related statutes, with emphasis on basic environmental chemistry, soil science, microbiology, and plant science. Adequate knowledge of chemistry is an essential component of designing a cleanup activity, and a certain degree of proficiency is required in order to appreciate the reactions of contaminant(s) in soil and water, and to formulate appropriate solutions for an environmental contamination episode.

The first portion of this book provides a background for several salient aspects of site remediation, that is, chemical properties of inorganic and organic environmental contaminants; properties of soils as relates to remediation; and basics of environmental site assessments. The second portion presents field remediation technologies in detail. Included are theory of operation, practical (i.e., field) considerations, and possible environmental impacts and other consequences of use of these technologies. Most of the technologies covered in this book are those commonly employed in the remediation of NPL ("Superfund"), brownfield, and underground storage tank–affected sites. New and promising technologies are continually becoming available; hence, there is an effort to present several in this book. This project is not intended to serve as an engineering manual; the reader is referred to several excellent books already available on this subject.

CHAPTER 1

How Did We Get Here? A Brief History

If we do not change our direction, we are likely to end up where we are headed.

—Chinese proverb

1.1 INTRODUCTION

A pollutant can be defined as any chemical or physical change to soil, water, or air that adversely affects biota and/or materials. When we use such a definition, it follows that pollutants have been released to the biosphere since the Earth's earliest days. Volcanic eruptions have released tons of mercury, hydrogen sulfide, hydrocarbons, and siliceous ash; forest fires have pumped carbon monoxide and particulate matter to the atmosphere; and soil and pollen have been widely dispersed.

As humans began to exercise dominion over the earth, they also began to have an impact on local, regional, and global ecosystems. However, the impact has been relatively insignificant for most of hominids' time on the planet. For example, early *Homo sapiens* are believed to be responsible for the extinction of several species of large mammals, and for local damage to ecosystems (e.g., by deliberately setting large forest fires to drive out game animals). Much later, when the Romans discovered the thermally insulating properties of asbestos, this mineral was mined and used extensively. Likewise, the Romans mined and smelted thousands of tons of lead for uses ranging from military supplies to linings for wine bottles. It has been suggested that lead exposure may have contributed to the fall of the Roman Empire.

Figure 1.1.   *Illustration of carding, drawing, and roving that appeared in* History of Cotton Manufacture, *Edward Baine, 1835*

Not until the Industrial Revolution of the eighteenth century, however, were humans responsible for environmental impacts on a massive scale. Machine labor replaced human labor (Fig. 1.1) and populations surged to urban centers. Global population began its exponential climb (to which there is as yet no leveling off). The costs of this revolution included air and water pollution, respiratory and other ailments, dehumanization, and so on.

By World War I, chemical manufacture had become sophisticated and efficient. Some of the earliest polymers entered the world. Chemical weapons such as chlorine and phosgene gas were used on a large scale in the trenches of Belgium and France. By World War II, plastics were used extensively in war (for example, in bomber nose cones and parachutes) and somewhat less at home. Chlorinated organic pesticides began to re-place the conventional inorganic pesticides. The insecticide DDT, dubbed by Winston Churchill the "atom bomb of the insect world," saved millions of lives by controlling disease-carrying body lice and mosquitoes.

For the first half of the twentieth century, contaminants released to soil, water and air caused isolated damage, or else were absorbed into the bios-phere (at least temporarily). As the manufacture and use of anthropogenic chemicals increased, however, so did exposure, the doses received, and ultimately, damage to public health and the environment.

Release of mercury into Japan's Minamata Bay and the Agano River in the 1950s and 1960s resulted in the occurrence of a severe and debilitat-ing disease that came to be known as Minamata disease. Nervous system dysfunction including loss of motor functions and hearing was common and severe. Infants born to exposed mothers were found to be severely palsied, with mental retardation. The source of the mercury was found to be indiscriminate waste dumping by local industry.

During the postwar boom and into the 1960s, technology and manufacturing soared, with a concurrent awakening of American environmental consciousness. Photochemical smog, an artifact of industrialization and comfortable lifestyles (e.g., massive, inefficient automobiles possessing little or no pollution control) became a regular summer occurrence in many cities (Fig. 1.2). Emissions from homes heated by coal, fuel oil, or wood also contributed to local air pollution. Household wastes were incinerated in urban apartment units with little or no air pollution control. A study of sediments in Central Park Lake, New York City, correlated the accumulation of lead, tin, and zinc with the use of incinerators (Chillrud et al. 1999). Congress passed the Clean Air Act (CAA) in 1963 to regulate the production of air pollutants and to set emissions standards. The CAA has since evolved from a set of principles designed to guide states in controlling sources of air pollution (the 1967 Air Quality Act), to a set of detailed control requirements (the 1970, 1977, and 1990 amendments to the CAA) that the federal government implements and the states administer. The CAA of 1970 set specific goals for emission reductions and ambient air quality improvement. National ambient air quality standards (NAAQS), considered the centerpiece of the act, were established primarily to protect public health and secondarily to protect materials and vegetation (Phillips and Lokey 1995). The NAAQS was established for six pollutants: sulfur dioxide, nitrogen oxides, particulate matter, carbon monoxide, ozone, and lead.

Figure 1.2.   *Smog event over urban skyline*
U.S. Environmental Protection Agency.

By the late 1960s to early 1970s, concerns were heightened with regard to the management of both domestic and toxic chemical wastes. The New York City waste haulers' strikes made city dwellers painfully aware of the direct, acute hazards associated with ordinary household solid waste as mountains of refuse quickly grew on city sidewalks. Many coastal cities had disposed of municipal solid wastes and sewage sludges by dumping from barges on or beyond the continental shelf. In addition, the dumping of industrial wastes was carried out legally until 1970. Hazardous and radioactive materials were routinely dumped off the coasts of Massachusetts, Delaware, Maryland, and California (Hess 1993).

With the first Earth Day (1970) came a collective call for more responsible environmental management. Recycling programs became popular in many communities. President Nixon signed the National Environmental Policy Act (NEPA) into law, paving the way for the establishment of the U.S. Environmental Protection Agency (EPA).

The Clean Water Act has its origins in the Federal Water Pollution Control Act (FWPCA), enacted by Congress in 1972. This statute required the EPA to establish nationwide effluent standards on an industry-by-industry basis. The act established the National Pollutant Discharge Elimination System (NPDES) permit program, which was administered by individual states after federal authorization. The EPA, in carrying out the 1972 act, focused on the control of conventional pollutants such as biological oxygen demand and suspended solids, rather than toxic pollutants. The FWPCA developed a uniform nationwide approach for the protection of the nation's surface water by eliminating discharges of pollutants (toxic, chemical, physical, and thermal) into navigable waters. The act included a permit program, national effluent limitations, water quality standards, special provisions for oil and toxic substance spills, and grant programs for the construction of publicly owned treatment works (Paschal 1995). This framework remains in effect.

The Safe Drinking Water Act (SDWA), enacted in 1974, authorized the EPA to regulate contaminants in public drinking water systems. The act greatly expanded federal authority over drinking water quality. The EPA was given the responsibility of setting standards for levels of contaminants in public drinking water systems and regulating underground injection wells. The regulations established maximum contaminant levels (MCLs) and monitoring requirements for heavy metals, certain pesticides, bacteriological contaminants, fluorides, and turbidity (Williams 1997).

In 1990, primarily in response to the Exxon Valdez oil spill, Congress overhauled the oil spill provisions of the Clean Water Act, thus creating the Oil Pollution Act (OPA) of 1990. Issues surrounding tanker safety and oil pollution liability had been addressed in debates in Congress over the course of the previous twenty years, and the act brought about sweeping changes in the oil production and transportation industry. Its stringent requirements resulted in the restructuring of the industry, created immediate demand for oil-spill prevention and response technology, and catalyzed the establishment of numerous requirements at the federal, state, and local levels (Olney 1997).

Legislation addressing the management of wastes dates back as far as the Rivers and Harbors Act of 1899 (Carlson 1995). The Solid Waste Disposal Act of 1965 and the Resource Recovery Act of 1970 were designed to address the management of municipal solid wastes. These acts, however, did little to establish firm regulations; rather, guidelines were prepared and incentives (i.e., grant programs) were made available to municipalities. By 1976, the Resource Conservation and Recovery Act (RCRA) was enacted to address the responsible management of both solid (i.e., municipal) and hazardous wastes; however, the most muscle was included for the latter. Subtitle C is the centerpiece of RCRA as regards hazardous waste management. Management of hazardous wastes was to be "from cradle to grave," meaning that the waste, once produced by a generator, must be tracked throughout its journey to its final destination, a treatment or permanent disposal facility. This created a paper trail known as the *manifest system*. RCRA requirements include the identification of hazardous wastes and the quantifying of wastes. Extensive requirements for generators, transporters, and treatment, storage, and disposal (TSD) facilities were established.

RCRA has been amended several times since its enactment, most importantly by the Hazardous and Solid Waste Amendments of 1984 (HSWA). The HSWA mandated far-reaching changes to the RCRA program. The requirements for waste generators varied significantly, depending on the monthly amount of wastes produced. The EPA was required to regulate another 200,000 companies that produce relatively small quantities of hazardous waste. Stringent requirements were established for hazardous waste incineration systems; landfill design, construction, and operation; waste minimization; and a national land disposal ban program (Case 1997).

Figure 1.3. *Leaking underground storage tanks removed from an abandoned petroleum refinery*

Underground storage tanks (USTs) are now widely recognized as a source of soil and groundwater contamination at thousands of sites throughout the United States. USTs have contaminated the subsurface via several avenues. Some tanks and piping simply corroded or structurally failed during years of use. In other cases, spills occurred when tanks were emptied or when they overflowed during filling (Fig. 1.3). In 1988 the EPA estimated the existence of over two million UST systems (which include both the underground tank and piping connected to it) located at over 700,000 facilities nationwide. EPA estimated that roughly 75% of UST systems posed a significant potential for leakage and environmental harm because the systems were constructed of steel without corrosion protection (Nardi 1997). Since 1988, there has been a comprehensive effort to register USTs, assess sites suspected of leaks, remove old and leaking tanks, and clean up contaminated soil and groundwater.

The Emergency Planning and Community Right-to-Know Act (EPCRA) of 1986 was initiated as a result of the Bhopal, India, incident of December 1984, in which methyl isocyanate, a potent toxin used in certain pesticides and polymers, was released from a Union Carbide facility, killing over 2,000 local residents and injuring many thousands more. A year later, a similar release occurred from another Union Carbide facility in Institute, West Virginia. Casualties in the latter event were, however, low. EPCRA was a rider attached to SARA (Superfund Amendments and Reauthorization Act) and authorized a nationwide program of emergency planning and reporting as protection against accidents involving extremely hazardous chemicals (Lopez-Cepero 1995).

The Toxic Substances Control Act (TSCA) was enacted in 1976, in large part due to the discovery of extensive soil, water, and structural contamination by polychlorinated biphenyls (PCBs) and no coherent regulations to control PCB material. TSCA authorizes the EPA to: (1) obtain data from industry regarding the production, use, and health effects of chemical substances and mixtures, and (2) regulate the manufacture, processing, and distribution in commerce, as well as use and disposal of a chemical substance or mixture (U.S. GAO 2005). The act has been amended three times, each amendment resulting in an additional title. TSCA now contains four titles: I—Control of Toxic Substances; II—Asbestos Hazard Emergency Response Act; III—Indoor Radon Abatement Act; and IV—Lead-Based Paint Exposure Reduction Act.

By the late 1970s, there were numerous accounts of chemical "time bombs" that had been carelessly buried in the ground, often from unknown sources. One of the most notorious scenarios occurred in Niagara Falls, New York. In the 1940s and 1950s, the Hooker Chemical Company had used a number of disposal areas within the city for disposal of over one hundred thousand tons of hazardous petrochemical wastes. Wastes were placed in the abandoned Love Canal, in a large unlined pit on Hooker's property, and in other dumps throughout the city (Fig. 1.4). At this time, no comprehensive legislation addressing hazardous waste disposal existed in the United States. As a result, such wastes were frequently placed directly into the ground, with no pretreatment. An internal Hooker memorandum warned company officials: "Do not dig anywhere near this site . . . may be thousands of buried drums and tanks . . . might have fire or reaction if we dig up this junk."

Figure 1.4.   *The Love Canal (N.Y.) neighborhood during cleanup activities in the late 1970s*
U.S. Environmental Protection Agency.

By the mid-1970s chemicals had migrated from their disposal sites. Land was subsiding in areas where containers deteriorated; noxious fumes were detected in homes; and liquids seeped into basements, surface soil, and water. The incidences of cancer, certain birth defects, and psychological problems were all well above the national average. President Jimmy Carter declared a public health emergency for the site. Homes directly adjacent to the Love Canal were purchased by the state of New York and residents were evacuated. Numerous lawsuits were brought against Hooker Chemical, by both the U.S. government and local citizens. Issues of liability and compensation were tied up in the court system for years. Some of the difficulties related to settlement were the fact that Hooker signed a disclaimer in 1952, stating that the company assumed no liability in the event of injury to persons or loss of property resulting from the land transaction. Furthermore, there was simply no law covering the assignment of liability to responsible parties in the event of land contamination. This and similar incidents—for example, Times Beach, Missouri; Valley of the Drums, Kentucky (Fig. 1.5); Kin-Buc Landfill, New Jersey (Fig. 1.6)—became potent catalysts for the Superfund legislation.

An estimated 36,000 severely contaminated sites exist in the United States; however, some federal agencies claim the number to be much higher (Figs. 1.7, 1.8). The U.S. Government Accountability Office estimates there to be over 400,000 sites that are in need of cleanup. As of late 2006 a total of 1,241 sites were placed on the Superfund list (National Priorities List, or NPL): 1,083 nonfederal and 158 federal, with an additional 59 proposed. Sites occur on private property, company property, and

Figure 1.5.   *Valley of the Drums, Kentucky*
U.S. Environmental Protection Agency.

Figure 1.6.   *Kin-Buc Landfill, New Jersey*
NOAA Office of Response and Restoration.

Figure 1.7.   *Indiscriminate disposal of hazardous wastes into unsuitable locations (such as the open pit shown here) has resulted in significant soil and groundwater contamination*
U.S. Environmental Protection Agency.

Figure 1.8.   *Drums of hazardous wastes at this facility have been stockpiled improperly over long periods, resulting in severe soil contamination*
U.S. Environmental Protection Agency.

many federal lands (Department of Defense, Department of Energy, etc.). Beyond the federal list, states and cities possess their own lists of priority sites for cleanup.

1.2. BROWNFIELDS

The U.S. EPA Region 5 defines brownfields as "abandoned, idled or underused industrial and commercial sites where expansion or redevelopment is complicated by real or perceived environmental contamination that can add cost, time or uncertainty to a redevelopment project." The U.S. Office of Technology Assessment definition includes a site whose redevelopment may be hindered not only by potential contamination, but also by poor location, old or obsolete infrastructure, or other less tangible factors often linked to neighborhood decline (Fig. 1.9).

Brownfields routinely are associated with distressed urban areas, particularly central cities and inner suburbs that once were heavily industrialized, but subsequently were vacated. A small percentage of brownfield sites may be contaminated to the degree that they are candidates for the NPL under CERCLA.

The stigmatic impacts of brownfields on communities are manifold. Potential investors, concerned about liability, have avoided developing abandoned industrial sites. Real-estate buyers are reluctant to invest in brownfields, thus further diminishing the brownfields' value. Communities lose out on property tax revenues. Many states, eager to boost local economies, are seeking to revitalize brownfields by providing economic incentives for their assessment and redevelopment (Davis and Margolis 1997).

1.3 CERCLA AND THE SUPERFUND

The Comprehensive Environmental Response, Compensation, and Liability Act of 1980 (CERCLA) was enacted to address contamination from past disposal activities. The act established a federal cleanup program (Superfund) to finance the cleanup of contaminated sites and set guidelines for cleaning sites, and it established a system of assigning legal and financial liability for responsible parties.

The Superfund now totals over $1.6 billion. Monies to create the fund are based primarily on a tax on industries ("the polluter pays" strategy),

Figure 1.9. Brownfields range in size from an abandoned corner gasoline station to large industrial facilities

and a small portion is derived from individual income taxes. However, cleanup costs for uncontrolled and abandoned U.S. hazardous-waste sites are estimated to exceed $350 billion. Because the Superfund cannot remediate all sites, the U.S. EPA has formulated a system for the determination of potentially responsible parties, or PRPs.

1.3.1. Liability

With the enactment of CERCLA, there is no longer any question as to liability for a site that is contaminated from past improper disposal of wastes. CERCLA establishes four classes of PRPs liable for environmental investigation and cleanup costs:

- the current owner or operator of a facility
- person(s) who owned or operated a facility at the time of disposal of any hazardous substances
- person(s) who arranged for disposal or treatment of hazardous substances owned by such person(s)
- person(s) who transported hazardous substances to treatment or disposal facilities

CERCLA declares that these parties are liable for all costs of removal or remedial action incurred by the U.S. government. They are also responsible for damages for injury to, destruction of, or loss of natural resources, including the costs for assessing them. PRPs are also liable for the costs of any health assessments conducted.

Liability under CERCLA is joint and several, which essentially means that all PRPs, at the outset at least, hold an equal share of liability. This relieves the government of proving the individual contributions of each PRP to the site. Courts have experienced difficulty in determining the amount of environmental harm caused by each party at a site where wastes of varying toxicities and migratory potential commingle (Rockwood and Harrison 1993). CERCLA allows a PRP that is liable to the government for cleanup and investigation costs to seek contribution from other PRPs. The CERCLA liability procedure was adopted by Congress to promote prompt cost recovery and equitable allocation of liability. However, the process has resulted in inequality and complexity, which causes delay, increases transaction costs, and results in inequitable allocations of liability.

EPA's policy addresses cleanup cost allocation on a case-by-case basis, maintaining maximum flexibility to propose solutions (Butler et al. 1993).

Throughout the history of Superfund, PRPs have searched for ways to distribute the costs of cleanup as broadly as possible. Until recently, PRPs focused their efforts on other industrial PRPs and their insurance companies. PRPs have recently focused on spreading Superfund costs to U.S. taxpayers via local governments. Approximately 20% of the sites listed on the NPL are municipal sites, a category that includes sites owned or operated by municipal governments, as well as privately owned sites that routinely accept MSW for disposal. The majority of these sites are landfills that have become contaminated by the codisposal of industrial hazardous waste or sewage sludges with MSW. The MSW or sewage sludge sent to landfills is typically of low toxicity. Hazardous substances constitute less than 0.5% of the materials contained in ordinary MSW. However, under Superfund case law, wastes are included in the liability framework if they contain even minimal amounts of hazardous substances. Industrial PRPs sued by the federal or state government at these sites are suing for contribution cities whose citizens produced MSW that was brought to the site (Steinzor and Lintner 1992).

1.3.2. The Innocent Purchaser Defense

If a purchaser of land found subsequently to be severely contaminated can show that "due diligence" was exercised in a property assessment prior to the transaction, his liability may be reduced. Due diligence involves an appropriate investigation in previous ownership and uses of the property. Such an investigation often takes the form of an environmental site assessment; however, there is no single standardized method for conducting such an investigation. The assessment process is outlined in chapter 5.

1.3.3. Removal Action versus Remediation

If a site is contaminated to the point of being placed on the NPL, a CERCLA-authorized action is conducted. Such an action is designated as either a short-term removal action or a long-term remedial response. A removal action involves cleanup or other actions taken in response to emergency conditions, an immediate threat to human health and the environment, or interim actions on a short-term basis. For the long term, remedial action is designed to stop or reduce a significant release of hazardous substances.

1.3.3.1. Removal Action

Examples of removal actions include installation of fences, waste seg-regation, evacuation of threatened populations, and construction of temporary containment systems (Fig. 1.10). The following factors are considered in determining whether to order a removal action (Wagner 1991):

- exposure of populations, animals, or food chains to contaminants
- contamination of drinking water supplies or sensitive ecosystems
- hazardous substances in storage that pose a threat of release
- high levels of hazardous substances at or near the soil surface that may migrate
- weather conditions that may cause hazardous substances to be released or migrate
- threat of fire or explosion
- availability of other federal or state response mechanisms to respond to the release

Figure 1.10. *Removal action in progress at a Superfund site*
U.S. Environmental Protection Agency.

1.3.3.2. Remedial Action

The remedial action is a lengthy and meticulous operation whose purpose is to permanently remove, destroy, or isolate the hazard at the site. The basic elements of the CERCLA remedial action process include:

- site discovery
- preliminary investigation
- site investigation
- hazard ranking system analysis
- listing on the National Priorities List
- remedial investigation
- feasibility study
- remedy selection
- record of decision
- remedial design/remedial action

Remedial designs range from the very simple to the highly complex. Because each site's characteristics, history, and complexity of contamination are unique, designs are prepared on a case-by-case basis. Decisions on the specific remediation method are influenced by technical considerations, degree of present hazard of the site to local populations and ecosystems, and political considerations.

As noted earlier, a total of 1,241 hazardous-waste sites in the United States have been assigned the highest priority for cleanup. Since the enactment of CERCLA in 1980, a total of 312 of these sites have been closed (remediated). In some cases, this means that contaminants were neutralized, detoxified, or removed. In other cases it may simply mean that the site of concern has been covered over with an impermeable cap and is subjected to long-term monitoring of groundwater and soil.

The EPA has placed much emphasis on the application of innovative technologies for site remediation. The Superfund Amendments and Reauthorization Act (SARA) requires the use of remedial technologies that permanently and significantly reduce the volume, toxicity, or mobility of contaminated materials at affected sites. In recent years, in fact, the number of Superfund Records of Decision for sites has been greatest for the novel techniques over the conventional technologies.

1.4. "IT AIN'T OVER 'TIL IT'S OVER."—YOGI BERRA

Since Earth Day 1970, the U.S. government and numerous state governments have enacted stringent, comprehensive regulations with far-reaching benefits in terms of protection of public health, soil, water, air, and ecosystems. Some states have made much greater strides than others.

Contaminated sites continue to be discovered throughout the United States. Additionally, illegal and improper waste disposal continues as unscrupulous owners, operators, and employees seek the lowest-cost methods for waste disposal. The following abbreviated list presents some recent news reports:

"Excavators Find Toxic Waste at Former Plant," *Bismarck Tribune*, July 17, 2006

Excavations at the property of the former Reserve Mining Co. in Silver Bay, Minnesota, have unearthed thousands of 55-gallon drums of contaminated lubricating grease and other toxic industrial wastes. More than 2,400 barrels have been found so far and 322 tons of contaminated soil has been removed. The Minnesota Pollution Control Agency estimates there may be another 2,000 barrels and tons more grease to remove. Tests on the gear lubricant in the barrels show levels of 270 milligrams per liter of lead, far above the federal standard of 5 milligrams per liter to be considered hazardous waste. Tests show that the waste has contaminated the groundwater immediately below the dump but has not yet reached nearby streams or Lake Superior. Reserve established an environmental fund of $2 million in bankruptcy requirements, but that has been used up and money for the cleanup is coming from the state's Superfund.

"Buried Toxins Resurface—In Fight over Power Plant Opponents Cite Company's Role in Dumping," *Pittsburgh Post-Gazette*, August 28, 2006

Twenty-seven years after the largest midnight dumping scheme was uncovered in Pennsylvania, the site remains a toxic mess with 4,000 barrels of hazardous waste unaccounted for. In 1979, a Findlay waste-hauling company was caught dumping and backfilling toxic waste into a Washington County strip mine. Three companies involved on the site were pressured by the Department of Environmental Resources to clean up the contamination but criminal charges were never filed. Only 500 barrels have been removed from the site while a remaining 4,000 are believed to still be buried there. The 55-gallon barrels are suspected to contain amino, alkyd, and polyester liquid resins. These resins are made of styrene, xylene, formaldehyde, and various benzene forms; all are toxic, hazardous and flammable. Strong odors from the mine are indicative that the toxic waste has more than likely spilled from damaged drums into the backfill. DER officials are continuing to evaluate the 27-year old mystery.

"Lead Levels High near Gun Site," *Ithaca Journal*, **September 14, 2006, at www.theithacajournal.com/apps/pbcs.dll/article?AID=/20060914/ NEWS01/609140369/1002 (accessed June 11, 2007)**

Soil samples taken from a property adjacent to the Ithaca Gun Factory found levels of lead contamination as high as 184,000 ppm and arsenic levels as high as 2,210 ppm. Levels of cadmium and chromium also exceeded federal standards. The pollution was a result of improper disposal of ammunition used to test weapons made at the factory, which had been in operation for 124 years. The property was placed on the Superfund list in 2000 and experienced a $4.8 million dollar cleanup effort from 2002–2004. The EPA removed more than 2,700 tons of contaminated soil from the site but did not finish the job. Tarps had been placed over the contaminated soil temporarily until the property owner was able to remove it.

"Poison under the Pavement," *Earth Island Journal* **21 (2): 40–41**

In Greenpoint, New York, from 17 to 30 million gallons of petroleum products are migrating under the surface. The vapors from these products contain dangerous levels of explosive and carcinogenic chemicals. This release is almost 50% bigger than the *Exxon Valdez* spill in 1989. In 1995 a pipeline and pump were installed and 3.5 million gallons of oil have been removed, but the cleanup of the remainder could take 20 more years to complete.

"Lethal Cyanide Spill in Ghana Outrages Gold Mining Communities," *Environment News Service*, **July 5, 2006**

A cyanide spill in Ghana has posed serious threats to local populations and wildlife. The release has caused numerous fish kills and has made many people sick. This is not the first time the Bogosu Gold Ltd. Company has harmed the local environment, and citizens in surrounding villages are demanding an environmental audit. The cyanide was specifically used for extracting gold from rock tailings. The contaminated tailing apparently spilled into local soils and water. The company then applied neutralizing chemicals such as hydrogen peroxide into the stream to detoxify the water. The national environmental protection agency has become involved and is conducting further testing.

"DEM Files Pollution Charges," September 8, 2006, at www.projo.com/ news/content/projo_20060908_pollute8.31dd243.html (accessed December 1, 2006)

In Providence, Rhode Island, the Department of Environmental Management reports criminal charges against N.E. Environmental Services and two of its executives for allowing pollutants to enter groundwater in Smithfield. The recycling company, that formerly recycled antifreeze and oil filters, discharged these pollutants from April through February 2005. The spills became apparent when odors were detected from a stream. Glycol, an alcohol used in antifreeze, was found in the septic system and spread to nearby wetlands, causing damage to wildlife and plants.

"Lead Contamination Causes Warnings," *State Journal-Register* **(Springfield, IL), September 28, 2006**

Tests completed this summer found high levels of lead contamination on 20 to 25 residential properties near a former zinc smelting plant in Montgomery County, state and federal environmental officials said Wednesday. Homeowners have been advised of the tests. "Lead contamination is mostly about not ingesting it. If you have little kids, they shouldn't be playing in the dirt," said Mick Hans, a spokesman for the U.S. Environmental Protection Agency regional office in Chicago. He added that people living in areas of suspected contamination are advised to wash away soil such as from garden vegetables, but that lead contamination generally is not considered an airborne hazard.

"Fairbanks Motorsports Park Shut Down for Asbestos Contamination, at www.mesolink.org/mesothelioma-news/ 09-28-05.html (accessed October 5, 2006)

A decision has been made by officials to close the Fairbanks Motorsports Park until further notice following the discovery of asbestos contamination at the site. The asbestos originates from illegally dumped soil that was contaminated with the hazardous substance, which is known to cause a number of health problems including a deadly cancer known as mesothelioma. The illegal dumping of the contaminated soil, which surrounds a dirt bike racing track, is currently being investigated by the Environmental Protection Authority. It has been confirmed that the soil in question was found to be missing from a Mitchell industrial waste holding yard last week. An EPA spokesperson confirmed that the soil had been used in the construction of noise barriers.

"ADEQ Director Owens Announces $45,000 Penalty against Arizona Water Company for Hazardous Waste Violations," January 7, 2005, at www.azdeq.gov/function/news/2005/jan.html (accessed October 4, 2006)

Arizona Department of Environmental Quality (ADEQ) Director Steve Owens today announced a $45,000 civil penalty as part of a settlement with Arizona Water Company for violations of the state's hazardous waste laws. During a January 2003 inspection of the company's Coolidge facility, ADEQ staff discovered that Arizona Water Company had illegally discharged hazardous wastewater directly to the soil, failed to properly characterize lead-containing hazardous waste and failed to meet basic hazardous waste labeling requirements. ADEQ issued a Notice of Violation to Arizona Water Company in February 2003 for these offenses following inspection of the Coolidge facility.

"Lead, Arsenic, and Polycyclic Aromatic Hydrocarbons in Soil and House Dust in the Communities Surrounding the Sydney, Nova Scotia, Tar Ponds," *Environmental Health Perspectives* **112 (1): 35–41**

As a result of 87 years of steel production, the Sydney, Nova Scotia tar ponds are considered to be "Canada's worst contaminated site." Coal tar, a product of the coke process, was released directly into Muggah Creek, thus creating the infamous tar ponds. Compared to Nova Scotia and the rest of Canada, Sydney shows significantly higher rates of cancer, cancer mortality and congenital anomalies. Levels of lead, arsenic and PAHs were evaluated using background contaminant levels obtained outside of the study area and beneath a 100-year-old house. The study reveals that there is significant home, groundwater and soil contamination in the study areas. The current tar pond remediation policy does not include these homes, which pose a significant health risk to their occupants, but it is recommended that these sites be added.

"Government Survey Shows Abandoned WWII Chemical Weapons Pose Risk to Residents Nationwide," Associated Press Tokyo, November 28, 2003

The Japanese government completed a survey of abandoned chemical weapons in 140 locations around the country. Approximately one-third appear to have leaked and contaminated soil and water resources in the area. The survey was initiated after a number of residents in various locations were poisoned. Mustard gas and lewisite (a chemical similar to arsenic) were the primary chemicals manufactured during the war. Cleanup of the weapons and contaminated sites is being arranged by the appropriate government agency.

"EPA Orders Local Man to Pay for Illegal Dumping in Cook County Preserve Site," EPA Environmental News, February 23, 1999

On December 23, 1998, a Chicago-area man was charged with dumping 22 55-gallon drums of paint waste off the boat dock in the Cook County Forest Preserve. The paint wastes are considered hazardous since they are ignitable. The soil on the site has been excavated and disposed in a hazardous waste landfill.

"Toxic Soup under Navy Base Creeps toward Water Supply," Los Angeles Times, February 22, 1999

In the 1960s and 1970s rocket boosters for NASA were built and cleaned at Seal Beach, CA. This has resulted in a plume of TCE (trichloroethylene) that is 195 feet deep and 2,500 feet wide. This is a concern to the community that uses the groundwater for drinking since the TCE is a cancer-causing toxic solvent. TCE levels were found to be 165,000 ppb and the federal drinking limit is 5 ppb. The Navy is currently removing and treating some of the material and continuously monitoring the surrounding area drinking water.

"Toxic Home Costs Orkin Millions," *Tampa Tribune*, November 21, 1998

Orkin Exterminating Co. illegally used the pesticide chlordane for termite control after it was banned in 1988. Chlordane was used from 1948 to 1988. Chlordane cannot be decomposed by the human body, can accumulate, and can affect the neurological, reproductive, and immune systems. Orkin treated a historic home with chlordane in 1993. The house was subsequently condemned for occupation due to chlordane contamination. The couple that lived in the house was awarded $2 million in settlement for the case.

"EPA to Remove 700,000 Tons of Soil," *St. Louis Post-Dispatch*, October 16, 1998

With further testing of a roadway site contaminated with dioxin, the EPA has determined that dioxin contamination extends into a nearby neighborhood. To clean up the site, 700,000 tons of soil will have to be removed. Some residents in the area have relocated at the request of the EPA.

"Record Dioxin Levels Found in Osaka," *Daily Yomiuri*, September 23, 1998

In Osaka, Japan, record-breaking levels of dioxin were found in soil near a water-cooling system of a garbage incinerator. The most recent testing at the site indicates that the soil is contaminated with 52,000 nanograms of dioxin per gram of soil. This level is thousands of times higher than the amount that would be fatal to adult human beings. It is thought that the dioxin was concentrated as exhaust gas went through a purification system for the removal of hydrogen chloride. The contaminated water was continually recycled leading to the progressively higher levels of dioxin.

"Water Contaminated in Seven States," *Chemical Market Reporter*, September 14, 1998

In the states of California, Nevada, Utah, Texas, New York, Maryland, and Arkansas perchlorate has been found in the groundwater. Perchlorate is used in fireworks, munitions, and rocket fuel. At high enough levels perchlorate can interfere with the thyroid gland's ability to produce hormones and regulate metabolism. Research is underway to determine the effects of a low level of perchlorate such as those being found in groundwater in these states.

"Coast Guard and Toxic Batteries," *New York Times*, September 2, 1998

The U.S. Coast guard has been dumping used batteries in U.S. lakes and rivers for decades. The Coast Guard claims that these batteries are of no threat to humans or marine life, but it is well known that the heavy metal lead is in batteries and that consumption of lead can harm humans. Currently the Coast Guard is being sued in order to force the organization to clean up the batteries.

"Asbestos Action," *New Hampshire Business Review*, June 19, 1998

A river in Nashua, New Hampshire, has asbestos-contaminated sediment resulting from the discharge of asbestos-laden wastewater. The wastewater treatment plant received the asbestos from an asbestos materials manufacturing facility. Contamination in the river included both the sediments in the river and the shoreline extending 800 feet downstream from the wastewater treatment facility. The cleanup project involves the excavation of the contaminated sediments and removal to a special hazardous waste cell at the city landfill. The cleanup cost is $2.6 million.

"More Dioxin Contamination Sites Discovered," *Kansas City Star*, June 14, 1998

Dioxin-contaminated soil has been turning up in several areas in Missouri. The culprit seems to be a waste oil hauler who disposed of dioxin contaminated waste oil by spraying it onto roadways, and in one case, a horse arena. The EPA had just shut down an incinerator operation for the disposal of dioxin contaminated soil when a new roadway site and the horse arena site were found. The two new sites were discovered as the result of tips from the public. The cost of cleaning up the sites is estimated at $10 million. Residents near the sites were tested for dioxin levels, but it was determined that their blood dioxin levels were normal. Together, the two sites contain 12,000 tons of contaminated soil that will have to be treated.

"Benzene in Wells Traced to Old Gas Station,"
Star Tribune, **May 15, 1998**

Gasoline storage tanks in Paynesville, Minnesota, are blamed for benzene contamination of several wells in the area. The old storage tanks have since been removed along with 1,500 cubic yards of contaminated soil. A well has been installed to extract any remaining contamination.

"AlliedSignal to Save $50m in Ohio Site Clean-up,"
Haznews, **January 1998**

A total of 457,000 cubic yards of soil are contaminated with polycyclic aromatic hydrocarbons at the site of former wastewater treatments lagoons for AlliedSignal. Included as contaminants at the site are tar, coal and coke fines. The EPA has proposed a clean-up level of 1 mg/kg for land that is to be used for residential purposes, and 100 mg/kg for land that will be made into wetlands. Bioremediation is proposed as a possibility to get to the 100 mg/kg level, but is not likely to be effective at reducing contamination to the 1 mg/kg level.

QUESTIONS

1. Which act promulgated by the U.S. Congress created the "innocent landowner defense" for a property buyer who is concerned about environmental issues, as a means of protection? Under this act the purchaser may attempt to show "due diligence" in conducting a property investigation.
2. Which of the following is correct? PRPs under a CERCLA situation may include: (a) owner or operator of the facility; (b) owner of the

hazardous storage facility; (c) the hazardous waste generator; (d) transporter of the hazardous substance; (e) all of the above.

3. In assessing cleanup costs among multiple PRPs at an EPA-funded cleanup, how does the EPA apportion costs?

4. A primary goal of CERCLA is to establish a mechanism to respond to releases of hazardous substances at uncontrolled waste sites. True or false?

5. CERCLA liability does not necessarily involve proving negligence. True or false? Explain.

6. Search the brownfields database in your community. How many sites are listed? What are the primary industry types (e.g., heavy industry, petrochemical, manufacturing, gasoline stations)? What types of contaminants occur?

7. Do NPL sites exist in your county or state? Check the U.S. EPA website for NPL sites and determine: (1) the site history, including production activities; (2) waste types generated; (3) Record of Decision. Have the sites been remediated?

8. CERCLA liability is strict, joint and several, and retroactive. Define and/or explain these three components of liability. You may want to check the EPA website, www.epa.gov/superfund/ or some of the references listed in this chapter.

REFERENCES

Butler, J. C. III, M. W. Schneider, G. R. Hall, and M. E. Burton. 1993. Allocating Superfund costs: Cleaning up the controversy. *Environmental Law Reporter* 23:10133–44.

Case, D. R. 1997. Resource Conservation and Recovery Act. In *Environmental Law Handbook*, 14th ed., ed. T. F. P. Sullivan. Rockville, MD: Government Institutes.

Carlson, R. L. 1995. RCRA Overview. In *Handbook on Hazardous Materials Management*, ed. D. B. Cox. Rockville, MD: Institute of Hazardous Materials Management.

Chillrud, S. N., R. F. Bopp, H. J. Simpson, J. M. Ross, E. L. Shuster, D. A. Chaky, D. C. Walsh, C. C. Choy, L. Tolley, and A. Yarme. 1999. Twentieth-century atmospheric metal fluxes into Central Park Lake, New York City. *Environmental Science & Technology* 33:657–61.

Davis, T. S., and K. D. Margolis. 1997. *Brownfields: A Comprehensive Guide to Redeveloping Contaminated Property*. Chicago: Section of Natural Resources, Energy, and Environmental Law, American Bar Association.

Hess, K. 1993. *Environmental Site Assessments, Phase 1: A Basic Guide*. Boca Raton, FL: CRC Press.

Lopez-Cepero, B. D. 1995. Emergency Planning and Community Right-to-Know Act of 1986. In *Handbook on Hazardous Materials Management. Institute of Hazardous Materials Management*, ed. D. B. Cox. Rockville, MD: Institute of Hazardous Materials Management.

Nardi, K. J. 1997. Underground storage tanks. In *Environmental Law Handbook*, 14th ed., ed. T. F. P. Sullivan. Rockville, MD: Government Institutes.

Olney, A. P. 1997. Oil Pollution Act. In *Environmental Law Handbook*, 14th ed., ed. T. F. P. Sullivan. Rockville, MD: Government Institutes.

Paschal, E. F. Jr. 1995. Clean Water Act. In *Handbook on Hazardous Materials Management. Institute of Hazardous Materials Management*, ed. D. B. Cox. Rockville, MD: Institute of Hazardous Materials Management.

Phillips, J. W., and J. D. Lokey. 1995. Toxic air pollution control through the Clean Air Act. In *Handbook on Hazardous Materials Management. Institute of Hazardous Materials Management*, ed. D. B. Cox. Rockville, MD: Institute of Hazardous Materials Management.

Rockwood, L. L., and J. L. Harrison. 1993. The Alcan decisions: Causation through the back door. *Environmental Law Reporter* 23:10542–45.

Steinzor, R. I., and M. F. Lintner. 1992. Should taxpayers pay the cost of Superfund? *Environmental Law Reporter* 22:10089–90.

U.S. Government Accountability Office. 2005. *Chemical Regulation: Approaches in the United States, Canada, and the European Union*. GAO-06-217R, November 4, 2005. See: www.gao.gov/docsearch/abstract.php?rptno=GAO-06-217R.

Wagner, T. P. 1991. *The Complete Guide to the Hazardous Waste Regulations*. 2nd ed. New York: Van Nostrand Reinhold.

Williams, S. E. 1997. Safe Drinking Water Act. In *Environmental Law Handbook*, 14th ed., ed. T. F. P. Sullivan. Rockville, MD: Government Institutes.

CHAPTER 2

Chemistry of Common Contaminant Elements

Life should be like the precious metals, weigh much in little bulk.

—Seneca

2.1. INTRODUCTION

Many sites in industrialized nations are contaminated with potentially toxic metals such as cadmium, chromium, mercury, and lead. Certain metals, when concentrated in soil and sediments, pose a threat to public health and the environment. Metals enter the biosphere from disposal of wastes in landfills or uncontrolled dumps; from atmospheric fallout; and from spills and leaks in factories, mines, distribution facilities, or during transportation (Smith et al. 1995; U.S. EPA 1995). Metals can subsequently become attached to particulates (soil, dust, fly ash) and carried in air currents; leached through the soil profile; carried away in surface runoff; accumulate in plants to the point at which they become phytotoxic; and be translocated through the food chain. Metal contamination of soils by anthropogenic inputs has been discovered in industrial areas, mine sites, urban areas, near metal smelters, and in waste-disposal areas along roadsides (Fig. 2.1).

As part of a thorough environmental assessment and remediation program for an affected site, soil testing should be conducted in order to measure total concentrations of metals and the chemical forms (species) present. It is also important to measure background metal levels to assess the degree of contamination. Soils are composed of mineral and organic

Figure 2.1. *Abandoned coal surface mine, eastern United States. Soil material is extremely acidic, resulting in metal solubilization and mobility.*

constituents that vary in composition laterally as well as down the profile. It is therefore not easy to establish a minimum concentration below which a soil may be considered uncontaminated by a particular pollutant. Average amounts of trace contaminants found in soils are given in Table 2.1.

The mobility of trace elements in soils is controlled by several chemical and physical phenomena. For example, finer-sized soil fractions (clays, silts, metal oxides, organic matter) bind metals by cation exchange and specific adsorption (Cline et al. 1993). For contamination situations in which metal contamination is very high, that is, thousands

Table 2.1.   Distribution of trace elements in world soils

Element	Common Range	Average
	mg/kg	
Arsenic (As)	1–50	5
Cadmium (Cd)	0.01–0.70	0.06
Chromium (Cr)	1–1,000	100
Lead (Pb)	2–200	10
Mercury (Hg)	0.01–0.3	0.03
Barium (Ba)	100–3,000	430
Boron (B)	2–100	10
Copper (Cu)	2–100	30
Manganese (Mn)	20–3,000	600
Nickel (Ni)	5–500	40
Selenium (Se)	0.1–2	0.3
Silver (Ag)	0.01–5	0.05
Tin (Sn)	2–200	10
Zinc (Zn)	10–300	50

Source: U.S. Environmental Protection Agency 1995.

of mg/kg, the sorption capacity of soils is exceeded, and the contamination will be present as discrete metal-mineral phases (Kabata-Pendias 2001; Davis and Singh 1995). Metal ions can be immobilized in such soils by the formation of insoluble precipitates, incorporation into the crystalline structure of clays and metal oxides, and/or by physical entrapment in the immobile water within soil pores (Moore et al. 1993). Conversely, metals can become mobilized under acidic pH regimes, under reducing conditions, and in high salt-content soils. Soil organic matter content, redox state, and pH are all relevant to the mobility and availability of metals in soil. The significance of these properties is discussed below and in subsequent chapters.

In this chapter, the chemical properties and reactions of several common metallic and semimetallic contaminants are presented, with emphasis on mobility/immobility, toxicity, transformations in the biosphere, and remediation practices.

2.2. THE ELEMENTS

2.2.1. Arsenic

Based on its position in the periodic table, arsenic (As) is a semimetal, or metalloid, and possesses attributes of both metals and nonmetals. Arsenic is widely distributed throughout the biosphere, occurring in over 200 mineral species including native As, sulfides, sulfosalts, and oxides (Woolson 1992). As with many of the minerals discussed in this chapter, arsenic is highly chalcophilic, which means that it can crystallize in a reducing environment to form sulfide species. Significant anthropogenic sources of As to the biosphere include: metal processing including smelting of copper, lead, and zinc ores; processing of sulfur and phosphorus minerals; coal combustion; land application of contaminated biosolids; and the use of As pesticide sprays (Kabata-Pendias 2001; U.S. EPA 1994). The worldwide range of As in natural soils is < 1 to 95 mg/kg; however, the As content of contaminated soils has been reported to be as high as 2,000 mg/kg (Kabata-Pendias 2001).

Arsenic is present in contaminated sites as As_2O_3 or compounds derived therefrom. Arsenic also may occur in such organometallic forms as methylarsinic acid, $H_2AsO_3CH_3$, an ingredient in many pesticides, as well as arsine, AsH_3, and its methyl derivatives including dimethylarsine

As(CH$_3$)$_2$ (Smith et al. 1995). The chemistry of As in soil, sediments, and water is somewhat complex. Its oxidation states include $-3, 0, +3$, and $+5$. The As(V) compounds predominate in aerobic soils and sediments; As(III) compounds occur in slightly reduced soils; and arsine, methylated arsines, and elemental As predominate under very reduced conditions. Under most conditions As(V) is present as the H$_2$AsO$_4^-$ species, while As(III) as the H$_3$AsO$_3$ species is dominant in low pH and reducing environments (Crecelius et al. 1986). The anions AsO$_2^-$, AsO$_4^{3-}$, HasO$_4^{2-}$, and H$_2$AsO$_3^-$ are the most common mobile forms of As. Arsine and methylated derivatives are highly volatile and will vaporize after formation.

Arsenic compounds in soils, sediments, and water undergo complex transformations, including oxidation-reduction, ligand exchange, and biotransformation. These processes are affected by pH, salinity, oxidation-reduction status, types and amounts of anions present, clay and hydrous oxide contents, sulfide concentrations, and composition of microorganisms. The various biological and chemical transformations that control the mobility and availability of As are shown in Figure 2.2.

Many As compounds adsorb strongly onto soils and sediments, specifically clays, oxides, hydroxides, and organic matter; therefore, leaching is minimal (Moore et al. 1988; Welch et al. 1988). Arsenates (AsO$_4^{3-}$) have a chemical behavior similar to phosphates; that is, they are sorbed by Fe and Al oxides, aluminosilicates, and layer silicate clays (McBride 1994). Arsenates are also readily fixed by phosphate gels, Ca, and humus. The most strongly sorbing solids for As, however, are Fe and Al oxides (Kabata-Pendias 2001; Huang 1975).

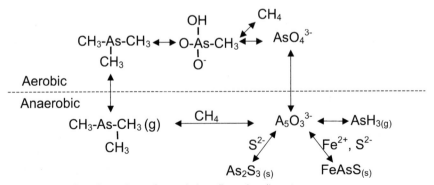

Figure 2.2. *Transformations of arsenic in soils and sediments*

Several plant species, including some established on mine wastes and other As-contaminated media, have been found to tolerate high levels of tissue As. Many plants apparently take up soil As passively. A fairly linear relationship between soil As concentration and plant uptake of As has been reported. Plants are also capable of translocating root As to above-ground biomass. The toxicity of As to plants depends on the concentration of soluble As in soil. However, plant response may also be related to total soil As and additionally to soil properties. For example, significant growth reduction may occur with 1,000 mg/kg As in clayey soil; however, in a sandy soil 100 mg/kg As is equally toxic (Kabata-Pendias 2001; Woolson et al. 1973). Arsenic toxicity has been noted in plants growing on mine waste, on soils treated with arsenical pesticides, and on soils amended with biosolids (i.e., sewage sludge). Symptoms of As toxicity include leaf wilting, root discoloration, and cell plasmolysis. The most common symptom, however, is growth reduction (Kabata-Pendias 2001).

Depending on soil properties and pollution source, plants may accumulate extremely large amounts of As. Kabata-Pendias (2001) reports tissue As levels in some plants as high as 6,000 mg/kg dry weight. Arsenic poisoning from plants to animals is relatively uncommon; however, negative health effects of high As concentration in crop and forage plants are possible.

The toxicity of As in soils may be overcome in several ways, depending on As pollution sources and soil properties. In flooded soils (e.g., rice paddies), increasing the oxidation state limits As bioavailability (Hanada et al. 1975; U.S. HHS 1992). Application of materials that precipitate As in soil (e.g., ferrous sulfate, calcium carbonate) can also be employed effectively (U.S. HHS 1992).

2.2.2. Barium

Barium (Ba) and its compounds are used in several industrial and other applications, including: oil and gas drilling muds; insecticides; plastic stabilizers; paint, glass, and rubber manufacture; lubricating oils; and jet fuels. Barium compounds continue to have important medical uses (Smith et al. 1995; U.S. HHS 1992; Dixon and Weed 1977).

Barium sulfate (barite, $BaSO_4$) and barium carbonate (witherite, $BaCO_3$) occur in ore deposits and comprise approximately 0.05% of the

Earth's crust. The average Ba concentration in soils is higher than that of most of the trace elements, with a worldwide range of 19 to over 2,300 mg/kg (Kabata-Pendias 2001). Barium occurs naturally in drinking water and foods, as a result of dissolution and normal cation exchange reactions at the soil-root interface. Barium occurs only in the $+2$ oxidation state. In soils it associates geochemically with feldspars and biotites. The Ba^{2+} ion substitutes readily for K^+ in these structures, because their ionic radii are similar (1.35 and 1.33 A° for Ba^{2+} and K^+, respectively; Dixon and Weed 1977). As soils weather, released Ba^{2+} can occur as the dissolved cation. It can also be immobilized by precipitation with sulfate or carbonate, concentration into Mn and P concretions, specific adsorption onto oxides and hydroxides, or by fixation on high–charge layer silicate clays such as smectites and vermiculites (Smith et al. 1995; Kabata-Pendias 2001).

Barium mobility in soils is a function of soil characteristics such as cation exchange capacity (CEC) and $CaCO_3$ content. In soils with high CEC values, Ba mobility is limited due to adsorption. Clay and humus exchange sites have a preferential cation exchange selectivity for Ba^{2+} over Ca^{2+} and Mg^{2+}. High $CaCO_3$ content limits mobility by precipitating Ba as $BaCO_3$. In the presence of sulfate ions, Ba precipitates as $BaSO_4$. Barium also forms salts of low solubility with arsenate, chromate, hydroxide, and phosphate ions. As a result, Ba is relatively immobile in soils (Welc et al. 1988). Barium may be mobilized under certain conditions, however. Its concentrations in soil solutions show substantial variation, for example depending on soil texture (Kabata-Pendias 2001). In the presence of Cl^- ions, Ba is mobile and is more likely to be leached into groundwater because of the solubility of $BaCl_2$ compounds. In soil water, Ba can form complexes with natural organics such as fatty acids in landfill leachates (Smith et al. 1995).

Relative to the amount found in soils, little Ba is concentrated by plants. Barium is a common component of plant tissue; however, it is not considered to be an essential element for plant growth. Tissue Ba content ranges from 1 to 198 mg/kg (dry weight), being the highest in leaves of cereals and legumes and the lowest in grains and fruits. The highest concentrations of Ba, up to 10,000 mg/kg (dw), are reported for various trees and shrubs (Chaudry et al. 1977; Shacklette et al. 1978). There are limited reports of toxic Ba concentrations in plants. Concentrations considered to be toxic have ranged from 220 mg/kg to as much as 1%–2% (dw) (Chaudry et al. 1977; Uminska 1993). Plants may take up Ba easily from acid soils. Toxicity effects of Ba to plants may be reduced by the addition of Ca, Mg, and S salts to the growth medium. Antagonistic interactions between these elements and Ba may occur in both plant tissue and soils (Kabata-Pendias 2001).

2.2.3. Cadmium

Cadmium (Cd) occurs in the Earth's crust as sulfide ores of lead, zinc, and copper. Significant Cd releases to the biosphere have resulted from: the smelting of metallic sulfide ores; burning of fossil fuels; incineration of municipal solid waste (MSW); metal plating operations; and disposal of Cd-containing wastes such as biosolids, Ni-Cd batteries, and Cd-plated steel. Cigarette smoking is also a Cd source; tobacco takes up soil Cd, some of which is entrained in smoke. Most smokers reportedly possess about twice the Cd concentration in their bodies as do nonsmokers. Cadmium does not often occur in significant levels in water, although it can leach into groundwater from waste disposal sites (U.S. EPA 1994).

In soil, Cd concentrations in excess of about 1 mg/kg are considered to be evidence of anthropogenic pollution (Uminska 1993; Chaudry et al. 1977). The range of Cd in natural soils is 0.06 to 1.1 mg/kg (McBride 1994), and levels in contaminated sites have reached as high as 0.15% (Kabata-Pendias 2001).

Cadmium is rarely found in nature as the pure metal. At contaminated sites, Cd exists primarily as the Cd(II) ion (the predominant oxidation state in nature), Cd-CN^- complexes, or $Cd(OH)_2$, depending on pH and waste processing prior to disposal (U.S. EPA 1995). During weathering Cd readily solubilizes. The most significant environmental factors that control Cd ion mobility are pH and oxidation-reduction potential. Cadmium is most mobile in soils at pH values at or below 5.0, whereas in neutral and alkaline soil Cd is rather immobile. At pH values less than 8.0, it exists as the Cd^{2+} ion. In addition, it may form complex ions such as $CdCl^+$, $CdHCO_3^+$, $CdCl_4^{2-}$, $Cd(OH)_3^-$, and $Cd(OH)_4^{2-}$ and organic chelates. There may occur monovalent hydroxy ion species (e.g., $CdOH^+$) that do not readily occupy cation exchange sites. In the alkaline pH range, Cd^{2+} precipitates as $Cd(OH)_2$ and the less soluble $CdCO_3$. The Cd^{2+} ion can also coprecipitate with $CaCO_3$ (McBride 1994). In strongly oxidizing environments Cd is likely to form minerals such as CdO and $CdCO_3$ and may also accumulate in phosphate and other deposits (Kabata-Pendias 2001). Under reducing conditions and in the presence of sulfides, CdS forms. Cadmium will also precipitate with arsenate, chromate, phosphate, selenate, and selenite, with solubilities being a function of pH and geochemistry (U.S. EPA 1995).

Cadmium adsorption often correlates with the CEC of clay minerals, carbonate minerals, oxides, and organic matter in soils (Smith et al. 1995). Various anions such as chloride and sulfate complex with Cd, maintaining it in solution. Conversely, the presence of other soil cations (Ca^{2+}, Mg^{2+}, Fe^{2+}, etc.) reduces Cd sorption because of competitive adsorption.

Cadmium is associated with Zn in its geochemistry. The Cd^{2+} cation is more mobile than Zn^{2+} in acidic oxidizing conditions. This mobility is attributed to weak adsorption of Cd to organic matter, silicate clays, and oxides unless the pH is greater than 6.0. At high concentrations, Cd complexes with humic substances or other organic molecules. Soil microbial activity is believed to influence the transformations of Cd in soils. Cadmium does not form volatile compounds.

Because Cd is readily available to plants from both air and soil sources, its concentration rapidly increases in plants grown in polluted areas (Smith et al. 1995). Furthermore, the origin of soil Cd is an important factor controlling its solubility and phytoavailability. Oats absorbed a much higher proportion of anthropogenic Cd (added as CdO) than that of lithogenic origin (Grupe and Kuntze 1987). A great proportion of soil Cd accumulates in root tissues (Pichtel et al. 2000; Kabata-Pendias 1979), although it is known to occur in substantial amounts in shoot tissues of many leafy vegetables.

Cadmium is considered a toxic element to plants, with the main cause of toxicity the disruption of enzyme activities. The greatest concern regarding plant uptake, however, is as a Cd reservoir and a pathway to humans and animals. Thus, tolerance of some plant species to higher Cd levels poses a public health risk (Smith et al. 1995). In human and animal nutrition, Cd is a cumulative poison. Cadmium accumulates in food crops and grasses, and in domestic livestock and wildlife (Smith et al. 1995; U.S. EPA 1994). The application of sewage sludge to soil may increase soil Cd levels; this process can result in elevated Cd levels in crops. The U.S. Environmental Protection Agency has set guidelines for the application of sewage sludges and other materials to agricultural soils in efforts to limit Cd to food and feed crops (U.S. EPA 1983).

Liming a soil beyond a pH of 7.0 will result in the formation of relatively immobile Cd species (e.g., hydroxides, oxides, and carbonates). This reaction is relevant for the development of reclamation techniques for the management of Cd-enriched soils (Smith et al. 1995; Laxen 1985).

2.2.4. Chromium

Significant sources of chromium (Cr) to the biosphere include the chemical manufacturing industry and combustion of fossil fuels (natural gas, oil, and coal). Other sources include wastewaters from electroplating, leather tanning, and textile industries; incineration of municipal solid waste (MSW) and sewage sludge; cement manufacture; and emissions from air conditioning cooling towers that use Cr compounds as rust inhibitors (U.S. EPA 1994; Nriagu 1988). The variability in the oxidation states of Cr in soils is significant in terms of public health and environmental hazard. Chromium exhibits variable oxidation states (from 0 to +6); however, it exists primarily in three forms: metallic chromium (Cr(0)), trivalent (Cr[III]), and hexavalent (Cr[VI]). Chromium occurs in natural soils primarily as the trivalent and hexavalent species, in concentrations ranging from 7 to 221 mg/kg (McBride 1994). The Cr(VI) ion, common in industrial uses, forms anions such as chromate (CrO_4^{2-}), bichromate ($HCrO_4^-$), or dichromate ($Cr_2O_7^{2-}$). These remain soluble in soils and sediments; thus, the risk of groundwater contamination is significant (Nivas et al. 1996). Hexavalent Cr readily passes through cell membranes and can damage DNA; hence, it is carcinogenic. Most soil Cr, however, exists as Cr(III) (chromic) and occurs within mineral structures or as mixed Cr(III) and Fe(III) oxides. In general, Cr(III) resembles Fe(III) and Al(III) in ionic size and in geochemical properties; for example, Cr(III) readily substitutes for Fe(III) in mineral structures (Kabata-Pendias 2001; McBride 1994). The compounds of Cr(III) are considered to be stable in soils because they are only slightly mobile in acid media and, by pH 5.5, have precipitated. Aqueous concentrations are generally below water quality standards. The Cr(III) species is therefore less of a public health and environmental concern. In contrast, Cr(VI) is unstable in soils and is easily mobilized in both acid and alkaline conditions

(Kabata-Pendias 2001). The environmental behavior of Cr depends on various factors including soil pH, oxidation state, mineralogical properties, and the presence of organic matter. Chromium behavior is governed strongly by both soil pH and redox potential (James and Bartlett 1983a; Bartlett and Kimble 1976a; 1976b). The adsorption of chromate by soils and subsurface materials is rather poorly understood. The CrO_4^{2-} anion may be adsorbed to Fe and Al oxides and with other positively charged colloids. Chromate may also be adsorbed by ligand exchange, and $HCrO_4^-$ may behave similarly to $H_2PO_4^-$ (James and Bartlett 1983b). Reduction of Cr(VI) to Cr(III) with subsequent precipitation or adsorption of the trivalent species may occur in the presence of reductive solids, Fe(II), and organic material (Bartlett and Kimble 1976b; James and Bartlett 1983c). Soil pH also affects the rate of reduction of Cr(VI) to Cr(III). Conversely, some Cr(III) can be oxidized to chromate, CrO_4^{2-} at high pH (Bartlett and James 1979). This oxidation is promoted by the presence of Mn (McBride 1994). Soil organic matter is known to mobilize a portion of soil Cr (James and Bartlett 1983c).

Chromium is a required element in human and animal nutrition. Stimulating effects of Cr on plants have been observed by several authors; however, phytotoxicity of Cr is a common phenomenon. The form most available to plants is Cr(VI), which is also toxic to plants and animals. There is evidence that Cr(VI) cations can be transformed in plant cells into Cr(III), which react with DNA and protein compounds. The Cr(VI) compounds exhibit a mutagenic effect on *Bacillus subtilis* cells while Cr(III) compounds result in only slight mutagenic activities (Pacha and Galimska-Stypa 1988). Organic exudates from the plant root (e.g., acids) may reduce Cr(VI) in the rhizosphere. The Cr(III) species is generally unavailable to plants and, due to low solubility, Cr(III) compounds are not translocated through cell membranes (Smith et al. 1995; Tobin et al. 1984). The minimal mobility of soil Cr (typically as trivalent) may be responsible for an inadequate Cr supply to plants.

Remediation of Cr-contaminated soil apparently is closely linked to oxidation state. For soils enriched in Cr(VI), washing with hot water has been found to be effective (Ososkov and Bozzelli 1994). In the case of Cr(III) contamination, however, removal processes become much more complex due to the formation of insoluble complex ions and precipitates. Some researchers have experienced modest success with simple dissolution of Cr minerals using chelating agents (e.g., EDTA, NTA) and acids (HCl)

(Pichtel and Pichtel 1997). Others (Thirumalai Nivas et al. 1996) have applied anionic surfactants to soils to remove Cr as colloidal micelles.

2.2.5. Lead

Lead (Pb) has highly chalcophilic properties; its primary form in nature is galena, PbS. Lead is released to the biosphere primarily from metal smelting and processing, secondary metals production, Pb battery manufacturing, pigment and chemical manufacturing, and disposal of Pb-containing waste. Specific Pb sources include industrial waste and construction debris buried in landfills, high-explosive burn sites, firing ranges, and disposal and storage of lead acid batteries (Pichtel 2005).

The fate of anthropogenic Pb in soils has recently been of much concern because this metal is hazardous to humans and animals from two sources: the food chain and soil dust inhalation and/or ingestion.

Lead enters the soil in various and complex compounds. During weathering of natural Pb sulfides, slow oxidation processes tend to form carbonates, oxides, hydroxides, and other minerals, and Pb is also incorporated into clay minerals. Soil material at battery processing sites likely contains $PbSO_4$ with various metallic Pb forms. Lead ingots (90%–95% Pb) can be recovered (Fig. 2.3), and metallic Pb battery components such as electrode screens, terminals, plates, or chips are commonly found. Lead concentrations of up to 30% have been reported for soil intermingled with battery casing scrap and associated Pb compounds (Royer et al. 1992). The main Pb pollutants emitted from smelters occur in mineral forms (e.g., PbS, PbO, $PbSO_4$, and $PbO\cdot PbSO_4$; see Fig. 2.4), while Pb

Figure 2.3. Lead ingots unearthed at an automotive battery recycling facility. (Photo by Mark Steele.)

Figure 2.4. *Scanning electron micrograph of soil at a battery recycling facility. The mixed aggregates contain both anglesite (PbSO₄) and metallic Pb.*

in auto exhausts is mainly in the form of halide salts (e.g., PbBr, PbBrCl, Pb(OH)Br, and $(PbO)_2PbBr_2$). Tetramethyl lead, a relatively volatile organolead compound, may form as a result of biological alkylation of organic and inorganic Pb by microorganisms in anaerobic sediments (Smith et al. 1995).

An upper limit for the Pb content of a normal soil is approximately 70 mg/kg. However, due to widespread Pb pollution, most soils are likely to be enriched in this metal, especially in the surface horizon (Smith et al. 1995; Kabata-Pendias 2001; Davies 1977). It is therefore difficult to locate a truly noncontaminated soil.

Lead occurs mainly as Pb(0), Pb(II), and, to a lesser degree, the Pb(IV) species. Lead is reported to be the least mobile of the heavy metals. Contamination of soils with Pb is mainly an irreversible and, therefore, a cumulative process in surface soils. Several observations of the Pb balance in various ecosystems show that the input of this metal greatly exceeds its output (Smith et al. 1995).

After being released to a contaminated site, most Pb is retained strongly by soil; very little is transported into surface water or groundwater. The fate of Pb is affected by adsorption, ion exchange, precipitation, and complexation to organic matter. In soils, Pb forms stable complexes with both inorganic (e.g., Cl^-, CO_3^{2-}) and organic (e.g., humic and fulvic acid) ligands (Bodek et al. 1988). Soluble Pb may react with carbonates, sulfides, sulfates, and phosphates to form low-solubility compounds (Smith et al. 1995). The adsorption of Pb is highly dependent on the kinds of ligand involved in the formation of hydroxy complexes of Pb (e.g., $PbOH^-$ and $Pb_4[OH_4]^{4+}$). Farrah and Pickering (1977) discuss possible mechanisms of adsorption of hydroxy species and suggest that Pb sorption on montmorillonite is a cation exchange process, while on kaolinite and illite Pb is competitively adsorbed. Abd-Elfattah and Wada (1981) found a higher selective adsorption of Pb by Fe oxides, halloysite, and imogolite than by humus, kaolinite, and montmorillonite. In other studies, the greatest affinity to sorb Pb was reported for Mn oxides. Lead is also associated with Al hydroxides. In some soils Pb may be highly concentrated in calcium carbonate particles or in phosphate concretions. In soil with high organic matter content and a pH ranging from 6.0 to 8.0, Pb may form insoluble organic complexes; if the soil has less organic matter at the same pH, hydrous lead oxide complexes or lead carbonate or lead phosphate precipitates may form.

Increasing amounts of Pb in surface soils have been reported for various terrestrial ecosystems. Concern about Pb contamination of soils had been minimal for years because the relative insolubility of adsorbed and precipitated forms of Pb in soils has been commonly accepted. However, some forms have been found to be available for plant uptake (Pichtel et al. 2000; Pichtel and Salt 1998; J. Pichtel and Anderson 1997). Furthermore, certain soil and plant factors (e.g., low pH, low P content of soil, organic ligands) are known to promote both Pb uptake by roots and Pb translocation to plant tops. Of environmental significance is the ability of plants to absorb Pb from soil and air, even though Pb is believed to be the metal of least bioavailability and the most highly accumulated metal in root tissues. The levels of Pb in soils that are toxic to plants are a function of plant species, Pb concentration, and Pb species; thus, amounts will vary over a wide range. Several authors have reported concentrations ranging from 100 to several thousand mg/kg (Kabata-Pendias 2001; Pichtel et al. 2000; Pichtel and Salt 1998).

Several plant species and genotypes are adapted to growth in high Pb concentrations in soils. A number of species and ecotypes (as well as bacterial species) are known to possess Pb-tolerance mechanisms (Yangh et al. 2005; Thurman 1991; Verkleij and Schat 1990). This is reflected by variable amounts in plants, as well as a varied distribution of Pb between roots and above-ground biomass (Kabata-Pendias 2001). The highest bioaccumulation of Pb generally is reported for leafy vegetables (mainly lettuce) grown in proximity to nonferrous metal smelters where plants are exposed to Pb sources in both soil and air. In these locations, highly contaminated lettuce may contain up to 0.15% Pb (dw) (Smith et al. 1995; Roberts et al. 1974). Lead has also been found to accumulate in certain crops grown on biosolids-amended soils (Pichtel and Anderson 1997).

The mode of Pb uptake into plants is passive (Zimdahl 1975; Hughes et al. 1980). Lead, although not readily soluble in soil, is absorbed mainly by root hairs and is stored to a considerable degree in cell walls (Kabata-Pendias 2001). When Pb is present in soluble forms in nutrient solutions, plant roots are able to take up great amounts, the rate increasing with increasing concentration in the solutions and with time. The translocation of Pb from roots to tops is typically limited, however (Smith et al. 1995; Zimdahl 1975). Airborne Pb, a major source of Pb pollution, is also readily taken up by plants through foliage (Kabata-Pendias 2001).

Adequate soil phosphorus (P) content is known to reduce the effects of Pb toxicity. This interference is due to the ability of Pb to form insoluble phosphates in both plant tissues and in soils. Sulfur is known to inhibit the transport of Pb from roots to shoots. Sulfur deficiency markedly increases the Pb movement into the tops (Smith et al. 1995; Jones et al. 1973). Recent studies (Huang et al. 2005) have demonstrated that arbuscular mycorrhizal fungi could protect host plants from the phytotoxicity of excessive lead by changing the speciation from the bioavailable to the nonbioavailable form. This might illustrate that mycorrhiza have a unique mechanism for protecting their host from excessive lead phytotoxicity by chelating lead in the roots.

The solubility of Pb can be greatly decreased by liming. A high soil pH may precipitate Pb as hydroxide, phosphate, or carbonate, as well as promote the formation of Pb-organic complexes that are rather stable.

2.2.6. Mercury

Mercury (Hg) is a chalcophile and, in unweathered rocks is commonly found as cinnabar, HgS. Sources of soil contamination with Hg include metal processing industries, certain chemical works (especially chloralkali), and the use of fungicides containing Hg. Sewage sludges and other wastes may also be sources of Hg contamination. Mercury has been used in the gold amalgamation process in gold mining in the Brazilian Amazon basin (Olivera et al.; Malm et al. 1990). Common secondary Hg sources are spent batteries, fluorescent lamps, switches, dental amalgams, measuring devices, and laboratory and electrolytic refining wastes.

Background levels of Hg in soils are difficult to estimate due to widespread Hg pollution. The background contents of soil Hg are estimated to range between 50 and 300 µg/kg, depending on soil type. Thus, Hg contents in excess of these values should be considered an indicator of anthropogenic contamination (Kabata-Pendias 2001).

At contaminated sites, Hg exists in the mercuric (Hg[II]), mercurous (Hg$_2$[II]), elemental (Hg[0]), or alkylated form (e.g., methyl and ethyl mercury). The behavior of Hg in contaminated soils is of concern because its bioavailability poses a significant health hazard. In soils and surface water, solid forms partition to colloidal particles whereas volatile forms (e.g., metallic mercury and dimethylmercury) are released to the atmosphere. Mercury exists primarily in the mercuric and mercurous forms as complexes with varying water solubilities. In soils and sediments, sorption is one of the most important controlling pathways for removal of Hg from solution.

Mercury is strongly sorbed to humic materials and is retained by soils mainly as slightly mobile organocomplexes. In acid conditions, Hg is leached from soil profiles in the form of organic complexes. Other removal mechanisms include flocculation and coprecipitation with sulfides. Hg(OH)$_2$ is likely to predominate over other aqueous species at a pH near or above neutrality. Some investigators believe that Hg(OH)$_2$ is the preferred sorbed species (Kabata-Pendias 2001).

The most important transformation process in the environmental fate of Hg is biotransformation. Any Hg form entering sediments, groundwater, or surface water under the appropriate conditions can be microbially converted to the methylmercuric ion. Sulfur-reducing bacteria are responsible for most Hg methylation in the environment, with anaerobic conditions favoring their activity. The methylation of elemental Hg plays a key role in environmental cycling of Hg. Methylated Hg, the most common Hg form, is mobile and readily taken up by organisms including some higher plants. Humic substances are known to mediate the chemical methylation of inorganic Hg by releasing labile methyl groups. Methylation of Hg can also occur abiotically. Mercury methylation processes have apparently been involved in earlier events of catastrophic Hg poisoning. Methylmercury, being soluble and mobile, rapidly enters the aquatic food chain (Baralkiewicz et al. 2006; Webb et al.). Concentrations of methylmercury in carnivorous fish can be 10,000 to 100,000 times the concentrations found in ambient waters (Callahan et al. 1979).

Volatile elemental Hg may be formed through the demethylation of methylmercury or the reduction of inorganic Hg, with anaerobic conditions favoring the reactions (Smith et al. 1995; see Fig. 2.5). Rapid conversion of organic Hg and Hg^{2+} ions to the elemental state (Hg^0) in contact with humic substances may occur. Several types of bacteria and yeasts have been shown to promote the reduction of cationic Hg^{2+} to the elemental state (Hg^0).

Plants take up Hg easily from solution culture. There is also evidence that high soil Hg concentrations increase Hg contents of certain plants (Moreno-Jimenez et al. 2006). The rate is highest for roots, but leaves and grains also accumulate much Hg. Various organic Hg compounds (methyl, ethyl, phenyl) added to soil are partly decomposed or adsorbed by soil constituents. However, all these compounds, having a relatively small

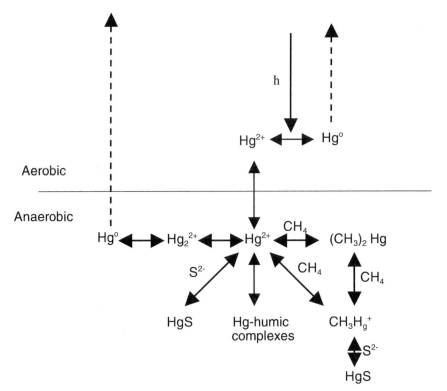

Figure 2.5. *Transformations of mercury in soils and sediments*

degree of dissociation and adsorbability, are readily taken up by plants. Methyl-Hg is the most available, while phenyl- and sulfide-Hg are the least available Hg forms to plants. Plants are known to directly absorb Hg vapor (Ericksen and Gustin 2004; Ericksen et al. 2003).

The distribution of Hg in plants has been studied because of the potential for Hg entry into the food chain. Therefore, much information is available related to the Hg content of plant foods. The background levels of Hg in vegetables and fruits vary from 2.6 to 86 μg/kg (dw). Plants grown in contaminated sites may accumulate much higher than normal amounts of Hg, however. Certain plant species, lichens, carrots, lettuce, and mushrooms, in particular, are likely to take up more Hg than other plants grown at the same sites. Also, some parts of plants have a greater ability to absorb Hg, as is the case of apple flesh (Kabata-Pendias 2001).

Plants differ in their ability to take up Hg and can also develop a tolerance to high Hg concentrations in their tissues when grown in soils overlying Hg deposits. The Hg tolerance mechanism of the physiological barrier is not known; however, it is probably related to the inactivation of Hg at membrane sites (Kabata-Pendias 2001).

Regarding plant growth on contaminated soils, there is the additional concern for the generation of methyl-Hg from microbial methylation of Hg by bacteria and fungi under both aerobic and anaerobic soil conditions. Even simple Hg salts or metallic Hg create a hazard to plants and soil biota from the toxic nature of Hg vapor (Kabata-Pendias 2001). The symptoms of Hg toxicity are, most commonly, a stunting of seedling growth and root development and an inhibition of photosynthesis and, as a consequence, a reduction in yield. Mercury accumulated in root tissue inhibits K^+ uptake by plants.

Mercury uptake by plant roots may be minimized by neutralizing the soil pH with liming materials. Also, sulfur-containing compounds and rock phosphates may inactivate mercurial fungicides or elemental Hg in soils.

2.2.7. Nickel

Anthropogenic sources of nickel (Ni), from industrial activity in particular, have resulted in a significant increase in the Ni content of soils. Nickel is released in the emissions from mining and metal-processing operations, from municipal waste incineration, and from the combustion of coal and oil. Land application of biosolids and certain phosphate fertilizers may also be significant sources of Ni. Sources to water include stormwater runoff, wastewater from municipal sewage treatment plants, and leachate from landfill sites (U.S. EPA 1994). Worldwide soil Ni concentrations range from 0.2 to 450 mg/kg. The highest Ni contents occur in clay and loamy soils. Nickel is also elevated in soils over basic and volcanic rocks, and in some organic-rich soils (Kabata-Pendias 2001).

The +2 oxidation state is the only stable Ni form in the environment. In surface soil horizons, Ni occurs mainly in organically bound forms, part of which may be soluble chelates. Nickel species such as Ni^{2+}, $NiOH^+$, $HNiO^-_2$, and $Ni(OH)^-_3$ also occur.

Generally, the solubility of soil Ni is inversely related to soil pH. Nickel sorption on Fe and Mn oxides is especially pH-dependent, probably because $NiOH^+$ is preferentially sorbed (Kabata-Pendias 2001).

Environmental Ni pollution greatly influences its concentrations in plants. In ecosystems where Ni is an airborne pollutant, plant tops are likely to concentrate the most Ni, which can be washed from leaf surfaces. Biosolids have also been shown to be a source of Ni to plants. Nickel in sludge that is present mainly in organic chelated forms is readily available to plants (Pichtel and Anderson 1997) and therefore may be phytotoxic. As Ni is readily mobile in plants, berries and grains are reported to contain elevated Ni concentrations (Kabata-Pendias 1995).

The soluble, adsorbed (exchangeable), and organically bound fractions of soil Ni are the forms most available to plants (Pichtel and Anderson 1997). Nickel is readily taken up by plants from soils and, until certain concentrations in plant tissues are reached, the adsorption is positively correlated with soil Ni concentrations. Both plant and pedological factors affect Ni uptake by plants, but the most significant factor is soil pH (Kabata-Pendias 1995).

Nickel is a rather toxic element to plants. The mechanism of Ni toxicity is not well understood, although restricted growth of plants and injuries caused by excess concentrations have been observed. Elevated concentrations in plant tissues may inhibit photosynthesis and transpiration. The most common symptom of Ni phytotoxicity is chlorosis. With plants under Ni stress, the absorption of nutrients, root development, and metabolism are restricted. In addition, low N_2 fixation by soybean plants may be caused by Ni excesses (Kabata-Pendias 2001).

Generally the range of excessive or toxic amounts of Ni in most plant species varies from 10 to 100 mg/kg (dw). Most sensitive species are affected by much lower Ni concentrations, ranging from 10 to 30 mg/kg (dw). Several species are known for their great tolerance and hyperaccumulation of Ni (Nkoane et al. 2005; Massoura et al. 2004; Brooks et al. 1974). Hutchinson and Whitby (1974) reported 902 mg/kg Ni in the grass *Deschampsia flexuosa*, and Peterson (1975) measured 1,780 mg/kg Ni in *Silene acaulis*.

Soil treatments, such as additions of lime, phosphate, or humified organic matter, decrease Ni availability to plants (Kabata-Pendias 2001).

2.2.8. Selenium

Excessive levels of selenium (Se) in soil have been determined both in naturally Se-enriched areas (typically semiarid and arid environs) and in industrial areas where Se is released to the atmosphere. Examples of the former include various coal deposits and clay-rich sediments. Examples of the latter include certain metal-processing operations, the combustion of coal, and MSW incineration. Several emissions, including Se-enriched fly ash, may be a significant source of Se, which is relatively available to plants (Kabata-Pendias 2001). Soil Se ranges worldwide from 0.05 to 1.27 mg/kg (McBride 1994).

Selenium, a chalcophile, tends to be associated with sulfide minerals in rocks. Natural weathering results in the oxidation of insoluble reduced forms, including elemental Se (Se^{o}), selenides (Se^{2-}), and selenium sulfides, to the more soluble selenites (SeO_3^{2-}) and selenates (SeO_4^{2-}).

Several oxidation states are possible for Se in soils, and the soil oxidation-reduction potential strongly affects Se behavior. In alkaline, oxidized soils, the selenates predominate. They bond weakly to oxides and other minerals, so that Se mobility in neutral to alkaline soils is high. In slightly acid oxidized soils, selenites are common; these are of lower mobility than selenates. This is because of the ability of SeO_3^{2-} to chemisorb strongly onto oxides and aluminosilicates, particularly Fe oxides and montmorillonite, respectively, and to precipitate as the insoluble ferric selenite. In reducing environments, that is, wet or organic-rich soils, the insoluble reduced forms (selenides and Se-sulfides) predominate so that Se mobility and bioavailability are low. Under reducing conditions biological methylation of Se may occur; this process may form volatile compounds (e.g., dimethyl selenides).

The solubility of Se in most soils is rather low; therefore, many agricultural areas produce crop plants and forage low in Se content. However, in naturally Se-enriched soils, in calcareous soils, in arid zones, and in contaminated soils in industrial areas Se as selenate may be accumulated by plants in concentrations high enough to be toxic to grazing livestock. Some legumes (e.g., sweetclover) grown on coal ash are known to contain as much as 200 mg/kg (dw) Se. Grass grown in the vicinity of a P fertilizer plant contained up to 1.2 mg/kg (Gough and Severson 1979; Gutenmann et al. 1976).

The application of P, S, and N may detoxify Se, which may be a result either of depressing Se uptake by roots or of establishing a more favorable ratio of Se to these elements. The application of S is an important remedial treatment on Se-enriched soils (Kabata-Pendias 2001; Johnson 1975).

2.2.9. Zinc

Zinc ores include zinc sphalerite or zinc blende (ZnS and marmatite, ZnS with some Fe). Zinc is extracted from ores by roasting to form zinc oxide (ZnO). The main use of Zn is as a corrosion-resistant coating on iron or steel. Zinc metal is used to make the casings of zinc-carbon dry cell batteries, sacrificial anodes, and die-cast parts. Brass alloy is used in shell casings, tubing, and electrical equipment. Zinc dust is used in priming compounds, paints, alkaline dry cell batteries, and metals processing.

Soil contamination with Zn has reached very high concentrations in certain areas. Zinc is released to the atmosphere as dust and fumes from zinc production facilities, automobile emissions, and fuel combustion. Additional sources in air include MSW incineration, coal combustion, smelter operations, and some metalworking industries. Zinc in the atmosphere is often deposited in soils and vegetation. Municipal biosolids applied to cropland can also be enriched with trace metals including Zn. Hazardous-waste sites are additional sources: Zn has been found in over 700 of the 1,300 National Priorities List (NPL) hazardous-waste sites (U.S. EPA 1994). These sources, along with releases of Zn through metal corrosion and tire wear, contribute to urban runoff contamination.

Zinc occurs naturally in soils in amounts ranging from 17 to 125 mg/kg. The most common and mobile Zn form in soil is Zn^{2+}, but other ionic species may occur. The factors controlling Zn mobility in soils are similar to those for Cu, but Zn appears to occur in more readily soluble forms (Lindsay 1972). Clay minerals, hydrous oxides, and pH are among the most important factors controlling Zn solubility in soils. Of lesser importance are precipitation as hydroxide, carbonate, and sulfide compounds, and complexation by organic matter. Zinc can enter some layer silicate clays (e.g., montmorillonite) and become immobilized. Soil organic matter is known to be capable of binding Zn in stable forms (Kabata-Pendias 2001). Because Zn is adsorbed by mineral and organic moieties, its accumulation in surface horizons is fairly common.

Zinc is considered to be readily soluble relative to the other heavy metals in soils. Zinc is most readily mobile and available in acid-light (sandy, loamy) mineral soils. Acid leaching will result in active Zn mobilization. Solubility and availability of Zn is inversely correlated with Ca-saturation and P compounds present in soils. This relationship presumably is a result of both adsorption and precipitation processes (Kabata-Pendias 2001).

Zinc is an essential trace element in the growth of both plants and animals (Smith et al. 1995). Toxicity and tolerance in plants have recently been of special concern because the prolonged use of Zn fertilizers, as well as its input from industrial pollution, has resulted in an increase in Zn content of surface soils. Several plant species and genotypes are known to possess a great tolerance of soil Zn. Some genotypes grown in Zn-rich soils or in areas of heavy atmospheric Zn deposition may accumulate extremely large amounts without showing symptoms of toxicity (Thurman 1991; Verkleij and Schat 1990). Zinc is not considered to be highly phytotoxic. Zinc-Cd interactions are common in the literature, with reports both of antagonism and synergism between the two elements in the uptake-transport processes (Smith et al. 1995; He et al. 2004).

Additional concerns related to Zn pollution are changes in metal speciation. For example, in soil (pH 6.8) amended with Zn-enriched compost (composted biosolids, composted muncipal solid waste), an increase was observed of easily available Zn species and weakly bound or exchangeable Zn species (Pichtel and Anderson 1997). Soluble Zn-organic complexes that occur particularly in municipal biosolids are very mobile in soils and therefore are readily available to plants (Lavado et al. 2005). Amelioration of Zn-contaminated soils is commonly based on controlling its availability by the addition of lime or organic matter or both.

QUESTIONS

1. The toxicity of heavy metals depends in large part on its form, for example, ionic versus organically bound. Explain.

2. Explain the factors affecting Cd mobility in the environment. Include soil pH, oxidation-reduction status, clay mineralogy, and other factors.

3. Which chromium species, for example, $+3$ versus $+6$, is a suspected mutagen? An essential trace element? Discuss the factors that result in transformation of one species to the other.

4. Which heavy metals/metalloids are known to form methylated compounds? What is the environmental significance of such methylation reactions?

5. Volcanic eruptions are a significant source of which metal(s) to the biosphere?

6. Which metal is more mobile in soils, all other factors being equal: Cd or Pb? Explain your reasoning.

7. Due to widespread Pb pollution, most soils may very likely be somewhat enriched in this metal. True or false? Discuss.

8. Choose the correct answer: Lead can enter food via: (a) uptake from soil and transport through the food chain; (b) lead in solder inside food cans; (c) plant uptake of Pb-containing dusts; (d) all of the above.

9. Choose the correct answer: Lead in water can be from (a) piping using lead solder connections; (b) contamination in aquifers supplying the wells; (c) industrial residue; (d) all of the above.

10. What is (are) the common form(s) of lead in soils?

11. What benefits of lead-based paint made it so popular? Discuss.

12. Pb may be present in soils and aquatic ecosystems in the Pb^{2+} form. True or false?

13. Water chemistry (e.g., hard versus soft water) may influence Pb availability in water. True or false? Explain.

14. Lead is an airborne contaminant as well as a water (i.e., ingestion) hazard. Which is of greater concern?

15. Lead will not readily leach from soil; that is, rainfall and other natural conditions will not promote the downward movement of Pb out of the soil profile. Explain the processes responsible for this phenomenon.

16. Mercury is the most volatile of all the heavy metals. True or false?

17. Which form(s) of mercury is (are) readily mobile and easily taken up by organisms?

18. How do Hg species react with humic materials—is sorption possible? Discuss.

REFERENCES

Abd-Elfattah, A., and K. Wada. 1981. Adsorption of lead, copper, zinc, cobalt and cadmium by soils that differ in cation-exchange materials. *J. Soil Science* 32:271.

Baralkiewicz, D., H. Gramowska, and R. Golstrodyn. 2006. Distribution of total mercury and methyl mercury in water, sediment and fish from Swarzedzkie lake. *Chemistry and Ecology* 22 (1): 59–64.

Bartlett, R. J., and B. James. 1979. Behavior of chromium in soils: III. Oxidation. *Journal of Environmental Quality* 8:31–35.

Bartlett, R. J., and J. M. Kimble. 1976a. Behavior of chromium in soils: I. Trivalent forms. *Journal of Environmental Quality* 5:379–83.

———. 1976b. Behavior of chromium in soils: II. Hexavalent forms. *Journal of Environmental Quality* 5:383–86.

Bodek, I., W. J. Lyman, W. F. Reehl, and D. H. Rosenblatt. 1988. *Environmental Inorganic Chemistry: Properties, Processes, and Estimation Methods*. Elmsford, NY: Pergamon.

Brooks, R. R., J. Lee, and T. Jaffre. 1974. Some New Zealand and New Caledonian plant accumulators of nickel. *J. Ecol.* 62:493–98.

Callahan, M. A., M. W. Slimak, and N. W. Gabel. 1979. *Water-Related Environmental Fate of 129 Priority Pollutants*. Vol. 1, *Introduction and Technical Background, Metals, and Inorganics, Pesticides and PCBs*. EPA-440/4-79-029a, Report to U.S. Environmental Protection Agency, Office of Water Planning and Standards, Washington, DC. Springfield, VA: Versar Incorporated.

Chaudry, F. M., A. Wallace, and R. T. Mueller. 1977. Barium toxicity in plants. *Commun. Soil Sci. Plant Anal.* 8:795–97.

Cline, S. R., B. E. Reed, and M. Matsumoto. 1993. In *Hazardous and Industrial Wastes. Proceedings of the 25th Mid-Atlantic Industrial Waste Conference*, ed. A. Davis. Lancaster, PA: Technomic.

Crecelius, E. A., N. S. Bloom, C. E. Cowan, and E. A. Jenne. 1986. Speciation of selenium and arsenic in natural waters and sediments. Arsenic speciation. EPRI project 2020-2, Battelle Pacific North Lab, Sequim, WA, 32.

Davies, B.E. 1977. Heavy metal pollution of British agricultural soils with special reference to the role of lead and copper mining. In *Proceedings of the International Seminar on Soil Environment and Fertility Management in Intensive Agriculture*, Tokyo, 394.

Davis, A., and I. Singh. 1995. Washing of zinc(II) from a contaminated soil column. *Journal of Environmental Engineering* 121:174–85.

Dixon, J. B., and S. B. Weed. 1977. *Minerals in Soil Environments*. Madison, WI: Soil Science Society.

Ericksen, J. A., and M. S. Gustin. 2004. Foliar exchange of mercury as a function of soil and air mercury concentrations. *Science of the Total Environment* 324 (1–3): 271–79.

Ericksen, J. A., S. E. Lindberg, J. S. Coleman, M. S. Gustin, D. E. Schorran, and D. W. Johnson. 2003. Accumulation of atmospheric mercury in forest foliage. *Atmospheric Environment*. 37 (12): 1613–22.

Farrah, H., and W. F. Pickering. 1977. The sorption of lead and cadmium species by clay minerals. *Aust. J. Chem*. 30:1417.

Gough, L. P., and R. C. Severson. 1979. Impact of point source emission from phosphate processing on the element content of plants and soils. In *Trace Substances Environmental Health*, vol. 10, ed. D. D. Hemphill, 225. Univ. Missouri, Columbia. Soda Spring, Idaho.

Grupe, M., and H. Kuntze. 1987. Zur Ni-mobilitat einer geogen belasteten Braunerde. *Mitteilungen der Deutschen Bodenkunklichen Gesellschaft* 55:333.

Gutenmann, W. H., C. A. Bache, W. D. Youngs, and D. J. Lisk. 1976. Selenium in fly ash. *Science* 191:966.

Hanada, S., M. Nakano, H. Saitoh, and T. Mochizuki. 1975. Studies on the pollution of apple orchard surface soils and its improvement in relation to inorganic spray residues. *Bulletin of the Faculty of Agriculture, Kagoshima University* (Hirosal University, Japan) 25:13.

He, P. P., X. Y. Lv, and G. Y. Wang. 2004. Effects of Se and Zn supplementation on the antagonism against Pb and Cd in vegetables. *Environment International* 30(2), 167–72.

Huang, P. M. 1975. Retention of arsenic by hydroxy-aluminum on surface of micaceous mineral colloids. *Soil Science Society of America Proceedings* 39:271.

Huang, Y., S. Tao, and Y.-J.Chen. 2005. The role of arbuscular mycorrhiza on change of heavy metal speciation in rhizosphere of maize in wastewater irrigated agriculture soil. *Journal of Environmental Sciences* 17 (2): 276–80.

Hughes, M. K., N. W. Lepp, and D. A. Phipps. 1980. Aerial heavy metal pollution and terrestrial ecosystems. *Advances in Ecological Research* 11:217.

Hutchinson, T. C., and L. M. Whitby. 1974. Heavy-metal pollution in the Sudbury mining and smelting region of Canada. I. Soil and vegetation contamination by nickel, copper, and other metals. *Environmental Conservation* 1:123–32.

James, B. R., and R. J. Bartlett. 1983a. Behavior chromium in soils: VI. Interactions between oxidation-reduction and organic complexation. *Journal of Environmental Quality* 12:173–76.

———. 1983b. Behavior of chromium in soils: VII. Adsorption and reduction of hexavalent forms. *Journal of Environmental Quality* 12:177–81.

———. 1983c. Behavior chromium in soils: V. Fate of organically complexed Cr(III) added to soil. *Journal of Environmental Quality* 12:169–72.

Johnson, C. M. 1975. Selenium in soils and plants: contrasts in conditions providing safe but adequate amounts of selenium in the food chain. In *Trace Elements in Soil-Plant-Animal Systems*, ed. D. J. D. Nicholas and A. R. Egan, 165. New York: Academic Press.

Jones, L. H. P., S. C. Jarvis, and D. W. Cowling. 1973. Lead uptake from soils by perennial ryegrass and its relation to the supply of an essential element (sulphur). *Plant Soil* 38:605.

Kabata-Pendias, A. 1979. Effects of inorganic air pollutants on the chemical balance of agricultural ecosystems. United Nations ECE Symposium on Effects of Air-Borne Pollution on Vegetation, Warsaw, August 20, 134.

———. 2001. *Trace Elements in Soil and Plants*. 3rd ed. Boca Raton, FL: CRC Press.

Kitigashi, K., and I. Yamane, eds. 1981. *Heavy Metal Pollution in Soils of Japan*. Tokyo: Japan Science Society Press.

Lavado, R. S., M. B. Rodríguez, and M. A. Taboada. 2005. Treatment with biosolids affects soil availability and plant uptake of potentially toxic elements. *Agriculture, Ecosystems and Environment* 109 (3–4): 360–64.

Laxen, D. P. H. 1985. Trace metal adsorption/coprecipitation on hydrous ferric oxide under realistic conditions. *Water Research* 19:1229–32.

Lindsay, W. L. 1972. Zinc in soils and plant nutrition. *Advances in Agronomy* 24:147.

Malm, O., W. C. Pfeiffer, C. M. M. Souza, and R. Reuther. 1990. Mercury pollution due to gold mining in the Madeira River Basin, Brazil. *Ambio* 19:11–15.

Massoura, S. T., G. Exhevarria, E. Leclerc-Cessac, and J. L Morel. 2004. Response of excluder, indicator, and hyperaccumulator plants to nickel availability in soils. *Australian Journal of Soil Research* 42 (8): 933–38.

McBride, M. B. 1994. *Environmental Chemistry of Soils*. New York: Oxford University Press.

Miller, W. P., and W. W. McFee. 1983. Distribution of cadmium, zinc, copper, and lead in soils of industrial northwestern Indiana. *Journal of Evironmental Quality* 12:29–33.

Moore, J. N., W. H. Ficklin, and C. Johns. 1988. Partioning of arsenic and metals in reducing sulfidic sediments. *Environmental Science & Technology* 22:432–37.

Moore, R. E., B. E. Reed, and M. Matsumoto. 1993. In *Hazardous and Industrial Wastes. Proceedings of the 25th Mid-Atlantic Industrial Waste Conference*, ed. A. Davis. Lancaster, PA: Technomic.

Moreno-Jimenez, E., R. Millan, J. M. Penalosa, E. Esteban, R. Gamarra, and R. O. Carpena-Ruiz. 2006. Mercury bioaccumulation and phytotoxicity in two wild plant species of Almaden area. *Chemosphere* 63 (11): 1969–73.

Nivas, D. A., B.-J. Sabatini, Shiau, and J. H. Harwell. 1996. Surfactant enhanced remediation of subsurface chromium contamination. *Water Research* 30 (3): 511–20.

Nkoane, B. B. M., W. Lund, G. M. Sawula, and G. Wibetoe. 2005. Identification of Cu and Ni indicator plants form mineralised locations in Botswana. *Journal of Geochemical Exploration* 86 (3): 130–42.

Nriagu, J. O. 1988. Production and uses of chromium. In *Chromium in the Natural and Human Environments, Advances in Environmental Science and Technology*, vol. 20, ed. J. O. Nriagu and E. Nieboer. New York: Wiley-Interscience.

Olivera, L. J., L. D. Hylander, and S. E. De Castro. Mercury behavior in a tropical environment: The case of small-scale gold mining in Poconé, Brazil. *Environmental Practice* 6 (2): 121–34.

Ososkov, V., and J. W. Bozzelli. 1994. Removal of Cr(VI) from chromium contaminated sites by washing with hot water. *Hazardous Waste and Hazardous Materials* 11:511–17.

Pacha, J., and R. Galimska-Stypa. 1988. Mutagenic properties of selected tri- and hexavalent chromium compounds. *Acta Biologica* (Katowice, Poland) 9:30.

Peterson, P. J. 1975. Element accumulation by plants and their tolerance of toxic mineral roles. In *International Conference on Heavy Metals in the Environment*. Vol. 2, *Pathways and Cycling*, ed. T. C. Hutchinson. Toronto: Institute for Environmental Studies, University of Toronto.

Pichtel, J. 2005. Phytoextraction of lead-contaminated soils: Current experience. In *Heavy Metal Contamination of Soils: Problems and Remedies*, ed. I. Ahmad, S. Hayat, and J. Pichtel. Enfield, NH: Science Publishers.

Pichtel, J., and M. Anderson. 1997. Trace metal bioavailability in municipal solid waste and sewage sludge composts. *Bioresource Technology* 60:223–29.

Pichtel, J., K. Kuroiwa, and H. T. Sawyerr. 2000. Distribution of Pb, Cd and Ba in soils and plants of two contaminated sites. *Environmental Pollution* 110:171–78.

Pichtel, J., and T. M. Pichtel. 1997. Comparison of solvents for ex-situ removal of Cr and Pb from contaminated soil. *Environmental Engineering Science* 14:97–103.

Pichtel, J., and C. A. Salt. 1998. Vegetative growth and trace metal accumulation on metalliferous wastes. *Journal of Environmental Quality* 27:618–24.

Roberts, T. M., W. Gizyn, and T. C. Hutchinson. 1974. Lead contamination of air, soil, vegetation, and people in the vicinity of secondary lead smelters. In *Trace Subst. Environ. Health*, 8:155, ed. D. D. Henry. Columbia: University of Missouri Press.

Royer, M. D., A. Selvakumar, and R. Gaire. 1992. Control technologies for remediation of contaminated soil and waste deposits at Superfund lead battery recyling sites. *Journal of the Air and Waste Management Association* 42:970–80.

Shacklette, H. T., J. A. Erdman, and T. F. Harms. 1978. Trace elements in plant foodstuffs. In *Toxicity of Heavy Metals in the Environment*, part 1, ed. F. W. Oehme. New York: Marcel Dekker.

Smith, L. A., J. L. Means, A. Chen, B. Alleman, C. C. Chapman, J. S. Tixier, S. E. Brauning, A. R. Gavaskar, and M. D. Royer. 1995. *Remedial Options for Metals-Contaminated Soils*. Boca Raton, FL: CRC Press.

Thirumalai Nivas, B., D. A. Sabatini, B. Shiau, and J. H. Harwell. 1996. Surfactant enhanced remediation of subsurface chromium contamination. *Water Research* 30: 511.

Thurman, D. A. 1991. Mechanism of metal tolerance in higher plants. In *Effect of Heavy Metal Pollution on Plants*. Vol. 2, *Metals in the Environment*, ed. N. W. Lepp, 239–49. London: Applied Science Publishers.

Tobin, J. M., D. G. Cooper, and R. J. Neufeld. 1984. Uptake of metal ions by *Rhizopus arrhizus*. *Applied and Environmental Microbiology* 47:821.

Uminska, R. 1993. Cadmium contents of cultivated soils exposed to contamination in Poland. *Environmental Geochemistry and Health* 15:15–19.

U.S. Department of Health and Human Services. 1992. Toxicological profile for barium and compounds. Clement International Corporation. Washington, DC: Agency for Toxic Substances and Disease Registry.

U.S. Environmental Protection Agency. 1983. *Process Design Manual. Land Application of Municipal Sludge*. EPA-625/1-83-016.

———. 1994. *Common Chemicals Found at Superfund Sites*. EPA 540/R-94/044. Washington, DC: Office of Solid Waste and Emergency Response.

———. 1995. *Contaminants and Remedial Options at Selected Metal-Contaminated Sites*. EPA/540/R-95/512. Cincinnati: National Risk Management Research Laboratory.

Verkleij, J. A. C., and H. Schat. 1990. Mechanisms of metal tolerance in higher plants. In *Heavy Metal Tolerance in Plants: Evolutionary Aspects*, ed. J. A. Shaw, 179–93. Boca Raton, FL: CRC Press

Webb, M. A. H., C. B. Schreck, M. Plume, C. Wong, D. T. Gunderson, G. W. Feist, M. S. Fitzpatrick, and E. P. Forester. Mercury concentrations in gonad, liver, and muscle of white sturgeon *Acipenser transmontanus* in the lower Columbia River. *Archives of Environmental Contamination and Toxicology* 50 (3):443–51.

Welch, A. H., M. S. Lico, and J. L. Hughes. 1988. Arsenic in groundwater of the western United States. *Groundwater* 26:333–47.

Woolson, E. A. 1992. Introduction to arsenic chemistry and analysis. In *Arsenic and Mercury. Workshop on Removal, Recovery, Treatment and Disposal.* EPA/600/R-92/105.

Woolson, E. A., J. H. Axley, and P. C. Kearney. 1973. The chemistry and phytotoxicity of arsenic in soils II. Effects of time and phosphorus. *Soil Science Society of America Proceedings* 37:254.

Yang, G., J. Wu, and Y. Tang. 2005. Research advances in plant resistance mechanisms under lead stress. *Chinese Journal of Ecology* 24 (12):1507–12.

Zimdahl, R. L. 1975. Entry and movement in vegetation of lead derived from air and soil sources. Paper presented at the 68th annual meeting of the Air Pollution Control Association, Boston, June 15.

CHAPTER 3

Hydrocarbon Chemistry and Properties

There are thousands of different chemicals in the environment that may cause adverse human health effects. Little is known about the toxicological properties of most of these chemicals.

—U.S. Environmental Protection Agency, "Unfinished Business: A Comparative Assessment of Environmental Problems," 1987

My father rode a camel; I drive a car; my son flies a jet; his son will ride a camel.

—Saudi saying

3.1. INTRODUCTION

Organic chemicals are the foundation of numerous industries including: fuel refining; plastics manufacture; paint, solvent, and pesticide manufacture; dry cleaning; asphalt production; detergents; and electronics. The use of organics worldwide has soared since Second World War II and improper use and accidents are of increasing concern. Many of these compounds, for example, fuels such as gasoline, have contaminated soil and water from improper use or storage. Also common is the spillage of motor oil onto soil due to improper handling. Contamination both on land and in water has occurred as a result of accidents during petroleum transport (pipelines, ships, trucks). Enormous quantities of pesticides, solvents, and other petrochemicals are used on the commercial and individual scale in the United States, and transport and application of these chemicals is of public health and environmental concern.

Certain petroleum hydrocarbons are acutely hazardous to public health or the biosphere, either via explosion hazard, defatting of biological tissue, direct toxicity, or simple asphyxiation. Long-term exposure to hydrocarbon compounds such as benzene (a common gasoline additive) or benzo[a] pyrene (a component of diesel exhaust fumes, tobacco smoke, and charbroiled food) is known to increase cancer risk.

Hazardous waste-contaminated sites are often mixtures of heterogeneous organic compounds that may be at least partially water soluble, resistant to bacterial degradation, and/or toxic in small doses. Understanding the chemical nature of organic contaminants is important in assessing the routes of exposure and the feasibility and method(s) of remediation. Operators need to know which compounds are expected to be toxic, which will float upon or sink within an aquifer, which will volatilize, and so on. Therefore, it is appropriate to look at the chemistry of petroleum hydrocarbons and at the relevant properties of some common petroleum products.

Petroleum products are mixtures of hydrocarbons; that is, they are a class of chemical compounds that contain the elements hydrogen and carbon. Although there is a broad range of compounds, the general categories of hydrocarbons encountered in nature as well as in commercial use are rather predictable. In order to successfully implement a remediation program for a hydrocarbon-affected site, a thorough understanding of the chemical and physical properties of the hydrocarbon(s) is essential.

3.2. STRUCTURE AND NOMENCLATURE

Organic chemistry is the study of carbon-containing compounds including hydrocarbons that are bound by a covalent bond. This bond is one in which electrons are shared between similar or chemically similar atoms (e.g., $C-C$; $C=O$; $C-N$, etc.) as opposed to bonds such as ionic (electrostatic), which involve the attraction of oppositely charged ions (e.g., K^+Cl^-).

Hydrocarbon molecules are composed of carbon and hydrogen in a myriad of combinations. An important rule of thumb for the correct representation of organic structures is that, in a stable hydrocarbon molecule, *carbon always, ALWAYS has four bonds*!

3.2.1. Aliphatic Hydrocarbons

The aliphatics are a category of straight-chain or branched hydrocarbons that can be divided into three groups depending on the number of bonds between adjacent carbon atoms. Alkanes contain only single bonds between adjacent carbon atoms, alkenes possess a double bond, and alkynes contain a triple bond. In those molecules having a combination of bonds, the compound is classified based on the highest number of bonds.

3.2.2. Alkanes

Alkanes possess a single bond between all carbon atoms. They may occur as straight chains, branched chains, or cyclic alkanes. The general formula for straight-chain alkanes is C_nH_{2n+2}. The simplest alkane is methane, CH_4.

We can build on this simple foundation and create a two-carbon chain:

$$
\begin{array}{c}
\text{H} \quad \text{H} \\
| \quad | \\
\text{H}-\text{C}-\text{C}-\text{H, also represented as } CH_3CH_3 \text{ or } C_2H_6, \text{ ethane.} \\
| \quad | \\
\text{H} \quad \text{H}
\end{array}
$$

Adding a single C to the chain (and observing the "four bonds to carbon" rule), we continue:

$$
\begin{array}{c}
\text{H} \quad \text{H} \quad \text{H} \\
| \quad | \quad | \\
\text{H}-\text{C}-\text{C}-\text{C}-\text{H} \quad \text{or} \quad CH_3(CH_2)CH_3 \quad \text{or} \quad C_3H_8, \text{ propane} \\
| \quad | \quad | \\
\text{H} \quad \text{H} \quad \text{H}
\end{array}
$$

$CH_3(CH_2)_2CH_3$ butane
$CH_3(CH_2)_3CH_3$ pentane
$CH_3(CH_2)_4CH_3$ hexane
$CH_3(CH_2)_5CH_3$ heptane
$CH_3(CH_2)_6CH_3$ octane
$CH_3(CH_2)_7CH_3$ nonane
$CH_3(CH_2)_8CH_3$ decane

.

.

.

$CH_3(CH_2)_{14}CH_3$ hexadecane, etc.

Methane, ethane, and propane possess low molecular weights, have very low boiling points, and are the primary components of natural gas, a common fuel.

The above alkanes are all known as normal, or *n*-alkanes, which indicate that the molecule exists as a straight chain without branches. Branched alkanes may be represented by the prefix *iso-*, for example, isobutane,

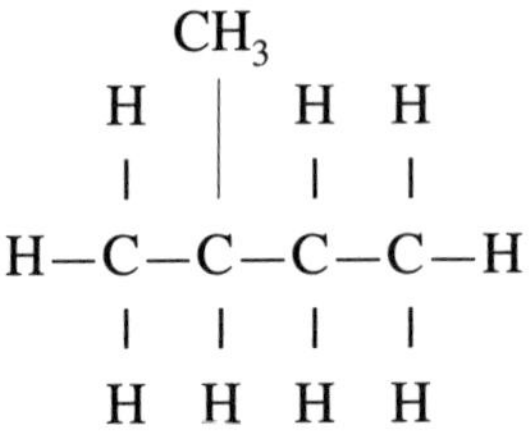

$$
\begin{array}{ccccc}
 & & CH_3 & & \\
H & & | & H & H \\
| & & | & | & | \\
H-C&-&C&-C&-C-H \\
| & & | & | & | \\
H & & H & H & H \\
\end{array}
$$

Branched isomers of hydrocarbons are important in gasoline formulations because they burn at a higher rate compared to the corresponding *n*-alkane; that is, they have a higher octane number. This number is essentially a rating of a fuel sample, used to indicate antiknock performance in motor vehicle engines. The higher the octane number, the higher the resistance to engine knock.

Alkanes also occur in cyclical structures, for example, cyclohexane, C_6H_{12}:

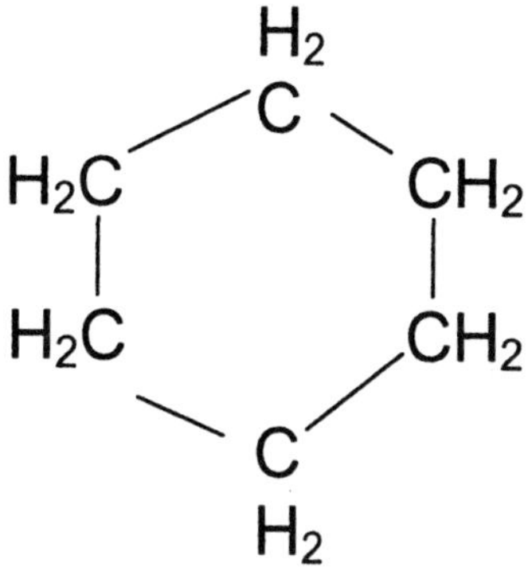

$$
\begin{array}{c}
\text{H}_2 \\
\text{C} \\
\text{H}_2\text{C} \qquad \text{CH}_2 \\
\text{H}_2\text{C} \qquad \text{CH}_2 \\
\text{C} \\
\text{H}_2
\end{array}
$$

or abbreviated as:

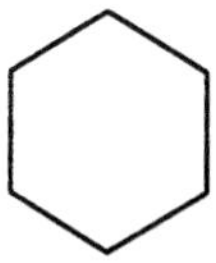

Where each apex of the hexagon is a carbon atom. Two H atoms are understood at each apex in order to form a total of four bonds to each C. Cyclohexane is a common component of gasoline.

3.2.3. Substitution in Aliphatics

In industrial, petrochemical, and other applications, aliphatics may contain substituents bound to the base molecule. For example, alkyl halides contain a halogen atom in place of a hydrogen:

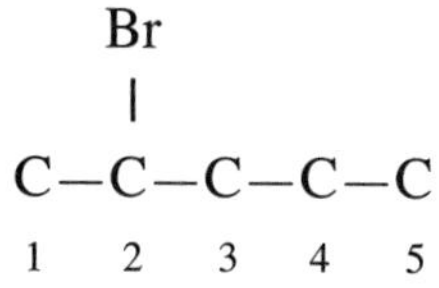

$$
\begin{array}{c}
\text{Br} \\
| \\
\text{C}-\text{C}-\text{C}-\text{C}-\text{C} \\
1 \quad 2 \quad 3 \quad 4 \quad 5
\end{array}
$$

which is 2-bromopentane. The halogens comprise Group VIIB of the Periodic Table and include F, Cl, Br, I, and At. Note that, in the structure above, the "2-" indicates the carbon position to which the substituent (in this case, the Br atom) is attached. Numbering is such that we arrive at the smallest possible number for a substituent location. The molecule:

$$\begin{matrix} & & & & \text{F} & & \\ & & & & | & & \\ \text{C}-\text{C}-\text{C}-\text{C}-\text{C}-\text{C}-\text{C} \\ 7 & 6 & 5 & 4 & 3 & 2 & 1 \end{matrix}$$

is 3-fluoroheptane, *not* 5-fluoroheptane.

Another example is carbon tetrachloride, a common industrial solvent, which is essentially a substituted methane:

carbon tetrachloride

It should be noted that the simple addition of a halide to a hydrocarbon molecule will drastically alter its chemical and physical properties including boiling point, water solubility, and vapor pressure, among others. Halides bound to hydrocarbons typically impart heat resistance to the molecule and greatly restrict biodegradation.

3.2.4. Alkenes

An alkene, also known as an olefin, contains at least one double bond between adjacent carbons and is considered *unsaturated* (that is, not all C atoms are "saturated" with H atoms). The general formula for alkenes is C_nH_{2n}. The name of the alkene ends in -*ene* or -*ylene*.

$$H_2C=CH_2 \text{ is ethene (or ethylene)}$$

$$\begin{matrix} & & \text{H} & & \\ & & | & & \\ \text{H}-\text{C}=\text{C}-\text{C}-\text{H} & \text{is 1-propene} \\ & & \text{H} & & \end{matrix}$$

$$H-C=C-C-C-H \text{ is 1-butene}$$

with H atoms shown on the carbons

$CH_2CH=CHCH_2$ is 2-butene.

Alkenyl halides contain at least one halogen atom and one carbon-carbon double bond. Examples include trichloroethylene (TCE) and tetrachloroethylene (or perchloroethylene, PCE), which are common solvents:

trichloroethylene   tetrachloroethylene

3.2.5. Alkynes

An alkyne contains at least one triple bond in the molecule. The general formula is C_nH_{2-n}. The triple bond is a high-energy bond; thus, alkynes are often used for high-temperature flames as in the case of ethyne (acetylene) in welding. Examples of alkynes include:

$$H-C\equiv C-H \qquad\qquad H-C\equiv C-CH$$

ethyne   propyne

3.2.6. Aromatic Hydrocarbons

Aromatic hydrocarbons comprise a unique category of hydrocarbons in that all such molecules possess the C_6H_6 (benzene) ring, represented as:

Single and double bonds alternate between adjacent carbons. Furthermore, these bonds are not permanent; rather, they are continuously alternating at extremely high speeds. This continuous transition between single and double bonds is termed *resonance*, which imparts a high degree of stability to aromatic compounds. As we shall see in subsequent chapters, aromatic hydrocarbons are often difficult to decompose by chemical or biological processes.

Examples of aromatic compounds are naphthalene, anthracene, cumene, and benzo[a]pyrene:

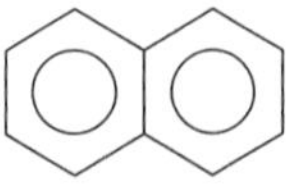

naphthalene 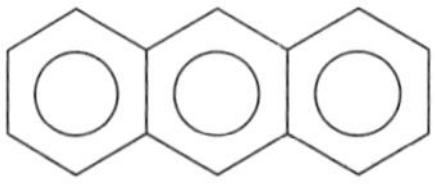   anthracene 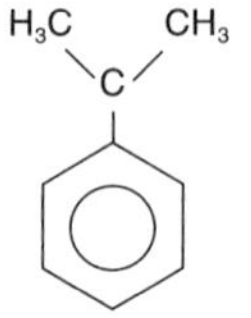   cumene 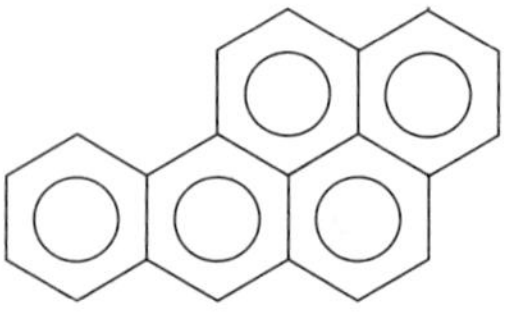   benzo[a]pyrene

3.2.7. Alkylaromatics

This group of hydrocarbons consists of aromatic compounds that contain an alkyl group in place of a hydrogen attached to a ring carbon. An alkyl group is simply an alkyl radical bound covalently to the aromatic. Examples of alkylaromatics are shown below:

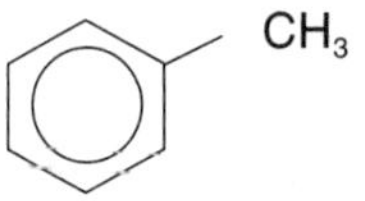

methylbenzene 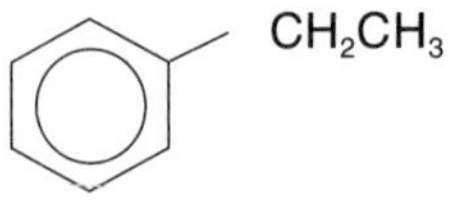   ethylbenzene

Ethylbenzene is a common component in gasoline blends.

3.2.8. Polycyclic Aromatic Hydrocarbons

Polycyclic aromatic hydrocarbons (PAHs), or polynuclear aromatic hydrocarbons (PNAs), are characterized by two or more fused benzene rings. Naphthalene, anthracene, and benzo[a]pyrene, shown above, are common examples of PAHs. These compounds are ubiquitous pollutants in many products and in combustion gases. Diesel fuels and exhausts from gasoline and diesel engines contain PAHs. In other applications, PAHs are sometimes called "coal tars" and are present in tobacco smoke. Some PAHs are known to be potent human carcinogens, for example:

- benz[*a*]anthracene
- benzo[*b*]fluoranthene
- benzo[*j*]fluoranthene
- benzo[*k*]fluoranthene
- benzo[*a*]pyrene
- indeno[*1,2,3-cd*]pyrene
- dibenz[*a,h*]anthracene
- chrysene

PAHs are not effectively degraded by microbial action and are strongly adsorbed onto soil particles, particularly onto clays; therefore, they are difficult to remediate. However, due to adsorption processes and due to their very low water solubilities and vapor pressures they are not highly mobile through soils or groundwater. Some recent studies have shown that certain PAHs can be decomposed under anaerobic conditions (Robinson et al. 2006; Ambrosoli et al. 2005).

3.2.9. Substituted Aromatics

A number of substituents in the form of organic groups or inorganics — for example, halogens — may be bound to a benzene ring and impart unique properties (e.g., altered water solubility, toxicity). Some common substituted aromatics include:

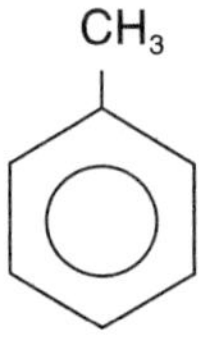

toluene 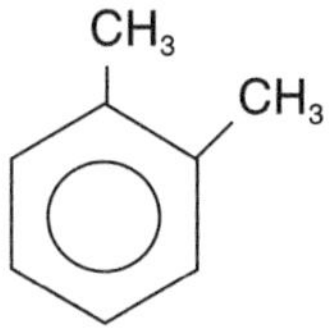   xylene 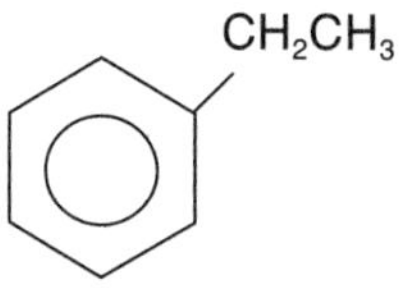   ethylbenzene 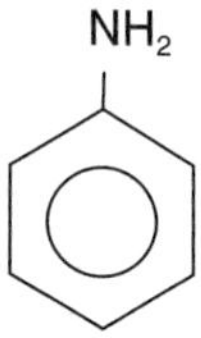   aniline

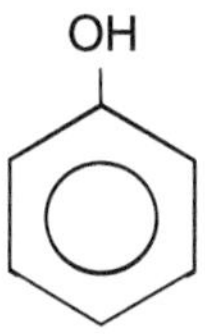

phenol 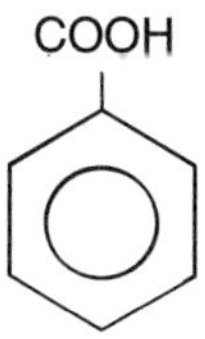   benzoic acid

The substituents on the benzene ring are numbered from 1 to 6, as in the case of 1,2,3-trichlorobenzene and 2,4,6-trichlorophenol:

1,2,3-trichlorobenzene   2,4,6-trichlorophenol

As with the numbering of substituents on aliphatic chains, those on aromatic molecules are numbered to provide the lowest values. If there is only one additional functional group attached to an already substituted ring the isomer is instead named by using the prefixes *ortho-*, *meta-*, and *para-* (*o-*, *m-*, and *p-*, respectively).

o-, *m-*, and *p-* positions to a ring.

p-nitrophenol   *m*-chlorobenzoic acid   *o*-bromotoluene

3.3. PROPERTIES OF HYDROCARBON FUELS

Industrialized societies are strongly dependent on petroleum products as fuels and in the production of numerous consumer, industrial, agricultural, defense, and other products. The most common uses include: fuels for vehicles and industry, heating oils, lubricants, as raw materials in manufacturing petrochemicals and pharmaceuticals, and solvents. About 65% of the petroleum used as fuel is in the form of gasoline in automobiles. Thus, petroleum products are extremely common and are the source of many soil and water contamination events.

3.3.1. Composition

Crude petroleum is a complex mixture of thousands of compounds, most of which are hydrocarbons. The detailed composition of crude petroleum depends on the origin and location of the petroleum fields; however, there are many similarities among diverse sources (Table 3.1).

Table 3.1.   Characteristics of crude petroleum components as a function of source

Characteristic or Component	Prudhoe Bay	Louisiana, USA	Kuwait
API gravity (20°C) (°API)	27.8	34.5	31.4
Sulfur (wt %)	0.94	0.25	2.44
Nitrogen (wt %)	0.23	0.69	0.14
Naptha fraction (wt %)	23.2	18.6	22.7
Paraffins	12.5	8.8	16.2
Naphthenes	7.4	7.7	4.1
Aromatics	3.2	2.1	2.4
Benzenes	0.3	0.2	0.1
Toluene	0.6	0.4	0.4
C_8 aromatics	0.5	0.7	0.8
C_9 aromatics	0.06	0.5	0.6
C_{10} aromatics	—	0.2	0.3
C_{11} aromatics	—	0.1	0.1
Indans	—	—	0.1
High-boiling fraction (wt %)	76.8	81.4	77.3
Saturates	14.4	56.3	34.0
n-paraffins	5.8	5.2	4.7
Isoparaffins		14.0	13.2
1-ring cycloparaffins	9.9	12.4	6.2
2-ring cycloparaffins	7.7	9.4	4.5
3-ring cycloparaffins	5.5	6.8	3.3
4-ring cycloparaffins	5.4	4.8	1.8
5-ring cycloparaffins	—	3.2	0.4

Source: Clark and Brown 1977; reproduced with kind permission of Elsevier Press, Inc.

Table 3.2. Hydrocarbon products from petroleum

	Number of Carbon Atoms	Boiling Point (°C)	Uses
Petroleum gases	1 to 4	< 5	Heating fuel, petrochemicals
Petroleum gases	4 to 10	35–80	Solvents, petrochemicals
Gasoline	5 to 13	20–225	Fuel
Kerosene	10 to 16	180–260	Fuel, lighting
Lubricating oils	20 to 50	350–600	Lubrication
Paraffin	23 to 29	50–60 (m.p.)	Wax
Asphalt	> 100	Viscous liquids	Paving, roofing materials
Coke	> 100	Solid	Solid fuel

Light crudes tend to contain more gasoline, naphtha, and kerosene fractions, and the heavy crudes more gas oil and residue. Typical fractions recovered from the distillation of a crude petroleum sample are shown in Table 3.2. The most abundant hydrocarbon is usually a composite of alkanes designated by the formula C_nH_{2n+2}. In petroleum, the alkane composition varies from methane, CH_4, to molecules having about 100 carbons. Most petroleum alkanes are of two types: a long, continuous chain of carbons, or one main chain with short branches, for example, 2-methylhexane:

$$CH_3$$

2-methyhexane

Petroleum also contains cycloalkanes, mainly those with five or six carbons per ring:

$$CH_3$$

methylcyclopentane   cyclohexane

Petroleum contains aromatic hydrocarbons such as benzene and derivatives where one or two hydrogens have been replaced by methyl or ethyl groups (for example, toluene and ethylbenzene). An additional, albeit unwanted, component of petroleum is sulfur, S. This element occurs in organic compounds arising from the original depositional environment. Sulfur is notorious as an environmental pollutant and is associated with acid precipitation. The S atom is chemically bonded to hydrocarbon molecules; therefore, it is not readily removed from petroleum. Petroleum is commonly labeled as being *sweet* or *sour* crude, which is a reflection of its S content. Low-S (about 0.5% S) is sweet, and high-S (2.5% or more) is sour. Finally, a range of metals, some of which are potentially hazardous to human health and the biosphere, occur in crude petroleum (again a product of the environment in which the petroleum has formed). Most of these metals, however, typically are present in concentrations less than 1 mg/L (Speight 1980).

3.3.2. Refining

Crude petroleum must be refined to separate its diverse constituents into useful fractions. These fractions are often further distilled to produce a specific commercial product. Petroleum hydrocarbons in crude oil possess different boiling points, according to the number and arrangement of carbon atoms in their molecules. Fractional distillation, accomplished in a distillation tower (Fig. 3.1), uses the difference in boiling point to separate the hydrocarbons in crude oil. Crude petroleum is pumped into a furnace where it is heated to approximately 750°F. At this point some of the petroleum has already vaporized. The combined liquid and vapor is then transferred to the base of the distillation tower and heated further. The fractionating column is cooler at the top than the bottom, so the vapors cool as they rise. An array of perforated caps is situated within the tower. Heated vapors migrate upward and will pass through the openings while liquids will fall. The perforations are fitted with cooled condensers allowing vapors to condense to a liquid.

The highest boiling vapors condense first and are collected as a liquid. Lower and lower boiling compounds are collected successively up the tower. The highest boiling fractions are heavy, high-molecular weight hydrocarbons that have properties suitable for lubricants and heating oils. Asphalts or paraffins also occur depending on the source of the petroleum. Vapors condensing in the middle range, or "middle distillates," are used for heavier fuels, diesel and jet fuels, and other commercial products such as

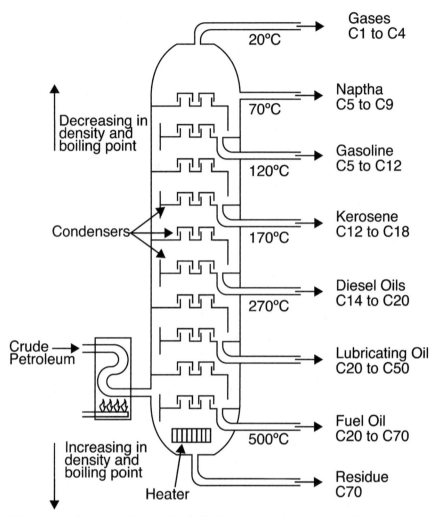

Figure 3.1. *Schematic diagram of a distillation tower used to refine petroleum*

kerosene. The next-lighter hydrocarbons occur in the C_4 to C_9 range and are used in gasoline. The lightest hydrocarbons, approximately C_1 to C_3, are gases at room temperature and are used in heating gas mixtures (Fig. 3.2).

Lowering the pressure over a liquid will lower its boiling point. Heavy residues from the fractionating column are subsequently distilled under a vacuum. As a result the heavier fractions can be further separated without high temperatures that might break them down. These residues are then passed on to a cracking unit, or used to obtain lubricating oils or blended into industrial fuels.

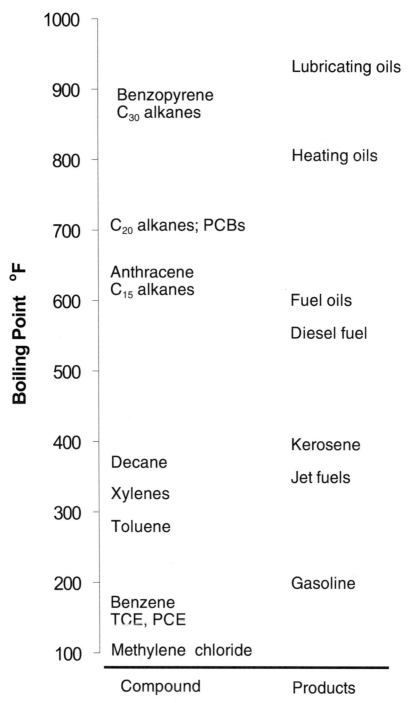

Figure 3.2. *Boiling point distribution of petroleum products*

3.3.3. Gasoline

Fuels are complex mixtures of as many as several hundred chemical compounds with molecular weights ranging between C_4 and C_{12}. Most gasoline blends contain from 50 to 150 compounds that are specifically formulated for burn rate (octane number), volatility (for consistent starts and performance in hot and cold weather), and emission control (by the addition of oxygenated compounds) (Speight 1980). Table 3.3 provides a typical distribution of aliphatic and aromatic compounds for automotive gasoline.

Gasoline fuels are formulated to burn at a certain rate, termed *octane number*. Power output is maximized by optimizing the rate at which a fuel burns inside the cylinders of an engine. The octane scale designates *n*-heptane an octane number of zero, and iso-octane an octane number of 100. Lead-containing compounds such as tetramethyllead and tetraethyllead had commonly been used to increase a fuel's octane number. These were convenient additives, as they did not affect any other fuel properties, for example vapor pressure. As a fuel burns, tetraethyl lead converts to lead(II) oxide:

$$2Pb(C_2H_5)_{4(l)} + 27O_{2(g)} \rightarrow 2PbO_{(s)} + 16CO_{2(g)} + 20H_2O_{(l)} \quad (2.1)$$

The lead(II) oxide will occur in the cylinders and is carried out with the exhaust gases (Meyer 1989). Other hazardous compounds including ethylene dichloride, EDC, and ethylene dibromide, EDB, were added as Pb scavengers to prevent buildup of lead oxide deposits. In the cylinder, EDC combines with Pb to produce lead chloride, $PbCl_2$, a volatile compound that is carried out of the engine with the exhaust (Cole 1994). As a result of public health concerns related to leaded compounds, the U.S. Environmental Protection Agency (EPA) banned the use of Pb additives in fuels in 1973.

Aromatic compounds also increase the octane rating of gasoline blends. Aromatics including benzene and alkylbenzenes have been used in place of Pb to increase octane number. Benzene, toluene, ethylbenzene, and xylene are collectively termed the BTEX compounds and some premium blends contain up to 50% aromatics. BTEX is more reactive than the alkanes typically occurring in fuels and result in the formation of photochemical smog (Rappenglück et al. 2000). In countries where catalytic converters are not required in automobiles, an increase in BTEX concentrations in outdoor air may occur. Aromatic compounds

Table 3.3. Major components of gasoline

Component	Percent by Weight	Component
n-alkanes		Octane enhancers
C_5	3.0	methyl t-butyl ether (MTBE)
C_6	11.6	t-butyl alcohol (TBA)
C_7	1.2	ethanol
C_9	0.7	methanol
C_{10}–C_{13}	0.8	
Total n-alkanes	17.3	Antioxidants
Branched alkanes	2.2	n,n'-dialkylphenylenediamines
C_4	15.1	2,6 dialkyl and 2,4,6-
C_5	8.0	trialkylphenols
C_6	1.9	butylated methyl, ethyl, and
C_7	1.8	dimethyl phenols
C_8	2.1	triethylene tetramine di
C_9	1.0	(monononylphenolate)
C_{10}–C_{13}		Metal deactivators
		n,n'-disalicylidene-1,2-
		ethanediamine
		n,n'-disalicylidene-
		propanediamine
		n,n'-disalicylidene-
		cyclohexanediamine
		disalicylidene-N-methyl-
		dipropylenetriamine
Total branched alkanes	32.0	Ignition controllers
cycloalkanes		tri-o-cresylphosphate (TOCP)
C_6	3.0	Icing inhibitors
C_7	1.4	isopropyl alcohol
C_8	0.6	Detergents/dispersants
		alkylamine phosphates
Total cycloalkanes	5.0	Poly-isobutene amines
Olefins		long-chain alkyl phenols
C_6	1.8	long-chain alcohols
Total olefins	1.8	long-chain carboxylic acids
		long-chain amines
		Corrosion inhibitors
Aromatics	7.6	carboxylic acids
benzene	3.2	phosphoric acids
toluene	4.8	sulfonic acids
xylenes	6.6	
ethylbenzene	1.4	
C_3-benzenes	4.2	
C_4-benzenes	7.6	
others	2.7	
Total aromatics	30.5	

Source: Agency for Toxic Substances and Disease Registry 2006.

are hazardous to human health; therefore, BTEX and cumenes are listed under RCRA Subtitle C regulations as hazardous substances (40 CFR 2004). The octane value of a fuel can be enhanced via blending in other organic substances with high octane numbers such as MTBE, which was introduced into fuels in 1979. Methanol is used to produce the oxygenated additive MTBE, methyl tert-butyl ether:

$$
\begin{array}{c}
CH_3 \\
| \\
H_3C-O-C-CH_3 \\
| \\
CH_3
\end{array}
$$

MTBE

Ethanol is used to produce the corresponding ethyl tert-butyl ether that is also blended with gasoline. Both ethers have octane numbers over 100. In addition to improving fuel combustion the use of MTBE reduces generation of carbon monoxide. MTBE is an oxygenated fuel and produces less CO during combustion than do hydrocarbons. Some gasolines in U.S. cities had contained up to 15% MTBE (Cole 1994). Controversy has recently surrounded MTBE use as this water-soluble compound has been linked with contamination of drinking water supplies via leaking underground storage tanks, pipelines, and marine engines. For this reason efforts are under way to phase MTBE out of gasoline blends.

There is a conflict between the EPA's toxicity characteristic rule and the petroleum exemption under RCRA and CERCLA. Gasoline is obviously hazardous as a result of its flammability and toxicity. Under some conditions petroleum contamination can be hazardous in the workplace since the more volatile products constitute a fire and explosive hazard. Some petroleum compounds are toxic, especially compounds routinely occurring in gasolines, for example, benzene. Despite these obvious hazards, gasoline and gasoline-contaminated debris have been exempted from hazardous regulations by the U.S. EPA.

3.3.4. Diesel Fuel

Diesel fuels rank second to gasoline as a fuel for internal combustion engines, with a demand of about 25% that of gasoline. Diesel engines require that a fuel self-ignite during compression in the cylinder. A measure of ignition quality is the cetane number, which corresponds to the percent of cetane, or *n*-hexadecane ($C_{16}H_{34}$) in a mixture of cetane and heptamethylnonane. The cetane number, partly a function of the paraffin, olefin, naphthalene, and aromatic composition, is also a measure of the tendency of an fuel to knock in an engine. Paraffins have low self-ignition temperatures; this makes them desirable in a diesel fuel. Diesel fuels contain a heavier range of hydrocarbons compared to gasoline and are in the C_{10} to C_{18} range. Diesel fuel blends are a compromise between ease of starting (high volatility) and good fuel economy (low volatility).

3.3.5. Kerosene

Kerosene originated as a straight-run petroleum fraction that boiled between about 400°F and 500°F and has been used as a fuel oil since the petroleum refining industry began. Kerosene is defined as a petroleum distillate and must be free of aromatic and unsaturated hydrocarbons, which are potential smoke producers. The desirable components are saturated hydrocarbons. Kerosene is composed mainly of hydrocarbons containing C_{12} or higher compounds.

3.3.6. Fuel Oil

Domestic fuel oils are those commonly used in homes and include stove oil and furnace fuel oil. They are so-called distillate fuels, because they are vaporized during the distillation process and thus possess a distinct boiling range. The gas oil range hydrocarbons possess a number of characteristics that make them desirable for heating oil; for example, they possess a higher calorific content than the lighter hydrocarbons such as kerosene or naphtha (Speight 1980).

3.3.7. Lubricating Oils

Lubricating oils are distinguished from other fractions of crude oil by their high (> 750°F) boiling point and high viscosity. Materials suitable for production of lubricating oils are hydrocarbons containing as many as 40 carbons per molecule. In these oils there is a predominance of normal and branched paraffins. There are also polycycloparaffins, whose rings are commonly condensed. Mono-, di-, and trinuclear aromatics are the main component of the aromatic portion, for example naphthalene and phenanthrene:

naphthalene   phenanthrene

Lubricating oils typically possess a high additive content. These compounds are included in an oil blend to improve both physical and chemical properties. Additive content can be as high as 20%, the most important being detergents and dispersants (Vazquez-Duhalt 1989).

Enormous quantities of waste lubricating oils are produced from maintenance of motor vehicle engines and industrial machinery. The world production of used motor oil is estimated at approximately 25 to 28 million tons in addition to 12–15 million tons lost yearly during engine operation (Vazquez-Duhalt 1989). These oils are of particular concern because many are known to be contaminated with a suite of metals, inorganics, and organic molecules. For example, some used automobile oils are known to contain Pb, As, and Ba, as well as PAHs, many of which are known carcinogens. These oils are not, unfortunately, managed as RCRA hazardous wastes in the United States as a result of the EPA's petroleum exemption. They are managed under other regulations, however, which were formulated to restrict their release to the biosphere. For example, the U.S. EPA's Used Oil Management Standards, enacted in 1992, prohibit the use of waste oil for dust control or weed control (U.S. EPA 1994).

Aliphatic compounds comprise about 73% to 80% of the total weight of used motor oil. This fraction is composed of alkanes and cycloalkanes of one to six rings. Monoaromatics and diaromatics make up another 11%–15% and 2%–5% of the weight, respectively (Vazquez-Duhalt 1989).

3.4 PETROCHEMICALS

Natural gas and crude distillates from petroleum refining are used as feedstocks to manufacture a wide variety of petrochemicals that are subsequently used in the manufacture of consumer goods.

The basic petrochemicals manufactured by cracking, reforming, and other processes include alkenes (for example, ethylene, propylene, butylenes, butadiene) and aromatics (benzene, toluene, xylenes). Some petrochemical plants may also have additional (e.g., alcohol) compound manufacturing units on-site. The base petrochemicals or products derived from them, along with other raw materials, are converted to a wide range of products. Some common examples include (World Bank Group 1998):

- plastics such as low-density polyethylene, high-density polyethylene, polypropylene, polystyrene, and polyvinyl chloride
- synthetic fibers such as polyester and acrylic
- engineering polymers such as acrylonitrile, butadiene, and styrene
- rubbers including styrene, butadiene rubber, and polybutadiene rubber
- solvents
- industrial chemicals, including those used for the manufacture of detergents, coatings, dyes, agrochemicals (pesticides), pharmaceuticals, and explosives

Some single-carbon compounds manufactured at petrochemical plants include methanol, formaldehyde, and halogenated hydrocarbons. Alkenes (olefins) are typically manufactured from the steam cracking of hydrocarbons such as naphtha. Major alkenes produced include ethylene, propylene, butadiene, and acetylene. Benzene is generally recovered from cracker streams at petrochemical plants. The major aromatic hydrocarbons manufactured include benzene, toluene, xylene, and naphthalene. The alkenes, alkenes, and aromatics produced are used in the manufacture of a wide range of products and are shown in Table 3.4.

3.4. CHEMICAL AND PHYSICAL PROPERTIES OF FUELS AND PETROCHEMICALS

From the standpoint of delineation of a contaminant plume and prognosis for success in remediation, important physical properties of petroleum

Table 3.4. Uses of alkanes, alkenes, aromatics, and related hydrocarbons in petrochemical applications

General Category	Compound	Applications
C-1 alkanes	Formaldehyde	Manufacture of plastic resins including phenolic, urea, and melamine resins. Bakelite, Formica, methanol
	Halogenated hydrocarbons	Manufacture of solvents, refrigerants, and degreasing agents
Alkenes	Ethylene	Low-density polyethylene, high-density polyethylene, polystyrene, polyvinyl chloride, ethylene glycol, ethanolamines, nonionic detergents
	Butadiene	Manufacture of nitrile rubber and styrene butadiene rubber
	Butanol	Additive in hydraulic and brake fluids and perfumes; manufacture of solvents (methyl ethyl ketone)
	Various	Acetone (solvent)
		Acrylonitrile (manufacture of acrylic fibers and nitrile rubber)
		Ethanol amines (solvents)
		Polyisoprene (for synthetic rubber manufacture)
		Polyvinyl acetate (used in plastics)
		Polypropylene
		Isopropanol (solvent and in pharmaceuticals manufacturing)
		Propylene glycol (used in pharmaceuticals manufacturing)
		Polyurethane
Aromatics	Benzene	Solvent; manufacture of phenol, styrene, aniline, nitrobenzene, detergents, pesticides (e.g., hexachlorobenzene), cyclohexane (intermediate in synthetic fiber manufacture), caprolactam (used in the manufacture of nylon)
	Toluene	Solvent in paints, rubber, and plastic cements
		Feedstock in the manufacture of organic chemicals, explosives, detergents, and polyurethane foams
	Xylenes	Manufacture of explosives (TNT), alkyd resins, plasticizers
	Naphthalene	Manufacture of dyes, pharmaceuticals, insecticides, mothballs, phthalic anhydride (used in the manufacture of alkyd resins, plasticizers, and polyester)
	Phenol	Thermoset plastics
		Solvent; manufacture of pesticides, pharmaceuticals, dyestuffs
	Styrene	Manufacture of synthetic rubber and polystyrene resins.
	Phthalic anhydride	Manufacture of alkyd resins and plasticizers (e.g., phthalates)
	Maleic anhydride	Manufacture of polyesters and alkyd resins, malathion
	Nitrobenzene	Manufacture of aniline, benzidine, dyestuffs
		Solvent in polishes
	Aniline	Manufacture of azo dyes, and rubber chemicals such as antioxidants

Source: Adapted from: World Bank Group 1998.

Table 3.5.   Physical and chemical properties of selected hydrocarbons

Product	Vapor Pressure mm Hg 20°C	Vapor Density Air = 1	Flashpoint °C	Flammability % by Volume LE	UEL	Solubility in H₂O 20°C, ppm
Gasoline	450	3–4	−30–43	1.4	7.6	50–100
Benzene	100	2.8	−11	1.3	7.9	1,790
Toluene	36	3.1	4	1.2	7.1	515
Ethylbenzene	10	3.7	18	0.8	6.7	75
Xylene	21	3.7	27	1.1	7.0	150
n-Hexane	124	3.0	−40	1.2	7.1	12
Jet fuel JP-4	103–155	5.5	−10–35	1.3	8.0	< 1
Diesel	< 1	4.5	40–65	1.3	6.0	< 1
Kerosene	1	4.5	40–75	1.4	6.0	< 1
Light fuel oil	50	3–7	40–100	nf[1]		< 1
Heavy fuel oil	neg.	< 0.1	65–130	1.0	5.0	< 1
Lubricating oil	< 0.1	1	150–225	nf		< 1ppb
Used oil	—	—	> 100	nf		< ppb
Carbon tetrachloride	91	5.3	N/A	nf		neg.
Tricholorethylene	57.8	4.5	N/A	12.5	90	neg.
Chloroform	167	4.1	N/A	nf		1.8g/100mL
Pentachlorophenol	40@ 221°C	9.2	—	nf		neg.
Methylene chloride	400@75°C	2.9	N/A	nf		1.32%

[1]Relatively nonflammable.

compounds are solubility in water, specific gravity, viscosity, and vapor pressure (Table 3.5).

3.4.1. Solubility

Petroleum hydrocarbons are, with few exceptions, insoluble in water. The maximum solubility of benzene is 1,750 μg/L (1,750 ppb) of water. That amount is, however, sufficient to be harmful to human health. The U.S. EPA limit for benzene in groundwater is 5 μg/L (Table 3.6). Solubility in most cases can be considered to be inversely proportional to molecular weight; lighter hydrocarbons are more soluble in water than are higher molecular weight compounds. Lighter hydrocarbons, that is, C_4 to C_8 including the aromatics, are relatively soluble. Gasoline is the only petroleum product in common use that contains constituents that are sufficiently soluble in water to cause health problems. The aromatic compounds, that is, benzene and alkyl benzenes, are the primary concern.

Table 3.6.   Maximum Concentration Limits (MCLs) of selected organic compounds in drinking water

Compound	Empirical Formula	Molecular Weight	Solubility* mg/L	MCL mg/L
Benzene	C_6H_6	78.1	1,800	0.005
Toluene	C_7H_8	92.2	500	2
Xylenes	C_8H_{10}	106.2	198	10
Ethylbenzene	C_8H_{10}	106.2	150	0.7
Pentachlorophenol	C_6OHCl_5	266.3	20	0.2
Carbon tetrachloride	CCl_4	153.8	800	0.005
Trichloroethylene	C_2HCl_3	131.4	1.1	0.005
Ethylenedibromide	$C_2H_4Br_2$	187.9	4,000	0.00005
Tetrachlorodibenzo[p]dioxin	$C_{12}H_2O_2Cl_4$	322	0.0002	0.00000005
Vinyl chloride	C_2H_3Cl	62.5	2,792	0.002

*In water, 20°C

Source: 40 CFR 2003.

Solubility is also a practical concern from a remediation perspective. Contaminants must be in soluble form in order for microorganisms to attack molecules for catabolism (degradation). Nonpolar compounds tend to be hydrophobic and partition into the organic component of a soil. The result is that nonpolar compounds are less mobile in soils and groundwater.

3.4.2. Specific Gravity

Specific gravity is the density of a substance compared with the density of water; hence it has no units. Petroleum products are less dense than water and will float. For example, gasoline has a specific gravity of approximately 0.73, and no. 2 fuel oil about 0.90. Petroleum products have been designated as *light nonaqueous phase liquids*, or LNAPLs. A halogenated hydrocarbon, for example, CCl_4, has a specific gravity of 1.59 and is labeled a *dense nonaqueous phase liquid* (DNAPL). LNAPLs are relatively easy to locate and recover in the subsurface environment because they tend to float on the water table. In contrast, DNAPLs sink to bedrock and are neither easy to find nor recover.

3.4.3. Viscosity

Viscosity is a measure of the resistance of the substance to gravity flow, that is, a measure of the ease with which hydrocarbons flow through soils. Only gasoline is of sufficiently low viscosity to migrate rapidly in most soils. Diesel and jet fuel will migrate, but more slowly than gasoline. A fuel oil release can thus be treated much less aggressively than, say, a gasoline release because the fuel oil is not going to migrate from the site as rapidly.

3.4.4. Vapor Pressure

Vapor pressure, or volatility, is the tendency of a molecule to leave the surface of a liquid (Fig. 3.3). This property is approximately the inverse of boiling point; likewise, it is the inverse of molecular weight. Some refined petroleum products, especially gasolines, vaporize readily and have flashpoints at room temperature or below it. At the other end of the spectrum are heavy viscous products such as lubricating oils and fuel oils that vaporize minimally (Cole 1994).

3.4.5. Explosive Limits

The lower explosive limit (LEL) is defined as the lowest percent by volume of a mixture of explosive gases in air that will propagate a flame at 25°C and atmospheric pressure. Gasoline is explosive when present in the range of 1.4% to 7.6% by volume in air. At concentrations greater than 7.6% gasoline vapor will not explode, as the air-vapor mixture is considered "rich." This 7.6% threshold is the upper explosive limit (UEL), defined as the maximum concentration of a gas above which the substance will not explode when exposed to a source of ignition. The

Figure 3.3.   *There are right ways and wrong ways to assess a compound's vapor pressure!*
U.S. Environmental Protection Agency

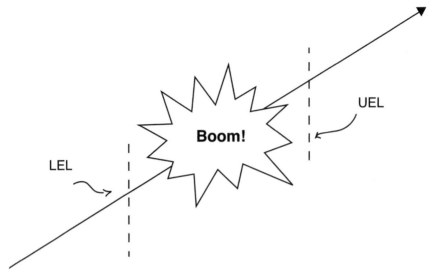

Figure 3.4. *Schematic representation of LELs and UELs*

explosive hazard range occurs between the LEL and the UEL (Fig. 3.4). It must be noted that at gasoline concentrations above the UEL fire may still be possible, and asphyxiation will occur. In addition, a sudden dilution of the gasoline vapors within the local atmosphere can bring the mixture back within the explosive range.

3.4.6. Flashpoint

Whereas explosive limits address concentrations, flashpoint relates to *temperature*, that is, the lowest temperature at which a flame will propagate through the vapor of a combustible material. In other words, flashpoint is the minimum temperature at which the liquid produces a sufficient concentration of vapor that it forms an ignitable mixture with air.

The source of ignition need not be an open flame, but could be static electricity or other electrical discharge.

QUESTIONS

1. Choose the correct answer: A hydrophobic compound: (a) has a defatting effect on biological tissue; b) is soluble in fats; (c) is soluble in oils; (d) is insoluble in water; (e) is nonpolar: (f) all of the above.

2. Heavy (high-molecular weight) petroleum hydrocarbons are usually insoluble in water. True or false?

3. Choose the correct answer: A substance that is immiscible: (a) will not dissolve in water; (b) is heavier than water; (c) in insoluble in fats.

4. Define a fuel's octane number.

5. Discuss some of the major octane boosters used in fuels to increase octane number. Discuss also any known or suspected health and environmental threats.

6. During a UST excavation, would a hydrocarbon with a vapor density of 1.25 be expected to rise, sink, or remain stable?

7. PCBs are readily absorbed into the body but are slowly metabolized and excreted. Explain why this occurs.

8. Hydrocarbons are good solvents for fatty substances. They are also good degreasers. True or false?

9. All other factors being equal, why are aromatic hydrocarbons more difficult to chemically degrade as compared with an alkane with a similar number of carbon atoms?

10. All other factors being equal, why is a large PAH molecule (ten fused rings) more difficult to decompose as compared with a mixed aromatic-alkane of similar molecular weight?

11. How do flashpoint and explosive limits differ for a hydrocarbon substance?

12. A field technician must enter a closed underground storage tank (UST) in order to remove petroleum sludges. The UST had formerly stored diesel fuel. What hazards should the worker be aware of prior to tank entry? Refer to Tables 3.3 and 3.4. Consider both immediate and long-term effects.

REFERENCES

Agency for Toxic Substances and Disease Registry. 2006. *Toxicological Profile Information Sheet. Gasoline.* See: www.atsdr.cdc.gov/toxprofiles/tp72-c3.pdf.

Ambrosoli R., F. A. Marsan, L. Petruzzelli, and J. L. Minati. 2005. Anaerobic PAH degradation in soil by a mixed bacterial consortium under dentrifying conditions. *Chemosphere* 60 (9): 1231–36.

Clark, R. C., and D. W. Brown. 1977. Petroleum: Properties and analyses in biotic and abiotic systems. In *Effects of Petroleum on Arctic and Subarctic Marine Environments and*

Organisms, ed. D. W. Brown, R. C. Clark Jr., N. L. Karrick, and W. D. MacLeod. New York: Academic Press.

Cole, G. M. 1994. *Assessment and Remediation of Petroleum Contaminated Sites*. Boca Raton, FL: CRC Press.

40 CFR. 2003. *Part 141.50. Maximum Contaminant Level Goals for Organic Contaminants*. Washington, DC: U.S. Government Printing Office.

———. *Part 261. Identification and Listing of Hazardous Waste*. Washington, DC: U.S. Government Printing Office.

Meyer, E. 1989. *Chemistry of Hazardous Materials*. 2nd ed. Englewood Cliffs, NJ: Prentice Hall.

Rappenglück B., P. Oyola, I. Olaeta, and P. Fabian P. 2000. The evolution of photochemical smog in the metropolitan area of Santiago de Chile. *Journal of Applied Meteorology* 39 (3): 275–90.

Robinson, J., R. Kalin, R. Thomas, S. Wallace, and P. Daly. 2006. In situ bioremediation of cyanide, PAHs and organic compounds using an engineered SEquenced REactive BARrier (SEREBAR). *Land Contamination and Reclamation* 14 (2): 478–82.

Speight, J. G. 1980. *The Chemistry and Technology of Petroleum*. New York: Marcel Dekker.

U.S. Environmental Protection Agency. 1994. *Environmental Regulations and Technology. Managing Used Motor Oil*. EPA/625/R-94/010.

Vazquez-Duhalt, R. 1989. Environmental impact of used motor oil. *Science of the Total Environment* 79:1–23.

World Bank Group 1998. *Petrochemicals Manufacturing. Pollution Prevention and Abatement Handbook*. See: ifcln1.ifc.org/ifcext/enviro.nsf/AttachmentsByTitle/gui_petrochem_WB/$FILE/petrochm_PPAH.pdf#search=%22petrochemicals%22.

CHAPTER 4

Subsurface Properties and Remediation

We know more about the movement of celestial bodies than about the soil underfoot.

—Leonardo Da Vinci

For all things come from earth, and all things end by becoming earth.

—Xenophanes

4.1. INTRODUCTION

At a site contaminated with organic and/or inorganic chemicals, the importance of understanding the physical and chemical properties of local soil and subsurface materials cannot be overstated. Soil and subsurface properties play critical roles in: (1) determining the potential for contaminant migration, including vertical and horizontal distribution of contaminants; (2) altering the toxicity of contaminants; and (3) planning and implementation of a remediation program. Soils are highly variable with depth, over large geographic regions, and even over short distances. Soils will vary significantly in their capacity for mobilizing solutes, for adsorbing organic and inorganic compounds, and for chemical and biological degradation of contaminants. In order to optimize remediation success, therefore, it is essential to possess a thorough knowledge of the subsurface conditions present in the affected area.

Soils are composed of inorganic solids (clay, silt, sand, and gravel), organic matter, and void space. The inorganic solids are produced as a result of long-term weathering of the parent geologic material. Soils are classified by texture, which is a function of their sand, silt, and clay content. There is a wide range of ratios and many classification schemes for particle size analysis (Fig. 4.1). The organic matter content may range from less than 1%, common for soils in arid regions, to more than 50% in peaty deposits. Air and water occupy the pore spaces between particles. Pore space may comprise from 25% to 60% of noncompacted soils.

4.2. RELEVANT CHEMISTRY AND MINERALOGY

4.2.1. pH

Soil pH strongly influences the availability of nutrients and the mobility of metals. It therefore follows that pH is directly associated with plant and microbial growth and activity. The optimum pH range for most crop plants, and also for many microbial populations, is approximately 5.5 to 8.0. Soils become acidic in regions where there is sufficient precipitation to leach exchangeable base-forming cations (Ca^{2+}, Mg^{2+}, K^+, Na^+) from the profile. The two cations that are primarily responsible for soil acidity are H^+ and Al^{3+}. In cases of extreme acidity, aluminum solubilizes into the soil solution as Al^{3+}, which contributes to acidity via hydrolysis reactions.

$$Al^{3+} + H_2O \rightarrow Al(OH)^{2+} + H^+ \qquad (4.1)$$

The H^+ ions are released into the soil solution, thus lowering the pH.

Under mildly acidic conditions, Al may occur as such aluminum hydroxy ions as $Al(OH)^{2+}$. In the soil solution they produce H^+ ions by hydrolysis reactions.

$$Al(OH)^{2+} + H_2O \rightarrow Al(OH)_2^+ + H^+ \qquad (4.2)$$

$$Al(OH)_2^+ + H_2O \rightarrow Al(OH)_3 + H^+ \qquad (4.3)$$

Soils are alkaline when the colloids experience a high degree of saturation with basic cations. Most metals precipitate, and are therefore less mobile, under neutral to high pH. Soil pH can be lowered by the addition of mineral acids, for example, sulfuric, nitric, or hydrochloric; ferrous or aluminum sulfate; or elemental sulfur. Conversely, pH can be increased by the addition of limestone ($CaCO_3$) or related materials, for example, CaO, $Ca(OH)_2$, etc.

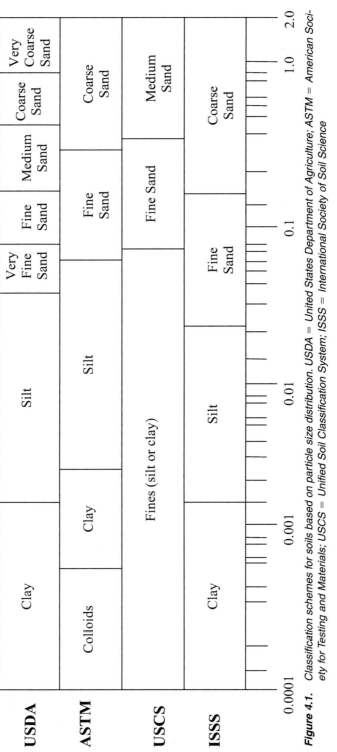

Figure 4.1. Classification schemes for soils based on particle size distribution. USDA = United States Department of Agriculture; ASTM = American Society for Testing and Materials; USCS = Unified Soil Classification System; ISSS = International Society of Soil Science

Soils possess a resistance to pH change that is known as *buffering ca-pacity*. In a soil, an equilibrium exists between residual, exchangeable, and soluble forms of acidity:

$$\text{Colloid-Al]} \leftrightarrow\leftrightarrow \text{Colloid]-Al}^{3+} \leftrightarrow\leftrightarrow \text{Al}^{3+} \qquad (4.4)$$
$$\text{residual} \qquad\qquad \text{exchangeable} \qquad \text{soluble}$$

If a small amount of base is applied to the soil to neutralize the H^+ ions in solution, the acid cations are replenished from exchangeable and possibly residual forms. The overall result is a very minor change in soil pH. The pH change will be appreciable only when enough base is added to neutralize the H^+ and Al^{3+} occurring in the exchangeable and residual storehouses. It follows that soils with a high CEC tend to have the greatest buffering capacities. A number of simple laboratory tests are available to measure a soil's buffering capacity.

4.2.2. Oxidation-Reduction Status

The redox potential of the soil (oxidation-reduction potential, Eh) is directly related to the concentration of O_2 in the gas and liquid phases. The O_2 concentration is a function of the rate of gas exchange with the atmosphere, and the rate of respiration by soil microorganisms and plant roots. Respiration may deplete O_2, lowering the redox potential and creating anaerobic (i.e., reducing) conditions. These conditions will restrict aerobic reactions and may promote anaerobic processes such as denitrification, sulfate reduction, and fermentation. Many reduced forms of polyvalent metal cations are more soluble (and thus more mobile) than their oxidized forms. Well-aerated soils have an Eh of about 0.8 to 0.4 V; moderately reduced soils are about 0.4 to 0.1 V; reduced soils measure about 0.1 to -0.1 V; and highly reduced soils are about -0.1 to -0.3 V. Redox potentials are difficult to measure and are not widely used in the field.

4.3. THE COLLOIDAL FRACTION

Soils are capable of adsorption of nutrients, contaminant elements, and other charged components due primarily to the presence of colloidal particles of varied compositions. A *colloid* is defined as a particle measuring less than 1μm across. Because of their extremely small size, soil colloids possess an enormous external surface area per unit weight. The external surface area of 1 gram of colloidal clay is about 1,000 times that of 1 gram of coarse sand. Some colloids, especially certain silicate clays, possess extensive internal surfaces as well. These surfaces occur between the crystal units of each particle, and the internal surface often exceeds the external surface area. The total surface area of soil colloids ranges from 10 m^2/g for clays with only external surfaces, to more than 800 m^2/g for clays with internal surfaces (Brady and Weil 2002).

Colloidal surfaces, both external and internal, are extremely reactive chemically by virtue of the presence of permanent electrical charges. For most soil colloids, electronegative charges predominate. The presence and intensity of these influence the attraction and repulsion of particles toward each other, thereby influencing a wide range of physical and chemical properties. Surface charges also play a critical role in the adsorption or repulsion of contaminant elements, especially metallic cations. The four major types of colloids present in soils are layer silicate clays, iron and aluminum oxides, allophane and similar amorphous clays, and humus.

4.3.1. Silicate Clays

Layer silicate clays occur as a result of the weathering of minerals such as pyroxenes and amphiboles, felspars, muscovite, olivine, and volcanic ash (silicate glass). Silicate clays are the most prominent inorganic colloids in soils of temperate regions and occur in soils of the tropics as well. Repeating, crystalline layers characterize these minerals. Each particle is composed of a series of layers composed of horizontally oriented sheets of silicon, aluminum, magnesium, and/or iron atoms bound together by oxygen and hydroxy groups. The general composition of these clays is illustrated by the formula for the clay kaolinite, $Si_2Al_2O_5(OH)_4$.

The exact composition and the internal arrangement of the atoms in a specified crystal determine its surface charge and other properties, for example the capacity to retain and exchange ions. Physical properties will also be affected; for example, some colloidal clays experience extensive shrinking and swelling with changes in moisture status while others are much less affected.

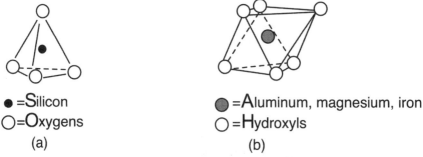

● =Silicon   ● =Aluminum, magnesium, iron
○=Oxygens   ○ =Hydroxyls
(a)   (b)

Figure 4.2.   *The basic structural units of 1:1 and 2:1 type clays: (a) a silica tetrahedron, and (b) an aluminum octahedron*

The most common and important silicate clays are the phyllosilicates. These clays are composed of two distinct sheets, one dominated by silicon, the other by aluminum and/or magnesium. The basic building block for the silica-dominated sheet is a four-sided unit (tetrahedron) composed of one silicon atom surrounded by four oxygen atoms (Fig. 4.2). An interlocking array of these tetrahedra linked together creates the tetrahedral sheet. Aluminum and/or magnesium ions are the key cations in the second type of sheet. An aluminum or magnesium ion is surrounded by six oxygen atoms or hydroxy groups, resulting in an eight-sided unit, or octahedron (Fig. 4.2). Numerous octahedra linked together comprise the octahedral sheet. The tetrahedral and octahedral sheets are the fundamental structural units of silicate clays.

The so-called 1:1-type minerals are composed of one Si tetrahedra sheet attached to one Al octahedra sheet; hence the term *1:1-type clay*. The 1:1 structure is fixed; that is, no expansion occurs between layers when the clay is wet. Cations and water molecules cannot penetrate between the structural layers of a 1:1 clay particle. The surface area of these clays is thus limited to the external surface. In contrast with the other categories of silicate clays, the 1:1 clays demonstrate very little plasticity (capability of being molded), cohesion, shrinkage, and swelling. In soils, kaolinite is the dominant member of the 1:1 clay minerals, which also include halloysite, nacrite, and dickite.

The crystal layers of 2:1 clays are characterized by an Al octahedral sheet sandwiched between two Si tetrahedral sheets (Fig. 4.3). The smectite group experiences significant interlayer expansion that occurs by swelling when the minerals are wet. Water can enter the interlayer space

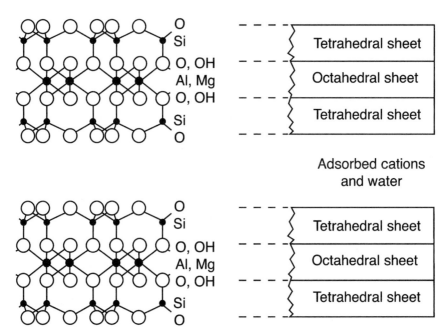

Figure 4.3.   Schematic of a 2:1 silicate clay showing two Si tetrahedral sheets surrounding one Al octahedral sheet

and force the layers apart. Montmorillonite is the most prominent member of the smectite group. Beidellite, nontronite, and saponite also occur in this category. The smectites also possess the properties of high plasticity and cohesion, and marked swelling and shrinkage between wetting and drying. Wide cracks form upon drying of smectite-dominated soils (e.g., Vertisols). Dry aggregates are very hard, making soils difficult to work in the field. Vermiculites are also 2:1-type minerals. Water molecules, along with Mg and other ions, are strongly adsorbed in the interlayer space of vermiculites; however, they act as bridges holding the units together. The extent of swelling is, therefore, less for vermiculites as compared to smectites.

4.3.2. Hydrous Oxides

Hydrous oxides of iron and aluminum are dominant colloids in the highly weathered soils of the tropics and semitropics and are also present in significant quantities in some temperate region soils. Examples of common iron and aluminum oxides are gibbsite ($Al_2O_3 \cdot 3H_2O$) and goethite

($Fe_2O_3 \cdot H_2O$). The formulas also may be written in the hydroxide form, that is, gibbsite is $Al(OH)_3$ and goethite is $FeOOH$. Some of these colloids possess distinct crystalline structures whereas others are amorphous. Hydrous oxides possess a significant pH-dependent charge; in other words, the exchange capacity is strongly influenced by soil pH. Strongly acidic soil solutions tend to impart a positive charge to hydrous oxides because H^+ and Al^{3+} ions saturate the colloidal surfaces. Under more alkaline conditions, these cations are stripped away, revealing a significant cation exchange capacity.

4.3.3. Allophane and Other Amorphous Colloids

In many soils significant quantities of amorphous colloidal matter occur. One of the more significant amorphous aluminum silicate colloids is allophane. This mineral is prevalent in soils developed from volcanic ash and has the general composition $Al_2O_3 2SiO_2 H_2O$. Allophane has a high capacity to absorb cations as well as anions.

4.3.4. Humic Colloids

Soil organic matter is generally composed of 25% to 35% polysaccharides and proteinlike compounds that are readily decomposed by microorganisms and therefore experience a short half-life in soils. About 65% to 75% of soil organic matter is composed of humic materials, which are a diverse assortment of secondary hydrocarbon molecules formed from the decomposition of plant and animal tissue deposited to soil. Humic colloids are complex mixtures of high molecular weight hydrocarbons, which are resistant to decomposition. There is no single chemical formula or structure that will accurately describe the colloidal structure and organization of humus. Humus is not a single compound; rather, it is a range of compounds having drastically differing chemistries and molecular weights (Fig. 4.4). Put simply, humus colloids are highly charged organic and amorphous rather than crystalline micelles, and possess a significant electrical charge.

Soils high in organic matter are capable of adsorbing significant quantities of organic contaminants. The organic molecule and the humic compound will be attracted to each other due to their nonpolar nature. Such adsorption will slow contaminant movement and, in many cases, result in

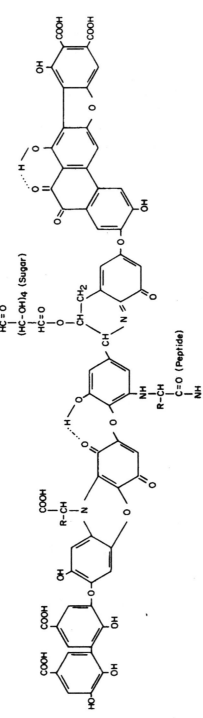

Figure 4.4. *Hypothetical structure of a humus molecule. (Reproduced with kind permission of the American Society of Agronomy.)* Mortvedt, Giordano, and Lindsay 1972.

the incorporation of certain contaminants over the long term. Soil organic matter usually has a substantial CEC and may have a significant anion exchange capacity as well. Anion exchange capacity, however, is usually much less than CEC. Increased soil organic levels will favor microbial activity due to increased nutrient supply (especially N, P, and S), CEC, tilth, water-holding capacity, and available carbon.

The negative electrical charges occurring in humus are associated with partially dissociated hydroxyl ($-OH$), carboxyl ($-COOH$), and phenolic groups (Table 4.1). These groups are associated with sheets of benzene rings or carbon chains of varying size and complexity (Fig. 4.4). As is the case for Fe and Al oxides, the negative charge occuring in humus is highly dependent on soil pH. Under very acid conditions the negative charge is relatively low because H^+ ions saturate the negative charges. With an increase in pH, however, H^+ ions dissociate from the carboxyl groups and subsequently from the hydroxyl and phenolic groups. This dissociation results in a greatly increased negative charge on the colloid. Under neutral to alkaline conditions the CEC of humus per unit weight greatly exceeds that of the silicate clays.

4.5. THE BIOLOGICAL COMPONENT

Soil materials possess a significant biotic component. Many groups of microorganisms occur in soils; however, the most significant include bacteria, actinomycetes, fungi, algae, and protozoa. The first three groups comprise the microorganisms most responsible for the transformations of organic matter, including hydrocarbon contaminants, in soils. These organisms are essential to nutrient cycling of ecosystems including C, N, P, and S. Active microorganisms decompose plant and animal tissue, converting them to cellular biomass, secondary materials (humus), CO_2, and other gases via mineralization, immobilization, and humification reactions. The biological component of soil and its reactions are discussed in more detail in chapter 11, "Microbial Remediation."

4.6. RELEVANT PHYSICAL PROPERTIES

Soil and subsurface materials recovered for analysis during a Phase II subsurface investigation may occur in many forms. Classification of these

Table 4.1. Functional and structural groups of humus

Alcohol	$R\text{-}CH_2OH$
Aldehyde	$\begin{matrix} H \\ R\text{-}C\text{=}O \end{matrix}$
Amino	$R\text{-}NH_2$
Amine	$\begin{matrix} H \\ R\text{-}C\text{-}NH_2 \\ H \end{matrix}$
Amide	$R\text{-}\overset{\displaystyle O}{\overset{\|}{C}}\text{-}NH_2$
Carboxyl	$R\text{-}\overset{\displaystyle O}{\overset{\|}{C}}\text{-}OH$
Carboxylate	$R\text{-}\overset{\displaystyle O}{C}\text{-}O^-$
Enol	$R\text{-}CH\text{=}CH\text{-}OH$
Ether	$R\text{-}CH_2\text{-}O\text{-}CH_2\text{-}R'$
Ester	$R\text{-}\overset{\displaystyle O}{\overset{\|}{C}}\text{-}O\text{-}R'$
Ketone	$R\text{-}\overset{\displaystyle O}{\overset{\|}{C}}\text{-}R'$
Keto acid	$R\text{-}\overset{\displaystyle O}{\overset{\|}{C}}\text{-}COOH$
Quinone	
Hydroquinone	
Peptide	$\begin{matrix} & & & H \\ & H \; H & | & H \\ ^+H\,N\text{-}\,C\text{-}\,C\text{-}\,N\text{-}\,C\text{-}\,COOH \\ & & \| \\ & & O \end{matrix}$

materials can provide an understanding of the hydrologic regime present at the site. These materials may be formed as soils develop from the weathering of bedrock underlying the site, fill materials placed in the subsurface during grading the site or backfilling an excavation, consolidated or unconsolidated sediments, igneous rock, or other sources. When formed naturally or installed, each of these geologic types possesses certain hydrologic properties. These properties may be altered during processes of lithification (the consolidation of sediment); through dissolution (the process through which caverns are formed); through weathering; and through fracturing (Pope and Matthews 1993).

4.6.1. Basic Hydrogeology

Soil and groundwater are key avenues for the transport of aqueous and nonaqueous contaminants. Water from direct application, precipitation, or runoff infiltrate through the soil surface; some will be stored in the upper horizons while some will percolate downward by the force of gravity until impermeable material is encountered. This subsurface material is sufficiently impermeable and tight that groundwater cannot flow through it. Materials that prohibit the passage of water to a well or spring are termed *aquitards*, *aquicludes*, or *confining layers*. Aquitards generally consist of clay and silt or unfractured, dense rock. From this point of confinement, percolating water fills all pore spaces until the lowermost soil is completely saturated. This *saturated zone* rises as water continues to fill the pore spaces. The top of the saturated zone is designated the *water table*. Above this is a zone in which water is held through adhesion, that is, capillary action between the soil grains. This is the *capillary fringe*. Above the capillary fringe is a zone of unsaturated soil, referred to as the *vadose zone* (Fig. 4.5).

An *aquifer* is a geologic stratum that has the ability to store and transmit large volumes of water and can supply significant quantities to a well or spring. Aquifers are typically composed of sand and gravel or fractured rock. At the water table, groundwater is subject to atmospheric pressure and the aquifer is termed *unconfined*. Most aquifers impacted by contamination from hazardous substances are shallow, unconfined bodies; that is, they are open to the land surface. Municipal water supply wells do not typically withdraw water from unconfined aquifers; however, domestic wells will sometimes tap into these. Groundwater in shal-

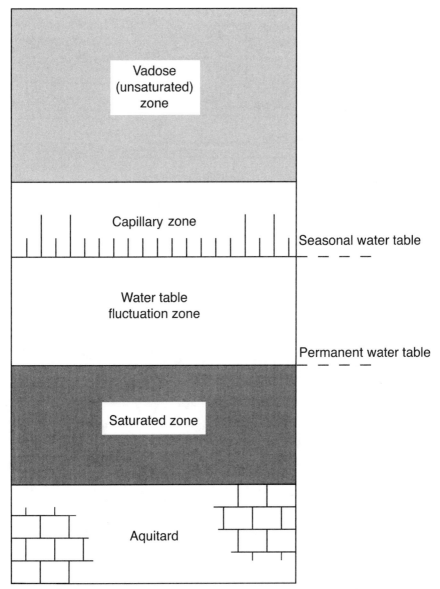

Figure 4.5. Cross-section of a soil column showing differing moisture regimes

low, unconfined aquifers may also discharge into rivers, wetlands, or other surface water bodies (Fig. 4.6). An aquifer may also outcrop in one area, then dip beneath an impermeable layer, becoming confined at some distance downgradient. Artesian groundwater conditions develop when an aquifer is overlaid by an aquitard. The aquitard acts as a rigid cover

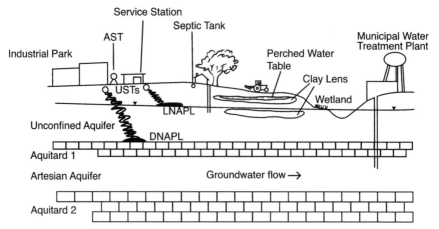

Figure 4.6. *Unconfined and confined aquifers and examples of possible contamination sources*

over the groundwater reservoir, and the water will experience pressure greater than atmospheric pressure; therefore, when a well is completed in an artesian aquifer, the water will rise in the well to a height above the top of the aquifer. These *confined aquifers* are a significant groundwater resource and tend to be isolated from contamination.

Groundwater is by no means static. The direction of groundwater flow is determined by measuring the elevations of the water table. This is accomplished by installing an array of monitoring wells. The top of the well casing is surveyed. The depth to water in each well is measured, and this value is subtracted from the top of casing elevation to determine the water table elevation. The water table elevations can be plotted on a site map to generate a water table contour map (Fig. 4.7). Water will flow perpendicular to the contour lines from higher to lower elevations. Low-density contaminants (LNAPL) will flow in the same direction as the groundwater. High-density organic solvents (DNAPL) will not be significantly affected by groundwater flow gradients; rather, they will flow from higher to lower elevations along the top of the aquiclude.

The location of recharge and discharge points partly controls the flow of groundwater. Recharge occurs as rain falls onto the surface, infiltrates, and percolates downward to the groundwater. Recharge occurs more readily where the surface soil or rock is permeable and the surface topography is relatively flat. Determining the depth and type of aquifers, groundwater transport velocities, and proximity of receptors (rivers,

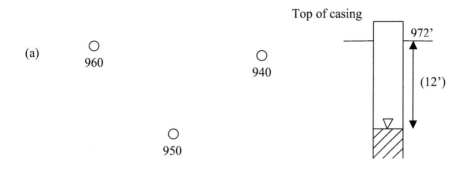

(a)

Top of casing

960   940

950

972'

(12')

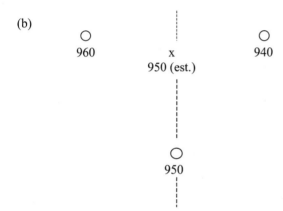

(b)

960   x   940
950 (est.)

950

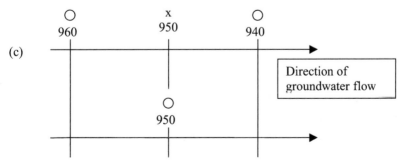

(c)

960   x   940
950

Direction of
groundwater flow

950

Figure 4.7. *Triangulation method for the estimation of groundwater flow direction*

lakes, etc.) is essential in the Phase II environmental assessment (see chapter 5, "Environmental Site Assessments").

4.6.2. Porosity

In site assessment and remediation activities it is important for the operator to determine properties of porosity, permeability, and hydraulic conductivity of subsurface materials. These parameters are all closely related. Porosity is the ratio of the pore space of the soil to the total soil volume. A strata having a porosity of 38% means that 38% of the total volume occurs as open space. Pore spaces may be classified according to size as *micropores* and *macropores*. The porosity of sandy soils consists mainly of macropores while clayey soils contain mostly micropores. Air, water, hydrocarbon vapors, and other contaminants occupy the pore spaces. The ratio of micropores to macropores influences the movement of soil water and gases. The ratio is also very important to a number of remediation activities; for example, certain aqueous contaminants can be literally flushed out of a soil under the proper conditions. If the soil has adequate porosity, especially as macropores, the flushing solution may be recharged fairly quickly and remediation is rapid, all other factors being equal. In the case of in situ bioremediation the ratios of soil gas and water, which are a function of porosity, greatly influence microbial activity.

Typically, more rounded particles such as gravel, sand, and silt, especially those having uniform particle sizes (sorted) have higher porosities than soils containing the platy clay minerals. Soils containing a mixture of grain sizes (poorly sorted) will also experience low porosities because the smaller particles fill void spaces between the larger ones.

4.6.3. Permeability

Permeability is the ability of the soil or subsurface strata to transport fluids. The more open and interconnected the pores in the rock, the higher the permeability. Permeability is expressed in units of length per time—centimeters per second or feet per day. In general, the larger the grain size, the larger the pore size and therefore the higher the porosity and permeability (Fig. 4.8). Porosity and permeability usually correlate; that is, the higher the porosity the greater the permeability. There are exceptions to

Permeability, cm/sec

10^2	10	1	10^{-1}	10^{-2}	10^{-3}	10^{-4}	10^{-5}	10^{-6}	10^{-7}	10^{-8}	10^{-9}

Clean gravel	Clean sands; mixtures of clean sands and gravels	Very fine sands; silts; mixtures of sand, silt, and clay; glacial fill; stratified clays; etc.	Unweathered clays

10^6	10^5	10^4	10^3	10^2	10	1	10^{-1}	10^{-2}	10^{-3}	10^{-4}	10^{-5}

Permeability, gal/day/ft^2

Figure 4.8.   *Abilities of different soil size fractions to transmit water*
U.S. Environmental Protection Agency 1989.

this association, however. Clays which have very small grain size may have porosities of 40% to 50% but are generally impermeable.

4.6.4. Hydraulic Conductivity

Hydraulic conductivity is a function of the properties of both the porous medium and the fluid passing through it. Typically, the hydraulic conductivity has higher values for gravel and sand and lower values for clay. Thus, even though clay-rich soils may have high porosities, they usually have lower hydraulic conductivities because the pore diameters in clay-rich soil are much smaller.

Henri Darcy, a French engineer living in the nineteenth century, made one of the earliest descriptions of groundwater flow. He observed a relationship between the volume of water flowing through sand and properties of the sand.

$$Q/t = KA \, dH/dL \qquad (4.1)$$

where Q is the volume of flow per unit time, t, through a column of a given cross-sectional area of flow, A. The flow is under a pressure gradient dH/dL, and the change in water level over a given length is L. K is the saturated hydraulic conductivity, a proportionality constant (Fig. 4.9).

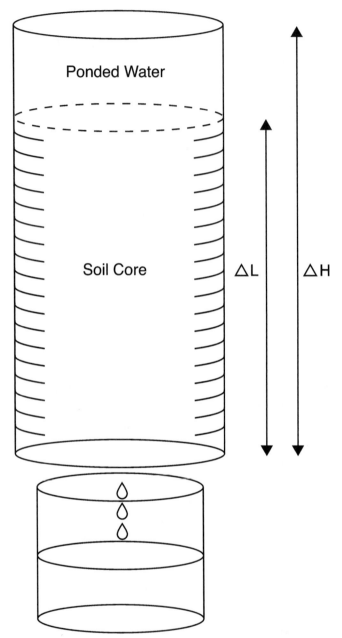

Figure 4.9. *Schematic of a soil column used to calculate saturated hydraulic conductivity*

Darcy's law calculates the volumetric flow rate through a unit cross section of the aquifer, not the actual velocity of water movement. The equation is rewritten in order to solve for the hydraulic conductivity:

$$K = \frac{Q \, \Delta L}{A \, \Delta H} \tag{4.2}$$

Example 4.1. Soil material is being considered for use as a lagoon liner. An intact core (6 cm diameter) is collected from a site and brought to the laboratory. The soil column measures 20 cm tall with a head of 2 cm water that is ponded on the top of the soil column. After the system has reached equilibrium, a total of 172 mL is collected per hour. Calculate the K_s.

$$K = \frac{Q \, \Delta L}{A \, \Delta H}$$

$$K = \frac{(172/60/60) \times (10 \text{cm})}{28.3 \text{ cm}^3 \times (12 \text{ cm})}$$

$$K = 1.4 \times 10^{-3} \text{ cm/sec}$$

The path of groundwater flow is dependent on the type of material through which the groundwater flows. For example, the pore spaces between sand grains are generally continuously connected. Flow of groundwater through sand or similar porous material is referred to as *porous-media flow*. In contrast, in a rock such as basalt the amount of pore space is very small and the pores are not interconnected; therefore, flow cannot occur. If the basalt is fractured, water can flow through the cracks. This type of medium influences the flow paths of the groundwater. In general, porous media do not restrict flow, while fractured media place extreme constraints on flow paths (Government Institutes 1993).

Hydraulic properties determine the feasibility of adding or removing materials such as water, air, and nutrients to the soil. Soil hydraulic conductivities of about 1.0×10^{-4} to 1.0×10^{-6} cm/sec are favorable for adding or removing materials. Soils with conductivities above this range undergoing a remediation program require careful management to prevent excessive drainage or contaminant migration off-site. Conductivities below this range tend to impair movement of reagents, air, and water, thus limiting the speed and effectiveness of remediation (Pope and Matthews 1993).

The hydraulic conductivity of saturated soils is dependent on grain size and particle sorting and is relatively stable over time. Hydraulic conductivity in unsaturated soil is influenced by grain size and sorting, as well as by the soil water content. At low water content, soil water moves mostly in response to adhesive and cohesive forces, which comprise the soil's matric potential. Soluble contaminants in unsaturated soil move in the thin films of water surrounding the soil particles. The thicker the film of water (e.g., the wetter the soil), the larger the path for contaminant movement and the greater amount of contaminant that can move in a given period of time (Pope and Matthews 1993).

4.6.5. Water-holding Capacity

The ability of a soil to hold moisture is determined primarily by its proportion of clay and organic matter. These colloids hold more water relative to their volume than do coarse-grained materials such as sands. The ratio of air and water in soil voids influences a number of chemical and biological processes in the soil. The activity of aerobic microorganisms is maximized when the soil moisture level measures about 70% to 80% of field capacity. Relatively dry soils tend to adsorb contaminants more strongly than moist soils because water competes with contaminants for adsorption sites. In an unsaturated soil, water and water-soluble compounds tend to move in all directions in response to matric potential (a reflection of adhesion of the water molecule to solids and cohesion of water molecules to each other). In wet soils, water and water-soluble components are most strongly influenced by the force of gravity. Nonaqueous-phase liquids (NAPLs) move through moist (not wet) soils rather quickly; dry soils tend to adsorb NAPL, and water in a completely wet soil will impede NAPL migration.

QUESTIONS

1. The two cations that are primarily responsible for soil acidity are H^+ and Al^{3+}. Explain how these cations are chemically interrelated as regards soil pH.
2. Explain why a soil pH measurement (with a glass electrode pH meter) does not provide a satisfactory estimate of the amount of liming material required to *change* soil pH.

3. Choose the correct answer: Clay and humus are significant to soils because of: (a) high cation exchange capacity; (b) serving as a significant nutrient storehouse; (c) high surface area per unit volume; (d) high water-holding capacity; (e) all of the above.
4. Most soil N, P, and S is held in the soil in organic, that is, humus-incorporated forms. True or false?
5. Humus is not a single molecule; rather, it contains a range of chemical substances and is quite variable. Explain.
6. What type(s) of colloids occur in soils of the temperate regions? Of the humid tropics? How might the electrical charges differ between the colloids of these two regions?
7. Soil material is being assessed as a possible liner for a chemical waste lagoon. A soil core was collected and brought to the laboratory. A 10 cm tall section of soil has 2 cm of water continuously ponded on it. The area of the core surface is 78 cm^2. A total of 62 mL H_2O is collected per hour. Calculate the Ks. The upper limit for Ks for lagoon liners is 1×10^{-8} cm/sec. Is this soil suitable for a liner?

REFERENCES

Brady, N. C., and R. R. Weil. 2002. *The Nature and Properties of Soils.* 13th ed. Upper Saddle River, NJ: Prentice Hall.

Government Institutes. 1993. *Environmental Science and Technology Handbook.* Rockville, MD.

Mortvedt, J. J., P. M. Giordano, and W. L. Lindsay. 1972. *Micronutrients in Agriculture.* Madison, WI: American Society of Agronomy.

Pope, D. F., and J. E. Matthews. 1993. *Bioremediation Using the Land Treatment Concept.* EPA/600/R-93/164. Washington, DC: U.S. Environmental Protection Agency, Office of Research and Development.

U.S. Environmental Protection Agency. 1989. Requirements for hazardous waste landfill design, construction and closure. Seminar publication. EPA/625/4-89/022. Cincinnati: Center for Environmental Research Information.

CHAPTER 5

Environmental Site Assessments

Dr. Watson: This is indeed a mystery. What do you imagine that it means?

Sherlock Holmes: I have no data yet. It is a capital mistake to draw conclusions before one has data. Invariably one begins to twist facts to suit theories, rather than theories to suit facts.

—Sir Arthur Conan Doyle, from "A Scandal in Bohemia,"
in *The Adventures of Sherlock Holmes*

5.1. INTRODUCTION

The purpose of the environmental site assessment (ESA) is to determine the presence, if any, of a hazardous condition existing on a parcel of land. This investigation is conducted primarily to avoid the liability and costs associated for the cleanup of a site that is later found to be contaminated with toxic materials. Almost all commercial transactions must now be accompanied by at least a so-called phase I environmental assessment. If a site is found to be in need of remediation, the information from an ESA facilitates the planning process for sampling, analysis, and remediation activities.

The ESA provides for a thorough assessment of on-site conditions and operations. Site conditions are compared with regulatory requirements to determine compliance. Hazardous substances and conditions are identified. The potential for human exposure and any risk and liability involved for the owners, operators, and other relevant parties should be included. Finally, recommended future courses of action (i.e., remedial action) if any, for the site are provided. Ultimately, the ESA process will produce a detailed report of findings. This will serve as a guide for future decisions as to the disposition of the property.

The ESA process is achieved via a review of regulatory and technical records, on-site inspection, mapping, sampling and analysis, interviews with site owners and managers, and finally, report preparation. The ESA has conventionally been divided into three phases. Phase I is a general problem identification; this is where historical records and documents are gathered, integrated, and analyzed. The phase I is a period of speculation; that is, the assessor keeps in mind that any scenario is possible for the site in question. The end result includes declaring a probability for contamination. Sampling is relatively uncommon during phase I with the possible exceptions of asbestos in building materials, radon sampling in buildings, and lead sampling in drinking water.

A detailed site characterization is involved in the phase II ESA. The basic purpose is to confirm or deny any suspicions that may have arisen during the phase I assessment. Additional historical research and information gathering takes place during phase II. Sampling and analysis may be extensive (Fig. 5.1). Soils may be sampled at the surface or to great depths; likewise, geologic strata may be recovered from core sampling. Surface water and groundwater may be collected and analyzed for concentrations of suspected contaminants. During phase II there is often a thorough survey to detect the presence of asbestos in building materials. Other specialized activities may involve analysis of a wildlife habitat by a biologist, audits of facility records of product use and waste management, and even tracking of suspicious activities by a private investigator (Hess 1993). The phase II ESA, by virtue of the time and resources involved, will prove to be a much more costly undertaking than the phase I.

A phase III ESA occurs after suspicions have been confirmed. By this point contamination has been identified and the assessor must now determine its extent. This may be accomplished by more extensive sampling of soil, strata, and water resources on and adjacent to the property. Often, a phase III becomes incorporated within the actual remediation activity. For example, containment barriers may be installed and groundwater may be extracted while additional monitoring wells are installed and soil cores collected.

There is often no clear delineation between the above three phases. For example, some modified phase I ESAs may involve extensive soil sam-

Figure 5.1.   *The phase II environmental site assessment involves extensive data collection for soil, water, building materials, and hazardous materials at a site*

pling. The decision as to degree of assessment is arranged between client and assessor.

The driving force behind ESAs is the Superfund Amendments and Reauthorization Act (SARA), which provides an incentive for environmental diligence in commercial property transactions. The so-called innocent purchaser or innocent landowner defense has placed much emphasis on identifying "recognized environmental conditions" in such transactions. "Recognized environmental conditions" are defined by ASTM (American Society for Testing and Materials 2005) as

> the likely presence of any hazardous substances or petroleum products on a property under conditions that indicate an existing release, a past release, or a material threat of a release of any hazardous substances or petroleum products into structures on the property or into the ground, groundwater or surface water of the property. The term includes hazardous substances or petroleum products even under the conditions in compliance with the laws.

Petroleum products are included in this definition because courts have extended CERCLA liability to petroleum-contaminated sites.

Clients of ESAs are primarily buyers of property (about 75% of all cases). Other clients include the property seller, the lending institution, and corporate shareholders. All these parties are concerned as to whether the property can be a liability due to the presence of hazardous substances.

The degree or depth of a site assessment is often a function of land use. If the assessor is reasonably confident that the site has been undeveloped or used solely as agricultural land for the previous five decades, then a somewhat less rigorous approach regarding the extent of the records search and site reconnaissance may be justified. Conversely, however, if the site is a brownfield with a long and not-so-stellar history of heavy industry and documented releases in the area, the assessment may be slow, cautious, and meticulous.

5.2. THE PHASE I ESA

Some of the key requirements of phase I assessments are to (Hess 1993):

- identify potential environmental liability on a property scheduled for a transaction;
- identify hazardous materials that might be disturbed and released during subsequent construction activities. Hazardous substances pose a reduced risk if left undisturbed. Early identification allows alternative plans for excavation;
- provide information about environmental conditions during planning stages, so that alternative designs can be formulated to avoid complications and reduce costs;
- ensure worker and public safety via exposure to soil, water, and air contamination;
- demonstrate that due diligence was exercised in case of unexpected problems and/or litigation. This aspect is critical in property transfers.

The components of an ESA will vary as a function of the site in question, client needs, and possible costs. However, the assessors should, in all cases, search and review the following:

Physical Setting

Topographic characteristics provide important information about surface drainage and the possibilities for contaminant transport. A United States Geological Survey (USGS) topographic quadrangle map will indicate surface contours, the presence of waterways, roads, and rail lines, and several other man-made features (e.g., quarries and large buildings) (Fig. 5.2). The

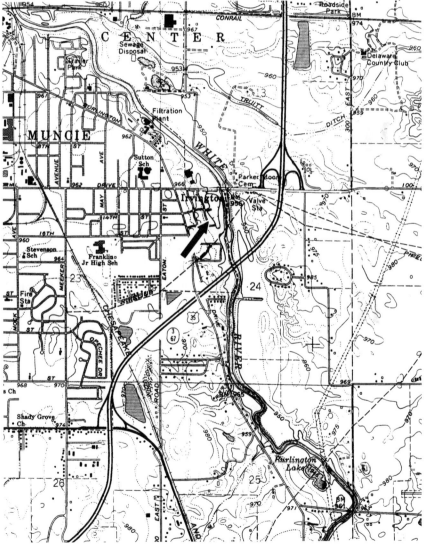

Figure 5.2. *Portion of a USGS topographic map showing area of study, a former excavation site*

topographic map will help the assessor predict directional movements of contaminants, thus identifying possible receptors (reservoirs, wetlands, homes, etc.) affected by contaminant transport. The topographic map will also provide information on proximity to population centers. It must be remembered that the parcel in question is not an isolated area; activities on neighboring properties may be affecting your site. Likewise, your parcel may be impacting neighboring land, populations, and other receptors.

Geologic Characteristics

The USGS and the USDA provide maps on soil, surficial deposits, and bedrock types for a selected area (Figs. 5.2 and 5.3). These data will pro-

Figure 5.3.   *USDA soils map of area of study*

vide additional clues as to the possibility for contaminant migration; for example, do there occur fractures or solution cavities that will cause rapid migration, or is the substrata relatively level and impermeable? Are the local soils sandy loams or dense clays? Is the water table close to the surface or at a significant depth? In many soil surveys so-called *made land*, which is soil composed of fill materials of uncertain origin, may be indicated on the soil survey (Fig. 5.3). USGS, state natural resources, and other maps will provide hydrogeologic data, for example depth to groundwater and the presence of perched water tables (Fig. 5.4).

Site History

Learning the identity of the previous site owners can provide the assessor with knowledge of the range of commercial and industrial activities carried out. The assessor must therefore review the chain of title. All ESAs require a thorough title search; the process involves visits to the county assessor's office to determine the chronological list of individuals and companies that owned and operated the property. Past or present operations at the site (i.e., petrochemical manufacturing versus a woodlot) will influence the extent to which the assessor must review. If the site occurs in an

Table 5.1.   Examples of sites and facilities posing significant environmental risk

Site or Facility	Possible Hazards
Petroleum and petrochemical facilities	Oils, fuels, resins, solvents, corrosives, chlorine
Manufacturing plants	Solvents, corrosives, reactives, resins, baghouse dusts
Waste-accumulation sites	Solvents, used oil, metals, acids
Metal plating	Cr, Cd, Cu, Ni, Pb, Zn, acids, alkalis, cyanide
Metal smelters, foundries	Metals, corrosives, paint, baghouse dust, resins, binders
Automobile battery recycling	Lead, other metals, acids
Automobile salvage yards	Waste oil, fuels, BTEX, MTBE, ethylene, glycol, tanks (propane, oxygen)
Uncontrolled or private dumps	Organic and inorganic solids and liquids
Photo processing and printing	Metals, solvents
Agricultural operations	Pesticides, fertilizers, unregulated dumps
Gasoline service stations	Gasoline, diesel fuel, BTEX, used oil
Dry cleaners	Solvents
Older buildings	Asbestos, lead-based paint
Coal and metal mines and spoils	Metals, acids

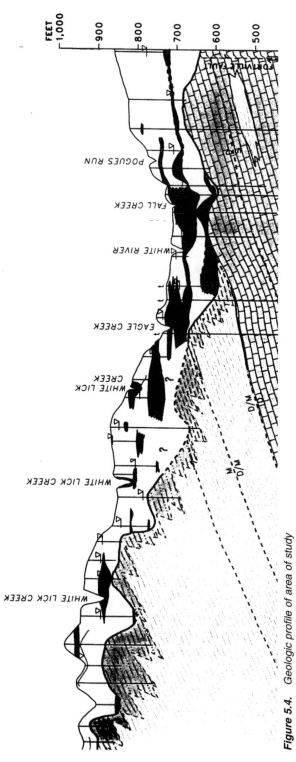

Figure 5.4. Geologic profile of area of study

area of heavy industry (e.g., a midwestern automotive or metalworking area), it may be necessary to search the title of ownership as far back as one hundred years. Title searches can be complicated at times; for example, if the property frequently changes hands, the property is part of several deeds, or the property is part of more than one county.

Aerial Photographs

Aerial photographs are kept on file at local Natural Resources Conservation (formerly Soil Conservation) Service offices and in various state natural resources and environmental offices. The photo review is another important tool for determining prior land usage (Fig. 5.5). The assessor should seek one aerial photo for the site for every five to ten years, going back at least fifty years. The site should be scrutinized for changes in topography, which may imply a disposal area. Also, the existence of man-made objects such as drums, Aboveground Storage Tanks (ASTs), Underground Storage Tanks (USTs), and buildings should be noted (Fig. 5.6). A man-made object will usually appear as a distinct entity as most possess sharp corners or straight edges. A good rule of thumb for identification of a natural versus a man-made structure is that natural formations almost always possess rounded, irregular, or diffuse shapes (Figs. 5.5 and 5.6).

Fire Insurance Maps

The Sanborn Fire Insurance Maps were originally formulated to assist insurance agents in assessing fire risk and the potential for the spread of fire. These maps have been developed for entire towns or sections of a city. They provide information on land use, structures, and occupants. Other useful information that may be gleaned from the maps includes type of construction (brick, asbestos, etc.), storage of raw materials, products manufactured or stored, and the presence of water mains and wells (Fig. 5.7).

Additional Resources

Other resources that a site assessor should consider in the historical-records search include architectural drawings of structures, local street directories, zoning records, building permits, and commercial directories.

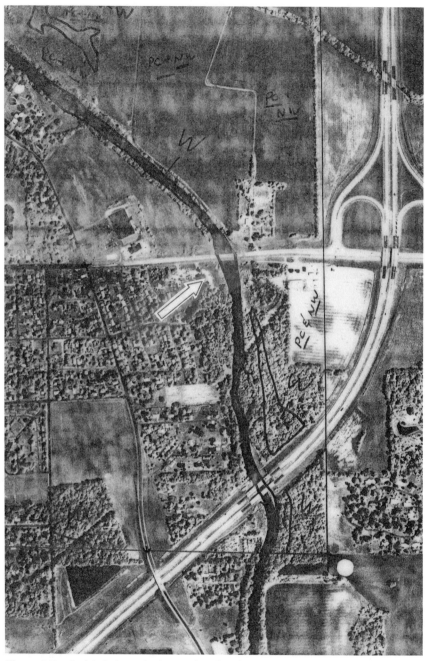

Figure 5.5. Aerial photograph of area of study, a former excavation site and current waste disposal site

Figure 5.6. *Aerial photograph of a derelict petroleum refinery showing storage tanks and buildings*

Relevant regulatory agency listings must be scrutinized to ascertain the documented presence of hazards or violations by federal, state, or county agencies. These listings are on file in each state's office of environmental protection. Such lists are usually available online and are updated regularly. Lists of highest priority for the assessor include the NPL (Superfund), Compensation and Liability Information System (CERCLIS), and RCRA lists; state hazardous-waste site lists, registered UST and Leaking underground storage tank (LUST) lists, and county health department violations lists (Table 5.2).

While at the state offices, the assessor should determine the history, if any, of permits or citations for the site. For example, have there been citations for improper disposal? Has a previous owner requested a permit for waste disposal? Has an NPDES permit been provided? This is an opportunity to confirm compliance with the state and federal occupational safety and health statutes and to describe any record of worker- or workplace-related environmental incidents.

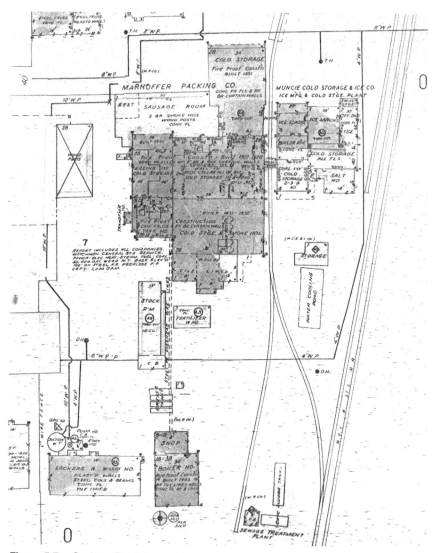

Figure 5.7.   Sanborn Fire Insurance Map

5.2.1. The Site Reconnaissance

Efforts to determine the possibility of site hazards by referring only to previously documented information are not adequate for a site assessment. A visit to the site is required in order to obtain firsthand observations of past or ongoing activities and occurrences. The purpose of a site walkover, then, is to locate specific problems at the site, if any, such as contaminated

Table 5.2.   Relevant data for the Phase I historical and records review

Federal Level
    National Priorities List (NPL) facilities list
    Comprehensive Environmental Response, Compensation
       and Liability Information System (CERCLIS) list
    RCRA treatment, storage, and disposal (TSD) facilities list
    Other RCRA lists
    • Large-quantity hazardous-waste generators
    • Small-quantity hazardous-waste generators
    • Hazardous-waste transporters
    SARA Title III Reports
    Emergency Response Notification System list

State Level
    State priority site list
    Unplanned release and spill databases
    Air emissions records
    Notices of violation or similar citations
    Hazardous-waste site list
    Landfill/solid waste-disposal site list
    Registered UST lists
    LUST lists

County Level
    Historical maps and plans
    Property surveys
    Building permits
    Landfill sites list
    Well records

Other Local Agencies
    Department of Health records
    Fire department hazardous materials emergency responses
    Sanitation department records
    Water quality agency records

Published Sources
    Aerial photos
    Fire Insurance directories (Sanborn Directories)
    City directory listings
    USGS topographical maps
    State or USGS groundwater survey maps
    State or USGS subsurface geology maps

areas that pose a liability to those with a financial interest in the property. The visual search is conducted for evidence of:

Current Use of the Site

Is the area undeveloped? Is it commercial, light industry, or heavy industry? The degree of development is related to the degree of potential hazard. For example, light manufacturing may produce small amounts of relatively nonhazardous solid wastes. In contrast, an established industrial facility may be responsible for the generation of solid and hazardous wastes, emissions control residues (e.g., baghouse dust), fugitive emissions, and process wastewater. Spills and other releases to soil and paved areas may have occurred.

Prior Use

Look for abandoned buildings and sheds that may be used to store hazardous materials. There are many documented cases where containers in old buildings have leaked as a result of corrosion and vandalism.

Hazardous Materials Storage and Use Areas

Hazardous waste may be stored in drums, bulk corrugated containers, tanks, or simply in lagoons, a common practice prior to the enactment of the RCRA regulations. Look for waste accumulation areas, storage sites, and disposal areas. This is also an opportunity to assess the overall condition of containers and storage areas; for example, note if drums are open or unlabeled, if they are rusting, and if there is evidence of previous spills (Fig. 5.8). Is the waste-storage area suitably covered to protect containers from precipitation? Is secondary containment available in the event of a release?

Figure 5.8. *Rusted drums found in a woodlot during an environmental site assessment*

Figure 5.9.   *USTs removed from closed petroleum refinery*

Underground Storage Tanks (USTs)
and Aboveground Storage Tanks (ASTs)

Both USTs and ASTs have been notorious sources of soil and water contamination (Fig. 5.9). Look for vent pipes, manways, and other covers that may indicate the presence of current or abandoned tanks. A depression within a paved-over area may indicate the presence of an old or abandoned UST. Evidence of hydrocarbon residues at or near the ground surface from previous spills and overfills may be visible.

Topography, Surface Water, and Wetlands

It is important to delineate drainage patterns in order to predict possible flow paths of surface water and any released contaminants on the land surface. Drains, surface water, and wetlands are likely receptors. The assessor should look for depressions, ditches, ponds, streams, and other low-elevation seeps. Unusual mounds or depressions may indicate the presence of dump areas. A sheen on the water table is a sign that free hydrocarbon product may be present. Product could be released from a UST, loose connections, or spills. Although a sheen on the water is generally not an indication of major contamination, it should indicate the need for further assessment as to the extent and degree of contamination, especially if drinking-water supplies occur locally.

Vegetation and Surface Soil

Soil and ground cover will provide subtle insights into activities on the site. Does the soil appear to be native to the area, or has fill material been brought in and graded over the site? The assessor should also look for stressed vegetation. Look for bare areas in fields otherwise having healthy vegetation. This may indicate spillage or disposal of toxic compounds. Discolored or stunted plants may simply be a result of inadequate soil fertility; however, they may also indicate the presence of heavy metals and/or hydrocarbons that pose toxic hazards to plants. Hydrocarbons can also cause moisture stress as NAPLs will tend to exclude water from soil pores. Stained soil and unusual odors are additional signs of hydrocarbons or other wastes in the soil (Fig. 5.10).

Figure 5.10.   *An uncontrolled landfill showing very poor drainage conditions with leaching from the soil surface*

Radon

This gas is a concern in closed buildings, especially in basements or first floors. Scan the property using radon canisters and report results of testing. If radon levels exceed the EPA action level a recommended response should be included.

Lead-Based Paint

It is estimated that 30 to 40 million older homes in the United States contain lead-based paint (LBP) (Fig. 5.11). Some LBP materials contain up to 50% Pb. About 75% of housing units in the United States built prior to 1980 were coated with LBP. In 1978, the manufacture and use of paints containing more than 0.06% Pb by weight on the interiors and exteriors of residential surfaces, toys, and furniture were banned.

Among the most common methods for testing LBP in buildings are laboratory analyses of paint chips and the use of portable X-ray fluorescence

Figure 5.11.   *Lead-based paint showing characteristic cubic-type cracks*

analyzers. For laboratory analysis, paint samples from several surfaces should be collected throughout the structure(s). Samples are removed by a heat gun, placed into plastic bags, labeled, and sent to a qualified laboratory for analysis. In the laboratory, samples are digested in concentrated acid and the dissolved extract is analyzed for total Pb content in an atomic absorption spectrophotometer. If the results exceed 0.5% Pb by weight the assessor's report should include a recommended response. More rapid methods exist to determine if Pb is present in paint, such as portable anodic stripping voltammetry and X-ray fluorescence detectors (Fig. 5.12). Both units provide fairly accurate, sensitive, and rapid values for Pb content on an intact surface. Both units are, however, rather expensive and require adequate training on the part of the user.

Lead in Water

Lead pipes are found in buildings built prior to the 1920s. Copper pipes and Pb solder (50% Sn, 50% Pb) came into common use in the 1950s. Lead solder has also been used in the construction of cisterns. The most common source of water contamination in structures is via Pb leaching from Cu pipes with Pb-soldered joints. In 1986, the use of Pb in public

Figure 5.12.   *An XRF detector is a useful and accurate means of field testing for the presence of lead. (Reproduced with kind permission of Thermo Electron Corporation, NITON Analyzers.)*

drinking water distribution systems was banned and the Pb content in brass was reduced to 8%.

Exposure to Pb-contaminated water systems is influenced by corrosiveness (i.e., pH, salt content) of the water, age of the Pb component (newer ones are more prone to leaching), quantity and surface area of the Pb-containing materials, and standing time and temperature of the water. The assessor should take one sample of water near a main to determine the Pb content entering the property and one sample of drinking water.

Asbestos-Containing Materials

Between 1900 and 1980, more than 30 million tons of asbestos were used in the United States. By some estimates 75% of all residential properties more than 30 years old, or those heated with steam or hot water, contain asbestos. Although banned for two decades, some asbestos-containing building materials are still available (Fig. 5.13). There is no argument about the utility of asbestos materials for building systems; among its useful properties are that it is fibrous (therefore it can be woven into

Figure 5.13.   *Asbestos floor tiles found during an environmental site assessment*

fabric), crystalline, thermally insulating, electrically insulating, thermally stable, and chemically stable.

The assessor should look for asbestos in a number of systems including:

- coverings for hot-water pipes and boilers
- heat reflectors such as those on wood stoves
- vinyl floor tiles and linoleum
- acoustical ceiling tiles
- siding on residential and commercial buildings
- roofing shingles and felts
- spray-on insulation or paint on walls and ceilings
- fuse boxes
- linings of air ducts

The asbestos-containing material (ACM) of greatest concern is that in a physical condition considered "friable." Asbestos is friable if it crumbles easily when subjected to hand pressure. The common types of ACMs that can contain friable asbestos include:

- a fluffy, sprayed-on material used for fireproofing, or a sprayed or troweled-on material that resembles a cement-like plaster and is used for fireproofing and soundproofing
- nonfriable asbestos wall board with sprayed- or troweled-on insulating material behind
- asbestos-based pipe or boiler insulation that may appear feltlike or cement-like

The assessor should sample suspect materials, send samples to a qualified lab, and include all results in the final report.

Miscellaneous

Additional considerations for the phase I walk-through include:

- business activities of nearby sites
- accessibility to the site
- suspicious features
- signs of misuse

- air emissions
- toxic chemicals
- PCB leakage from electrical equipment

It is important to note that the surrounding property should also be surveyed for hazardous materials, as a neighbor may have inadvertently or deliberately allowed contaminants to enter your site or facility.

5.2.2. Interviews

The phase I ESA should include interviews of personnel on-site regarding the current and prior use of the property. The assessor should inquire as to the types of activities, management of products and wastes, and regulatory compliance of operations. In the absence of knowledgeable on-site personnel, management or local officials can be interviewed. Typical individuals to interview regarding site operations include the property owner, managers, occupants, local governments, and, if possible, neighbors.

The facility assessor should inspect a number of useful records including registrations for underground storage tanks; material safety data sheets; community right-to-know plans; safety plans, spill prevention, countermeasure, and control plans; notices of violation; and hazardous-waste generator notices or reports.

5.2.3. Site Map

One of the products of the site reconnaissance is a detailed sketch of the property location. This should be prepared on computer-aided design software if possible. A USGS topographic map, enlarged, can serve as the base map for the site. Relevant details including drainage, structures, and potential hazards can be sketched onto the map. As emphasized earlier, it is necessary to examine property usage outside the immediate property boundaries; however, the assessor must set a reasonable limit as to how far this will be. Obtain a street map of the area and a property record ("street lot") map for the site and decide on a total search radius. For a phase I assessment the minimum search radius will depend on local conditions. The ASTM standard uses the term "search distance" because few properties have circular boundaries. Factors to consider in determining the minimum search distance include (Hess 1993):

- the density of use (urban industrial, urban commercial, suburban commercial, suburban multifamily, suburban residential, rural)
- potential migration routes
- distance to drinking water sources

In an urban industrial area a phase I search might extend a half mile or more. The main criterion for determining search distance is to ensure that potential sources of environmental risk have been covered.

5.2.4. The Report

Once all data is gathered the assessor prepares a report that provides detailed findings of the inspection. The report should include an executive summary listing the significant findings of the inspection as well as topographic, geologic, and surface maps, as well as other appropriate appendixes. All contacted sources should be listed. If phase II testing is recommended, this is to be included. The executive summary should include any limitations encountered in covering any relevant issues. After the assessor speaks with an attorney, the report should quantify potential environmental liabilities. If precise calculation is not possible, a range of potential costs should be provided (Hess 1993).

Even if no hazardous conditions are detected, the assessor should *never* guarantee that no hazardous substances exist on the property. The assessor is visiting and researching a site only briefly, and is therefore only observing a "snapshot" of the site. Unless every cubic inch of subsurface material is thoroughly analyzed and found to be uncontaminated, a site should not be declared as free from potential hazard—it is always possible that unwelcome surprises might be discovered at some later date.

5.3. BEYOND THE PHASE I

The phase II ESA is initiated only if the phase I has raised significant concerns about possible hazards on the property. The phase II investigation often includes the collection of extensive field data on soil, subsurface materials, groundwater, vegetation, and other materials on-site. As a result the phase II can be a costly and time-consuming activity. It is the intent of this chapter to provide only a brief glimpse into some of the more significant components of phase II. The reader is referred to several excellent references at the end of this chapter on the details of the phase II ESA.

Many variables will influence the behavior and movement of a contaminant plume. The downward and lateral migration of the contaminant through the subsurface depends on the actual quantity released, the physical properties of the product, and the structure and physical properties of the soil and rock through which the product is moving. In performing the phase II ESA it is essential to have a thorough understanding of characteristics of the release event, of the contaminant, and of the affected site. Since petroleum-related releases are by far the most common source of environmental contamination, this discussion will outline the phase II ESA process using petroleum hydrocarbons as the example contaminant.

5.3.1. Release Considerations

An initial step in the phase II investigation is to ascertain what contaminants were released. Knowledge of the type of the product released, its physical and chemical properties, and its major chemical constituents provides insight into subsurface behavior as well as the hazard potential to public health and environmental receptors. Petroleum products include a variety of fuel types, each having different physical and chemical properties. These properties must be known or estimated to make a judgment about its mobility—in other words, whether it will spread quickly as free liquid or vapor, its partitioning to various phases, and its potential for degradation.

The assessor must also determine the quantity of product released. This data will help to evaluate whether the contaminant has reached the water table, and it will be used to estimate the levels of contamination in all affected zones. Ascertaining the time since release is useful for estimating the quantity of product released. The composition and properties of the released material will change over time; volatile compounds evaporate, soluble constituents dissolve in infiltrating rainwater, and some constituents biodegrade. These physical, chemical, and biological changes that occur over time are collectively referred to as *weathering*. Weathering can result in a contaminant plume's having a dramatically different chemical composition compared with that which was originally released (Lyman et al. 1990).

After release into the soil, petroleum liquids transform between different phases: free product, vapor, dissolved product, and sorbed to soil colloids. The product may be present in all four phases at the same time. It is useful to know the relative proportions of contaminant in each phase, as hydrocarbons will vary in terms of mobility and feasibility of remediation depending on phase distribution.

As a petroleum release migrates from the site of origin, it fills soil pores. The plume percolates through the soil and a certain amount is retained within the pore space. The product in the soil that remains free-flowing and undissolved is termed *free product*. Because this is a hydrocarbon release, it is also labeled *nonaqueous phase liquid* (NAPL), as most hydrocarbons are nonpolar (that is, they do not react with water). Free product tends to migrate both vertically and horizontally due to gravity and capillary action. The migration occurs by successive permeation of larger areas, depending on the quantity of product discharged.

Infiltrating rainwater will dissolve some NAPL, thus promoting leaching through the soil toward the water table. Because of this slow dissolution, free product in the soil is a major concern in any site assessment and remediation program. As long as free product remains in the soil it is a potential source of contamination. For recent petroleum product releases (less than one year old), hydrocarbons are most likely to occur in the residual liquid (NAPL) phase rather than vapor and dissolved phases.

When free product reaches the water table it does not dissolve significantly. If the NAPL is less dense (i.e., has a lower specific gravity) than water, it is labeled a *light nonaqueous phase liquid* (LNAPL). Such free product tends to pool on the water table and may be carried along in the direction of groundwater flow. If, on the other hand, the NAPL is denser than water (*dense nonaqueous phase liquid*, or DNAPL), it will sink through the aquifer and accumulate at the point of an aquiclude such as bedrock. The product will flow along the bedrock surface until it penetrates a crevice or is blocked by a natural or man-made obstruction. The rate of free-product movement depends on the subsurface soil structure as well as the volume of the product released. Tighter soils such as clays restrict the flow, whereas sands and gravel allow rapid subsurface transport.

Hydrocarbon odors are a common initial clue that a release has occurred. The odor originates from vapors released as the volatile components of petroleum evaporate. Whether emanating from product within soil pores or floating on the water table, vapors migrate horizontally and upward along the paths of least resistance. Vapor migration can be blocked by buried structures; however, vapors will follow pathways through backfill material surrounding structures such as sewer and utility lines. Vapors can then accumulate in basements, underdrains, sewers, and water wells. In buildings the assessor must check for vapors, particularly in basements, that might have migrated through cracks in the foundation or through drains coming into the building. If vapors are detected when checking storm drains it is worth testing drains upgradient and downgradient to determine a pattern of migration. If higher levels of vapors are found upgradient, then the vapors may be originating from some other source. Portable field instrumentation for hydrocarbon vapor monitoring is discussed later in this chapter.

Soluble petroleum constituents will dissolve into both rainwater infiltrating through the unsaturated soil zone and groundwater. Some toxic constituents (e.g., benzene) are soluble in water yet are colorless, odorless, and tasteless in drinking water; therefore, the appropriate instrumentation is required for their detection.

Circumstances about a leak or spill will affect the behavior and movement of product released from a facility. All other considerations being equal, a rapid, high-volume leak can create a very different contaminant plume than will a slow leak. A high-volume release spreads laterally as well as downward; in contrast, a slow release moves downward via the macropores.

Much release information on the product type and amount released is available through interviews of owners and operators of the facility. Additionally, a review of facility records (e.g., product inventories, purchase and sales records, and tank tightness tests) will provide much useful data.

5.3.2. Contaminant Considerations

Numerous physical and chemical properties of the contaminant will dictate the overall mobility and toxicity of the plume. These properties will also influence the feasibility of a selected remediation program. Some of the more critical properties to assess in the phase II ESA are:

- water solubility
- viscosity
- specific gravity

- soil sorption coefficient
- biodegradability index
- vapor pressure
- vapor density

These properties can be measured directly in the laboratory (ASTM 1997) or can be inferred from published data. In many cases values may not be available for the bulk product; for example, gasoline composition will vary as a function of petroleum source, refinery, and blend. Often, however, one can consult default values, which provide generalized values for fuels. In some cases it may be advantageous to collect data for those components that pose a significant hazard and/or comprise a large volume of the plume (e.g., benzene and MTBE in a gasoline plume).

As mentioned in chapter 3, fuels are composed of a complex mixture of hydrocarbons, octane boosters, blending agents, detergents, and so on. For example, the molecular weight fractions of gasoline range from about C_4 to C_9. Gasoline contains aromatic compounds including benzene, toluene, ethylbenzene, and xylene (BTEX). These more volatile and toxic aromatic constituents are relatively mobile and water-soluble; they dissolve at least partially in infiltrating rainwater, travel through the soil, and can mix with groundwater. The most soluble components in gasoline are the oxygenated compounds such as ethanol and ethers, which are used as octane boosters. These latter compounds are added in concentrations as high as 11% by volume. MTBE is very mobile, soluble, and easy to detect. It partitions rapidly into the water phase and is not present in the vapor phase. Because of its high solubility, MTBE moves quickly out of the gasoline plume, forming a halo on the outer edges of the BTEX plume (NEIWPCC 1990). If MTBE is detected in groundwater, the assessor can infer that gasoline is present nearby because MTBE is used only in gasoline.

Middle distillate fuels such as diesel fuel, kerosene, jet fuel, and lighter fuel oils tend to be more dense, less volatile, less mobile, and less water soluble than gasoline. They also contain lower percentages of the more toxic aromatic compounds like BTEX. Heavier fuel oils and lubricants are even more dense and relatively insoluble and immobile in the subsurface environment than the middle distillates. The middle distillate and heavier fuels may be less volatile and less mobile, but they do migrate and do have the potential to cause substantial environmental contamination.

As gasoline weathers it experiences natural biodegradation, simple chemical oxidation, and transformation through the loss of the lighter, more volatile hydrocarbons. The heavier hydrocarbons are retained; thus, over time, the gasoline begins to take on the properties (including odors) of fuel oil. This will complicate the identification of the type of spill. Such aging may also affect the choice of field detection equipment used at a site. Aging does not proceed rapidly unless conditions are favorable. The aging process can be retarded by such factors as dense soils, barriers to vapor loss (e.g., paving), and/or high petroleum concentrations that inhibit bacterial breakdown.

In general, constituents with low molecular weights will move away from the source more quickly over time. This will occur either through volatilization or natural flushing by infiltrating rainwater. The more stable and less mobile constituents (typically, high-molecular weight compounds) remain near the source longer. Contaminant volatility, as measured by vapor pressure, indicates how readily it will transform from liquid to vapor. Contaminants with high vapor pressures partition readily into the vapor phase. Contaminant solubility is a measure of how readily it will dissolve in water (rainwater and pore water). Highly soluble contaminants will dissolve readily. Vapor analysis and soil sampling can be undertaken to determine in which phase most of the contamination is occurring. Soil material is often analyzed for total hydrocarbon concentration, while soil gas is sampled for evidence of hydrocarbon vapors.

Viscosity will affect the mobility and phase partitioning of a contaminant. A highly viscous constituent is likely to remain in the liquid phase (and perhaps sorbed to soil) rather than volatilize or dissolve. It will also remain in the unsaturated zone longer than a lower viscosity constituent. The extent to which a contaminant will sorb to soil particles depends on the phase (free liquid, vapor, or dissolved) and properties of the contaminant. The higher the pressure of a contaminant in the vapor phase, the greater the amount adsorbed. Sorption to colloids is inversely proportional to contaminant water solubility (i.e., the higher the solubility, the lower the degree of sorption). For soils with a high organic carbon content (greater than 0.1% by weight), sorption from aqueous solution is almost completely controlled by organic carbon (Lyman et al. 1990). A discussion of the chemical and physical properties of petroleum and petrochemicals appears in chapter 3.

5.3.3. Site Considerations

Site information embraces all relevant surficial, geologic, and hydro-geologic characteristics. It is important to be able to predict whether or not the release will migrate significantly and where it may spread. Some of this data may have already been compiled during the phase I ESA as part of the records search.

For a site assessment, published default values are available to enable assessors to estimate critical parameters on a timely basis. Representative geologic data such as that on file at the local USGS office may suffice to gain an approximate understanding of the subsurface. In most cases, however, measured data will greatly improve the precision of the findings (Figs. 5.14–5.16). Geologic characteristics can vary greatly, even over short distances, making accurate estimates of soil parameters difficult to determine without collecting extensive field data. Additionally, such data may be required to make a choice of corrective action technology.

A thorough understanding of local geologic and soil conditions is a crucial goal in the phase II ESA; the migration path and mobility factors are critical if the tank is located near a surface or groundwater source of a drinking water supply. In a relatively uniform soil formation, product migration is mainly downward. If a tank is located in a coarse to medium un-layered sandy soil, a gasoline release is apt to move rapidly toward the water table. In a layered subsurface, product migration has a more significant horizontal component. A subsurface clay lens will limit the downward movement of the product but will redirect the flow of the product laterally (Fig. 5.17). Migration through heterogeneous formations results

Figure 5.14. *Truck-mounted drilling system commonly used for split-spoon sampling of soils and for installation of groundwater monitoring wells (Photo by Julian C. Gray)*

Figure 5.15. *A split-spoon sample from a soil boring (Photo by Julian C. Gray)*

Figure 5.16. *An innovative system for sampling the subsurface. A direct push technology Geoprobe™ is pushed into the soil and withdraws vapor samples that are measured on-site for organics via a van-mounted gas chromatograph. The van also houses an inductively coupled plasma atomic emission spectrometer for analysis of individual elements. (Photo by Julian C. Gray.)*

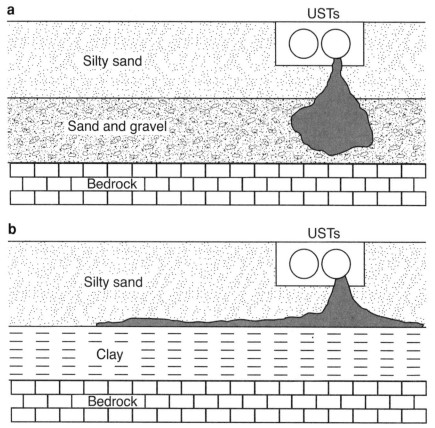

Figure 5.17. *Migration of NAPL as a function of soil type: (a) homogeneous sandy loam; (b) sandy loam underlain by a clay lens*

in gasoline plumes that vary in shape. Estimated migration should eventually be validated on a site-by-site basis through a detailed sampling program that would take place when a remedial action is implemented.

Some of the key parameters needed for a site assessment include:

- depth to groundwater
- depth to bedrock
- soil temperature
- moisture content
- particle size distribution/texture

- soil structure
- bulk density
- saturated hydraulic conductivity (K_s)
- unsaturated hydraulic conductivity

Optional parameters include:

- organic matter content
- cation exchange capacity
- soil microbial activity
- soil field capacity

Providing the specifics regarding measurement of the above parameters is beyond the scope of this book. The reader is referred to several references on measurement of site characteristics.

A shallow depth to groundwater can result in more contaminants leaving the unsaturated zone more rapidly than at a site with a thicker unsaturated zone. The greater the depth to groundwater, the greater the likelihood of detecting significant amounts of contaminants in the unsaturated zone in all four phases (NAPL, dissolved, vapor, sorbed).

The soil hydraulic conductivity (K_s) affects a contaminant's mobility, or ability to move away from the release site in the NAPL and dissolved phases. Soil air conductivity affects the mobility of contaminant vapors and is relatively analogous to K_s. Air and hydraulic conductivity vary from formation to formation in much the same way, with formations of low hydraulic conductivity generally having low air conductivity as well. Low conductivity, either hydraulic or air, indicates a greater probability of finding contaminants in all four phases close to the release site.

A high rainfall infiltration rate can enhance the transformation of the contaminant plume to different phases. Some hydrocarbons will dissolve in the infiltrating rainwater, thereby reducing the residual liquid portion of the contamination while increasing the amount of contamination dissolved in pore water.

The soil temperature also affects a contaminant's mobility. A contaminant's vapor pressure, and therefore the ease with which contaminants move into air spaces in soil, increases with increasing temperature. A greater percentage of the total amount of released contaminants is likely to be in the vapor phase in warmer regions or seasons. High soil temperatures also tend to reduce liquid viscosity, increasing ease of movement down through soil to the water table and out of the unsaturated zone. Last, higher soil temperatures will enhance the proliferation of indigenous microbial populations. A more diverse and active microbial consortia can decompose hydrocarbons more rapidly.

5.3.4. A Note on Field Sampling

Proper sample collection, preservation, and storage are essential if soil and water samples are being sent to a laboratory for analysis of volatile organic components (VOCs), total petroleum hydrocarbons (TPH), etc. Vapor losses and biodegradation of the sample should be minimized. Specifically, samples should be:

- collected with minimal disturbance to the soil. A soil sample exposed to the air will lose constituents by volatilization, and the presence of air will encourage biodegradation.
- preserved and sealed in a clean, vapor-tight jar as quickly and carefully as possible. Water samples should fill the jar completely, leaving no air bubbles. Samples should be collected in jars containing the appropriate chemical preservative (Csuros 1997).
- collected to avoid any cross-contamination. Sample-collection equipment should be decontaminated between samplings.
- labeled appropriately to correspond to the collection location at the site.
- immediately placed into an ice-filled cooler and transported to a qualified laboratory as soon as possible.
- properly stored at 4°C until analyzed. Holding time should be kept to a minimum.

Sampling of soil can be as simple as random collection of surface soils, to deep-drilling of soils over a surface grid pattern from a number of depths. The boreholes can later be converted to groundwater monitoring wells. The tests to be conducted on the environmental samples will vary with client, regulatory agency requirements, laboratory facilities and expertise, and other factors. Some of the more common tests for soil are listed in Table 5.3.

Table 5.3. Selected test methods for environmental samples

7190	Chromium FLAA
7191	Chromium GFAA
7196A	Chromium, hexavalent (Colorimetric)
7200	Cobalt FLAA
7210	Copper FLAA
7380	Iron FLAA
7420	Lead FLAA
7430	Lithium FLAA
7450	Magnesium FLAA
7460	Manganese FLAA
7470A	Mercury in liquid waste CVAA
7471A	Mercury in solid or semisolid waste CVAA
7480	Molybdenum FLAA
7520	Nickel FLAA
7550	Osmium FLAA
7740	Selenium GFAA
7760A	Silver FLAA
7770	Sodium FLAA
7780	Strontium FLAA
7840	Thallium FLAA
7950	Zinc FLAA
8011	EDB and DBCP by microextraction and GC
8015B	Nonhalogenated organics using GC/FID
8021B	Halogenated volatiles by GC using PID and ECD in series; capillary column technique
8081A	Organochlorine pesticides by capillary column GC
8082	PCBs by capillary GC
8100	Polynuclear aromatic hydrocarbons
8121	Chlorinated hydrocarbons by GC: capillary column technique
8141A	Organophosphorus compounds by GC: capillary column technique
8240/60	TPH
8240/60	BTEX (GC/MS)
8020 or 8240/60	VOCs
8240	MTBE (GC/MS)
8240	EDB, EDC (GC/MS)
8240	TML, TEL (GC/MS)
8260B	Volatile organic compounds by GC/MS
8270C	Semivolatile organic compounds by GC/MS
8275A	Semivolatile organic compounds (PAH and PCB) in soils/sludges and solid wastes using TE/GC/MS
8280A	Dioxins and furans by HRGC/LRMS
8290	Dioxins and furans by HRGC/LRMS
8310	Polynuclear aromatic hydrocarbons
8515	Colorimetric screening method for TNT in soil
9010A	Total and amenable cyanide (colorimetric manual)
9012A	Total and amenable cyanide (colorimetric automated UV)
9020B	Total organic halides (TOX)
9031	Extractable sulfides
9040B	pH electrometric measurement

(continued)

Table 5.3.   Selected test methods for environmental samples (*continued*)

9050A	Specific conductance
9056	Determination of inorganic anions by ion chromatography
9060	Total organic carbon (TOC)
9070	Total recoverable oil and grease
9071A	Oil and grease extraction method for sludge and sediment samples
9078	Screening test method for PCB in soil
9100	Saturated hydraulic conductivity, saturated leachate conductivity, and intrinsic permeability

Source: U.S. Environmental Protection Agency 1986.

5.3.5. Testing in the Field

The usefulness of the various types of field measurement equipment is contingent on the use of good field measurement procedures. There is a wide variety of field procedures currently being used. All of the general types and procedures are described in detail elsewhere.

Active soil vapor sampling and analysis measures the volatile hydrocarbon concentrations in a soil vapor sample that is collected in situ by pumping or withdrawing the sample into a field instrument for analysis. Soil vapor samples can be collected by: (1) using a drill or auger to install a borehole, inserting a portable instrument probe (see below), and taking a reading; (2) driving a hollow steel probe into the soil, collecting a sample using a gas-tight syringe, and injecting into a field instrument for analysis (Fig. 5.16); (3) driving a hollow steel probe into the soil and collecting a sample in a polyethylene bag for analysis with a portable field instrument; or (4) direct in-line sampling with a portable analytical field instrument (i.e., PID or FID) from a driven probe (NEIWPCC 1990).

Headspace analysis of soil or water involves collecting a sample, placing it in an airtight container, and analyzing the headspace vapor above the soil or water using a portable analytical instrument such as an FID or a PID (see below). This practice has its share of disadvantages; because there is no standard technique for its use, readings will vary drastically with different users. A variation of the technique is the dynamic headspace analysis of soil and water using a polyethylene bag; this technique involves collecting a sample, placing it in a reclosable freezer bag, agitating the sample to release vapors into the bag, then measuring the vapor concentration using analytical field instruments. The procedure includes generating a calibration curve using field standards to determine sample concentrations and conduct a quality-control check of analytical results.

The Hanby procedure involves the extraction of aromatic compounds from soil or water samples and yields a colorimetric indication of concentration and type of contaminants. Color indicates the type of compound and color intensity indicates the concentration (Hanby 2006). Training and practice are necessary for performing the analysis and for interpreting results.

Many states calibrate vapor detectors to a standard gas such as benzene, and set action levels from 100 parts per million (ppm) to 500 ppm. However, field testing instruments are most often used to obtain relative values. Values relative to one another will serve as guides in determining the extent of contamination and how much additional investigation is necessary, and cannot be used to obtain absolute values of contaminant levels.

Comparing results from field instruments with those from lab analyses is fraught with difficulty. As indicators of contamination, the techniques are equivalent, given satisfactory field technique. However, the numbers obtained from these techniques are not the same because most field instruments test for different groups of compounds, while labs analyze for individual constituents (NEIWPCC 1990).

The following paragraphs provide a brief description of some commonly used field testing instruments.

5.3.6. Field Testing Instruments

Colorimetric detector tubes are among the simplest field testing tools for environmental contamination. The tubes are designed for the measurement of a single, specific vapor or gas in air. Each tube is a short length of glass tubing that contains a specific chemical packing (Fig. 5.18). Air is drawn through the tube by a hand pump. As the contaminated air is pulled through the tube it reacts with the detector reagents to produce a color in the packing material. The length and intensity of the color is proportional to the concentration of the contaminant. The accuracy and detection range of a specific tube are stated in the manufacturer's technical literature. These tubes are relatively inexpensive and easy to transport, use, and interpret (NEIWPCC 1990).

The photoionization detector (PID) relies on the ionization of hydrocarbons to detect and measure the presence of organic vapors. An ultraviolet light beam within the instrument is used to ionize organic vapor molecules. The air sample is drawn through the instrument probe past

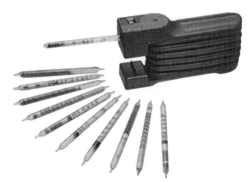

Figure 5.18. *Draeger Tubes for colorimetric analysis of vapors (Reproduced with kind permission of Draeger Safety, Inc.)*

the lamp by an internal pump. If the ultraviolet (UV) light can excite the air sample and cause it to ionize, a signal is produced on the instrument readout. The strength of the signal is a measure of the concentration. Some PIDs have interchangeable UV lamps that are sensitive to different ranges of compounds. All of the PID lamps have a specific sensitivity to BTEX. Different UV lamps can be used to detect different volatile constituents. The detection range for these instruments ranges from about 0.2 to 2,000 ppm.

Because PIDs do not detect alkanes such as methane, they can be useful in detecting aromatic constituents released from USTs in areas where "natural" methane may exist (e.g., septic fields, sewer lines). Ideal conditions for conducting PID analyses are dry weather and temperatures above 50°F. The responsiveness of PIDs decreases in moist conditions and high relative humidity (i.e., above 90%) (NEIWPCC 1990; IST 2006).

The flame ionization detector (FID) also measures the presence of organic gases and vapors. The FID uses a hydrogen flame to ionize molecules of volatile organic constituents present in the vapor sample. The ionized molecules produce a current that is proportional to the total volatile organic vapor concentration in the sample. The FID will detect the presence of volatile vapors including methane. FIDs are less sensitive than PIDs to relative humidity and temperature; however, excess carbon dioxide and depleted oxygen may extinguish the flame in the instrument. FIDs are also more sensitive to alkanes such as hexane and butane, which make up a higher fraction of gasoline than do the aromatics (NEIWPCC 1990).

A portable gas chromatograph (GC) uses a reactive separation column to isolate and analyze specific constituents in either a liquid or vapor phase in conjunction with a PID or FID detection system. A GC is a substantial improvement over the PID and FID in terms of accuracy, resolution, and technical sophistication. A portable GC consists of a sample injection system, a separation column, an output detector, and a detection system. A GC/FID system contains a combustible gas supply for the flame; a GC/PID system contains a UV lamp.

The vapor sample is injected into the GC and carried through the sample column by an inert carrier gas such as helium. The individual hydrocarbon contaminants travel through the column at unique speeds, thus reaching the detector at different times. Under ideal circumstances each component is separated by the time it enters the detector. Typically, the lightest constituents elute first, followed by progressively heavier constituents. The detection process is translated into a chromatogram, which shows the length of time from injection to maximum peak height. The peak height from baseline to the top of the peak is proportional to the concentration of a constituent (Fig. 5.19).

The portable GC is an extremely versatile and powerful tool for use in the field. However, performance of the GC is greatly dependent on the operator's capabilities; the instrument requires a substantial level of skill to operate and interpret the results.

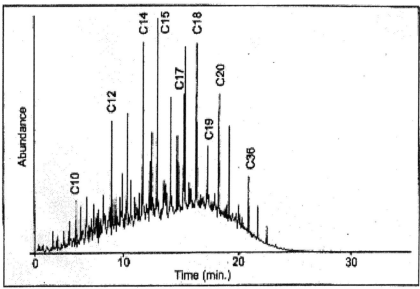

Figure 5.19. *Sample gas chromatograph of diesel fuel that had been weathered in soil for 100 days*

QUESTIONS

1. Environmental site assessments (ESAs) associated with a property transfer are common in light of CERCLA. List possible clients of an ESA.

2. What specific qualities have made asbestos enormously popular in construction and other applications for centuries?

3. Which of the following is considered a common type of material that can contain friable asbestos and may signal the need for further testing? (a) wall board with sprayed- or troweled-on material on the back that serves as insulation; (b) fluffy, sprayed-on material used for fireproofing ceilings or walls; (c) oils used to lubricate sliding doors; (d) wall insulation with a foamy texture; (e) all of the above

4. In what materials and equipment can PCBs can be found?

5. List four important industrial properties of PCBs.

6. PCBs are regulated under: (a) Resource Conservation and Recovery Act (RCRA); (b) Superfund Amendments and Reauthorization Act (SARA); (c) Toxic Substances Control Act (TSCA); (d) Safe Drinking Water Act (SDWA); (e) Federal Insecticide, Fungicide, and Rodenticide Act (FIFRA); (f) Lead Based Poisoning Prevention Act (LBPPA); (g) all of the above

7. An LNAPL will sink in an aquifer but will not dissolve in the water. True or false?

8. A phase I environmental inspection includes deep subsurface sampling combined with thorough chemical, physical, and biological testing of soils, groundwater, and geologic materials. True or false? Defend your answer.

9. The Hi-Jinx Petrochemical Company is preparing to sell 2.5 acres of its industrial complex east of town. The prospective buyer has hired you to assess the site for possible liabilities. Mark (T/F) those items that are essential to assess *in the phase I ESA*: (a) aerial photographs for the past five years; (b) fire insurance maps; (c) NPL, UST, and LUST lists; (d) citations and notices of violation; (e) detailed soil borings and groundwater and geologic analyses; (f) asbestos analysis of floor-, wall-, and pipe-insulation samples.

10. During the site reconnaissance you discover an area of buried drums, most of which appear to be unlabeled, rusting, and possibly

leaking. There is a slight odor of solvents. A limited phase II ESA, *at least* analyzing the above area, is strongly recommended. True or false?

There are several structures at the Hi-Jinx site: one production facility, a tank farm, two warehouses, and an unidentified building. All were constructed prior to 1955.
Use this information to answer questions 11–13.

11. Asbestos containing material (ACM) should be a concern for the site assessor. True or false?
12. LBP should be a concern, both inside and outside the structures. True or false?
13. It is possible that unregistered USTs may occur on-site. True or false?
14. Will soil acidity/alkalinity significantly affect movement of NAPL? Why or why not?
15. You are investigating a potentially hazardous atmosphere in a UST. Oxygen levels measure approximately 15% and there is a known risk from gasoline and benzene vapors at this site. What type of detector would you recommend using for simple field analysis of these vapors? Why?
16. Search the UST and LUST databases for your community. Where are the LUSTs located? What is the status of their cleanup?
17. Locate a commercial or industrial facility in or near your county. Compile the following information for the site and/or surroundings: (a) bedrock geology; (b) surficial geology; (c) soil types and descriptions; (d) presence of one or more aquifers; (e) depth to groundwater. These data can be found in a web search.
18. For the site located in question 17, locate: (a) the presence, if any, of USTs; (b) LUSTs; (c) NPDES permits; (d) waste-disposal permits, (c) TRI listings; (f) NPL listings. Most or all of this data can be found in a web search.

REFERENCES

American Society for Testing and Materials. 1997. *ASTM Standards Relating to Environmental Site Characterization*.West Conshohocken, PA: ASTM.

———. 2005. *Standard Practice for Environmental Site Assessments: Phase I Environmental Site Assessment Process*. E1527-00. West Conshohocken, PA: ASTM.

Csuros, M. 1997. *Environmental Sampling and Analysis for Technicians*. Boca Raton, FL: CRC Press.

Hanby. 2006. Hanby Environmental Laboratory Procedures. See: www.hanbytest.com/.

Hess, K. 1993. *Environmental Site Assessments, Phase I: A Basic Guide*. Boca Raton, FL: CRC Press.

International Sensor Technology. 2006. Photoionization detectors. See: www.intlsensor .com/pdf/photoionization.pdf.

Lyman, W., D. Noonan, and P. Reidy. 1990. *Cleanup of Petroleum Contaminated Soils and Underground Storage Tanks*. Park Ridge, NJ: Noyes.

New England Interstate Water Pollution Control Commission. 1990. *What Do We Have Here? An Inspector's Guide to Site Assessment at Tank Closure*. Boston: NEIWPCC.

U.S. Environmental Protection Agency. 1986. *Test Methods for Evaluating Solid Waste, Physical/Chemical Methods*. SW-846. Washington, DC.

APPENDIX TO CHAPTER 5

Phase II ESA Activity

In this exercise, a portion of the Hi-Jinx Chemical Company is known to have experienced contamination of the subsurface. You are to assess well logs for the site, which is known to be contaminated from both disposal of industrial waste (ca. 1947–1958) and leakage of several underground storage tanks (possibly over the past decade). The USTs had stored number 2 heating oil for use in several boilers adjacent to Building 7. The waste dumps contained primarily a mixed metallic waste in acidic solutions.

Refer to the website http://www.govinstpress.com/books/Pichtel/ for the site plan and complete well logs.

Tasks

1. Print the site plan (Fig. A.1.). Based on the well log information, draw the approximate groundwater contours. Draw arrows indicating the direction of groundwater flow.
2. Based on well log data (pH readings, metal concentrations, direction of groundwater flow), indicate the approximate location of the waste dump(s).
3. Draw cross-sectional diagrams of the site along transects A-A', B-B', and C-C'. Describe any trends in soil properties (e.g., clay or sand lenses), acid plumes, hydrocarbon plumes. As an example of how to draw the cross-sectional figure, refer to Figure A.2.

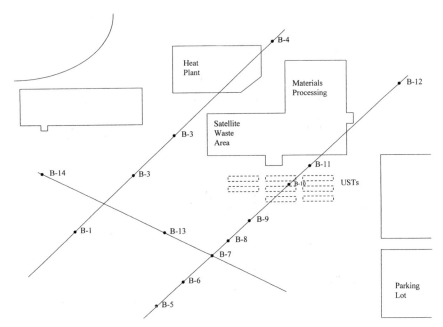

Figure A.1.

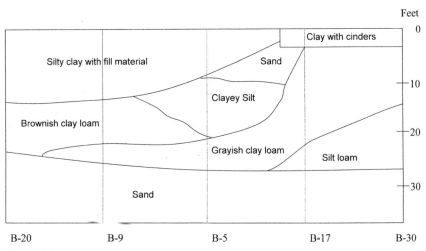

Figure A.2.

CHAPTER 6

Isolation of the Contaminant Plume

This monument will outlast metal and I made it
more durable than the King's seat, higher than the pyramids.
Gnaw of the wind and rain? Impotent.
The flow of the years to break it, however many.

Ezra Pound, "This Monument Will Outlast"

6.1 INTRODUCTION

If a plume of hazardous contaminants drifts beyond the vadose zone and
contacts groundwater, its rate of migration may greatly accelerate, increasing any threat of public health or environmental damage. Contaminants
from a site can enter groundwater via several avenues: infiltration of precipitation or run-on from the surface; groundwater migration into the contaminated zone; and migration of contaminants as free liquids through soil.

Some contaminants are *immiscible* hydrocarbons, which are less dense
than water (LNAPLs or "floaters") and will float on the groundwater
table. Other contaminants (hydrocarbon "mixers" and a number of metals,
salts, and anions) will readily combine with groundwater. In certain situations any or all of the above contaminants can be carried along with
groundwater, which is by no means a static body. In order to control contaminant migration it may be necessary to contain the plume and prevent
additional dissolution of hazardous constituents by water entering the
contamination zone. During such an isolation period engineers, scientists,
and regulatory officials can formulate a detailed remediation program.

Before a specific containment technique is selected and established in the field it is essential to identify all significant contaminants, thoroughly assess the site hydrogeology, and understand the behavior of the contaminants in soil, groundwater, and other environmental media. A thorough environmental site assessment will provide the operator with an understanding of the site geology and hydrology and the properties and behavior of the contaminants in the subsurface.

A number of systems are available to isolate the affected area so that contaminants are contained, either for permanent isolation or for removal or treatment at a later date. Isolation techniques are commonly used in association with so-called pump-and-treat systems, which lower the water table and remove affected groundwater. Such systems pump the groundwater from within the contained area for eventual treatment. Specific systems that can effectively limit the spread of the contaminant include: diverting the flow of groundwater; subsurface barriers placed in the direction of flow to control lateral spread; and placement of an impermeable cap on the land surface to reduce infiltration of precipitation and run-on (U.S. EPA 1989). Each technique varies in terms of effectiveness, logistics of installation, and overall cost. These techniques have the common purpose of isolating the contaminant; they do not remediate the site per se; that is, they do not remove or destroy the contaminant.

6.2. DIVERTING GROUNDWATER FLOW

6.2.1. Groundwater Pumping

The vertical or horizontal movement of groundwater can be altered by the injection of water into a substratum or by the extraction of groundwater from selected locations. This can ultimately serve to divert, contain, or remove a contaminant plume. An array of extraction wells is positioned downgradient from a contaminated zone and functions to remove groundwater and contaminants (Fig. 6.1). Another approach is to inject water directly into the subsurface to literally push the plume away from an area requiring protection, such as a public drinking-water source or an ecologically sensitive area (Fig. 6.2) (U.S. EPA 1989). Pumping techniques comprise an *active* strategy for diverting groundwater. A disadvantage of this technique, then, is that continuous operation and ongoing maintenance

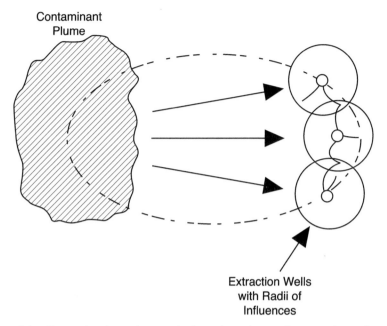

Figure 6.1.   *Removal and containment of a hazardous plume using extraction wells*
U.S. Environmental Protection Agency 1985.

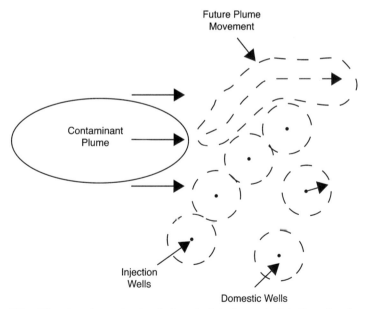

Figure 6.2.   *Diversion of a contaminant plume by injecting water into the subsurface*
U.S. Environmental Protection Agency 1985.

are required for the entire period of the remedial activity, which can prove costly for lengthy operations.

6.2.2. Subsurface Drains

In contrast to pumping techniques, subsurface drains comprise a passive system that does not require substantial maintenance. Subsurface drains are permeable regions established in or near a contaminated zone with the purpose of intercepting groundwater flow. The water is collected at a low point and pumped or drained by gravity to a collection basin or storage tank. The collected liquids are subsequently treated and released. Subsurface drains can also isolate a contaminated area by intercepting uncontaminated groundwater before it comes into contact with the site (Fig. 6.3) (U.S. EPA 1989).

6.3. SUBSURFACE BARRIERS

Low-permeability barriers can serve as a practical and permanent, albeit cumbersome, isolation technique for an affected site. Barriers block the flow of uncontaminated groundwater from entering a contaminated site. Additionally they can prevent contaminated liquids from migrating from a site. When enclosed by such a barrier, contaminated liquids can be recovered under controlled conditions for eventual treatment. Barriers include slurry walls, grout curtains, and sheet piling. These barriers comprise a *passive* means of containment, whereas groundwater pumping and subsurface drains control both pollutant migration and extract contaminated groundwater for subsequent treatment. In order to serve

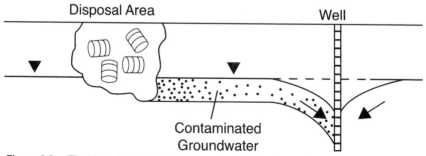

Figure 6.3.   *The Use of subsurface drainage to contain a hazardous plume*

as an effective barrier, walls are constructed of low-permeability materials. Wall materials can be either soluble or insoluble and are selected based on site considerations, installation logistics, and cost factors. Typical materials include soil-bentonite mixtures, cement-bentonite mixtures, or rigid sheet materials (e.g., steel). Prior to the selection of materials, a chemical analysis of wall and contaminant compatibility is necessary (U.S. EPA 1989).

The overall effectiveness of barriers can be significantly improved by curbing surface infiltration. This is often accomplished by installing surface caps prior to or during the installation of barriers (see below). The placement of a low-permeability barrier usually involves substantial earth moving, is energy- and labor-intensive, and is expensive. However, once installed, it is a long-term, low-maintenance containment system.

6.3.1. Slurry Walls

Slurry walls are a common installation for reducing groundwater flow in unconsolidated materials. Slurry walls are rigid underground physical barriers formed by pumping slurry into a deep vertical trench during excavation, allowing the slurry to set, and back-filling with native soil or other suitable material. Several materials are suitable in the construction of the slurry wall depending on the chemical and physical nature of the contaminants and on the strength required. Slurries are commonly constructed with Portland cement, a cement-bentonite mixture, or a soil-bentonite mix. The trench is excavated by standard construction equipment such as a backhoe. The slurry hydraulically shores the trench walls to prevent collapse.

Once the lateral extent and physical and chemical properties of the contaminant plume are determined, the positioning of the wall is decided. If contaminants are soluble and/or mobile in water—for example, metals, salts, and certain organics ("mixers")—a slurry wall can be connected ("keyed") to a low-permeability stratum such as bedrock (Figs. 6.4–6.6). If installed properly, this will stop the flow of all liquids; however, it will not be feasible in locations of deep bedrock. In the case of floating contaminants, such as LNAPL, a wall can be constructed "hanging" (Fig. 6.7). However, any soluble contaminants in the water can, in theory, pass beneath the wall. A keyed slurry wall would therefore be appropriate.

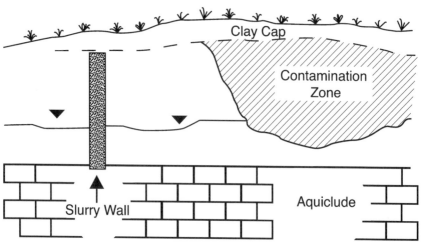

Figure 6.4. *Cross-section of a keyed-in slurry wall*

Figure 6.5. *A trencher making its first cut from the ground surface. The trenching boom is 27 ft long.*
U.S. Environmental Protection Agency 2006a.

Figure 6.6. *The trencher is cutting the barrier wall 24 ft deep, through the upper aquifer and 2 ft into the confining clay layer below. The trenching boom is obscured by the sand and slurry mix being thrown up in the center of the photo. The engineer on the right is taking atmospheric readings to confirm safe breathing conditions. The hose in the foreground is feeding clean water, which assists in soil cutting and hydrating the bentonite in the trench.*
U.S. Environmental Protection Agency 2006a.

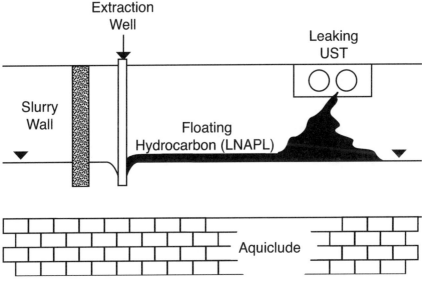

Figure 6.7.   *Cross-section of a hanging slurry wall*

Slurry walls can be placed upgradient or downgradient of the contaminant site, or it can completely encircle the affected area (Figs. 6.8 and 6.9). Circumferential walls are common for small plumes and have advantages over linear walls (U.S. EPA 1989, 1991; Smith et al. 1995). They reduce the amount of uncontaminated groundwater entering the affected area from upgradient, and also prevent the downgradient migration

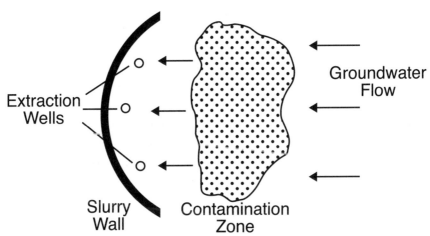

Figure 6.8.   *Slurry wall positioned downgradient of a contaminant plume*
U.S. Environmental Protection Agency 1989.

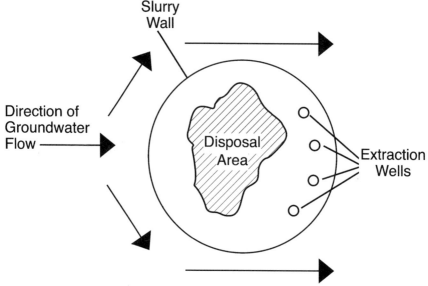

Figure 6.9.   *Placement of a circumferential slurry wall*
U.S. Environmental Protection Agency 1989.

of contaminants. Additionally, the use of circumferential walls in association with extraction wells within the perimeter can maintain the hydraulic gradient in an inward direction, which will prevent the escape of contaminants (Smith et al. 1995).

Several practical issues must be addressed in the design of a slurry wall. Compatibility of wall materials and contaminant must be determined. The presence of reactive or incompatible contaminants in a soil may damage a slurry wall and limit its reliability. For example, soil-bentonite mixtures can be damaged by strong acids or bases, sulfates, or strong electrolyte solutions (Smith et al. 1995; U.S. EPA 1991). Furthermore, in soils contaminated with hydrophobic compounds (NAPL), insufficient contact may occur between slurry material and soil. It is often beneficial to remove as much free product as possible prior to installation of the wall. Slurry walls must also be compatible with the native soils, geologic strata, and groundwater. Permeability of the proposed slurry mixture with soil and geologic material from the site should be tested in the laboratory. Site conditions and wall construction materials should also be used to determine the optimum configuration of the slurry wall. Site topography will affect choice of slurry materials. A soil-bentonite mixture will flow readily; therefore, a site using this slurry material must be nearly level. In contrast, concrete-bentonite mixtures, which set rather quickly, are suitable for sites with irregular topography (Smith et al. 1995).

6.3.2. Grout Curtains

Grout curtains are rigid underground barriers formed by injecting grout into porous rock or soil through wells. As with a slurry wall, the grout curtain will contain affected groundwater, divert a chemical plume, and divert groundwater flow around an affected area. Grouts are commonly composed of particulate materials (e.g., Portland cement) or soluble chemicals (sodium silicate). Some grouts are organic and contain polymers or bitumen.

Construction of a grout barrier is accomplished by pressure-injecting the grouting material through a pipe into the strata to be sealed. The injection points are usually arranged in lines of primary and secondary grout holes (Fig. 6.10). During or after drilling, the necessary amount of grout is injected into one row of holes and allowed to permeate into the surrounding

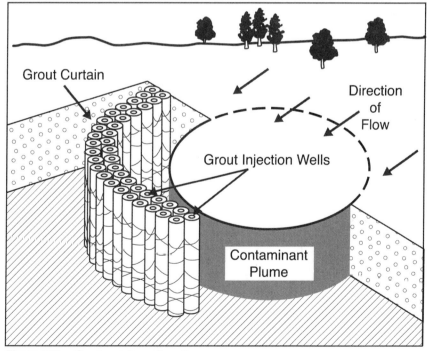

Figure 6.10.   *Grout curtain configuration*
U.S. Environmental Protection Agency 1985.

soil. After the grout has had time to set, the secondary holes are injected. The spacing of the injection points is calculated based on factors including soil permeability, grout viscosity, and set time of the grout. The points must be spaced to allow the grout injection radii from adjacent injection points to overlap (Smith et al. 1995). After injection the grout solidifies in place to reduce water flow and strengthen the formation. Each borehole should be drilled into the underlying bedrock if possible, thereby locking in the structure and preventing flow of water-soluble or heavy immiscible contaminants below the curtain.

Grouting has a higher cost relative to that of slurry walls. Cement has probably been used more than any other grouting material. The addition of clay to the grout can expand the grout's range of usage. Clays have been widely used in grouts because of their relatively low cost.

6.3.3. Sheet Piling

Sheet piling barrier walls involve driving rigid sheets into the ground to form a physical barrier to groundwater movement. These sheets are typically composed of steel or concrete that can be interlocked or sealed to form a continuous impermeable barrier. Steel sheet piling is more commonly used than concrete because of its resistance to shock and physical stress, because it is more effective overall at groundwater cutoff, and because it is less costly.

Sheet piles are seldom used as a groundwater barrier at contaminated sites because the integrity of the wall is variable (Smith et al. 1995; U.S. EPA 1991). Sheet piling is more commonly employed for temporary dewatering in other construction, for example, removal of a UST (Fig. 6.11), or for erosion protection. Another drawback to sheet piling is that rocky soils and other obstructions (e.g., buried drums) damage and deflect the piles, thus lessening its ineffectiveness as a groundwater barrier. Sheet piling does allow for some leakage through the interlocking joints. Such leakage should be taken into consideration when predicting the permeability of the formation.

6.4. CAPPING

At a hazardous site the control of infiltrating water is important in order to prevent solubilization of constituents within the plume. Capping sys-

Figure 6.11.   *Steel sheet piling used for containing a plume of heating oil at a UST site*

tems are employed in order to reduce surface water infiltration, provide a
stable surface over contaminated soil, and to improve aesthetics. Several
cap materials and designs are in use ranging from simple, single layers of
compacted clay to complex multilayer systems. In cases where remedial
treatments are not recommended due to cost or feasibility concerns, permanent caps can provide long-term isolation of contaminants and prevent
mobilization of soluble compounds. Capping may also be used for temporary isolation of contaminants during the selection of final treatment
technology. Surface water control practices (ditches, berms, etc.) are often
used in association with caps in order to control rainwater drainage and
run-on/runoff around the site.

Selection of the capping materials and design depends on remedial objectives, risk factors, and site cleanup goals. Other factors include the local
availability and cost of cover materials, the chemical and physical nature
of the contaminants being covered, climate, and projected future use of the
site. The design of caps usually conforms to the standards in 40 CFR 264,
in which closure requirements for RCRA landfills are provided. These
standards include minimum liquid migration rates, requirements for maintenance of covers, site drainage, resistance to settling, and other damage.

6.4.1. Synthetic Membranes

A synthetic membrane cap is installed as a series of overlapping sheets over a prepared surface, after which the sheets are sealed. Membrane materials include polymers, rubber, coated fabrics, and others. Success in use of synthetic membranes depends on the compatibility of the polymer with the contaminants, proper installation including seaming and placement to prevent damage, and protection against weathering and root penetration. Seaming of sheets is critical to success as this is a common source of leakage. Edges can be seamed by the use of heat guns (fusion seams), chemical adhesives, and extrusion seams (Fig. 6.12). The major benefits of synthetic membranes are their extremely low permeabilities and variability of composition to match a particular situation. A range of polymer types is available that can be selected for compatibility with a particular contaminant. Common polymers include:

- HDPE (high-density polyethylene)
- VLDPE (very low-density polyethylene)
- PVC (polyvinyl chloride)
- CSPE (chlorosulfonated polyethylene)
- urethane
- polypropylene
- proprietary formulations

Membranes may vary in thickness from 30 to 45 mils (1 mil = $\frac{1}{1000}$ inch).

Limitations of synthetic membranes include cost and their potential for failure in the long-term due to damage caused by puncturing, tearing, or weathering. These limitations can be minimized by proper design and installation.

6.4.2. Low-Permeability Soils

This cap is composed of fine-grained soils (for example, clays, silty clays) that, when compacted, maintain a K_s of 10^{-6} to 10^{-7} cm/sec (0.1 ft/yr) or less. Benefits of such materials are that they may be locally available and are therefore relatively inexpensive. Furthermore, because they are natural materials, they will be durable over long periods.

a

b

Figure 6.12.   *Geomembrane cap installation. (a) Rolling out the geomembrane layer. Sand-*
bags hold edges in place against the wind. (b) Wedge seam sealer fuses the
seam. The sealer is self-propelling and the seam in advance of the sealer is
swept clean to facilitate a good seal.
U.S. Environmental Protection Agency 2006b.

A soil cap is installed after the site is prepared: Soil material is distributed and leveled, then the cap is covered by a clean soil later followed by
topsoil and vegetation. The soil should be limed and fertilized if necessary, then seeded and mulched immediately after placement to prevent
erosion. Deep-rooted vegetation, such as trees, should be avoided, as tap-
roots will eventually compromise the integrity of the liner. The vegetative
cover is typically a shallow-rooted grass or grass-legume mixture. The
benefit of a mixture of grasses and legumes is that a self-sustaining
ecosystem may eventually develop; that is, the legume will provide nitrogen to the grass crop. With time and vegetative turnover from year to year,
a minimal degree of maintenance may be required.

6.4.3. Multilayer Cap

The multilayer cap system is quite popular as a control against infiltration and for site closure. This also applies both to MSW landfills and

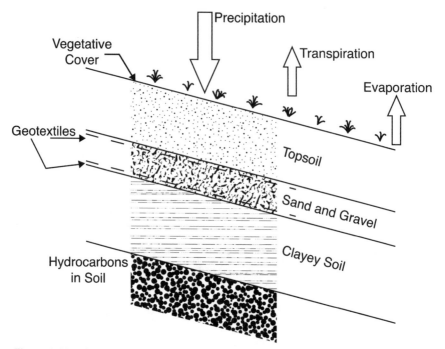

Figure 6.13.   *Cross-section of a typical multilayer cap system*

secure landfills for hazardous wastes. The cap minimizes infiltration, diverts water away from the site, and acts as a growth medium for vegetation. A typical multilayer cap system as shown in Figure 6.13 consists of three layers:

1. Sealing layer. Very low-permeability material is placed directly over the prepared site and is compacted, if appropriate, using heavy equipment. This layer serves as the barrier immediately overlying the contaminated materials. Its purpose is to prevent downward infiltration, and may be composed of compacted fine-grained soil materials or a flexible synthetic geomembrane. If the layer is composed of soil material, a layer of 18 to 24 in. is typically required. The sealing layer is protected from the action of weathering and root penetration by the overlying soil and drainage layers.
2. Drainage layer. This is a bed of porous material (e.g., sand, synthetic grid), which promotes the drainage of liquids that have penetrated the uppermost layer. This layer is designed and sloped so that flow

of infiltrating water will be carried laterally to the low points of the cap, ultimately to be removed from the site either by gravity flow or a sump. The drainage layer is typically about 18 to 24 in. thick.

3. Surface soil. This is a layer of native soil placed to a depth of 12 to 24 in. This layer supports vegetation and provides a cover for the drainage layer below. It should be of adequate fertility in order to promote long-term vegetative growth with minimal maintenance. It is essential to protect the cap and surface drainage layers from erosion damage. The use of appropriate grading for each construction material in addition to mulching and growing dense-rooted vegetation helps to protect caps from erosion.

6.5 OTHER PRACTICAL CONSIDERATIONS

6.5.1. General Design

The design of a containment system must address all vertical and horizontal migration pathways for contaminants, precipitation, and groundwater. Surface water run-on can be addressed by the utilization of diversion channels, drains, berms, and other physical barriers. During the design and construction phases of the containment system it is important to consider future use and use restrictions of the land. For example, future use of a capped area must not damage the integrity of the cap. The addition of active gradient controls (i.e., pump and treat) required by some installations will add to the long-term operating costs of these systems (U.S. EPA 1989).

The presence of a barrier such as a cap may actually hinder remediation efforts. For example, if the installation of monitoring wells or exhumation of materials should occur after capping, these physical changes will adversely affect the integrity of the cap.

6.5.2. Equipment

Generally, large earth-moving equipment is required for the installation of slurry walls and caps. Large bulldozers, backhoes, and earth-hauling machines are also used. Truck-mounted drills and augers are employed for grout curtain installation, and truck-mounted hammers for steel sheet piling.

6.5.3. Monitoring

The ultimate goal of containment is to halt the spread of contaminants in the subsurface following a release. In other words, containment involves holding hazardous materials in place. Monitoring therefore becomes important as a means for measuring effectiveness of the containment strategy. This may be accomplished by groundwater monitoring to measure water quality and groundwater depth, and visual inspections of caps for structural integrity. Groundwater monitoring should take place both up- and downgradient of the barrier walls in order to compare soil and water quality in contaminated and presumably noncontaminated zones. Long-term monitoring may be required to ensure that containment is effective.

The discussion and illustrations provided above address ideal situations. In the field, hydrogeologic characteristics will vary with distance, soils will be heterogeneous, and contaminants, particularly hydrocarbons, are expected to weather with time and will thus vary in terms of solubility, viscosity, biodegradability, and other variables.

6.6. TREATMENT OF GROUNDWATER (PUMP-AND-TREAT TECHNOLOGIES)

Up to this point, pumping for containment has implied no treatment of groundwater; rather, a plume is simply being isolated or diverted to either prevent groundwater contamination or limit additional contamination. Another objective of groundwater pumping, however, involves removal of dissolved contaminants from the subsurface.

Groundwater remediation became an environmental priority in the United States following the passage of RCRA and CERCLA. At the time, the most commonly used approach was to pump contaminated water to the surface and treat it using carbon filtration or air stripping (U.S. EPA 1996)—both termed *pump-and-treat* methods.

If groundwater is to be cleaned up, the desired level of treatment must be determined a priori. Next, the design and implementation of the groundwater pumping system are formulated, based on data evaluated in setting cleanup goals. The criteria for well design, pumping system, and treatment are dependent on site characteristics and contaminant type. Actual treatment may include the design of a train of processes such as gravity separation, air stripping, or carbon adsorption for the removal of specific contaminants (see below). An associated component of groundwater pump-and-treat is determining the termination requirements. Termination requirements are based on the cleanup goals defined in the initial stage of the remedial process. The termination criteria are also dependent on the specific site aspects revealed during remedial operations (FRTR 2006).

Groundwater monitoring is a required component of a groundwater extraction system, used so that the effectiveness of the overall treatment protocol can be assessed. Additionally, monitoring data will allow the operator to determine when termination requirements have been met and operations can cease. Groundwater sampled from wells and piezometers allows the operator to adjust the system in response to changes in subsurface conditions caused by the remediation activity.

The following groundwater treatments are commonly employed following pumping. These are briefly described below and some are described in detail in subsequent chapters.

6.6.1. Bioreactors

Extracted groundwater is transferred to a large reaction vessel where the contaminants come into intimate contact with aerobic heterotrophic microorganisms. Common reactor types include suspended growth or attached biological reactors. In suspended systems, for example, the activated sludge process, contaminated groundwater is circulated in an aeration basin. In attached systems, such as rotating biological contractors and trickling filters, microorganisms become established on an inert support matrix (see chapter 11). The aerobic microbial consortium decomposes the hydrocarbon contaminants as oxygen and nutrients (if necessary) are introduced.

6.6.2. Constructed Wetlands

Groundwater treatment via constructed wetlands uses natural geochemical and biological processes occurring within an artificial wetland ecosystem to accumulate and remove metals and other contaminants from influent waters; for example, microbial activity in the dense rhizosphere (root zone) decomposes hydrocarbons and immobilizes metals. Certain plant types will also take up metals from the water and soil.

6.6.3. Air Stripping

Air stripping involves the mass transfer of volatile contaminants from water to air. Volatile organics are partitioned from groundwater by increasing the surface area of the contaminated water exposed to air. For groundwater remediation, this process is typically conducted in a packed tower or aeration tank. The typical packed tower air stripper includes a spray nozzle at the top to distribute contaminated water over the packing in the column, a fan to force air countercurrent to the water flow, and a sump at the bottom of the tower to collect decontaminated water. Auxiliary equipment that can be added to the basic air stripper includes an air heater to improve removal efficiencies; automated control systems with safety features such as explosion-proof components; and air emission control and treatment systems such as activated carbon units, catalytic oxidizers, or thermal oxidizers.

6.6.4. Granulated Activated Carbon (GAC) Adsorption

During liquid phase carbon adsorption, groundwater is pumped through one or more canisters or columns containing activated carbon. When the concentration of contaminants in the effluent from the bed exceeds a certain level, the carbon can be regenerated in place, removed and regenerated at an off-site facility, or removed and disposed. The two most common reactor configurations for carbon adsorption systems are the fixed bed and the pulsed, or moving, bed. Adsorption by activated carbon has a long history of use in treating municipal, industrial, and hazardous wastes.

6.6.5. Ion Exchange

Ion exchange removes ions from the aqueous phase by the exchange of cations or anions between the contaminants and the exchange medium. Ion exchange materials may consist of resins made from synthetic organic materials that contain ionic functional groups to which exchangeable ions are attached. They also may be inorganic and natural polymeric materials. After the resin capacity has been exhausted, resins can be regenerated for reuse.

6.6.6. Precipitation

This discussion relates primarily to the removal of heavy metals including their radioactive isotopes from groundwater. Precipitation of metals has long been the method of choice for treating metal-laden industrial wastewaters. In groundwater treatment applications, metal precipitation involves conversion of soluble heavy metal salts to insoluble salts that will precipitate. The precipitate is then removed from the water by physical methods such as sedimentation or filtration. The process typically uses pH adjustment, addition of a chemical precipitant, and flocculation. Typically, metals precipitate from the solution as hydroxides, sulfides, or carbonates. The solubilities of the specific metal contaminants and the required cleanup standards will dictate the process used. In some cases the metallic sludges generated can be shipped to recyclers for metal recovery (FRTR 2006).

6.6.7. Sprinkler Irrigation

The recovered groundwater is collected and distributed over the top of the site. The organic contaminants in the groundwater are degraded by the microorganisms naturally occurring in the soil (see chapter 11).

QUESTIONS

1. The purpose of containment is to "buy time" and prevent off-site contaminant migration; containment is *not* remediation. True or false? Explain.
2. Choose the correct answer: Containment may be needed when there is danger of contamination of: (a) groundwater; (b) drinking water wells; (c) sanitary or storm sewers; (d) buildings; (e) all of the above.
3. List the layers (geologic materials) of a multilayer cap situated over contaminated soil (in order, from the ground *surface* down to the *deepest* layer) and describe their functions.

REFERENCES

Federal Remediation Technologies Roundtable. 2006. *Ground Water Pumping/Pump and Treat Remediation Technologies Screening Matrix and Reference Guide, Version 4.0.* See: www.frtr.gov/matrix2/section4/4-48.html. Accessed 9/06.

Smith, L. A., J. L. Means, A. Chen, B. Alleman, C. C. Chapman, J. S. Tixier, S. E. Brauning, A. R. Gavaskar, and M. D. Royer. 1995. *Remedial Options for Metals-Contaminated Soils.* Boca Raton, FL: CRC Press.

U.S. Environmental Protection Agency. 1985. *Handbook: Remedial Action at Waste Disposal Sites (Revised).* EPA/625/6-85/006. Washington, DC: Office of Solid Waste and Emergency Response.

————. 1989. *Corrective Action: Technologies and Applications.* Seminar publication EPA/625/4-89/020.

————. 1991. *Handbook: Stabilization Technologies for RCRA Corrective Actions.* EPA/625/6-91/026.

————. 1996. *Pump-and-Treat Ground-Water Remediation. A Guide for Decision Makers and Practitioners.* EPA/625/R-95/005.

————. 2006a. *Cleanup Sites. February 5, 2001 Field Update.* See: http://www.epa.gov/region5/sites/amerchem/fu20010205.htm.

————. 2006b. *Cleanup in Region 10. Kerr-McGee Photo Gallery.* See: yosemite.epa.gov/r10/cleanup.nsf/9f3c21896330b4898825687b007a0f33/ee48a36956b9520288256a7800009bce?OpenDocument.

CHAPTER 7

Extraction Processes

All will come out in the washing.

—Miguel de Cervantes Saavedra

7.1 INTRODUCTION

Extractive processes involve the elutriation of inorganic and/or organic contaminants from soil for eventual recovery, treatment, and disposal. Also known as *soil flushing*, *soil washing*, *chemical leaching*, *solution mining*, or *hydrometallurgical processes*, a chemical separation is conducted in which contaminants are solubilized or similarly desorbed from solid forms and recovered. This technology contrasts with physical processes, in which soil fines (silt- and clay-sized particles) are separated in water from coarser material by simple gravity-settling processes, following which the former fraction is disposed of as hazardous waste (U.S. EPA 1995).

In situ extraction processes are applicable for either the vadose zone or the saturated zone. The flushing solution is applied to the affected site via sprinklers or irrigation, or by subsurface injection. A sufficient period is allowed for the applied reagents to percolate downward and react with contaminants. The contaminants are subsequently mobilized by solubilization or formation of emulsions (Smith et al. 1995). The elutriate is collected in appropriately placed wells or subsurface drains, following which they are removed, treated, or recycled back to the site (Fig. 7.1).

Pretreatment steps include preparation of flushing solutions and installation of systems to deliver and recover the flushing solution. Surface

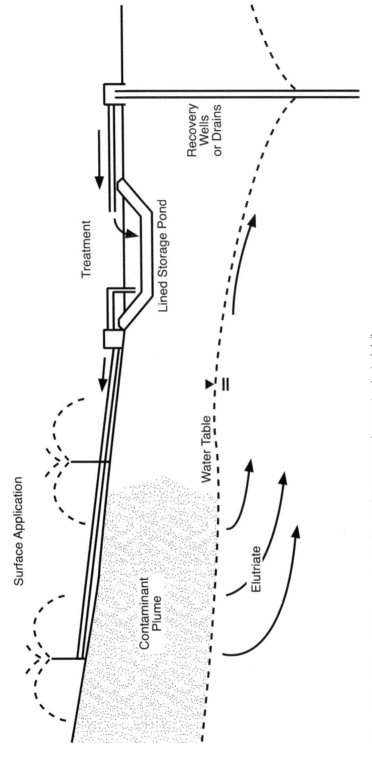

Figure 7.1. Schematic diagram of an in ditu glushing process in a vontaminated doil

grading, caps, or vertical barriers may be needed to control flow. Post-treatment steps may include disposal of treatment residuals, processing and reuse of flushing solution, and recovery and reuse of certain contaminants (e.g., metals). Both inorganics and organics are suitable for soil-flushing treatment if they are sufficiently soluble in an inexpensive solvent that is available in large volume. The selection of extracting solution must also conform with regulatory requirements because certain solutions pose public health and/or environmental risks if not properly managed.

An analogous process to soil flushing is its ex situ counterpart, *soil washing*. In this procedure, the contaminated soil is physically removed from the affected area—for example by backhoes—placed into a reactor vessel, and vigorously reacted with the washing solution. There may be repeated cycles of washing, centrifugation, and separation of soil material (Fig. 7.2). Eventually the residual extractant is rinsed out of the cleaned soil with H_2O and the soil is returned to the ground. The recovered extractant can be reused for additional washings.

To ensure a thorough level of treatment and compliance with regulatory requirements, extractive processes are often used in conjunction with other treatment technologies such as biodegradation, reaction with activated carbon, or chemical precipitation (Smith et al. 1995; U.S. EPA 1994a; 1994b).

7.2. EXTRACTING SOLUTIONS

Flushing solutions include water, acidic aqueous solutions, basic solutions, chelating agents, surfactants (i.e., detergents), oxidizing or reducing agents, and alcohols. The appropriate solution is chosen based on a variety of considerations including ability to react with contaminant, ease of handling, possible hazards with use, environmental and/or health hazard of the material, cost, and ease of recycling.

Raw water can be used to extract water-soluble or water-mobile constituents including simple salts and anions, for example, arsenate (AsO_4^{3-}), arsenite (AsO_3^{3-}), cyanide (CN^-), nitrate (NO_3^-), selenate (SeO_4^{2-}), etc. Acidic solutions are used for recovery of metals and for basic organic constituents including amines, ethers, and anilines. Basic solutions may be used for the removal of metals including zinc, tin, and lead, and for some phenols. Complexing and chelating agents are employed for

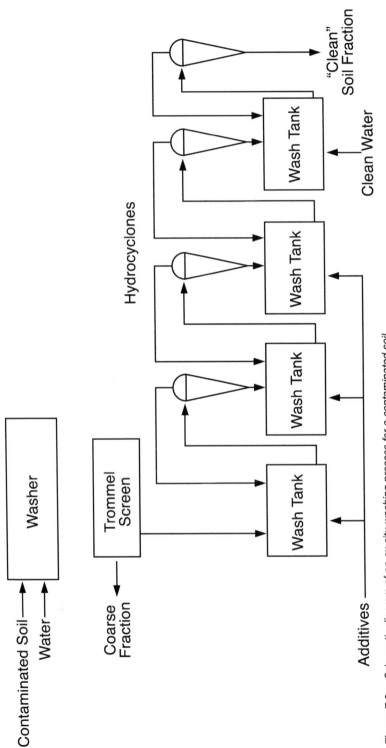

Figure 7.2. *Schematic diagram of an ex situ washing process for a contaminated soil* Griffiths 1995.

the removal of metals, and surfactants for nonaqueous or hydrophobic compounds. In limited cases, surfactants have been successful in the removal of selected metals (e.g., chromium) (Thirumalai Nivas et al. 1996). However, surfactants have shown most success in the solubilization and removal of organic contaminants.

7.3. FLUSHING METALS FROM SOIL

Metals at contaminated sites occur in complex forms, and mobility is controlled by numerous chemical and physical phenomena including soil type, pH, cation exchange capacity, particle size, and the presence of other inorganic or organic compounds (see chapter 2). Many of these factors are interdependent (Reed et al. 1995). Metal removal efficiencies during soil flushing depend not only on soil characteristics but also on metal concentration, chemistry of the metal(s), extractant chemistry, and overall processing conditions.

Metals that are minimally soluble in water often require acids, chelating agents, or other solvents for successful washing. Acids solubilize metals by either simple dissolution reactions of metal-containing solids, or by creating metal-hydrogen bonds on a crystal lattice, thereby allowing for metal removal from the solid surface. The most commonly used acids are hydrochloric, sulfuric, nitric, phosphoric, and carbonic acid. High extraction efficiencies, sometimes greater than 90%, have been reported with HCl for both artificially and field-contaminated soils (U.S. EPA 1994a; Reed et al. 1995; Tokunaga et al. 2005; Cline and Reed 1995; Tuin and Tels 1990). At a former automobile battery recycling facility Steele and Pichtel (1998) recovered 32% soil Pb, and Cd removal was 68% and 98% with 0.1 N and 1.0 N HCl, respectively. Tuin and Tels (1990) reported 75% and 81% Cd extraction efficiencies using HCl. The USEPA Acid Extraction Treatment System (AETS), which uses HCl, reduced both the total and TCLP Cd concentration in soil from the Palmerton (PA) Superfund site below regulatory standards (U.S. EPA 1994a).

Chelating agents such as ethylenedinitrilotetraacetic acid (EDTA), diethylene triamine pentaacetic acid (DTPA), nitrilotriacetic acid (NTA), N-(acetamido)iminodiacetic acid (ADA), and similar agents bond with the metallic cation to facilitate solubilization in the extraction medium (Tokunaga et al. 2005; Steele and Pichtel 1998; Khodadoust et al. 2005;

Bricker et al. 2001; Kayser et al. 2000). Others include cyclohexylene-dinitriloetetraacetic acid, ethyleneglycol-bis (β-aminoethyl ether) *N,N,N'N*-tetraacetic acid, EGTA (ethylenebis [oxyethylenetrinitrilo] tetraacetic acid) and ethyleneidaminedissuccinate (Grčman et al. 2003). Chelation mechanisms involve binding with the metal via multiple bonds (Fig. 7.3). Transition metals occurring in nature are typically characterized by the presence of at least one vacant *d*-orbital; hence, their cationic nature. This orbital is readily available for bonding, for example with an electron-rich π orbital of an organic ligand. Typically the N donor atoms of the chelant molecules are electron-rich; likewise, many chelant molecules contain a carboxylic acid or similar group which, when deprotonated, will bond with the cation. The ability to form highly stable metal complexes makes chelating agents like EDTA, DTPA, NTA, and ADA effective extractants for some metal-contaminated soils (Khodadoust et al. 2005; Gidarakos and Giannis 2006; Davis and Singh 1995; Cline et al. 1993).

Chelants vary in effectiveness of metal removal, a result of the presence of different numbers of reactive sites and differing degrees of bonding strength. Variability in removal efficiency is also a function of the presence of different solid forms of the metal in the soil, extracting solution pH, and potential interference from other cations that may complex with the chelant (Steele and Pichtel 1998; Brown and Elliott 1992; Elliott and Brown 1989; Hsieh et al. 1989; Shirk and Farrel 1985).

In a study of flushing a Superfund soil, EDTA was capable of removing virtually all of the nondetrital forms when at least a stoichiometric amount (1:1 molar ratio of chelant:metal) was present, and EDTA removed the equivalent of all nondetrital Cd (Steele and Pichtel 1998). Extraction efficiencies between 80% and 100% have been reported with EDTA for Cd sorbed on clay, calcium carbonate, and hydrous Fe oxides (Slavek and Pickering 1986; Pickering 1983; Farrah and Pickering 1978). Lead and Cd removal has been shown effective by ADA as well as by PDA (pyridine-2,6-dicarboxylic acid) (Steele and Pichtel 1998). Chen et al. (1995) reported 85% Pb extraction efficiency with PDA, and Macauley and Hong (1995) reported 95% Pb extraction efficiency from an artificially contaminated soil. Hong and Chen (1996) and Chen et al. (1995) noted over 90% Cd extraction efficiency with ADA and PDA.

Several researchers have tested naturally occurring molecules and analogs as potential chelating agents. Fischer (2002) tested the β-thiol

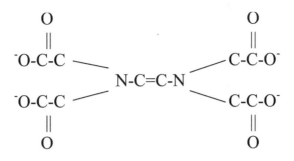

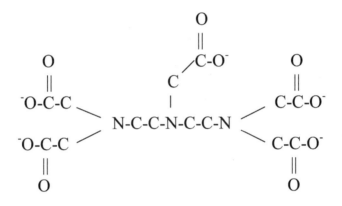

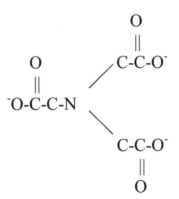

Figure 7.3. *Chemical structures of chelating agents EDTA, DTPA, and NTA*

group containing amino acids L-cysteine and L-penicillamine for their ability to release heavy metals (Cd, Cr, Cu, Hg, Ni, Pb, Zn) from peat, bentonite, and illite. Fischer and Bipp (2004) found, under optimized conditions, the following metal extraction degrees achieved with strongly alkaline D-gluconic acid solutions: Ni 43%, Cr 60%, Cd 63%, Zn 70%, Pb 80%, and Cu 84%. Evangelou et al. (2004) investigated the use of humic acids as an alternative to synthetic chelators.

In some cases surfactant molecules have enhanced metal extraction from soil. Pichtel and Pichtel (1997), Thirumalai Nivas et al. (1996), and Hessling et al. (1986) found several surfactants to be effective to varying degrees in solubilizing soil Cr as the chromate ion. The surfactant molecule, possessing a polar head and a nonpolar tail, has the ability to form micelles around Cr oxyions. Suggested solubilization mechanisms include ion exchange from soil colloids and simple dissolution of insoluble Cr phases (Thirumalai Nivas et al. 1996).

The applicability of water-soluble polymers as extractants for the remediation of heavy metal-contaminated soils has been studied (Sauer et al. 2004). Polyethylenimine (PEI) was functionalized with bromo- or chloroacetic acid to give an aminocarboxylate chelating group, which effectively binds lead. The resulting polymer, PEIC, is believed to have extraction properties similar to EDTA. Using soil from a Superfund site in New Mexico that contained approximately 10,000 mg/kg of Pb, the polymers removed more than 97% of soil lead. Subsequent experiments demonstrated that the selective extraction of lead could be controlled by varying polymer functionalization levels.

7.3.1. Chelant Recovery

The eventual separation of metal from the metal-extractant mixture is necessary for a soil extraction system to be complete and cost-effective. Several chemical and physical treatments are in use to recover the contaminants from the metal-chelant complex, thereby freeing the extracting solution for reuse. Treatment typically involves reaction of the metal-saturated chelant with an element that has a higher affinity for the organic ligand than the contaminant metal(s). For example, if Pb is removed from a soil as Pd-EDTA, the Pb can be desorbed from the complex by the addition of Ca. Calcium readily binds ligands at high pH (Bell 1977), thus freeing the contaminant metal to form a hydroxide solid (Tunay and Kabdasli 1994). Lead recovery from an EDTA-Pb complex was 70% and 62% at pH values of 11.0 and 12.0, respectively (Steele and Pichtel 1998). The corresponding recovery of Pb from an ADA-Pb complex and a PDA-Pb complex was over 95%. Brown and Elliott (1992) removed 40% of the Pb from an EDTA-Pb solution at pH 10.8 in the presence of 5 to 10 times more Ca^{2+} than Pb. Theoretically, the pH must be raised to 12.0 before the formation constant for Ca-EDTA exceeds that of Pb-EDTA (Ringbom 1963). Zeng et al. (2005) successfully used Na_2S combined with $Ca(OH)_2$ to precipitate the trace metals bound to EDTA, thus allowing it to be reused.

Once the metal is displaced from the complex, additional processing will be needed to remove impurities and concentrate the metal, in order to convert it to a marketable product. The most commonly used processing methods are precipitation and ion exchange. In some cases the metal salt or complex is reduced to the metallic form. Reduction can be accomplished by electrowinning or by reducing the metal using a reducing gas such as hydrogen (Zeng et al. 2005). If the end product is a metal-salt, it can be converted to a more marketable oxide or salt form via simple chemical processes.

7.4. FLUSHING ORGANICS FROM SOIL

Soil flushing has been employed for sites contaminated with hydrocarbons including wood preservatives (creosote, pentachlorophenol), PAHs (naphthalene, fluoranthene, pyrene, etc.), and some extremely toxic organics (chlorinated dibenzodioxins) (Urum et al. 2006; Mulligan and Eftekhari 2003; Leharne and Dong 2002; Betteker et al. 1993; U.S. EPA 1997).

A practical consideration for flushing organics from soil is the polarity of the contaminants. Many hydrocarbons are completely insoluble in water, whereas others may be only slightly soluble. Soluble (hydrophilic) organic contaminants often are easily removed from soil by flushing with water alone. Organics with octanol/water partition coefficients (K_{ow}) of less than 10 (log K_{ow} < 1) are highly soluble. Examples include low-molecular weight alcohols, phenols, and carboxylic acids.

The octanol-water partitioning coefficient (K_{ow}) is measured by mixing a test compound, for example a hydrocarbon mixture, with a solution of octanol (a C_8 hydrocarbon) and water and allowing the mixture to equilibrate. Separate aliquots of the octanol and water are removed and the concentration of the contaminant in each phase is measured. The coefficient is calculated as:

$$K_{ow} = [\text{contaminant in octanol}] / [\text{contaminant in water}]$$

Low-solubility (hydrophobic) organics may be removed with the assistance of a surfactant (Sposito et al. 1982; Tessier et al. 1979). Examples of hydrophobic compounds include petroleum products (gasoline, jet fuels, oil), aromatic solvents (benzene, toluene, ethylbenzene, xylene), semivolatiles (PAHs), chlorinated pesticides, chlorinated solvents (trichloroethene), and polychlorinated biphenyls (PCBs).

A schematic representation of a reaction of a surfactant molecule with a hydrocarbon contaminant is shown in Figure 7.4. Surfactants are useful

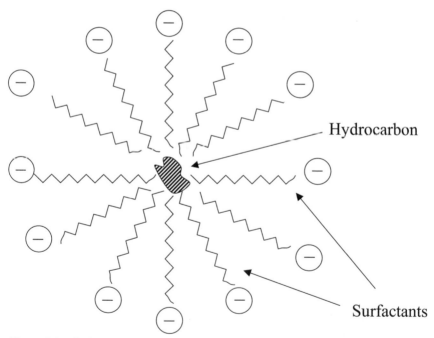

Figure 7.4. *Surfactant molecules sequestering contaminant molecule*

for solubilization of hydrophobic compounds because of their amphiphilic structure, meaning that one part of the molecule is a polar or ionic group (head) with a strong affinity for water, and the other part is a hydrocarbon group (tail) with an aversion to water:

$$
\begin{array}{c}
\text{H H H H H H H H H H O} \\
\text{| | | | | | | | | | |} \\
\text{H--C--C--C--C--C--C--C--C--C--C--S} = \text{O}^- \\
\text{| | | | | | | | | | |} \\
\text{H H H H H H H H H H O}
\end{array}
$$

    nonpolar   polar

In the presence of water-insoluble organics, the tail of the anion tends to dissolve in the organic molecule whereas the head remains in aqueous solution. Thus, the surfactant emulsifies, or suspends, organic material in water. Colloidal surfactant micelles, which can be removed in the process water, are formed.

Extraction of organics can be combined with other technologies such as bioremediation. For example, the BioGenesis soil-washing technology involves mixing excavated contaminated soil in a mobile washing unit. In the first stage, a proprietary surfactant solution is used to transfer organic compounds from the solid matrix to the liquid phase. The second stage involves biodegradation of residual hydrocarbons in the soil and the solubilized hydrocarbons (U.S. EPA 1993) (Fig. 7.5).

7.5. TECHNICAL/PRACTICAL CONSIDERATIONS IN SOIL FLUSHING

The feasibility of soil-flushing technology (and the level of treatment) is variable, depending on the appropriateness of solution for the contaminants; the ability to flood the soil with the flushing solution; the contact of flushing solution with waste constituents; the hydraulic conductivity of the soil; and the installation of collection wells or subsurface drains to recover all the applied liquids. Provisions must also be made for ultimate disposal of the elutriate. Some critical variables are outlined below.

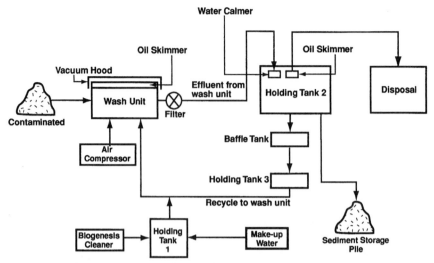

Figure 7.5. *Schematic diagram of the BioGenesis soil-washing technology*
U.S. Environmental Protection Agency 1993.

7.5.1. Contaminant Forms and Concentrations

It is essential to determine the total concentrations of those contaminant compounds present in the affected soil as well as their chemical forms. Typically, some detective work is required; that is, gleaning data from past disposal records, waste manifests, and so on, and amassing field analytical data. Numerous published methods are available for inorganic and organic analysis of soil and water (see chapter 5). The methods selected will be a function of regulatory requirements and client needs.

For many contaminants it is essential to know not only the total concentration, but which chemical species of contaminants occur as well. Partitioning of contaminant metals or organics occurs after release to the soil and involves the chemical redistribution of the contaminant within the soil matrix. The degree and range of redistribution is a function of the contaminant(s), the soil chemical and physical environment, and time. For example, after a soluble metal enters a soil it may adsorb to soil clay, organic matter, and hydrous oxides, and a portion may remain dissolved in the soil water. If the soil is in an oxidized state (i.e., high redox potential), the metal may crystallize as a hydroxide or carbonate, thus rendering it highly insoluble (and hence not amenable to extractive processes). In contrast, a reducing environment (e.g., a soil which is frequently saturated) will allow many metals to remain in solution. Such metal fractions are, therefore, readily leachable by extractive processes. If the plume is composed of hydrocarbons the effects of hydrocarbon weathering (i.e., partitioning into soluble, sorbed, and vapor phases) must also be considered. Therefore, a chemical analysis of the affected soil is needed, especially for aged releases.

The contaminant forms depend in part on the source of the contamination. For example, at a contaminated lead battery disposal facility, did soil Pb originate as soluble Pb salts, such as $PbSO_4$, or as PbO or metallic Pb? For $PbSO_4$, a relatively soluble salt, soil flushing is a relatively straightforward process. For the metallic species, however, soil extractive processes would be prohibitively slow and expensive, and probably not feasible.

Knowledge of partitioning (and ultimately knowledge of how much of a metal is readily extractable) can be gained from simple laboratory tests that separate a soil metal into specified fractions as a function of solubility in a particular solution. For example, researchers (Sposito et al. 1982) have developed a technique to determine exchangeable, adsorbed, organic-bound, carbonate-bound, and residual forms of a specific soil metal. The method involves sequential extraction of a soil sample with 0.05 M KNO_3, deionized H_2O, 0.5 M NaOH, 0.05 M Na_2EDTA, and hot (80°C) 4 M HNO_3. If soil metals are found to occur mostly in the KNO_3 and H_2O fractions they are considered exchangeable and water soluble, respectively, and extraction should be rapid and simple. If, however, most occurs in the HNO_3 fraction (as may be the case for Pb with spent battery casings), removal by extractive processes will not be feasible (Steele and Pichtel 1998).

Numerous other fractionation techniques for soil metals are available. Tessier et al. (1979) wrote an influential paper describing a five-step sequential extraction protocol for exchangeable, carbonatic, reducible, organic matter and sulfidic and residual metals. In a study by Keon et al. (2001), arsenic-bearing phases in sediment samples were quantitatively recovered by the following extractants in a sequential extraction procedure: As adsorbed on goethite, 1 M NaH_2PO_4; arsenic trioxide (As_2O_3), 10 M HF; arsenopyrite (FeAsS), 16 N HNO_3; amorphous As sulfide, 1 N HCl, 50 mM Ti-citrate-EDTA, and 16 N HNO_3; and orpiment (As_2S_3), hot concentrated HNO_3/H_2O_2. In a study by Ahnstrom and Parker (1999), cadmium was partitioned into five operationally defined fractions: 0.1 M $Sr(NO_3)_2$ (soluble-exchangeable); 1 M Na acetate, pH 5.0 (sorbed-carbonate); 5% NaOCl, pH 8.5 (oxidizable); 0.4 M oxalate + 0.1 M ascorbate (reducible); and 3 HNO_3:1 HCl (residual).

Metal concentration and overall concentration gradients will affect extraction success. At low metal concentrations, lower extraction efficiency may occur as a result of stronger binding, because binding energies associated with low sorption densities are substantial (Benjamin and Leckie 1981). The concentration gradient of the contaminant between soil and solution will also play a role in the extraction process. If the extracting solution is regularly removed and replaced, allowing for a greater concentration gradient, metal extraction is enhanced.

Soils and wastes that are amenable to soil flushing are those preferably containing one principal metal, where metals are readily soluble and extracted into an aqueous medium ($> 80\%$ extraction efficiencies) (Griffiths 1995).

7.5.2. Effects of Flushing Agent on Soil Properties

The addition of any flushing solution to the site requires knowledge and meticulous management of reactions that may adversely affect the soil system. For example, the application of sodium as dilute $NaOH$ to a soil may drastically restrict soil permeability. The Na^+ ion greatly expands the soil-diffuse double layer, resulting in the dispersal of soil particles and ultimately a complete loss of saturated hydraulic conductivity, K_s (Fig. 7.6). Therefore, extractive processes would no longer be applicable at this site. Similar dispersive effects may occur with excessive use of surfactants.

The addition of a fairly concentrated acid (e.g., 0.1 N HCl) will result in the dissolution of soil particles (particularly fines) with consequent loss of soil structure; eradication of the indigenous microbial populations that are responsible for nutrient turnover and the ultimate support of a stable soil; and dissolution of native soil metals, including nutrient bases (Ca^{2+}, Mg^{2+}, K^+, etc.). The solids that remain do not comprise a "soil" per se, but rather a mass of biologically inert solids. The dissolved soil solids will also pose a significant wastewater treatment issue because numerous soil constituents have been converted to the dissolved phase (Pichtel and Pichtel 1997). Laboratory tests, although serving as only a crude approximation of events in the field, should assess the impact of a flushing solution on soil properties.

7.5.3. Vertical and Lateral Distribution of Contamination

This data will be obtained via use of soil borings, noninvasive detection techniques (e.g., electromagnetic detection, ground-penetrating radar), groundwater analyses, and other field aspects of a phase II environmental

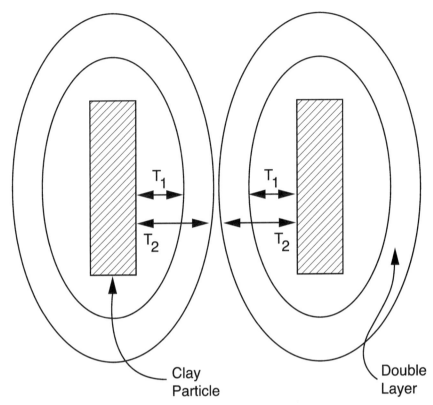

Figure 7.6.   *The diffuse double layer surrounding a clay particle. T_1 = thickness of the layer with an adsorbed divalent cation; T_2 = thickness with an adsorbed monovalent cation*

site assessment. Success of solubilization and removal with depth is a function of site characteristics such as K_s as well as engineering limitations such as depth of well installation. If the plume is relatively water soluble and very deep within the profile, soil flushing may not be feasible because control of flow will be difficult. Furthermore, construction of deep barrier walls will prove costly.

7.5.4. Suitability of Site to Flooding and Installation of Subsurface Drains

For in situ flushing to be effective, favorable hydrogeologic conditions are required, where flushing solutions with dissolved and suspended components can be readily applied, contained, and recovered. It is essential to possess a thorough knowledge of both surface and subsurface conditions prior to flushing. With insufficient preparation or when working with dense soils, surface runoff is a possibility. Conversely, in excessively drained soils migration of the flushing solution may continue through uncontaminated material and into groundwater, creating a much larger contamination problem than that which was first encountered.

In surficial layers, high clay content, high humic content, or high soil cation exchange capacity (> 5 to 10 meq/100 g) not only restricts site flooding but interferes with contaminant desorption. Soil K_s is a key physical parameter for determining the feasibility of using soil flushing. Soils with low K_s ($< 1 \times 10^{-5}$ cm/s) will limit the ability of flushing solutions to percolate through the soil within a reasonable time frame. Flushing processes will be most effective in permeable soils ($K_s \geq 1 \times 10^{-4}$ cm/s). Flushing technology is most applicable to permeable soils (approximately 30% or less silts + clays) (U.S. EPA 1991), because desorbed metals will be more quickly removed, allowing for a greater concentration gradient with fresh flushing solution.

For the subsurface, basic requirements include locating impermeable layers, areas of high K_s (e.g., sand or gravel lenses, fractures, discontinuities, etc.), and the presence of buried wastes, drums, USTs, and other large anthropogenic debris. This data will be obtained by the use of well logs, geologic and hydrogeologic maps, soil borings, noninvasive detection techniques (e.g., electromagnetic detection, ground-penetrating radar), groundwater analysis, and other routine components of the phase I and phase II environmental site assessments. Additionally, it is obviously essential to know the location of any utilities (electric, fiber optics, gas, water, steam, telephone, etc.) as such channels may have provided a path of rapid flow of the contaminant, and they may likewise cause unwanted dispersal of the flushing solution. Information on the locations of these conduits is available from local utilities.

Prior to field implementation of soil flushing, a thorough groundwater hydrologic study should be carried out. This should include information on seasonal fluctuations in water table, direction of groundwater flow, porosity, vertical and horizontal K_s, and infiltration.

7.5.5. Trafficability of the Site

Soils high in clay will form a "smeared" surface if vehicle traffic is heavy, and will limit downward migration of flushing solution. Excessively wet sites will not support heavy traffic and may require drainage.

7.5.6. Degree of Site Preparation

Many contaminated sites have served as waste dumps and may contain unconsolidated and large wastes (e.g., machine parts, steel drums, USTs). In order for soil flushing to be successful, contact between soil fines and the extracting solution must be maximized. Furthermore, paths of free flow should be eliminated; therefore, large debris should be removed from the site if at all possible. Surface drainage and controls of run-on and runoff may also be needed.

7.5.7. By-Products

In a system involving vigorous mixing and/or aeration (i.e., soil washing in reactor vessels), volatilization of hydrocarbon vapors is a common occurrence. Biological attack of hydrocarbon molecules will also promote weathering and subsequent vapor release. Off-gas collection and treatment may therefore be necessary.

7.6. THE GOOD AND THE BAD

There are many advantages to soil flushing. It is an extractive technology that results in the removal and reduction of contaminant content. This reduces future liability for the site operator and owner. In some cases there are possible economic benefits from the recovery of recyclable metals (radioactives, precious metals). Metals can be preconcentrated for recovery or can be recovered directly depending on metals and matrix. The process also produces a waste stream with lower volume and higher metals concentration, allowing metal recovery or more efficient treatment. In addition, the required equipment is relatively easily constructed and operated, and conventional fluid-processing equipment can be used. This includes irrigation systems, sprinklers, pumps, and extraction wells.

Soil flushing does not involve excavation, treatment, and disposal, which can be expensive and can be associated with certain hazards (e.g., wind dispersal of soil particles, mechanical hazards, etc.).

Soil flushing possesses its share of costs, however. Flushing will drastically alter the chemical, physical, and biological components of a soil and associated subsoil and aquifers. A solution composed of a fairly concentrated extractant is being forced through the site with the intention of contacting as much of the solid matrix as possible. Soil pH may be affected, the saturation of the cation exchange capacity by bases (Ca, Mg, K) will likely decrease, soil structure may be destroyed, and microbial activity will diminish. The continued saturation of the soil may result in a predominantly reducing environment.

The extracting solution used in the flushing process may itself become a pollutant. Flushing solutions may have toxic and other environmental impacts on the soil and water receiver systems. It is essential, at the completion of the remedial activity, to remove as much of the extracting solution as possible so that it does not become a local pollutant, and so that it does not migrate off-site. It may be useful to install subsurface containment barriers, such as sheet piling or slurry walls, in order to control the flow of the flushing solution and to create an essentially "closed" system (see chapter 6).

Remediation times will be long (from one to several years) due to the slowness of diffusion processes in the liquid phase. In order for the entire process to be cost effective and to reduce environmental impact, the flushing solution must be regenerated on-site and reused. Chelating agents are often expensive and difficult to recover from the flushing solution.

Bacterial fouling of infiltration and recovery systems and treatment units may be a problem, especially if high Fe concentrations are present in groundwater or if biodegradable reagents are being used (U.S. EPA 1990). Flushing additives may interfere with downstream wastewater treatment processes. For example, surfactants will inactivate or kill common heterotrophic bacterial populations that are employed in wastewater treatment plants for biochemical oxygen demand (BOD) removal.

Complex waste mixtures (e.g., several different metals or metals with organics) make formulating flushing solutions difficult. Each component may respond to treatment differently.

Several naturally occurring substances may interfere with soil washing and reduce extraction efficiency. For example, soil high in limestone will interfere with acid extraction because $CaCO_3$ will be dissolved along with the metals. A high soil organic matter content will hinder extraction by bases, and $Fe(OH)_3$ and $CaCO_3$ will interfere with chelating agent extraction. Since the process is highly waste-specific, treatability studies in the laboratory should be conducted prior to applying a procedure in the field.

Specialized acid-resistant equipment must be used for the acid-leaching process. Workers must be trained in safe handling procedures for flushing solutions, as many are potentially toxic, corrosive, or reactive.

7.7. CASE HISTORY

The King of Prussia Technical Corporation Superfund site, located in south-central New Jersey, began operations as a waste recycling facility in 1971. A primary function of the facility was to convert liquid industrial wastes to construction material and other uses. Six lagoons were constructed for waste treatment and approximately 15 million gal of acids and alkaline aqueous wastes were processed. Facility operations were halted and the site was abandoned in 1973 or 1974. Subsequent to closure, illegal dumping of solid and hazardous wastes apparently occurred (U.S. EPA 1995; 1994b ART 2006).

The site, measuring approximately 10 acres, is bordered mainly by pine forest. Site runoff flows via a swale toward nearby Great Egg Harbor River. Soil material is derived from the Outer Coastal Plain and is very sandy.

Soil and sediment at the site were found to be contaminated with several heavy metals including beryllium (Be), Cu, Cr, Ni, and Zn. Remedial alternatives considered for the site included (U.S. EPA 1995):

- no action
- limited action (site restrictions; installation of additional fencing)
- complete removal and off-site disposal of contaminated media
- limited excavation of sediments and soils followed by capping
- stabilization/solidification, either in situ or ex situ, of contaminated media followed by capping
- excavation of contaminated soils, sediments, and sludges followed by soil washing and return of "clean" soil to the site

After numerous technical reviews and pilot studies, soil washing was selected as the remedial option. Pilot studies using 990 tons of contaminated media showed that soil washing could effectively remove the contaminants from the site. Furthermore, the treated soil could be returned to its original location to restore site topography (Mann n.d.).

The highest concentration of surface (< 2 ft) contamination was located in sediments of the drainage swale. Maximum concentrations of Cr, Cu, and Hg were 8,010 mg/kg, 9,070 mg/kg, and 100 mg/kg, respectively. Subsurface (2–20 ft) contamination was highest in a zone of sludge-like material adjacent to the lagoons. The highest concentrations of contaminants in the sludge material were Cr at 11,300 mg/kg, Cu at 16,300 mg/kg, Pb at 389 mg/kg, and Ni at 11,100 mg/kg. The soils were found to contain

Figure 7.7.   *Plant assembly at the King of Prussia site. (Reproduced with kind permission of ART Engineering, LLC.)*

low concentrations of volatile and semivolatile organic compounds (U.S. EPA 1994a; ART 2006; 1993; Mann n.d.).

Selective excavation of metals-contaminated soils was conducted (Figs. 7.7–7.8). A total of 40,000 tons of material was excavated; however, only 20,000 tons exceeded the cleanup levels and required treatment. Selective

Figure 7.8.   *Hydrocyclone separation of contaminated soil. (Reproduced with kind permission of ART Engineering, LLC.)*

excavation of soil and sludge in and adjacent to the lagoons and the swale area involved the following steps:

1. Excavation of clean, overburden soils and transport to the stockpile area
2. Excavation and transportation of contaminated soils to the screening and blending area
3. Analysis of the contamination levels (using an X-ray fluorescence detector) in the trench bottom soils
4. Backfilling of the clean trench bottom with clean material (U.S. EPA 1995; Mann n.d.)

The soil washing system was designed to physically separate the metal-enriched soil fines from the larger particles, which were then reacted with water and surfactant. The system included the following processes:

1. Screening out the oversize fraction from the material to be treated by use of vibrating screens. Materials greater than 8-in. across, typically concrete, tree stumps, branches, etc., are periodically removed and stockpiled. The material that passes through the screens is directed to another mechanical screening unit to remove particles greater than 2 in. Materials passing through the screens ($<$ 2 in.) are then subjected to wet screening with high-pressure water sprays. The wet screening breaks up clods and forms a slurry.
2. Separating the screened soil/water slurry into coarse- and fine-grained material via a set of hydrocyclones (Fig. 7.9). Multiple

Figure 7.9.   *Soil feeding. (Reproduced with kind permission of ART Engineering, LLC.)*

cyclones achieved a separation efficiency of $> 99\%$ of the sands and fines. The hydrocyclones cut point was set at 40 microns, determined via a treatability study. The flow containing coarse-grained material was directed to the froth flotation stage, while the fine-grained material, presumably silt- and clay-sized, was processed into a sludge cake.

3. Froth flotation involves removing the contaminants from the coarse-grained material using air-flotation treatment units, specifically, an air-flotation tank equipped with mechanical aerators. The coarse-grained material is pumped into the tank, where a surfactant is added. The contaminants float within a froth and are removed from the surface of the flotation tank and sent to the sludge-management process. The cleaned underflow sands are sent to a cyclone and de-watering screens. Approximately 85% of the processed material (clean sand) from the site was used as backfill, while the water was recycled back to the wet screening process.

4. Sludge management involves treating the overflow from the hy-drocyclones, that is, fine-grained material and water. The overflow was pumped to clarifiers and a polymer added. The clarified solids were sent to a sludge thickener and ultimately to a filter press where the 15% to 20% solids influent was converted into a 50% to 60% dry solids filter cake. The filter cake was disposed off-site as a nonhazardous waste. The water from the sludge-management process was returned to the wet screening phase for reuse (U.S. EPA 1995; 1994b; ART 1993; 1992). The soil-washing unit can process 25 tons/hour.

The process oversize and clean sand from the soil-washing unit met the cleanup levels established for this situation (Table 7.1). The average concentrations of Be, Cu, Pb, Ni, and Zn in the clean sand and process oversize were at least an order of magnitude lower than the required cleanup levels. Cadmium, Hg, Se, and Ag were not detected in any process oversize samples; and As, Hg, Se, and Ag were not detected in any clean sand. Chromium, Cu, and Ni were concentrated in the sludge cake with individual contaminants measured at levels greater than 2,000 mg/kg (U.S. EPA 1995).

Approximately $7.7 million were expended on the soil-washing activity including off-site soil-disposal costs (U.S. EPA 1995; 1994b).

Table 7.1.   Treatment performance data for the King of Prussia Superfund site

Contaminant	Cleanup Level	Untreated Feed Soil (Range)	Clean Oversize Product (Average)	Clean Sand Product (Average)	Sludge Cake (Average)
			mg/kg		
As	190	n/a	0.62	nd	n/a
Be	485	n/a	5.9	1.9	n/a
Cd	107	n/a	nd	0.64	n/a
Cr	483	500–5,000	172	73	4,700
Cu	3,571	800–8,000	350	110	5,900
Pb	500	n/a	6.5	3.9	n/a
Hg	1	n/a	nd	nd	n/a
Ni	1,935	300–3,500	98	25	2,300
Ag	5	n/a	nd	nd	n/a
Zn	3,800	n/a	48	16	n/a

nd = not detected
n/a = samples were not collected
Sources: U.S. Environmental Protection Agency 1995; U.S. Environmental Protection Agency 1994b; Alternative Remedial Technologies, Inc. 1993.

QUESTIONS

1. List and discuss the specific benefits of conducting laboratory tests of an extracting solution prior to its application in a field situation.

2. Discuss three potential adverse effects from washing a soil with a moderately concentrated acid; with a surfactant solution.

3. List and discuss two soil components or compounds that may interfere with soil washing using EDTA.

4. Draw a surfactant molecule. How is it used in site remediation (on what types of contaminants)? How, specifically, does it function?

5. A permeable soil is contaminated with a hydrophobic (nonpolar) contaminant, for example, PCBs mixed with waste oil. Which would be an appropriate extracting solution? (a) water; (b) linear alkyl sulfate $CH_3[CH_2]_nCHOSO_3^-$; (c) dilute HNO_3; (d) dilute KOH.

6. The addition of dilute sodium hydroxide (NaOH) to a soil may be used for extraction of certain pollutants. What is one significant drawback to its use?

7. A soil-flushing solution may become a pollutant if it is used improperly and/or excessively. Explain and provide an example.

8. Explain how humus compounds are responsible for some metal chelation and complexation.

9. Soil flushing is an ideally suited process for a soil contaminated with several metals and mixed oils; all can be removed with one or two wash cycles. True or false? Justify your answer and provide an example.

REFERENCES

Ahnstrom, Z., and R. Parker. 1999. Development and assessment of a sequential extraction procedure for the fractionation of soil cadmium. *Soil Science Society of America Journal* 63 (6): 1650–58.

Alternative Remedial Technologies, Inc. 1992. *Soil Washing Demonstration Run for the King of Prussia Technical Site, December 14, 1992.*

———. 1993. *Site Operations Plan, The King of Prussia Technical Corporation Site, Winslow Township, New Jersey. July 26, 1993.*

———. 2006. *Soil Washing at King of Prussia (KOP) Superfund Site.* See: images.google .com/imgres?imgurl=http://www.art-engineering.com/Projects/KOP-Soil/ Image25.jpg&imgrefurl=http://www.art-engineering.com/Projects/KOP. Soil/Photos.htm&h=185&w=271&sz=16&hl=en&start=10&tbnid=AmMlm3Irh2_Qv M:&tbnh=77&tbnw=113&prev=/images%3Fq%3Dking%2Bof%2Bprussia%2Bsuper fund%2Bsite%26svnum%3D10%26hl%3Den%26lr%3D%26sa%3DN.

Bell, C. F. 1977. *Principles and Applications of Metal Chelation.* Oxford Chemistry Series. Oxford: Oxford University Press.

Benjamin, M. M., and J. O. Leckie. 1981. Multiple-site adsorption of Cd, Cu, Zn, and Pb on amorphous iron oxyhydroxide. *Journal of Colloid and Interface Science* 79:209–21.

Betteker, J., J. Sherrard, and D. Ludwig. 1993. Solidification/stabilization of contaminated dredged material. *Hazardous and Industrial Wastes* 25:93.

Bricker, T. J., J. Pichtel, H. J. Brown, and M. Simmons. 2001. Phytoextraction of Pb and Cd from a Superfund soil: Effects of amendments and croppings. *Journal of Environmental Science and Health* A36:1597–1610.

Brown, G. A., and H. A. Elliott. 1992. Influence of electrolytes on EDTA extraction of Pb from polluted soil. *Water, Air, and Soil Pollution* 62:157–65.

Chen, T. C., E. Macauley, and A. Hong. 1995. Selection and test of effective chelators for removal of heavy metals from contaminated soils. *Canadian Journal of Civil Engineering* 22:1185–97.

Cline, S. R., and B. E. Reed. 1995. Lead removal from soils via bench-scale soil washing techniques. *Journal of Environmental Engineering* 121:700–705.

Cline, S. R., B. E. Reed, and M. Matsumoto. 1993. Efficiencies of soil washing solutions for the remediation of lead contaminated soils. In *Hazardous and Industrial Wastes. Proceedings of the 25th Mid-Atlantic Industrial Waste Conference*, ed. A. Davis. Lancaster, PA: Technomic.

Davis, A. P., and I. Singh. 1995. Washing of zinc(II) from a contaminated soil column. *Journal of Environmental Engineering* 121:174–85.

Elliott, H. A. and G. A. Brown. 1989. Comparative evaluation of NTA and EDTA for extractive decontamination of Pb-polluted soils. *Water, Air, and Soil Pollution* 45:361–69.

Evangelou, M., H. Daghan, and A. Schaeffer. 2004. The influence of humic acids on the phytoextraction of cadmium from soil. *Chemosphere* 57 (3): 207–13.

Farrah, H., and W. F. Pickering. 1978. Extraction of heavy metal ions sorbed on clays. *Water, Air, and Soil Pollution* 9:491–98.

Fischer, K. 2002. Removal of heavy metals from soil components and soil by natural chelating agents. Part I: Displacement from clay minerals and peat by L-cysteine and L-penicillamine. *Water, Air, and Soil Pollution* 137 (1–4): 267–86.

Fischer, K., and H. P. Bipp. 2004. Removal of heavy metals from soil components and soils by natural chelating agents. Part II: Soil extraction by sugar acids. *Water, Air, and Soil Pollution* 138: 271–88.

Gidarakos, E., and A. Giannis. 2006. Chelate agents enhanced electrokinetic remediation for removal cadmium and zinc by conditioning catholyte pH. *Water, Air, and Soil Pollution* 172 (1–4): 295–312.

Grčman, H., D. Vodnik, S. Velikonja-Bolta, and D. Lestan. 2003. Ethylenediaminedissuccinate as a new chelate for environmentally safe enhanced lead phytoextraction. *Journal of Environmental Quality* 32:500–506.

Griffiths, R. A. 1995. Soil-washing technology and practice. *Journal of Hazardous Materials* 40:175–89.

Hessling, J. L., M. P. Esposito, R. P. Traver, and R. H. Snow. 1986. In *Metals Speciation, Separation, and Recovery.* Vol. 2, ed. J. W. Patterson and R. Passino. Chelsea, MI: Lewis.

Hong, A., and T. C. Chen. 1996. Chelating extraction and recovery of cadmium from soil using pyridine-2,6-dicarboxylic acid. *Water, Air, and Soil Pollution* 86:335–46.

Hsieh, H., M. Barnes, and E. Z. Aldridge. 1989. In *Physiochemical and Biological Detoxification of Hazardous Wastes.* Lancaster, PA: Technomic.

Kayser, A., K. Wenger, A. Keller, W. Attinger, H. R. Felix, S. K. Gupta, and R. Schulin. 2000. Enhancement of phytoextraction of Zn, Cd, and Cu from calcareous soil: The use of NTA and sulfur amendments. *Environmental Science and Technology* 34:1778–83.

Keon, N., H. Hemond, C. Swartz, D. Brabander, and C. Harvey. 2001. Validation of an arsenic sequential extraction method for evaluating mobility in sediments. *Environmental Science and Technology* 35 (13): 2778–84.

Khodadoust, A., K. Reddy, and K. Maturi. 2005. Effect of different extraction agents on metal and organic contaminant removal from a field soil. *Journal of Hazardous Materials* 117 (1): 15–24.

Leharne, S., and J. Dong. 2002. Investigations of surfactant facilitated removal of coal tar contaminants from manufactured gas works soils. IAHS-AISH: 311–18.

Macauley, E., and A. Hong. 1995. Chelation extraction of lead from soil using pyridine-2,6-dicarboxylic acid. *Journal of Hazardous Materials* 40:257–70.

Mann, M. J. n.d. Full-Scale Soil Washing at the King of Prussia (NJ) Technical Corporation Superfund Site. Alternative Remedial Technologies.

Mulligan, C., and F. Eftekhari. 2003. Remediation with surfactant foam of PCP-contaminated soil. *Engineering Geology* 70 (3–4): 269–79.

Pichtel, J., and T. M. Pichtel. 1997. Comparison of solvents for ex-situ removal of Cr and Pb from contaminated soil. *Environmental Engineering Science* 14:97–103.

Pickering, W. F. 1983. Extraction of copper, lead, zinc or cadmium ions sorbed on calcium carbonate. *Water, Air, and Soil Pollution* 20:299–309.

Rajput, V. S., S. Pilapitiya, M. E. Singley, and A. J. Higgins. 1989. Detoxification of hazardous waste contamination soils and residues by washing and biodegradation. In *Physiochemical and Biological Detoxification of Hazardous Wastes*. Lancaster, PA: Technomic.

Reed, B. E., R. E. Moore, and S. R. Cline. 1995. Soil flushing of a sandy loam contaminated with Pb(II), PbSO$_4$, PbCO$_3$, or Pb-naphthalene: Column results. *Journal of Soil Contamination* 4:243–67.

Ringbom, A. 1963. *Complexation in Analytical Chemistry*. New York: Wiley Interscience.

Sauer, N., E. Ehler, and B. Duran. 2004. Lead extraction from contaminated soil using water-soluble polymers *Journal of Environmental Engineering* 130 (5): 585–88.

Shirk, J. E., and C. W. Farrel. 1985. Approach to in-situ management of metals. In *Proceedings of the 8th Madison Waste Conference, Sept. 18–19, Madison, WI*.

Slavek, J., and W. F. Pickering. 1986. Extraction of metal ions sorbed on hydrous oxides of iron(III). *Water, Air, and Soil Pollution* 28:151–62.

Smith, L. A., J. L. Means, A. Chen, B. Alleman, C. C. Chapman, J. S. Tixier, S. E. Brauning, A. R. Gavaskar, and M. D. Royer. 1995. *Remedial Options for Metals-Contaminated Soils*. Boca Raton, FL: CRC Press.

Sposito, G., L. J. Lund, and A. C. Chang. 1982. Trace metal chemistry in arid-zone field soils amended with sewage sludge. I. Fractionation of Ni, Cu, Zn, Cd and Pd in solid phases. *Soil Sci. Soc. Am. J.* 46:260–64.

Steele, M. C., and J. Pichtel. 1998. Ex-situ remediation of a metal-contaminated Superfund soil using selective extractants. *Journal of Environmental Engineering* 124:639–45.

Tessier A., P. G. C. Campbell, and M. Bisson. 1979. Sequential extraction procedure for the speciation of particulate trace metals. *Anal. Chem.* 51:844–51.

Thirumalai Nivas, B., D. A. Sabatini, B. Shiau, and J. H. Harwell. 1996. Surfactant enhanced remediation of subsurface chromium contamination. *Water Research* 30:511.

Tokunaga S., S. W. Park, and M. Ulmanu. 2005. Extraction behaviour of metallic contaminants and soil constituents from contaminated soils. *Environmental Technology* 26 (6): 673–82.

Tuin, B. J. W., and Tels, M. 1990. Removing heavy metals from contaminated clay soils by extraction with hydrochloric acid, EDTA or hypochlorite solutions. *Environmental Technology Letters* 11:1039–52.

Tunay, O., and N. I. Kabdasli. 1994. Hydroxide precipitation of complexed metals. *Water Research* 28:2117–24.

Urum, K., S. McMenamy, S. Grigson, and T. Pekdemir. 2006. A comparison of the efficiency of different surfactants for removal of crude oil from contaminated soils. *Chemosphere* 62 (9): 1403–10.

U.S. Environmental Protection Agency. 1990. *Superfund Record of Decision, King of Prussia, New Jersey, September*.

——. 1991. *Guide for Conducting Treatability Studies Under CERCLA: Soil Washing Interim Guidance*. EPA/540/2-91/020A. Washington, DC.

———. 1993. *BIOGENESIS Soil Washing Technology: Innovative Technology Evaluation Report*. EPA/540/R-93/510. Office of Research and Development.

———. 1994a. *Acid Extraction Treatment System for Treatment of Metal Contaminated Soils*. EPA/540/SR-094/513. Cincinnati: Superfund Innovative Technology Evaluation.

———. 1994b. *Remedial Action Report: Soil Washing Remediation, King of Prussia Technical Corporation Site, Camden County, New Jersey, July*.

———. 1995. *Soil Washing at the King of Prussia Technical Corporation Superfund Site, Winslow Township, New Jersey. Cost and Performance Report*. Office of Solid Waste and Emergency Response, Technology Innovation Office.

———. 1997. *Treatment Technology Performance and Cost Data for Remediation of Wood Preserving Sites*. EPA/625/R-97/009. Office of Research and Development.

Zeng, Q., W. Hendershot, S. Sauve, and H. Allen. 2005. Recycling EDTA solutions used to remediate metal-polluted soils. *Environmental Pollution* 133 (2): 225–31.

CHAPTER 8

Solidification/Stabilization

Thoughts crystallize into habit and habit solidifies into circumstances.

—Bryan Adams

8.1. INTRODUCTION

Solidification and stabilization (S/S) technologies are employed in situations where large quantities of toxic and/or relatively immobile contaminants occur; large debris (e.g., drums, battery casings) are scattered extensively; and/or soil K_s is not suitable for flushing (i.e., very dense soil). An example of such a scenario may be a sprawling waste site laden to variable depths with lead-battery casings and free metals of varying chemistries and toxicities.

S/S technology is conducted by mixing contaminated soil, either in situ or ex situ, with a binding agent to form a crystalline or polymeric matrix that incorporates the contaminated materials. Inorganic binders include cement, cement kiln dust, fly ash, and blast furnace slag. Certain organic wastes can be immobilized by organic binders such as bitumen (asphalt), polyethylene, or urea-formaldehyde. During solidification, contaminants are immobilized within a solid matrix in the form of a monolithic block. Stabilization converts contaminants to a less- or a nonreactive form, typically by chemical processes. It follows that the S/S process does not remove contaminants from the affected soil; rather, it serves to physically sorb, encapsulate, or alter the physical or chemical form of the contaminants, producing a less leachable material.

S/S can: (1) improve the handling and other physical characteristics of the contaminated soil by converting a liquid or sludge to a solid; (2) decrease the toxicity of the soil by altering the contaminant's physical and chemical properties; (3) decrease the exposed surface area of contaminants, thereby reducing their solubility; and (4) limit the contact of transport fluids (groundwater, infiltrating rainwater) with contaminants (U.S. EPA 1995). Many wastes containing metal or inorganic contaminants are suitable for treatment with S/S technologies; however, potential interferences and incompatibilities must be addressed. The main technologies are grouped as inorganic (cement-based) S/S and organic polymerization (thermoplastic- and thermoset-based polymers).

8.2. CEMENT-BASED TECHNOLOGIES

In cement-based S/S, contaminated materials are mixed with a suitable ratio of cement or similar binder. Primary binder categories are cement and pozzolans. Examples of common pozzolans are fly ash, lime kiln dusts, pumice, and blast furnace slag. Cement-based S/S processes have been used for site remediation and hazardous-waste treatment more often than other S/S technologies. Cement-based S/S has been applied to plating wastes containing Cd, Cr, Cu, Pb, Ni, and Zn. Studies on contaminated soil treatment showed cement-based S/S effective for the immobilization of As, Pb, Cu, Zn, Cd, and Ni (Wareham and Mackenchnie 2006; Carmalin and Swaminatian 2005; Fitch and Cheeseman 2003; Vandercasteele et al. 2002). Cement has also been successful with organic-contaminated materials including PCBs, oily sludges, vinyl chloride, plastics, and sulfides (Yilmaz et al. 2003; Donnelly and Webster 1996; Benge and Webster 1994; Bettahar et al. 1999; Jones 1989; Tittlebaum et al. 1985). The composition of the cement or pozzolan, the type(s) of contaminants present, and the amount of water and aggregate added determine set time, cure time, pouring characteristics, and engineering properties (e.g., compressive strength) of the treated soil (U.S. EPA 1995; Kyu-Hong and Jagga 1989). Cement and pozzolan compositions, including those used in S/S, are classified according to ASTM standards (Smith et al. 1995; U.S. EPA 1989b).

Portland cements typically are composed of calcium silicates, aluminates, aluminoferrites, and sulfates. Cementation of the waste-binder mixture begins when the water is added, either separately or from the soil. Once the cement contacts water, hydration of tricalcium aluminate occurs, causing rapid setting. The water hydrates calcium silicates and aluminates to form calcium silicate-hydrate. Thin silicate fibers grow out from the cement grains and interweave, hardening the mixture. Hydration of tricalcium and dicalcium silicates results in the formation of crystalline calcium hydroxide and other minerals, which provide for strength development after setting (Means et al. 1995; U.S. EPA 1990b).

Pozzolanic reaction is a relatively inexpensive treatment for contaminated materials. In general, however, pozzolan-solidified soils are not considered as durable as Portland cement-treated soils (Bettahar et al. 1999; Means et al. 1995; Qian et al. 2006; Dermatas and Meng 2003; Kamon et al. 2000). With pozzolanic S/S, silica or silica alumina materials are used that have minimal cementation properties but can react with lime or cement to produce cement-like material. The primary mechanism is the physical entrapment of the contaminant in the pozzolan matrix. In contrast to lime-based materials, pozzolans contain significant amounts of silicates. The final product varies from a soft, fine-grained material to a hard, cohesive material similar to cement, depending on the amount of reagent added and the types and amounts of wastes treated (Kamon et al. 2000). Pozzolanic reactions are generally slower than cement reactions. Waste materials that have been stabilized/solidified with pozzolans include oily sludges, plating sludges containing various metals (Al, Ni, Cu, Pb, Cr, and As), waste acids, and creosote (Bettahar et al. 1999; U.S. EPA 1989b; Wareham and Mackenchnie 2006; Qiao et al. 2006). Inorganic binder systems using sodium silicate and cement/silicate have also been used in S/S (Andres et al. 2002; Carmalin and Swaminathan 2005; Montgomery et al. 1988; Spencer et al. 1982).

Numerous hydrolysis reactions affect the solubility of metals in S/S-treated soils and wastes. Hydrolyzed metals form several hydroxides, oxides, carbonates, and sulfates, among other species. The log K_{sp} values for certain metal-hydroxides are: Cd, 14.3; Cr(III), 30.2; Pb, 19.9; and Hg(II), 25.5, indicating very insoluble product formation (Means et al. 1995). Published solubility data is useful for deciding which form of a hazardous metal is most stable, and to what degree stabilization is possible given site conditions, available materials, and technology. Actual concentrations of precipitated species depends on several solution parameters including pH, redox potential, and composition of salts (Means et al. 1995). In a study of effectiveness of S/S (U.S. EPA 1990a), $Cd(OH)_2$ and $Pb(OH)_2$ have comparable stabilities; however, the degree of leaching differed for the two metals. Leaching of Pb was substantially higher than that of Cd due to the differing precipitation reactions for each metal hydroxide.

Additives may be used with cement-based S/S treatment to promote the immobilization of specific contaminants or to improve physical character-istics. Activated carbon, organophilic clay, silica compounds, and other sorbents are added to aid in the immobilization of organics (U.S. EPA 1990b; 1992; Gong and Bishop 2003). Soluble silicate additives are used to speed setting and reduce free water, and can precipitate lower-solubility forms of some metals. Sulfide molecules allow for reducing reactions and can form very low-solubility metal sulfides.

Advantages of cement-based processes include the availability of ma-terials locally, the low cost both of materials and mixing equipment, binder applicability to a wide range of waste types, knowledge of the hardening and setting reactions, ease of use in the field, use of naturally occurring materials as the binder, and flexibility for different applications (Means et al. 1995; McDaniel et al. 1990; Conner 1990).

8.3. ORGANIC STABILIZATION/SOLIDIFICATION

Organic stabilization/solidification with thermoplastic binders and or-ganic polymerization has been applied to certain hazardous wastes; how-ever, this has been used to a lesser degree than S/S with cements and poz-zolans (Smith et al. 1995; U.S. EPA 1990b).

Thermoplastic S/S is often a microencapsulation process in which the contaminated soil does not react chemically with the encapsulating mate-rial. A thermoplastic material such as asphalt (bitumen) or polyethylene is used to bind the waste constituents into a stabilized/solidified mass. The most common thermoplastic material for S/S is asphalt. The asphalt may be heated before it is mixed with a dry soil, or it may be applied at ambi-ent temperature. In the latter case compaction removes additional water from the aggregate/soil mixture. Bitumen may be used for stabilizing/so-lidifying oil- and gasoline-contaminated soils. The final consistency will vary depending on the density of the hydrocarbon mixed into the bitumen and the amount of aggregate added to the mixture. Thermoplastic encapsulation has also been applied to electroplating sludges, painting and re-finery sludges containing metals and organics, incinerator ash, baghouse dust, and radioactive wastes (Tittlebaum et al. 1985; U.S. EPA 1989b; Nagy et al. 1991).

Organic-based S/S can also use polymer formation to immobilize con-taminants. The technique involves drying and dispersing soil through a polymer matrix. The soil is mixed into a hot plastic mass that then cools, incorporating the soil within a solid block. The soil/thermoplastic mix is commonly extruded into a container, for example a metal drum, to provide a convenient form for transport and disposal. Other materials, such as poly-ethylene, polypropylene, urea formaldehyde, or paraffin can be employed for specific wastes (ASTM 1985). Organic polymerization has been used to treat radioactive wastes and has been applied to organic chlorides, phe-nols, paint sludges, cyanides, and As. Polymerization can also be applied to flue gas desulfurization sludge, electroplating sludges, Ni-Cd battery wastes, kepone-contaminated sludge, and certain chlorine product wastes (U.S. EPA 1989a; Kyles et al. 1987).

8.4. FIELD TECHNOLOGIES: EX SITU

S/S can be accomplished either ex situ or in situ. Vigorous mixing is usu-ally needed to disperse the binder in the soil matrix; therefore, S/S processes are often applied to excavated materials. Ex situ processing in-volves excavating the contaminated materials from the affected site, dry or wet screening to remove large debris and produce a well-graded size distribution, mixing soil with binder and water, removal and treatment of off-gases (if dusts or volatile gases are produced), and transfer of the treated materials to a disposal area (Fig. 8.1) (U.S. EPA 1995).

Ex situ S/S treatment can be accomplished in a fixed facility or in a mo-bile treatment plant transported to the site. Screening and crushing of the affected soil may be needed prior to blending operations, to handle over-size materials such as rocks and debris. Portable S/S plants have been de-veloped that include bulk chemical feed or other blending equipment. Pro-cessing rates for large portable plants range from 500 to over 1,000 tons per day (AFCEE 1992). Pilot-scale plants typically can process 100 tons per day and may be transported on one trailer (Smith et al. 1995).

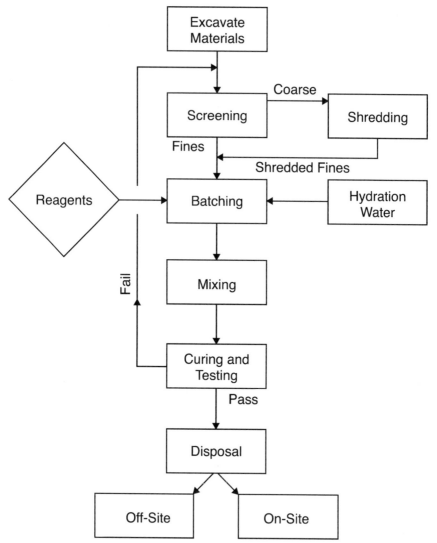

Figure 8.1.   *Treatment train for ex situ S/S of contaminated soil*
U.S. Environmental Protection Agency 1992.

Common approaches to mixing of the binder include in-drum mixing, in-plant mixing (e.g., rotary drum), and area mixing. In-drum mixing typically is used for highly toxic materials or small volumes of soil. The binder and soil are combined and mixed in a 55-gal drum. In-plant mixing can be either continuous or batch. Continuous processes often employ a pug mill mixer equipped with paddles attached to a horizontal rotating shaft to carry out the mixing. Batch operations typically use some form of drum mixer. For example, a rotary drum mixer is an inclined container that has internal baffles and rotates to mix the contents (Smith et al. 1995). Area mixing involves placing layers of binder and soil in a large containment area and then mixing with a backhoe or other earth-moving equipment.

The loading and mixing of waste and binder will result in particulate air emissions. If the contaminated material contains volatile organics, mixing operations and heating due to binder hydration will release organic vapors. Control of dust is often needed, and control of organic vapors is necessary in some situations.

8.5. IN SITU S/S TREATMENT

During in situ S/S treatment the binder material is introduced directly to a contaminated site by surface application or use of augers. A major advantage of in situ S/S is that it eliminates the labor, energy, and costs involved with soil excavation, transport, and replacement or disposal. Another advantage is that it is applicable at space-limited sites such as near buildings, pipes, tanks, and other obstructions. Furthermore, dust generation is greatly reduced. A critical challenge in utilizing in situ S/S is the complete and uniform mixing of the binder with the contaminated soil. Other disadvantages of auger methods are that they are not feasible in the presence of bedrock or boulders and are impeded in the presence of clays, oily sands, and cohesive soils. Poor progress under these circumstances may require the use of ex situ processes.

In situ chemical treatment reagents must not create an environmental or health hazard. Treatment systems can potentially introduce oxidizing, reducing, or neutralizing chemicals into the groundwater system; therefore, adequate knowledge of the subsurface environment is essential to avoid contamination. Also, injection of treatment chemicals may create the requirement for land disposal as per federal regulations. In such cases, the selection of reagents for chemical treatment will be limited by the Land Disposal Restrictions (LDRs) on introducing chemicals into the soil (U.S. EPA 1995; 40 CFR 1996).

The chemical forms of soil contaminants must also be considered during the treatment process. For example, Cr(VI), which is both toxic and mobile in soils, should first be reduced to the less hazardous Cr(III) species prior to in situ treatment. A common approach to Cr reduction involves acidification followed by reduction and neutralization. The Cr(VI) ion is a strong oxidizing agent under acidic conditions and in many cases readily converts to Cr(III). Acidification can be accomplished using mineral acids. With the pH adjusted to < 3.0, ferrous sulfate is added to convert Cr(VI) to Cr(III). After chemical reduction, solution pH is increased to > 7.0 to coprecipitate Cr(III) with ferric and ferrous iron (Conner 1990). The Cr(III) is also readily precipitated by hydroxide over a wide pH range. Other in situ Cr reducing agents include FeS, leaf litter, and acid compost. Treatments are also available for Cr reduction in neutral pH ranges. Possible Cr reduction reagents include sodium metabisulfite, sodium bisulfite, and ferrous ammonium sulfate (Jacobs 1992). Reduction at neutral pH generates less sludge, so the total waste volume is reduced.

In situ treatment processing involves reagent preparation, mixing of binder and contaminated soil, and off-gas treatment. The basic approaches for mixing binder with soil are in-place mixing, vertical auger mixing, and injection grouting. In-place mixing is applicable only to shallow or surface contamination. The process involves spreading and mixing binder reagents with contaminated soil by common earth-moving equipment (draglines, backhoes, dozers), and allowing the mixture to set and cure. Vertical auger application is adapted from the construction industry. A system of large-diameter crane-mounted augers injects and mixes binder into the soil (Figs. 8.2 and 8.3). Vertical augers loosen soil and mix in the binders. A 10-ft diameter auger mounted on a crawler crane is applicable. Dry reagents and water are pneumatically dispersed into the soil as the auger creates a pattern of overlapping 10-ft diameter columns (Fig. 8.4). Mixing can be accomplished to depths up to 40 ft and can process 500 to 1,000 yd^3 of soil per day. Deep drilling is also possible, reaching depths of up to 150 ft. A cluster of two to four augers, each up to 3 ft in diameter, is assembled to loosen subsoil and mix in the binder (Fig. 8.4) (U.S. EPA 1989b; 1997). During injection grouting, the binder containing dissolved or suspended treatment agents is forced into the contamination zone under pressure and allowed to permeate the soil. Grout injection can be applied to contaminated formations deep below the ground surface. The injected grout cures in place to form an in situ treated mass (U.S. EPA 1995).

Figure 8.2. *An engineer directs the positioning of multiple augers. Three augers overlap each other. Successful fixation of the contaminants requires that the soil be thoroughly mixed with the cementing mixtures. (Reproduced with kind permission of Boulanger and Duncan, University of California, Davis.)*
Boulanger and Duncan 2002.

Figure 8.3. *Close-up showing that the middle auger is recessed relative to the outer two augers. The grout, which is a mixture of cementing agents and water, is injected through ports near the ends of the augers. (Reproduced with kind permission of Boulanger and Duncan, University of California, Davis.)*
Boulanger and Duncan 2002.

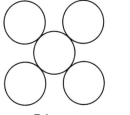
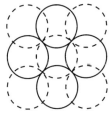
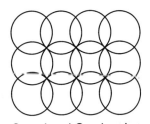

Primary   Secondary   Completed Overlapping

Figure 8.4. *Overlapping column arrangement in S/S-treated soil*
U.S. Environmental Protection Agency 1990a.

Figure 8.5.   *Augers advancing into the ground, mixing the soil. (Reproduced with kind permission of Boulanger and Duncan, University of California, Davis.)*
Boulanger and Duncan 2002.

After reagents are applied the site is allowed adequate time for binder setting and curing. Once the materials have cured, options can be considered for site development. If the site is located in an industrial area, it may be possible to build upon the surface, using the solidified matrix as a base. A layer of soil can also be distributed over the surface, which can be seeded.

8.6. TECHNICAL CONSIDERATIONS

S/S treatment is usually not applicable to wastes with volatile organic compounds or high levels of semivolatile organic compounds unless off-gas removal and treatment is employed. Otherwise, the waste can be prepared for S/S by steam stripping or incineration, depending on the types and concentrations of the organics (Smith et al. 1995). For a site contaminated with both metals and organics, pretreatment may be needed to transform the solids to forms more suitable for S/S. The addition of silicates or modified clays to the binder system may improve S/S performance with organics (U.S. EPA 1995). Other pretreatment steps may include screening for debris removal, size reduction, neutralization, Cr(VI) reduction, removal or destruction of organics, or physical separation. Post and treatment steps may include disposal of treated residuals, control of dust, collection, and treatment of off-gas.

Success of S/S can be evaluated depending on the desired final uses of the solidified materials. If the operator's goal is simple soil detoxification, the Toxicity Characteristics Leaching Procedure (TCLP) test should be conducted. This test provides a practical measure of the leachability of toxic elements within the treated mass. In addition, it may be necessary to test the permeability of the solidified materials. If the site is to be used for construction or similar engineered purposes, the durability of the cured materials must be measured, as well as other cement-industry requirements (for example, unconfined compressive strength, wet/dry, freeze/thaw). In some cases it may be necessary to inspect the material on a microstructural basis (Dermatas and Meng 2003; Vespa et al. 2006). Tests may include X-ray diffraction for crystalline structure, optical and scanning microscopy, and EDX (energy dispersive X-ray spectrometry) for elemental analysis of crystal structures.

8.7. OVERVIEW OF S/S TECHNOLOGIES

S/S technology is a widely accepted technology for the treatment of metal-, inorganic-, and certain organic-contaminated wastes. The technology can be conducted either ex situ or in situ depending on practical considerations (e.g., chemical and physical state of contaminants), available equipment, subsurface characteristics (presence of utilities and other structures), and cost. The overall process is relatively simple and inexpensive, and uses common chemicals and construction equipment. Simple materials, including certain nonhazardous industrial wastes (as in the case of pozzolans), can be employed as fixative materials.

The technology can simultaneously treat a wide variety of contaminants. This is especially true for inorganics of similar chemistry (for example, di- and trivalent metals). Some forms of chemical treatment such as oxidation, reduction, and pH neutralization are simple and inexpensive to implement, particularly for single-contaminant wastes. S/S improves the handling and physical characteristics of the wastes; in other words, sludges are transformed into solids. The technique reduces leaching of contaminants by decreasing surface area and reduces pollutant solubility in the treated waste, generally by chemical changes. The permeability of the treated area is significantly reduced. The stabilized material can be engineered to produce a subbase or slab for subsequent industrial use at the site. If a site is to be revegetated, however, placement of a soil cover of sufficient depth will be necessary.

Although S/S technology is relatively simple in principle, there are disadvantages to its use. No single binder is effective for the stabilization of all metals. In some situations one metal will be stabilized while a second metal concurrently becomes more soluble (e.g., cement will immobilize Pb but may increase the mobility of As). Potential for interferences and incompatibilities must be considered in pilot tests. General types of interferences include inhibition of bonding between waste and binder materials, retardation of setting, reduction in stability of the matrix resulting in leaching of contaminants, and reduction in the physical strength of the final product (U.S. EPA 1995). The operator must be aware of chemical incompatibilities; for example, the oxidation of soil containing reduced Cr, Hg, and Pb can convert these metals to more toxic or mobile forms; the neutralization of alkaline waste can increase metal mobilities by redissolving hydroxide precipitates; and the oxidation of certain organic wastes can increase toxicity due to by-products formed. Also, arsenic wastes are difficult to treat due to the complex chemistry or arsenic. Soils with unacceptable physical characteristics such as being too solid or too viscous to mix will cause difficulties for S/S. The technology does not reduce total contaminant content in the soil; volume expansion is an inevitable result of S/S treatment.

Complications for S/S are posed by materials containing organics. An oil and grease content $> 1\%$ interferes with contact between reactant and soil. Nonvolatile and semivolatile organics can be difficult to treat, and volatile organics are not readily treatable. Pretreatment is usually required. Many contaminants interfere with bonding between soil and binder (therefore increasing time of setting and decreasing durability); these include cyanides, arsenates, sulfates, sulfides, metals salts, and metal complexes (Means et al. 1995; U.S. EPA 1988). Wastes that contain organics as the primary contaminants will also cause difficulties. Some may be removed by volatilization processes; others may or may not react with the binder. The S/S process is very waste-specific, and site-specific treatability studies should be conducted.

Atmospheric emissions of dust and volatile organic compounds are a concern with S/S. Adding dry waste and a binder to a mixer can generate significant dust emissions. Volatilization and emission of volatile organic compounds may pose a hazard during mixing procedures, and emissions control may be required. Heat from exothermic binder hydration reactions can cause a rapid release of both dust and volatile organics.

There are some specific concerns regarding the use of in situ S/S. For example, delivering reagents to the subsurface and achieving uniform mixing and treatment in situ may be difficult. Further, in situ S/S has relatively slow treatment throughput compared to ex situ S/S.

8.8. CASE HISTORY

The Selma Pressure Treating (SPT) site was used for the chemical treatment of lumber since 1942. The site is located southeast of Fresno, California, in the San Joaquin River Valley. The SPT site covers 18 acres; however, the actual wood-treatment area measures 3 to 4 acres. The site is located less than a quarter-mile from homes and businesses. Groundwater resources near the site are classified as a beneficial use, sole-source aquifer. This aquifer provides the domestic water supply for surrounding communities and rural homes, and surface irrigation systems are also supplemented by this water (U.S. EPA 1992, 2005).

The original wood-preserving process involved dipping lumber into a mixture of pentachlorophenol (PCP) and oil, and allowing the excess fluid to drip as the wood dried on open storage racks. In 1965, site operators converted to a pressure-treating process that involved conditioning the lumber to reduce moisture content and increase permeability, followed by impregnating the wood with chemical preservatives. From 1942 to 1971, wastes from the treatment plant were disposed via:

- runoff into drainage ditches and a percolation ditch
- drainage into dry wells
- spillage on open ground
- placement into an unlined pond and a sludge pit
- disposal in an adjacent vineyard

The plant ceased operations in 1981.

Chemical preservatives used at the site included fluor-chromium-arsenate-phenol, Woodtox 140 RTU, heavy oil penta solution, LST concentrate, copper-8-quinolinoate, PCP, and chromated-copper-arsenate (CCA). A contaminated groundwater plume migrating from the site, along with soil contamination beneath the site, was identified. The primary metal contaminants were As, Cr, and Cu. PCP was also detected along with associated degradation and impurity products including polychlorinated dibenzo-p-dioxins (PCDD), polychlorinated dibenzofurans (PCDF), and chlorinated phenols. Hydrocarbon-related constituents were detected and included volatile organic compounds such as benzene, toluene, and xylene, and PAHs such as naphthalene and pyrene. These may have resulted from the use of diesel fuel as a carrier for the PCP. The highest levels of contamination occur in the first 5 ft of soil material (U.S. EPA 2005; 1992).

Federal and state agencies have been jointly involved in regulatory actions at the site since the 1970s. The U.S. EPA scored the site at 48.83 using the Hazard Ranking System (HRS) (U.S. EPA 2006), and the site was resultantly placed on the Superfund National Priorities List in 1983. Following a remedial investigation/feasibility study (RI/FS), a Record of Decision (ROD) was signed in 1988.

The Silicate Technology Corporation (STC) immobilization technology is a solidification/stabilization process that uses a proprietary organophilic material (FMS silicate) to adsorb organic compounds up to 20 times its weight. When combined with a cementitious binder material, the reagents selectively adsorb organic and inorganic contaminants and produce a high-strength monolith. The resulting solid materials have passed federal and state regulatory threshold levels for TCLP leachate tests. Leachability has also been found to decrease with age (U.S. EPA 1992; 2005).

A backhoe/front-end loader was used to collect contaminated soil from an unlined disposal pond. An approximately 300 ft^2 area was excavated to a depth of 3 ft. The excavation was lined with a layer of 20-mil HDPE and backfilled with 1 ft of sand overlain by 1 ft of crushed stone (1 in. diameter) and clean soil at the conclusion of the activity. Contaminated soils from the unlined waste disposal pond were transported directly to the processing area, where storage piles covered by 10-mil HDPE were placed prior to batch processing. Each batch was mixed in a batch mixer prior to the addition of reagents. A schematic of the process appears in Fig. 8.6. Materials and equipment at the site included:

- A 15 × 50 ft area lined with 20-mil HDPE liner to store the solidified waste. Treated waste was discharged into cardboard concrete forms mounted on pallets and placed in the storage area. The storage area was graded so that rainwater runoff from the solidified waste was collected.

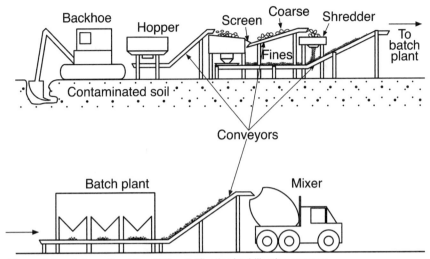

Figure 8.6.   *Schematic of the STC solidification/stabilization process*
U.S. Environmental Protection Agency 1992.

- Electric generators to supply power for process equipment, the support trailer, equipment, and other needs.
- Process and wash water for the treatment unit and decontamination, obtained from the facility potable water supply. About 220 gal of water were required per treated batch.
- A scale for weighing reagents and raw wastes.
- A heavy equipment decontamination area bermed and lined with 20-mil plastic for cleaning large equipment.
- A personnel decontamination station.
- A 3,000-gal tank to store decontamination water.
- A gasoline-powered high-pressure cleaner to clean the STC process equipment and other heavy equipment (U.S. EPA 1992; 2005).

Arsenic was found to be stabilized by the STC treatment under neutral leaching conditions. Acidic leaching resulted in greater As mobility in both the raw and treated waste. Increased mobility is due partly to the amphoteric nature of As; that is, its solubility increases as the leachate pH either decreases or increases away from neutrality. Using the TCLP, results for reduction in As ranged from 35% to 92%. Some of the soil As may have been reduced from the (V) to the (III) species during the raw-waste mixing process, thereby rendering the treated contaminants more mobile and easily leached under acidic TCLP conditions. The STC process was not effective in converting the arsenite to arsenate or a species that could be chemically immobilized; minor amounts of both arsenite and arsenate were detected in some of the treated waste (U.S. EPA 1992; 2005).

Pentachlorophenol (PCP) was the main organic contaminant of concern at the SPT site. Based on the information from a treatability study, samples were also analyzed for semivolatile organics such as tetrachlorophenol (TCP), phenanthrene, naphthalene, and phenol. These constituents were detected in negligible concentrations. PCP concentrations for the soil extracts varied as a result of the STC stabilization process (Table 8.1). All raw and treated waste concentrations were, however, below TCLP federal regulatory threshold levels of 100 ppm for PCP. Percent reductions of oil and grease in the treated wastes ranged from 32% to 52%. Although the treatment process was not highly effective in reducing the amount of extractable oil and grease, the presence of small quantities ($< 2\%$) of oil and grease did not adversely affect the solidification process (U.S. EPA 1992; 2005).

Raw waste samples had pH values ranging from 6.3 to 7.1. Treated wastes were very basic, with pH values of 12.5 to 12.6. The sand and water additives had pH values of 8.6 and 8.0, respectively, and the reagent mixture had a pH of 12.5.

Moisture content of the raw waste ranged from 3.9% to 5.8%, and moisture content of the treated wastes varied from 1.9% to 9.7% (Table 8.2). The treated reagent mixture had an average moisture content of 4.1%. Average bulk densities ranged from 1.42 to 1.54 g/cm^3 for the raw waste, and treated waste had bulk densities ranging from 1.55 to 1.62 g/cm^3. The treated reagent mixture had an average bulk density of 1.92 g/cm^3. Volume increased, ranging from 59% to 75%. Average permeability values for the treated waste ranged from 0.8×10^{-7} to 1.7×10^{-7} cm/sec. Average unconfined compressive strength (UCS), defined as the load per unit area, ranged from 259 to 347 psi for the treated wastes. These values are well below the ASTM and American Concrete Institute (ACI) minimum required UCS of 3,000 psi for the construction of sidewalks (ASTM 1991). However, values are well above the EPA minimum guideline of at least 50 psi for hazardous-waste solidification (U.S. EPA 1988).

Table 8.1.   TCLP results for selected analytes in the raw
and treated waste, Selma Pressure Treating
Superfund Site

Test	Batch	Raw Waste	Treated Waste
		mg/L	
PCP-TCLP	1	1.50	3.42
	2	2.27	< 0.25
	3	1.75	5.52
	4	2.28	0.90
PCP-TCLP	1	34.7	3.98
Distilled H_2O	2	40.0	0.58
	3	40.5	3.05
	4	79.9	120
As-TCLP	1	1.82	0.086
	3	1.06	0.101
	4	2.40	0.875
	5	3.33	0.548
As-TCLP	1	0.80	< 0.01
Distilled H_2O	3	0.73	< 0.01
	4	1.25	< 0.01
	5	1.07	0.011
As(V)	3	60.5	< 2.0
	4	19.5	21
	5	260	< 2.0
Cr-TCLP	1	0.13	0.245
	2	< 0.05	0.187
	3	0.10	0.287
	4	0.27	0.320
Cr-TCLP	1	0.19	< 0.05
	2	0.17	< 0.05
	3	0.07	0.056
	4	0.11	0.079
Cu-TCLP	1	3.42	0.09
	2	1.38	0.75
	3	6.53	0.10
	4	9.43	0.06
Cu-TCLP	1	0.45	0.031
	2	0.37	< 0.030
	3	0.99	0.054
	4	0.56	0.032

Source: U.S. Environmental Protection Agency 1992.

A few operational problems were encountered during the solidifica-
tion/stabilization activity:

1. Certain contaminated soils (PCP-contaminated materials) were not
   well mixed after treatment; the treated waste contained large (up to

Table 8.2.   Selected physical and engineering characteristics of the raw and treated
waste, Selma Pressure Treating Superfund Site

	Moisture Content		Bulk Density		Permeability	UCS
	Raw	Treated	Raw	Treated	Treated	Treated
Batch	%		g/cm³		cm/sec × 10⁻⁷	psi
1	5.8	2.6	1.42	1.57	1.7	301
3	5.7	1.9	1.54	1.55	1.5	278
4	4.2	9.7	1.54	1.58	0.9	259
5	3.9	8.8	1.54	1.62	0.8	347

Source: U.S. Environmental Protection Agency 1992.

2-in. diameter) aggregates of untreated waste. The problem was solved in subsequent batches by forcing the raw waste through a set of screens prior to treatment, reducing the raw waste aggregate size to about 0.04 to 0.08 in. (1–2 mm) diameter.

2. The generation of large amounts of contaminated dust from the movement of equipment, supplies, and site personnel. The dust caused fouling of the photoionization device used for air monitoring. The dust problem was remedied via application of water to the site from a water truck.

3. Generation of a dust cloud created upon initially mixing the dry reagents in the mixer. A tarp was secured over the top of the mixer after adding dry reagents (U.S. EPA 1992; 2005).

QUESTIONS

1. Describe the purpose of the TCLP. How can it be applied to solidified/stabilized contaminated soil material?
2. Locate ASTM standards for concrete testing. How do you expect solidified soil to differ from Portland cement in terms of UCS and other properties?
3. What, if any, is the effect of the presence of oily wastes on S/S of metal-contaminated soil?
4. Ideally, Cr(VI) should be reduced to Cr(III) prior to S/S. Explain why this is so.
5. Volume expansion inevitably results from S/S treatment. Identify a case study of S/S treatment of contaminated soil and provide data for volume expansion.

REFERENCES

Air Force Center for Environmental Excellence. 1992. *Remedial Technology Design, Performance and Cost Study*. Brooks Air Force Base, TX: Environmental Services Office.

American Society for Testing and Materials (ASTM). 1985. *Temperature Effects on Concrete*. Philadelphia: ASTM.

———. 1991. *Annual Book of ASTM Standards*. Philadelphia: ASTM.

Andres, A., J. Viguri, A. Irabien, M. F. de Velasco, A. Coz, and C. Ruiz. 2002. Treatment of foundry sludges by stabilization/solidification with cement and siliceous binders. *Fresenius Environmental Bulletin* 11 (10 B): 849–53.

Benge, O., and W. Webster. 1994. *Proceedings of the IADC/SPE Drilling Conference, Dallas, 1994*, 169–80.

Bettahar, M., J. Ducreax, G. Schafer, and F. Van Dorpe. 1999. Surfactant enhanced in situ remediation of LNAPL contaminated aquifers: Large scale studies on a controlled experimental site. *Transport in Porous Media* 37 (3): 255–76.

Boulanger, R. W., and Duncan, J. M. 2002. Geotechnical Engineering Photo Album. An Instructional Website to Complement Textbooks. University of California, Davis. cee.engr.ucdavis.edu/faculty/boulanger/geo_photo_album/index.html.

Carmalin, S., and K. Swaminatian. 2005. Leaching of metals on stabilization of metal sludge using cement based materials. *Journal of Environmental Sciences* 17 (1): 115–18.

Conner, J. R. 1990. *Chemical Fixation and Solidification of Hazardous Wastes*. New York: Van Nostrand Reinhold.

Dermatas, D., and X. Meng. 2003. Utilization of fly ash for stabilization/solidification of heavy metal contaminated soils. *Engineering Geology* 70 (3–4): 377–94.

Donnelly, J., and W. Webster. 1996. From sediment to solid. *Civil Engineering—ASCE* 66 (5): 41–43.

Fitch, J., and C. Cheeseman. 2003. Characterisation of environmentally exposed cement-based stabilised/solidified industrial waste. *Journal of Hazardous Materials* 101 (3): 239–55.

40 CFR. 1996. *Part 268. Land Disposal Restrictions*. Washington, DC: U.S. Government Printing Office.

Gong, P., and P. Bishop. 2003. Evaluation of organics leaching from solidified/stabilized hazardous wastes using a powder reactivated carbon additive. *Environmental Technology* 24 (4): 445–55.

Jacobs, J. H. 1992. Treatment and stabilization of a hexavalent chromium containing waste material. *Environ. Progr*. 11:123–26.

Jones, L. 1989. *Interference Mechanisms in Waste Stabilization/Solidification Processes, Project Summary*. EPA 600/S2-89/067. Cincinnati: Risk Reduction Engineering Laboratory.

Kamon, M., T. Katsumi, and Y. Sano. 2000. MSW fly ash stabilized with coal ash for geotechnical application. *Journal of Hazardous Materials* 76 (2–3): 265–83.

Kyles, J. H., K. C. Malinowski, and T. F. Stanczyk. 1987. Solidification/stabilization of hazardous waste—a comparison of conventional and novel techniques, toxic and hazardous wastes. In *Proceedings of the 19th Mid-Atlantic Industrial Waste Conference, June 21–23*, ed. J.C. Evans.

Kyu-Hong, A., and N. Jagga. 1989. Stabilization of heavy metal bearing sludges using ce-mentitious binders. In *Physiochemical and Biochemical Detoxification of Hazardous Wastes*. Lancaster, PA: Technomic.

McDaniel, E. W., R. D. Spence, and O. K. Tallent. 1990. Research needs in cement-based waste forms. Paper presented at the XIVth International Symposium on the Scientific Ba-sis for Nuclear Waste Management, Meeting of the Materials Research Society, Boston.

Means, J. L., L. A. Smith, K. W. Nehring, S. E. Brauning, A. R. Gavaskar, B. M. Sass, C. W. Wiles, and C. I. Mashni. 1995. *The Application of Stabilization/Solidification to Waste Materials*. Boca Raton, FL: CRC Press.

Montgomery, D., J. Sollars, and R. Perry. 1988. Cement-based solidification for the safe disposal of heavy metal contaminated sewage sludge. *Waste Management & Research* 6 (3): 217–26.

Nagy, B., et al. 1991. Organic matter and containment of uranium and fissiogenic isotopes at the Oklo natural reactors. *Nature* 354 (6353): 472–75.

Qian, G., J. Tay, Y. Cao, and P. Chui. 2006. Utilization of MSWI fly ash for stabiliza-tion/solidification of industrial waste sludge. *Journal of Hazardous Materials* 129 (1–3): 274–81.

Qiao, X., C. Poon, and C. Cheeseman. 2006. Use of flue gas desulphurisation (FGD) waste and rejected fly ash in waste stabilization/solidification systems. *Waste Management* 26 (2): 141–49.

Smith, L. A., J. L. Means, A. Chen, B. Alleman, C. C. Chapman, J. S. Tixier, S. E. Braun-ing, A. R. Gavaskar, and M. D. Royer. 1995. *Remedial Options for Metals-Contami-nated Soils*. Boca Raton, FL: CRC Press.

Spencer, R. W., R. H. Reifsnyder, and J. C. Falcone. 1982. Applications of soluble silicates and derivative materials in the management of hazardous wastes. In *National Confer-ence on the Management of Uncontrolled Hazardous Waste Sites*, ed. R. Sims and K. Wagner. Silver Springs, MD: HMCRI.

Tittlebaum, M. E., R. D. Seals, F. K. Cartledge, and S. Engles. 1985. *Critical Reviews in Environmental Control* 15:179–211.

U.S. Environmental Protection Agency. 1988. *Technology Screening Guide for Treatment of CERCLA Soils and Sludges*. EPA/540-2-88/04. Washington, DC: Office of Emer-gency and Remedial Response.

———. 1989a. *HAZCON Solidification Process, Douglassville, PA: Applications Analysis Report*. EPA/540/A5-89/001. Office of Research and Development.

———. 1989b. *Stabilization/Solidification of CERCLA and RECRA Wastes: Physical Tests, Chemical Testing Procedures, Technology Screening, and Field Activities*. EPA/625/6-89/022. Center for Environmental Research Information.

———. 1990a. *Handbook on In Situ Treatment of Hazardous Waste-Contaminated Soils*. EPA/540/2-90/002. Cincinnati: Risk Reduction Engineering Laboratory.

———. 1990b. *Morphology and Microchemistry of Solidified/Stabilized Hazardous Waste Systems*. EPA/600/02-89/056, NTIS No. PB90-134156/AS. Cincinnati: Risk Reduction Engineering Laboratory.

———. 1992. *Silicate Technology Corporation's Solidification/Stabilization Technology for Organic and Inorganic Contaminants in Soils: Applications Analysis Report*. EPA/540/AR-92/010. Office of Research and Development.

———. 1995. *Contaminants and Remedial Options at Selected Metal-Contaminated Sites.* EPA/540/R-95/512.

———. 1997. *Recent Developments for In Situ Treatment of Metal Contaminated Soils.* EPA-542-R-97-004. Office of Solid Waste and Emergency Response.

———. 2005. *Region 9: Superfund. Selma Treating Co.* See: yosemite.epa.gov/r9/sfund/ r9sfdocw.nsf/4b229bb0820cb8b888256f0000092946/f67ccbca080c9ad288257007005e 9435!OpenDocument.

———. 2006. *Introduction to the HRS.* See: www.epa.gov/superfund/programs/npl_hrs/ hrsint.htm.

Vandercasteele, C., G. Wauters, V. Dutre, and D. Geysen. 2002. Solidification/stabilisation of arsenic bearing fly ash from the metallurgical industry. Immobilisation mechanism of arsenic. *Waste Management* 22 (2): 143–46.

Vespa, M., M. Harfouche, E. Wieland, A. Scheidegger, R. Dahn, and D. Grolimund. 2006. Speciation of heavy metals in cement-stabilized waste forms: A micro-spectroscopic study. *Journal of Geochemical Exploration* 88(1–3): 77–80.

Wareham, D., and J. Mackenchnie. 2006. Solidification of New Zealand harbor sediments using cementitious materials. *Journal of Materials in Civil Engineering* 18 (2): 311–15.

Yilmaz, O., K. Unlu, and E. Cokca. 2003. Solidification/stabilization of hazardous wastes containing metals and organic contaminants. *Journal of Environmental Engineering* 129 (4): 366–76.

CHAPTER 9

Soil Vapor Extraction

The grand show is eternal. . . . Vapor is ever rising. Eternal sunrise, eternal dawn and gloaming, on sea and continents and islands, each in its turn, as the round earth rolls.

—John Muir

For what is your life? It is even a vapor, that appeareth for a little time, and then vanisheth away.

—James 4:14

9.1. INTRODUCTION

Soil vapor extraction (SVE, in situ volatilization, soil venting) involves the removal of volatile organic compounds from a contaminated subsurface by drawing air currents through a network of wells. This treatment applies to the vadose zone, specifically the interstitial spaces, where hydrocarbon vapors can become entrained in the flow of extracted air and removed from pores. Within the saturated zone, a modification of the technology, known as *air sparging*, is used to treat groundwater.

In the vadose zone, SVE extracts the vapor-phase components of gasoline, aviation gasoline, jet fuel, and certain solvents (e.g., naphthol spirits). Therefore, low-molecular weight, volatile contaminants are extracted more readily than are heavier contaminants. Lighter contaminants include butane, pentane, and hexane; the aromatics benzene, toluene, xylenes, ethylbenzene; and other alkylbenzenes. Diesel fuel, crude petroleum, heating oils, used oil, and fuel oil are poorly suited to vapor extraction.

A schematic of an SVE system is shown in Figure 9.1. Unit operations include:

1. An air heater, established upgradient of the injection port, to warm influent air. Warmed air will raise subsurface temperatures and serves two purposes: (a) to increase the volatilization rate of hydrocarbons directly, and (b) to stimulate indigenous microbiological activity, which can further work to decompose organics. In cold climates air heaters additionally serve as freeze protection for the system (EPRI 1988).
2. A grid network of slotted pipe allows air to flow through the system.
3. Induced draft fans establish the airflow through the vadose zone.
4. A vapor treatment unit recovers and treats volatilized hydrocarbons; this process minimizes emissions to the atmosphere. A number of techniques are available to oxidize or otherwise remove hydrocarbon emissions from the recovered air, and will be discussed later. The effluent from this unit must comply with air pollution standards.
5. Air flow meters, flow control valves, and sampling ports are included in the design to support air flow and assess the efficiency of the system (EPRI 1988).

9.2. SITE CHARACTERIZATION

Site investigation should begin with geophysical methods (an electromagnetic survey or ground-penetrating radar) to determine the location of nonaqueous phase liquids, followed by soil-gas monitoring to locate zones of highest concentrations, and conclude with soil sampling to determine the full extent of contamination and establish cleanup levels. Bench- and field-scale studies may be needed to determine treatability of the hydrocarbons. Using a cone penetrometer equipped with sensing devices (U.S. EPA 1996) can reduce the cost of sampling the soil matrix.

When a shallow water table is present, it is important to investigate the potential for rising of the water table, which can result in the removal of less vapor and more water and affect the overall efficiency of vapor extraction.

It is important to identify geologic formations that may occur between the surface and the base of the contaminant plume. These strata and

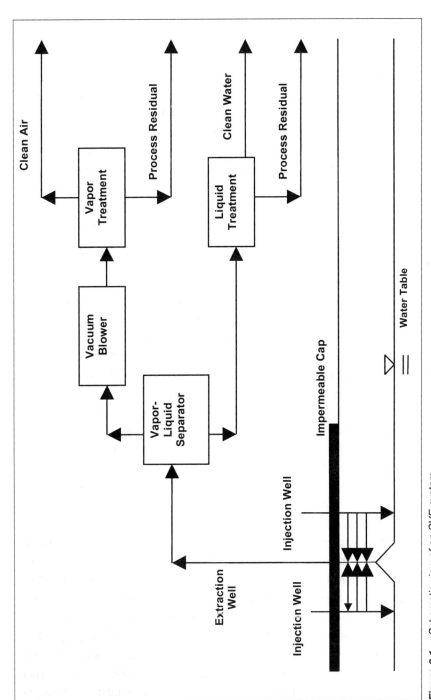

Figure 9.1. *Schematic view of an SVE system*
U.S. Environmental Protection Agency 1991.

components (i.e., clay lenses, large rocks and boulders, large cavities) can significantly impede vapor extraction. The most reliable way to identify these components is to evaluate descriptions of soil boring logs (either existing or those conducted as part of the evaluation). Blow counts recorded from drilling operations can indicate densely compacted layers that may impede vapor extraction. Geophysical surveys such as electrical resistivity can also be conducted to delineate the locations of geologic formations. After the contaminant plume and geologic formations have been identified they should be mapped. Such mapping can assist in determining the location of the SVE system (i.e., where the contaminants are of highest concentration) and if any geologic structures will interfere. To evaluate this relationship, both plan view and cross-sectional maps should be generated; a 3-D computer-generated map would prove illustrative.

Typically, soils and groundwater are analyzed for VOCs; base, neutral, and acid extractables (BNAs); and total petroleum hydrocarbons (TPH). For complex mixtures such as gasoline, diesel fuel, and solvent mixtures, it is more cost-effective to measure indicator compounds such as benzene, toluene, ethylbenzene, and xylenes (BTEX), or trichloroethylene rather than each compound present. The presence of vapor phase hydrocarbons in the subsurface can be determined by sampling, either by soil gas techniques or monitoring wells. As a general rule, benzene levels (as indicated by BTEX analysis) of approximately 200 ppm or greater indicate free gasoline. If the release has not aged significantly, free gasoline will contain a significant vapor phase. Biodegradation products should be considered as possible target compounds because they can be more toxic than the parent compound (e.g., TCE may be converted to vinyl chloride). Because SVE may not remove all contaminants, soils should be analyzed for less volatile or nonvolatile contaminants (BNAs and TPH) to assess the need to remediate by other methods (excavation, biotreatment, soil washing, etc.).

The presence of contaminants in groundwater indicates a potential for high mobility and increased health risks. The contaminants may be dissolved in the groundwater or may be moving downward as free organics through the saturated soil. LNAPL may be present as free product at the capillary fringe and DNAPL may occur as free product at the bottom of the aquifer. Determination of the extent of groundwater contamination aids in assessing the need for remediation by pump-and-treat technology (U.S. EPA 1991).

9.3. FIELD DESIGN CONSIDERATIONS

Successful volatilization requires the use of extraction wells and, frequently, injection wells (Fig. 9.2). The area from which a well extracts volatile compounds is termed the *zone of influence*. This area is rarely circular; however, such zones have often been assigned a *radius of influence*. The zone of influence of each well varies from 30 to 150 feet depending on soil type—for example, sandy versus clayey—(U.S. EPA 1991) and pumping rate.

Preheated air improves recovery, especially in colder weather, but this will increase the cost of operation. Steam injection has been used successfully in field tests but the hazard exists that the increased subsurface pressure would diffuse and spread the contamination.

Vapor extraction wells are similar to groundwater monitoring wells in terms of construction (Fig. 9.3). A typical well is constructed from slotted plastic pipe, usually PVC. Wells should be slotted only through the zone of contamination. The slot size and number of slots per inch should be chosen to maximize the open area of the pipe. The slotted area is often encased in a nylon sock in order to prevent entry of soil particles. A filter packing such as sand or gravel is placed between the borehole and pipe. The filter packing should be as coarse as possible. Any dust carried by the vapor flow can be removed by an aboveground filter. Bentonite pellets and a cement grout are placed above the filter packing. It is important that these be properly installed to prevent a vapor flow from "short-circuiting" (U.S. EPA 1991).

Well locations should be chosen to ensure adequate vapor flow through the contaminated zone while minimizing vapor flow through other zones. If one well is sufficient, it should be placed in the geometric center of the contaminated zone unless vapor flow channeling along a single direction is anticipated to occur. In that case the well should be placed in order to maximize airflow through the contaminated zone (Johnson et al. 1990). When multiple wells are used it is important to consider the effect that each well has on the vapor flow to all other wells. For example, if three extraction wells are required at a given site, a stagnant region may form in the middle of the wells. This problem can be alleviated by the insertion of either passive wells or forced injection wells within the zone of influence of the three wells (Fig. 9.2). A passive well is one that is open to the atmosphere. Groundwater monitoring wells can be used for such applications. Forced

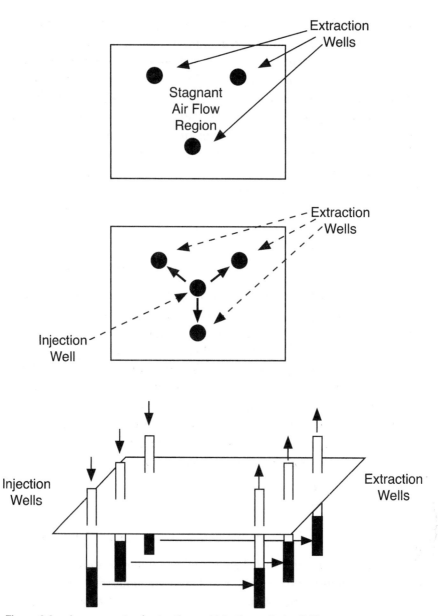

Figure 9.2. *Arrangements of extraction and injection wells for SVE*
Johnson et al. 1990.

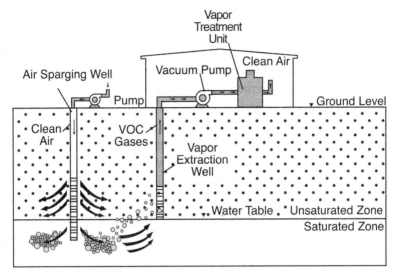

Figure 9.3. *Cross-section of an air sparging/vapor extraction well system*

injection wells are simply vapor wells into which air is pumped rather than removed. It is important that the locations of forced injection wells be carefully chosen so that vapors are captured by the extraction wells and not forced off-site (Johnson et al. 1990).

A variation to conventional SVE technology involves the use of horizontal extraction wells. This method has shown great promise in areas where drilling units may not be safe or feasible, for example in soils directly beneath an active facility. A drill bit is directed at a selected angle into the subsurface, eventually leveling and penetrating the contamination zone. The drill will subsequently be directed to return to the surface on the other side of the structure. Screened PVC tubing is then drawn through the drill holes (Fig. 9.4) (Conger and Trichel 1994). For shallow contamination zones (< 4 m below ground surface) vapor extraction trenches combined with surface seals may be more effective than vertical or horizontal wells. Trenches are usually limited to shallow soil zones.

Surface seals are sometimes used to control the vapor-flow paths. For a shallow treatment zone (< 5 m) the surface seal will have a significant effect on the vapor-flow paths (Fig. 9.5). For wells screened below 8 m, the influence of surface seals becomes less significant (Johnson et al. 1990). Depending on the characteristics of the site, different materials can be used to seal the surface. A geomembrane liner can be rolled over the site

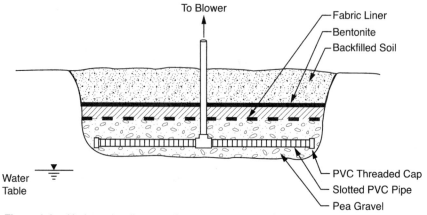

Figure 9.4. *Horizontal well system for the installation of SVE wells*
U.S. Environmental Protection Agency.

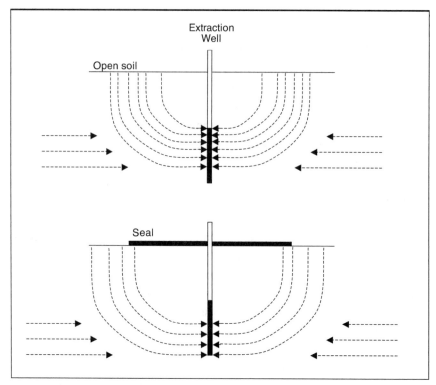

Figure 9.5. *A surface seal in an SVE system, promoting greater lateral flow of soil vapors*
Johnson et al. 1990.

Figure 9.6.   *Soil vapor extraction and sparge wells on Old Airport Tarmac. (Reproduced with kind permission of Global Technologies, a Division of Angvil Environmental Systems, Inc.*

and easily removed when the remediation program is complete. Geomembranes are readily available in a variety of materials, of which high-density polyethylene (HDPE) is the most common. The life of geomembranes can be shortened if exposed to sunlight. Alternatives to a synthetic membrane are clay or bentonite, which can be applied in any thickness. Clay liners are not easily removed, and both clay and geomembranes are susceptible to damage from personnel and equipment. A third alternative — the most common at commercial or industrial sites — is the use of a concrete or asphalt cap (Fig. 9.6). This alternative works well at sites that have been paved or will be paved (for example, an industrial park or gasoline station) (U.S. EPA 1996).

In most areas an air permit or exemption must be obtained, and exhaust air must be treated prior to release to the atmosphere. Common techniques for treating hydrocarbon-contaminated air include:

Condensation

Condensation can separate effluent VOCs from the carrier air and is usually accomplished by refrigeration. The efficiency of this technique is determined by the effect of temperature on the vapor pressure of the VOCs present. Condensation is most efficient for high-vapor concentrations. The technology becomes less efficient as the cleanup progresses and vapor concentrations decrease. The method may be ineffective during the last stages of the cleanup. Because vapors are not completely condensed, additional treatment steps may be required (U.S. EPA 1991).

Vapor Combustion Units

Vapors are incinerated and destruction efficiencies are typically $> 95\%$. A supplemental fuel such as natural gas is added before combustion, unless extraction well vapor concentrations are a few percent by volume. This process becomes less economical as vapor concentrations decrease below 10,000 ppm_v. Extraction rates of up to 50 lb of hydrocarbons per hour can be achieved (Cole 1994). In a similar mode, extracted vapors can be burned as a fuel supplement in an internal combustion engine. In this configuration the engine itself can be used to power the pump system, thereby providing for a free energy source for the system.

Catalytic Oxidation Units

Vapor streams are heated and then passed over a catalyst bed. Catalyzed metal powders, similar to those of automotive catalytic converter devices, are commonly employed. These devices remove hydrocarbons by oxidation to CO_2 and H_2O. Destruction efficiencies are typically $> 95\%$. These units are used for vapor concentrations $< 8,000$ ppm_v (Johnson et al. 1990). Catalytic systems are expensive to operate, due mostly to high maintenance costs.

Carbon Beds

Carbon can treat almost any vapor streams, but is economical only for very low emission rates (< 100 g/d). Granulated activated charcoal filters will clean exhaust air by chemical and physical adsorption of hydrocarbon vapors. Such filters are too expensive to serve as the primary hydrocarbon removal method. Weekly maintenance is required to replace saturated filters. Granulated activated charcoal filters require approximately 100 lb carbon for each 15 lb of hydrocarbons filtered (Cole 1994).

Chemical Oxidation

The collected vapors can be exposed to low concentrations of strong oxidants. Common oxidants include ozone, hydrogen peroxide, and ultraviolet (UV) radiation.

Biofilters

A filter material such as sphagnum moss is packed into a column and the packing material is inoculated with bacterial cultures and inorganic nutrients. Contaminated vapors are passed through the column and are adsorbed onto the high surface area of the filter material and/or degraded by bacterial action (Cole 1994; Diks and Ottengrat 1991).

Diffuser Stacks

These do not treat vapors per se, but are a low-cost solution for areas in which they are permitted. Stacks must be carefully designed to minimize health risks and maximize safety.

9.4. TECHNICAL CONSIDERATIONS

Removal of hydrocarbons from contaminated soil depends on a number of site-specific factors; that is, the controlling mechanisms for vapor and chemical diffusion are unique to the site. The primary factors include contaminant properties, site properties, and site-management practices (EPRI 1988; Johnson et al. 1990; Noonan and Curtis 1990; Jury 1986).

9.4.1. Contaminant-Specific

The chemical properties of the contaminants directly affect the manner in which they interact with the soil matrix. As discussed in chapter 3, petroleum products are complex mixtures of hundreds of hydrocarbon compounds. Different components possess a range of chemical and physical properties. As a result, some products will be more amenable than others to removal by SVE. Properties such as vapor pressure, solubility, concentration, viscosity, and octanol-water partitioning coefficient affect the susceptibility of chemicals to SVE. For example, compounds having high vapor pressure and low solubility in water are more efficiently removed from soil. The Henry's law constant, a measure of the equilibrium distribution between air and dilute solutions, is often used as an indicator of volatilization and thus the ease of removal. The more volatile compounds such as benzene will have a constant of approximately 0.25 or higher. Less volatile compounds such as naphthalene will have a constant closer to 0.02. Because of this property and the higher content of volatile organic compounds in gasoline, proportionally more gasoline will be removed by in situ volatilization than kerosene or heavy heating oils. Experimental results indicate that gasoline can be 100% removed within about 100 days from porous soil; however, fuel oil contaminants have been shown to be at high levels even after 120 days (EPRI 1988).

Petroleum hydrocarbons chemically weather with time, with a resulting partitioning into a number of phases. The most common phases are free product (NAPL), dissolved in water, sorbed to soil particles, and vapor phase (see chapter 5). The equilibrium distribution of phases in a soil depends in part on the extent to which the contaminants have aged. For example, fresh leaks in which gasoline is still largely in the bulk phase are more readily volatilized than older, aged releases containing higher percentages of heavier hydrocarbons. The extent to which the hydrocarbons are adsorbed onto soil particles will also play a role. Hydrocarbons are most strongly attracted to organic matter and clays and less strongly attracted to sands and gravels. Finally, the extent to which the liquid hydrocarbon phase has been smeared by fluctuating groundwater tables will affect partitioning in the subsurface (Cole 1994).

The relative biodegradability of the hydrocarbon mixture will also affect phase partitioning and therefore amenability to SVE. Some hydrocarbons that are rather biodegradable, for example MTBE, are transformed and will tend to partition into a number of phases including the vapor phase rather rapidly, thus becoming more available for volatilization.

9.4.2. Site-Specific

SVE is limited to the vadose zone. Soil water content influences the rate of volatilization by affecting the rates at which chemicals can diffuse through the vadose zone. Volatilization rates are generally greater from dry soil than wet soil. An increase in soil water content will decrease the rate at which volatile compounds are transported to the surface via vapor diffusion. The SVE method works slowly, or not at all, if any of the following conditions are present: (1) the contamination is mainly in groundwater; (2) groundwater is near the surface; or (3) groundwater levels fluctuate over short time periods, as for example during seasonal fluctuations (Turkall et al. 1992; Friesen 1990).

The rate at which hydrocarbon compounds volatilize and are transported to the surface is a function of both the travel distance and cross-sectional area available for flow. Porosity and permeability are important to the performance of the SVE system. Diffusion distance increases and cross-sectional flow area decreases with decreasing porosity. The coefficient of permeability is a function of porosity and ranges from a permeable 10^2 cm/sec (gravel) to 10^{-7} cm/sec (impermeable, homogeneous clay) (EPRI 1988).

High concentrations of clay will lower permeability significantly and therefore inhibit volatilization. In porous soil, extraction of volatiles can be rapid; in heavy clays the method has little use. The concentration of sorptive surfaces in the mineral and organic fractions of soils will affect volatilization. An increase in adsorption sites will result in an increase in the immobilization of hydrocarbons in soil. When hydrocarbons are sorbed onto clay surfaces or soil organic matter they are not available for volatilization until they can be desorbed (EPRI 1988).

Volatilization of hydrocarbon compounds will increase with increasing temperature. Additionally, increasing wind speed will decrease the boundary layer of relatively stagnant air at the ground/air interface. Depending on hydrocarbon characteristics, this will assist volatilization. Water evaporation at the soil surface strongly affects the upward flow of water through the unsaturated zone. Hydrocarbon compounds that are dissolved in water can thus be transported to the soil surface, enhancing volatilization by evaporation. Precipitation provides water for infiltration into the vadose zone. Hydrocarbon compounds that are more susceptible to leaching and less prone to soil adsorption will be affected (EPRI 1988).

9.4.3. Management-Specific

The management factors that alter soil conditions may influence volatilization. Soil management techniques that decrease leaching, increase

soil surface contaminant concentrations, or maximize soil aeration will enhance volatilization. Pumping rate, well positions, and well diameters all
influence the degree of vapor recovery from a site.

9.5. CASE HISTORY

The Fairchild Superfund site, located in southern San Jose, California, is a
former semiconductor manufacturing facility that operated from 1977 until 1983. In 1981, an underground organic solvent storage tank had failed,
and a mixture of solvents contaminated local soil and groundwater. An estimated 60,000 gal of solvents were released. Solvents detected in local
soils included trichloroethane (TCA), dichloroethene (DCE), isopropyl
alcohol (IPA), xylenes, acetone, freon-113, and PCE. Trichloroethane was
measured at concentrations up to 3,530 mg/kg and xylenes up to 941
mg/kg. The maximum concentration of total solvents in soil (including
TCA, 1,1-DCE, IPA, xylenes, acetone, Freon-113, and PCE) was 4,500
mg/kg (U.S. EPA 1995).

The site is located in an area that ranges from flat to gently sloping and
is underlain by several hundred feet of unconsolidated alluvial deposits
over bedrock. The alluvium formation consists of layers of water-bearing
sand and gravel alternating with more dense silt and silty clay layers.
Four aquifer systems have been identified in the alluvium; the shallow-
est at a depth ranging from 10 to 40 ft below ground surface (BGS), and
the next from 50 to 70 ft BGS. The alternating sand and gravel layers
range in thickness from several feet to 140 ft in thickness (U.S. EPA
1995; Canonie 1993).

Interim remedial cleanup activities began at the site in 1982. The company removed the damaged UST and excavated and disposed 3,400 yd^3 of
soil in a permitted hazardous waste facility. A groundwater extraction and
treatment system was installed to prevent further migration of contaminants and to extract contaminated groundwater from recovery wells. A
bentonite slurry wall was constructed around the site perimeter to contain
contaminated groundwater on-site within the shallower aquifers (U.S.
EPA 1992; 1989).

Soil vapor extraction was selected as the remedial alternative for contaminated soil at the Fairchild Superfund site based on treatability study
results and because it conserves more water than a pump-and-treat system
(i.e., there is less groundwater extraction) (U.S. EPA 1995; 1989).

The California Regional Quality Control Board established cleanup goals for the SVE remedial action for both individual vapor extraction wells and the overall SVE system. The board required air extraction from individual wells until the contaminant removal rate decreased to 10% or less of the initial removal rate, the contaminant removal rate declined at less than 1% per day for 10 consecutive days, or SVE system operation achieved a total contaminant removal rate of less than 10 lb/day (Canonie 1993).

The SVE system installed at the Fairchild site contained 39 extraction wells. The system included air inlet wells to provide additional air into the zone of contamination. The slurry wall and groundwater extraction system were used to control groundwater flow and to prevent contaminant migration. Groundwater was extracted from recovery wells within the slurry wall enclosures to lower the water elevation inside the wall. These activities also contained soil vapors for the SVE system.

The extraction wells were connected to a vapor extraction and treatment system consisting of vacuum pumps, a dehumidifier, and granular activated carbon (GAC) tanks. Two vacuum pumps with a capacity of approximately 4,500 cu ft per minute (cfm) at 20 in. Hg were used to remove soil vapors. Five GAC adsorption units were used to capture the organic compounds extracted in the soil vapors. Soil vapors were first directed to two 3,000-lb GAC beds operating in parallel followed by a second set of GAC beds in parallel, and then to a final, single 3,000-lb GAC bed (Canonie 1993; 1989).

Each extraction well was equipped with a submersible pump to remove groundwater that collected in the well. The pumps in the vapor extraction wells were connected by underground piping to a groundwater treatment system that consisted of air stripping and discharge to surface water.

The SVE system was designed to operate continuously five days a week. At any one time, the system operated a maximum of 25 of the 39 extraction wells (U.S. EPA 1995; Canonie 1993).

The SVE system removed approximately 16,000 lb of solvents from the soil during 16 months of operation (427 days totaling 9,800 hours of operation). The extraction rate was maximized at 130 lb/d early in the program (Fig. 9.7). The rate of contaminant extraction increased rapidly during the initial stages of system operation (two months) and then decreased to a more modest rate. The cleanup goal, that is, less than 10 lb/d contaminant removal rate, was achieved after eight months. The system

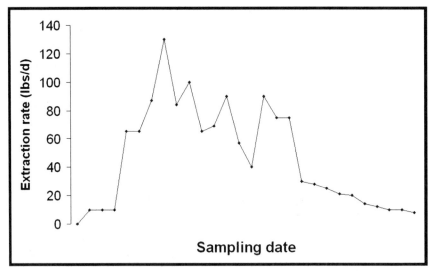

Figure 9.7. *Contaminant removal rate from the Fairchild Superfund site*
U.S. Environmental Protection Agency 1995.

was operated for eight months after the 10 lb/d goal was achieved to remove additional contaminants (i.e., to the point where the soil was believed to no longer leach contaminants to the groundwater). Less than
4 lb/d was extracted after 16 months. Cumulative mass of contaminants
removed over time is shown in Figure 9.8. A test designed to evaluate po-

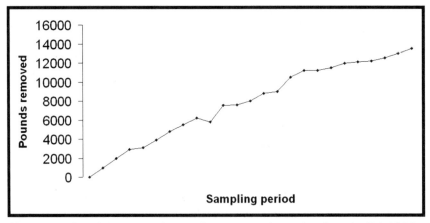

Figure 9.8. *Cumulative mass of contaminants removed over time from the Fairchild Superfund site*
U.S. Environmental Protection Agency 1995.

Table 9.1.   Analysis of soil contaminant concentrations at two times during the SVE process

Boring	TCA t_1	TCA t_2	DCE t_1	DCE t_2	Xylenes t_1	Xylenes t_2	Acetone t_1	Acetone t_2	IPA t_1	IPA t_2
					mg/kg					
1	3,530	416	16.6	2.2	941	462	18	281	nd	134
2	40.6	79	3.4	2.5	19.2	156	nd	1.5	nd	0.9
3	266	37.3	12.5	1.5	189	85.6	7.7	3.5	0.02	1.8
4	12.2	7.8	1.6	0.3	4.8	5.5	7.6	1.9	nd	nd
5	6.4	5.5	0.5	1.5	nd	1.2	nd	2.9	nd	0.4
6	1.1	0.1	.05	.01	nd	nd	nd	nd	nd	nd

t_1 = before remediaton
t_2 = after 18 months
nd = not detected

Source: U.S. Environmental Protection Agency 1995.

tential rebound in extraction wells revealed that shutting off extraction wells for two to six weeks did not cause soil vapor concentrations to increase (U.S. EPA 1995).

The concentration of many of the contaminants in soil borings had decreased after seven months of operation (Table 9.1). However, concentrations of several contaminants increased during this period, including acetone, TCA, xylenes, IPA, and TCE. The variation in contaminant concentrations in the soil may be attributed to variation in contamination across the areas where the soil borings were collected (U.S. EPA 1995).

Capital costs for the SVE program were $2,100,000 (not including costs for construction of the slurry wall or for aquifer pumping), and actual operation and maintenance costs totaled $1,800,000 for 16 months of operation. This corresponds to $240 per pound of contaminants removed and $93 per cu yd of soil treated. The actual costs for this project were 7% less than the projected costs because the time required for remediation was less than originally estimated (U.S. EPA 1995).

QUESTIONS

1. How does soil temperature influence success in SVE?
2. Soil pH will affect SVE success. True or false? Explain.

3. Explain the effect of soil texture on establishing the radius of influence.
4. Explain why a cap is useful to control flow of vapors during SVE.
5. How does air sparging differ from soil vapor extraction?
6. Explain how hydrocarbon vapors can be treated once they are extracted from the subsurface.

REFERENCES

Canonie Environmental. 1989. *Interim Design Report, In-Situ Soil Aeration System. Project 82-012.* March.

———. 1993. *Five-Year Status Report and Effectiveness Evaluation.* December.

Cole, G. M. 1994. *Assessment and Remediation of Petroleum Contaminated Sites.* Boca Raton, FL: CRC Press.

Conger, R. M., and K. Trichel. 1994. Drilling on your side. Soils. As cited in *Underground Tank Technology Update. University of Wisconsin-Madison, College of Engineering* 8:5–7. Madison, WI.

Diks, A., and R. Ottengrat. 1991. In *Situ and On-Site Bioreclamation, The Second International Symposium, April 5–8, 1993, San Diego.*

Electric Power Research Institute. 1988. *Remedial Technologies for Leaking Underground Storage Tanks.* Chelsea, MI: Lewis.

Friesen, K. A. 1990. Chemical changes of biodegraded gasoline in a laboratory simulation of the vadose zone. MS thesis, Colorado School of Mines.

Johnson, P. C., C. C. Stanley, M. W. Kemblowski, D. L. Byers, and J. D. Colthart. 1990. A practical approach to the design, operation, and monitoring of in situ soil-venting systems. *Ground Water Monitoring Review* 10 (2): 159–78.

Jury, W. A. 1986. *Volatilization from Soil,* and S. C. Hern and S. M. Melancon, *Guidelines for Field Testing Soil Fate and Transport Models. Final Report, Appendix B.* EPA 600/4-86-020.

Noonan D. C., and T. J. Curtis. 1990. *Groundwater Remediation and Petroleum, A Guide for Underground Storage Tanks.* Chelsea, MI: Lewis.

Turkall, R. M., G. A. Skowronski, and M. S. Abdel-Rahman. 1992. The effect of soil type of absorption of toluene and its bioavailability. In *Petroleum Contaminated Soils,* vol. 3, ed. P. T. Kostecki and E. J. Calabrese. Chelsea, MI: Lewis.

U.S. Environmental Protection Agency. 1989. *Superfund Record of Decision. Fairchild Semiconductor, S. San Jose, California, March.*

———. 1991. *Guide for Conducting Treatability Studies under CERCLA: Soil Vapor Extraction. Interim Guidance.* EPA/540/2-91-019A. Washington, DC: Office of Emergency and Remedial Response.

———. 1992. *Superfund Interim Site Close Out Report, Fairchild—San Jose, California. U.S. EPA Region IX, March 25.*

————. 1995. *Soil Vapor Extraction at the Fairchild Semiconductor Corporation Superfund Site, San Jose, California. Cost and Performance Report*. Washington, DC: Office of Solid Waste and Emergency Response, Technology Innovation Office.

————. 1996. *Engineering Forum Issue Paper: Soil Vapor Extraction Implementation Experiences*. Publication 9200.5-223FS EPA 540/F-95/030 PB95-963315. Washington, DC: Office of Solid Waste and Emergency Response.

————. 2004. How to Evaluate Alternative Cleanup Technologies for Underground Storage Tank Sites: A Guide for Corrective Action Plan Reviewers. (EPA 510-B-94-003; EPA 510-B-95-007; and EPA 510-R-04-002). See: http://www.epa.gov/OUST/pubs/tums.htm

CHAPTER 10

Permeable Reactive Barriers

The meeting of two personalities is like the contact of two chemical substances; if there is any reaction, both are transformed.

—C.G. Jung

10.1. INTRODUCTION

Pump-and-treat systems have found widespread application at affected sites and have become a standard technology for cleanup of contaminated groundwater (see chapter 6). Several drawbacks are noteworthy to this approach, however. A pump-and-treat system requires an external energy source that becomes costly when operated over long periods. Also, because much of the water initially extracted is uncontaminated, pump-and-treat may waste groundwater resources.

Even when properly operated, pump-and-treat systems have inherent limitations (Keely 1989): They may not work well with complex geologic materials or heterogeneous aquifers; they often stop reducing contamination long before reaching intended cleanup levels; and in some situations they can make sites more difficult to remediate by smearing contamination across the subsurface. To address such concerns, the installation of permeable reactive barriers (PRBs) downgradient of a contaminant plume may permit low cost, long-term treatment (Fig 10.1). These barriers allow the passage of groundwater while promoting the degradation or removal of contaminants by specific chemical and physical mechanisms, most commonly reduction, precipitation, and sorption. PRBs have been used to successfully treat or remove metallic, radioactive, nonmetallic (e.g., nitrates), and hydrocarbon contaminants from groundwater.

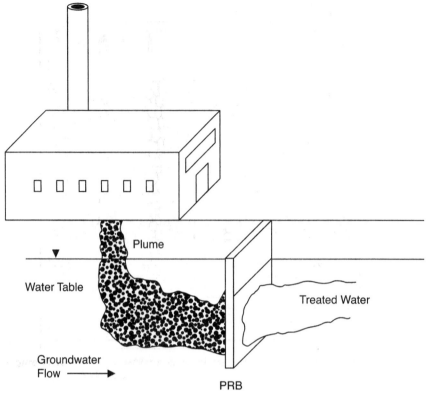

Figure 10.1.   *PRB Technology*

10.2. INSTALLATION AND CONFIGURATION OF PRBs

The PRB is installed across the flow path of a contaminant plume (Fig. 10.2). The reactive media is installed in order to be in intimate contact with the surrounding aquifer material. The reactive treatment zone either decomposes the contaminant or restricts its movement via employing reactants and agents including zero-valent iron (ZVI) or other reduced metals, zeolites, humic materials, chelating agents, sorbents, active microbial cells, and others. Several variations of PRB configurations, including a funnel-and-gate system (Fig. 10.2), are available and combine a permeable gate and impermeable funnel sections to capture wide contaminant plumes. The reactive cell (gate) portion is supplied with the necessary treatment media.

Continuous reactive barriers are useful when the plume is not wide and/or contaminant concentrations are low. Vertical sections of pea gravel can be installed upgradient of the reactive zone to promote uniform flow

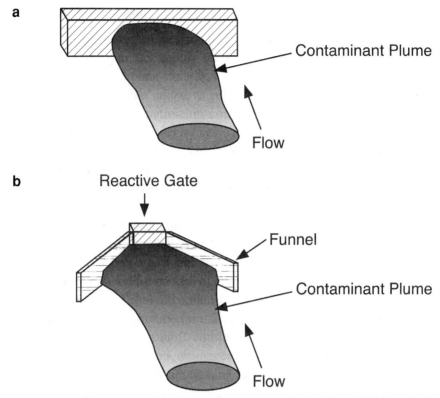

Figure 10.2. *Two PRB configurations: (a) continuous reactive barrier; and (b) funnel-and-gate system*

of the affected groundwater through the reactive zone. Some PRBs are installed as permanent or long-term units across the flow path of the contaminant plume. Some PRBs are installed as in situ reactors that are readily accessible for simple removal and replacement of reactive media. The wall may be used to provide permanent containment for relatively nonhazardous residues or to decrease the volume of the more toxic contaminants for subsequent treatment.

Design of the PRB system begins with collecting contaminated groundwater from the site and performing a bench-scale treatability study to determine flow rates, reaction intermediates, and products. The required residence time of the contaminants and reactive cell dimensions are determined using the treatability results, along with the aquifer properties (flow velocities, etc.) and computer modeling. Various construction methods can be used to install PRBs, such as trenching, caisson deployment,

Figure 10.3.   *Placement of reactive material into a gate structure of a bone-char phosphate barrier at Fry Canyon, Utah (USGS)*

clamshell digging, soil mixing, vertical hydraulic fracturing, or high-pressure jetting (U.S. EPA 1998) (Fig. 10.3).

A thorough site characterization is important to ensure proper design and installation of a reactive barrier. Characterization should include an evaluation of the surface features, structures, and buried utilities to ascertain whether the site is suitable for PRB installation. If the site is amenable, the characterization will help determine what types of PRB emplacement technologies are feasible.

The aerial and vertical extent of the plume, contaminant chemistry and concentrations, and flow direction and velocity of groundwater must be accurately determined to achieve the required treatment levels. Detailed information on subsurface permeability, fracturing, and aqueous geochemistry is needed for the PRB design. The plume must not pass over, under, or around the PRB, and the reactive zone must adequately treat the contaminant without rapidly clogging with precipitates or becoming passivated.

The key components of site characterization that should be evaluated before implementing a PRB include (U.S. EPA 1998):

- site hydrogeology
- site geochemistry
- contaminant types and concentrations
- site microbiological properties

10.3. TREATMENT MECHANISMS WITHIN PRBs FOR SPECIFIC CONTAMINANTS

Many reactive media or their combinations have been employed for use in PRBs, and numerous media are currently under investigation for a variety of contaminants. Iron metal, designated as Fe^o or zero-valent iron (ZVI), is the most common reactive media in the majority of field-scale and commercial PRB projects. The ZVI creates a low oxidation potential in groundwater, resulting in the precipitation of low-solubility minerals that remove some redox-sensitive contaminants (Morrison et al. 2001). Scrap iron is an inexpensive media that can be readily obtained in a granular form in the large quantities needed. It has the ability to reductively dehalogenate hydrocarbon compounds and reduce oxidized inorganic species (U.S. EPA 1998). Contaminants that have been successfully treated by ZVI and other media are listed in Table 10.1.

A range of biological and chemical mechanisms have been employed in PRBs to remove hydrocarbon and inorganic contaminants from groundwater, including abiotic reduction, chemical precipitation, sorption, ion exchange, and biotic reduction (Morrison et al. 2001). Their mechanisms of action on various groundwater contaminants are described below.

10.4. CONTAMINANTS SUITABLE TO PRB TREATMENT

10.4.1 Reductive Treatment of Halogenated Organic Compounds

A substantial body of research has been conducted on the degradation of chlorinated solvents, for example chloroform (CCl_4), TCE, and PCE, by reaction on the surface of iron (Fe^o) particles. The suggested degradation mechanism is abiotic reductive dehalogenation with a consequent oxidation of the Fe^o by the chlorinated hydrocarbon.

An interaction of anodic and cathodic reactions occurring at the Fe^o particle surface (Eqs. 10.1 and 10.2, respectively) results in the net reductive reaction (Eq. 10.3). Dechlorinated hydrocarbon products are generated as a result of the combined reactions (U.S. EPA 1998):

Anode $$Fe^o \rightarrow Fe^{2+} + 2e^- \tag{10.1}$$

Cathode $$RCl + 2e^- + H^+ \rightarrow RH + Cl^- \tag{10.2}$$

Net $$Fe^o + RCl + H^+ \rightarrow Fe^{2+} + RH + Cl^- \tag{10.3}$$

Table 10.1.   Contaminants that can be treated by PRBs

Organic Compounds		Inorganic Compounds	
Methanes	Tetrachloromethane	Trace metals	Antimony
	Tricholormethane		Chromium
	Dichloromethane		Nickel
			Lead
			Uranium
			Technetium
			Iron
			Manganese
			Selenium
			Copper
			Cobalt
			Cadmium
			Zinc
Ethanes	Hexachloroethane	Anion contaminants	Sulphate
	1,1,1-trichlorotethane		Nitrate
	1,1,2,-tricholormethane		Phosphate
	1,1-dichloroethane		Arsenic
Ethenes	Tetrachloroethane		
	Trichloroethene		
	cis-1,2-dichloroethene		
	trans-1,2-dichloroethene		
	1,1-dichloroethene		
	Vinyl chloride		
Propanes	1,2,3-trichloropropane		
	1,2-dichloropropane		
Aromatics	Benzene		
	Toluene		
	Ethylbenzene		
Other	Hexachlorobutadiene		
	1,2-dibromoethane		
	Freon 113		
	N-nitrosodimethylamine		

Source: U.S. Environmental Protection Agency 1998.

Sequential hydrogenolysis is considered the primary degradative pathway during the reductive dechlorination of chlorinated methanes (e.g., CCl_4). The majority of the carbon tetrachloride is converted to chloroform, which is eventually converted to methylene chloride (CH_2Cl_2) (Eq. 10.4) (U.S. EPA 1998; Roberts et al. 1996). No further reaction of methylene chloride has been detected in an unamended ZVI system (U.S. EPA 1998).

$$CCl_4 \rightarrow CHCl_3 + Cl^- \rightarrow CH_2Cl_2 + 2Cl^- \qquad (10.4)$$

Accurate mass balances have been determined for the transformation of several chlorinated ethenes (Orth and Gillham 1996). Using Fe^o, TCE is

Equation 10.5

reduced primarily to ethene and ethane via two interconnected degradation pathways, sequential hydrogenolysis, and reductive β-elimination (eq. 10.5) (U.S. EPA 1998; Roberts et al. 1996). The intermediate products, *cis*-dichloroethene (cDCE) and vinyl chloride, are produced in the sequential hydrogenolysis pathway and are slower to degrade than is TCE. In contrast, the chloroacetylene intermediate produced via the β-elimination pathway is a short-lived intermediate and is rapidly reduced to ethene. The β-elimination pathway accounts for the rapid conversion of TCE to ethene and ethane, with relatively minor intermediate product formation (U.S. EPA 1998).

Zero-valent iron is a mild reductant, and dehalogenation rates vary for different chlorinated solvents. Published data for the degradation rate of halogenated hydrocarbons indicate that the primary variable responsible affecting degradation rate is the surface area of iron per unit volume of pore water (U.S. EPA 1998; Johnson et al. 1996; Sivavec et al. 1995; Matheson and Tratnyek 1993).

10.4.1.1. Other Considerations with Reductive Dechlorination in PRBs

Incomplete dechlorination of a highly chlorinated hydrocarbon, for example tetrachloroethene, could result in the production of undesirable intermediates such as vinyl chloride, which is more hazardous and more persistent than the parent compound. Even very low concentrations of undesirable intermediates in the PRB effluent must be prevented. Thorough knowledge of contaminant types as well as subsurface conditions must therefore be determined a priori. Bench-scale testing of the PRB reactive material with the contaminants is essential prior to field application.

Typically, PRBs are designed to provide adequate residence time in the treatment zone for the degradation of the parent hydrocarbon compound and all toxic intermediate products generated. At sites where groundwater is contaminated with a mixture of chlorinated hydrocarbons, the PRB design is usually determined by the least reactive constituent. Highly halogenated hydrocarbons tend to be reduced more rapidly than the less halogenated congeners; likewise, dechlorination is more rapid on saturated carbons (for example, CCl_4) than on unsaturated carbons (for example, TCE or vinyl chloride) (U.S. EPA 1998).

Under aerobic conditions, dissolved oxygen is an effective terminal electron acceptor. Chlorinated hydrocarbons such as PCE and CCl_4, however, have oxidizing potentials very similar to that of oxygen (O_2). Should the affected groundwater have a relatively high Eh, oxygen could potentially compete with the chlorinated hydrocarbons as the oxidant (U.S. EPA 1998; Archer and Harter 1978; see Eq. 10.6).

$$2Fe^o + O_2 + 2H_2O \rightarrow 2Fe^{2+} + 4OH^- \qquad (10.6)$$

10.4.2. Reductive Treatment of Inorganic Anions

Anions and oxyanions of chromium (Cr), arsenic, selenium, technetium, and antimony are significant groundwater contaminants. Because of their negative charge, such anionic species are typically repulsed by negatively charged colloidal surfaces that usually predominate in soil and aquifers under neutral pH conditions (see chapter 4). The resulting high solubility of such anions results in a potential hazard to water supplies. PRB technology is often appropriate for the treatment and removal of these contaminants.

10.4.2.2. Chromate

As discussed in chapter 2, chromium typically occurs in soil, water, and sediments in two oxidation states, Cr(III) and Cr(VI). Trivalent Cr is relatively nontoxic and also serves as a micronutrient. It forms hydroxide precipitates under certain conditions and is also readily adsorbed by some minerals. Hexavalent Cr, on the other hand, is quite toxic and forms relatively soluble oxyanions, resulting in its persistence in contaminated aquifers (U.S. EPA 1998; Palmer and Puls 1994; Marsh et al. 2000).

Under typical groundwater pH and Eh conditions, Cr(VI) usually speciates as chromate, CrO_4^{2-}. Reduction of chromate to trivalent Cr species, followed by precipitation of insoluble Cr(III) hydroxide precipitates, has been studied extensively in PRBs. Several solid phases containing reduced iron, including Fe^o, promote the reduction and precipitation of Cr(VI) (U.S. EPA 1998; Gould 1982; Bowers et al. 1986; Bostick et al. 1999; Blowes and Ptacek 1992; Powell et al. 1994; Powell et al. 1995b). Iron-bearing oxyhydroxides (Eary and Rai 1989) and iron-bearing aluminosilicate minerals (Eary and Rai 1989; Kent et al. 1994) have also been successful in Cr(VI) reduction.

Rates of Cr(VI) reduction are dependent on the nature of the Fe^o (i.e., how it was manufactured, levels of impurities) and whether certain aluminosilicate-containing aquifer materials are present and mixed with the iron (Powell et al. 1995b; Powell et al. 1995a; Powell and Puls 1997). The overall reactions for Cr(VI) reduction by Fe^o and the subsequent precipitation of Cr(III) and Fe(III) oxyhydroxides are shown in Equations 10.7 and 10.8.

$$CrO_4^{2-} + Fe^o + 8H^+ \rightarrow Fe^{3+} + Cr^{3+} + 4H_2O \tag{10.7}$$

$$(1-x)Fe^{3+} + (x)Cr^{3+} + 2H_2O \rightarrow Fe_{(1-x)}Cr_xOOH(s) + 3H^+ \tag{10.8}$$

Cr(III) and Fe(III) hydroxide phases have been found to precipitate on the surface of reacted Fe, indicating coprecipitation and the likelihood of the formation of a solid phase having the general formula $(Cr_x, Fe_{1-x})(OH)_3$ (Powell et al. 1994; Powell et al. 1995b). Other studies indicate that the dominant mineral product generated is a mixed Fe-Cr oxyhydroxide phase with the mineral structure of goethite (FeOOH) as shown in equation 10.8 (U.S. EPA 1998).

Reduction and precipitation of soluble metals within a plume can also be accomplished by adding dissolved dithionite, $S_2O_4^{2-}$, into groundwater. The dithionite ion reduces solid-phase ferric iron (Eq. 10.9) (Morrison et al. 2002; Ammonette et al. 1994; Scott et al. 1998). Dithionite oxidizes to sulfite, SO_3^{2-}, as Fe(III) is reduced to Fe(II). As was the case with Fe°, ferrous iron Fe(II) will reduce Cr(VI) to Cr(III), which precipitates as a solid solution of Cr(III) and Fe(III) hydroxide (Eq. 10.10) (Morrison et al. 2002).

$$S_2O_4^{2-} + 2Fe^{3+}_{(s)} + 2H_2O \rightarrow 2SO_3^{2-} + 2Fe^{2+}_{(s)} + 4H^+ \qquad (10.9)$$

$$CrO_4^{2-} + 3Fe^{2+}_{(s)} + 5H^+ \rightarrow Cr(OH)_{3(s)} + 3Fe^{3+}_{(s)} + H_2O \qquad (10.10)$$

10.4.2.4. Arsenate

Arsenic (As) commonly occurs as a dissolved species in two oxidation states, As(V) and As(III), and less commonly in other oxidation states including As(0), As(-I), and As(-II) (see chapter 2). The As(V) oxidation state forms the mineral H_3AsO_4 and its dissociation products. The As(III) oxidation state forms H_3AsO_3. Arsenic reduction to the As° species followed by precipitation or incorporation into a secondary arsenic sulfide has been proposed as a treatment technique for soluble arsenic in groundwater (McRae et al. 1997). In batch tests conducted using Fe°, McRae et al. (1997) measured rapid reduction of As(V), from concentrations of 1,000 µg/L to < 3 µg/L. Similar experiments using As(III) and mixtures of As(III) and As(V) indicated equally rapid removal rates.

10.4.3. Reductive Treatment of Heavy Metals

Biotic treatment in PRBs has been developed for the reductive precipitation of heavy metals. A common objective is to convert soluble metals to insoluble metal sulfides. Biologically-mediated sulfate reduction has been used for decades to remove metal cations generated from acid mine drainage in natural and constructed wetlands. This mechanism has also been applied to treatment in permeable reactive barriers (Blowes et al. 1995; Waybrant et al. 1995; Benner et al. 1997; Blowes et al. 1997).

Biotic reduction is carried out by supplying an electron donor and nutrients for use by native microorganisms in the PRB. Possible electron donors include leaf mulch, sawdust, wheat straw, and other plant wastes; municipal solid waste (MSW) and MSW compost have been used as microbial nutrient sources (Benner et al. 1997). Dissolved sulfate serves as an electron acceptor. Biologically mediated reduction of sulfate to sulfide, with the concurrent formation of metal sulfides, occurs via Equations 10.11 and 10.12 (U.S. EPA 1998).

$$2CH_2O_x + SO_4^{2-} + 2H^+ \rightarrow 2CO_2 + 2H_2O + H_2S^- \quad (10.11)$$

$$Me^{2+} + H_2S^- \rightarrow MeS_{(s)} + H^+ \quad (10.12)$$

where CH_2O represents organic carbon and Me^{2+} represents a divalent soluble metal cation.

Reducing conditions created in the PRB result in the precipitation of metals and other redox-sensitive inorganic contaminants. Groundwater conditions (e.g., temperature) and the chemical milieu (pH, nutrient status, salinity) will affect the population and activities of microorganisms and the rate of sulfate reduction.

10.4.4. Chemical Precipitation of Metals

Groundwater contaminated with strong acids will contain significant concentrations of dissolved metals. For example, acid mine drainage (AMD) may achieve pH values as low as 2.0 and often contains high concentrations of soluble Fe, Al, and Mn.

Limestone, $CaCO_3$, and apatite have been used successfully in PRBs to precipitate groundwater metals (Golab et al. 2006; Skinner and Schutte 2006; Amos and Younger 2003). Limestone PRBs have been extensively used for treating AMD by both neutralizing acidity and precipitating dissolved metals, especially Fe.

Limestone dissolves in the acidic water, increases the alkalinity, and raises solution pH (Eq. 10.13). Metal contaminants precipitate as hydroxides (Eq. 10.14) or carbonates (Eq. (10.15) if pH has increased sufficiently (U.S. EPA 1998; Morrison et al. 2002).

$$CaCO_3 + H^+ \rightarrow HCO^-_3 + Ca^{2+} \quad (10.13)$$

$$Me^{2+} + 2(OH)^- \rightarrow Me(OH)_2 \quad (10.14)$$

$$Me^{2+} + HCO_3^- \rightarrow MeCO_3 + H^+ \qquad (10.15)$$

where Me=metal.

Phosphate from apatite stabilizes soluble Pb by forming hydroxypyromorphite [$Pb_{10}(PO_4)_6(OH)_2$], a low-solubility mineral (Ma et al. 1995). Apatite also accumulates Cd and Zn (Sneddon et al. 2006; Peld et al. 2004), but not as effectively as it does Pb (Morrison et al. 2002; Chen et al. 1997).

10.4.4.1. Uranium

In carbonate-dominated groundwater with moderate pH values, reductive precipitation proceeds as shown in Equation 10.16 (Morrison et al. 2002).

$$Fe^o + UO_2(CO_3)_2^{2-} + 2H^+ \rightarrow UO_2(s) + 2HCO_3^- + Fe^{2+} \qquad (10.16)$$

U^{6+} is additionally reduced by ferrous iron (Morrison et al. 2002).

Apatite has been used in PRBs to promote chemical precipitation and to accumulate uranium (Fuller et al. 2002). Commercial sources of apatite include mined phosphate rock deposits and bone material. Uranium (U) precipitates on the surface of phosphate particles was identified as meta-autunite [$Ca(UO_2)_2(PO_4)_2 \cdot 6.5H_2O$][14], which suggests mineral precipitation as the mechanism of U immobilization on apatite (Morrison et al. 2002).

10.4.5. Adsorptive Treatment of Metals

Inorganic anions that are not susceptible to reductive or precipitation processes must be removed from solution by other means. These anions, as well as redox-sensitive species, may be removed by adsorption onto mineral surfaces. Adsorption is a process involving the surface retention of ions to a solid surface. Most adsorption reactions are reversible and occur at relatively rapid rates. Some adsorption reactions are selective, with the attachment occurring at specific sites. Other adsorption reactions are less specific and therefore ions compete with each other for attachment sites (Morrison et al. 2002).

Several adsorbents are useful in PRBs to remove inorganic contaminants from groundwater. Amorphous ferric oxides (AFOs) have a high affinity for adsorption of U and metal contaminants by virtue of its high surface area per unit mass (Waite et al. 1994; His and Langmuirm 1985). Simon et al. (2003) found that hydroxyapatite could sorb more than 2,900 mg/kg uranium. Zeolites have also been used in PRBs to treat inorganic contaminants. Zeolites are a group of hydrated sodium aluminosilicates, either natural or synthetic, with significant ion exchange properties.

The use of sphagnum peat, limestone, and hydrated lime to remove U, As, Mo, and Se in laboratory batch tests was described by Thomson et al. (1991) and Longmire et al. (1991). Morrison and Spangler (1992, 1993) proposed the use of industrial byproducts as reactants to remove U, As, and Mo in precipitation or sorption PRBs (Morrison et al. 2002). Lee et al. (2004), using waste greensands from the iron foundry industry, measured high removal capacities for Zn. The mechanism is attributed to the action of clay, organic carbon, and residual iron particles. Furthermore, high pH values in the presence of clay and residual iron particles apparently enhance sorption and precipitation of Zn.

10.5. DESIRED CHARACTERISTICS OF PRB REACTIVE MEDIA

For optimal long-term treatment with minimal effects on the local environment, media employed in PRBs must be compatible with local soils, strata, and groundwater. In other words, the reactive media should cause no adverse chemical reactions nor generate any undesirable by-products when reacting with constituents in the contaminant plume. Likewise, the media itself must not become a source of contaminants. The material must also not pose a hazard to site workers handling the materials. The PRB media must, therefore, be well understood and characterized (U.S. EPA 1998).

To control treatment costs using PRBs, the media material should be readily available at a moderate cost, and the material should persist for long periods (i.e., it should not be highly soluble or depleted due to excessive reactivity). The PRB media must not restrict groundwater flow. This requires that particle size not be excessively small; similarly, the media should not consist of a wide range of particle sizes that might result in blocked intergranular spaces. The material should, therefore, be of uniform grain size (U.S. EPA 1998).

10.6. A NOTE ABOUT FE° LONGEVITY

The lifespan of effective ZVI-based PRBs is relatively unknown. Cost effectiveness is directly linked to longevity of the PRB reactant media.

The longevity of ZVI is potentially reduced by three phenomena (Morrison et al. 2002): (1) dissolution of the iron; (2) mineral precipitation leading to significant reduction in permeability; and (3) passivation of the ZVI (i.e., the changing of the chemically active surface of the metal to a much less reactive state) resulting from alteration of Fe° particle surfaces.

ZVI dissolves in the presence of oxygenated groundwater (Eq. 10.17). When sufficient oxygen is present in groundwater the Fe^{2+} generated in Equation 10.17 further oxidizes to Fe^{3+} (Eq. 10.19) and can precipitate as ferric hydroxide or (oxy)hydroxides (Eq. 10.20).

$$2Fe^{\circ}_{[ZVI]} + 4H^+ + O_2 \rightarrow 2H_2O + Fe^{2+} \tag{10.17}$$

$$2Fe^{\circ} + O_2 + 2H_2O \rightarrow 2Fe^{2+} + 4OH^- \tag{10.18}$$

$$4Fe^{2+} + 4H^+ + O_2 \rightarrow 4Fe^{3+} + 2H_2O \tag{10.19}$$

$$Fe^{3+} + 3OH^- \rightarrow Fe(OH)_{3(s)} \tag{10.20}$$

Iron corrosion (oxidation) can generate large quantities of iron oxides and (oxy)hydroxide precipitates, thus resulting in significant chemical and physical impacts within the reactive system (Powell et al. 1994; Powell et al. 1995b). The rapid consumption of dissolved O_2 at the entrance to an Fe barrier results in precipitate formation that might restrict system hydraulic conductivity upgradient of the reactive media (Mackenzie et al. 1997; MacKenzie et al. 1995). This mineralized zone resulted in low permeability in laboratory column experiments by Mackenzie et al. (1995), who suggested that placing high-porosity zones of ZVI mixed with gravel upgradient from the PRB can extend the life of the PRB. Upgradient gravel zones are commonly used in PRBs for this purpose (Morrison et al. 2002b; Naftz et al. 2002). Sulfide minerals may also precipitate in ZVI-based PRBs (see Eqs. 10.11–10.12) and further restrict permeability.

ZVI will also experience corrosion in the absence of O_2. Anaerobic corrosion of Fe by water (Eq. 10.21) is a slow process, however. Reaction 10.21 may increase solution pH, yielding ferrous (oxy)hydroxides in anaerobic systems (Eq. 10.22). The aqueous corrosion of iron is mediated by the layer of oxides, hydroxides, and oxyhydroxides that are present at the iron–water interface. The formation of these precipitates might coat the iron surface and limit its reduction-oxidation capabilities.

$$Fe^o + 2H_2O \rightarrow Fe^{2+} + H_2 + 2OH^- \tag{10.21}$$

$$Fe^{2+} + 2OH^- \rightarrow Fe(OH)_{2(s)} \tag{10.22}$$

Little is known about the phenomena of surface passivation. Minerals tend to precipitate on the ZVI surface, leading to surface deposit formation that is sufficiently thick to prevent electron transfer to continue (White and Peterson 1998).

10.7. SUMMARY OF PRB TECHNOLOGY

As with any remedial technology, it is essential to fully understand all variables that will influence successful implementation and remediation. A thorough understanding of local hydrogeology and plume boundaries is needed prior to PRB installation. The rate of groundwater flow through the reactive zone of the PRB must be determined. This is necessary to establish the groundwater/contaminant residence time per unit thickness of reactive media which, when combined with the contaminant transformation rate as it passes through the media, determines the required thickness of reactive media (U.S. EPA 1998).

The stability, mobility, and toxicity of the transformation products passing through the PRB must also be assessed. If these products are regulated compounds, they must not exit the reactive zone of the PRB without themselves being immobilized or transformed to innocuous compounds (U.S. EPA 1998).

10.8. ADVANTAGES OF PRB TECHNOLOGY

PRB technology has shown much promise in field treatment of contaminated aquifers. Some of its most significant advantages include (NFESC n.d.):

- passive in situ detoxification of groundwater
- uses no external energy source

- potential to treat contaminants to very low levels
- the land surface can be restored to its original function
- long-term unattended operation
- more cost-effective than pump-and-treat systems

10.9. DISADVANTAGES OF PRB TECHNOLOGY

The technology has some drawbacks worth noting, however:

- unknown long-term effects from chemical and/or biological precipitate formation
- construction complications from subsurface utilities and/or aboveground structures
- limited to depths of less than 50 ft using current construction technologies

QUESTIONS

1. Explain the process of decomposition of chlorinated hydrocarbons (for example, vinyl chloride) within a PRB. Are certain phases of the reaction more influenced by aerobic versus anaerobic conditions? Explain.
2. How can PRBs be constructed or maintained so that occlusion (clogging) of the upgradient side is limited?
3. Explain passivation. How can this process be overcome or at least limited in a ZVI-reactive barrier?

REFERENCES

Ammonette, J. E., J. E. Szecsody, H. T. Schaef, J. C. Templeton, Y. A. Gorby, and J. S. Fruchter. 1994. Abiotic reduction of aquifer materials by dithionite: A promising in-situ remediation technology. In *Thirty-Third Hanford Symposium on Health and the Environment, in-Situ Remediation: Scientific Basis for Current and Future Technologies*, ed. G. W. Gee and N. R. Wing, 851–81. Columbus, OH: Battelle.

Amos P. W., and P. L. Younger. 2003. Substrate characterization for a subsurface reactive barrier to treat colliery spoil leachate. *Water Research* 37 (1): 108–20.

Archer, W. L., and M. K. Harter. 1978. Reactivity of carbon tetrachloride with a series of metals. *Corrosion-National Association of Corrosion Engineers (NACE)* 34 (5): 159–62.

Benner, S. G., D. W. Blowes, and C. J. Ptacek. 1997. A full-scale porous reactive wall for prevention of acid mine drainage. *Ground Water Monitoring and Remediation* 17:99–107.

Blowes, D. W., and C. J. Ptacek. 1992. *Geochemical Remediation of Groundwater by Permeable Reactive Walls: Removal of Chromate by Reaction with Iron-Bearing Solids*. Dallas: Subsurface Restoration Conference, U.S. Environmental Protection Agency, Kerr Laboratory.

Blowes, D. W., C. J. Ptacek, C. J. Hanton-Fong, and J. L. Jambor. 1995. In situ remediation of chromium contaminated groundwater using zero-valent iron. Paper presented at the American Chemical Society, 209th National Meeting, Anaheim, California, April 2–7.

Blowes, D. W., R. W. Puls, T. A. Bennett, R. W. Gillham, C. J. Hanton-Fong, and C. J. Ptacek. 1997. *In-situ* porous reactive wall for treatment of Cr(VI) and trichloroethylene in groundwater. Paper presented at the International Containment Technology Conference and Exhibition, St. Petersburg, FL, February 9–12.

Bostick, W. D., R. J. Stevenson, R. J. Jarabek, and J. L. Conca. 1999. Use of apatite and bone char for the removal of soluble radionuclides in authentic and simulated DOE groundwater. *Advances in Environmental Research* 3:488–98.

Bowers, A. R., C. A. Ortiz, and R. J. Cardozo. 1986. Iron process for treatment of Cr(VI) wastewaters. *Metal Finishing* 84:37.

Chen, X., J. V. Wright, J. L. Conca, and L. M. Peurrung. 1997. Evaluation of heavy metal remediation using mineral apatite. *Water, Air, and Soil Pollution* 98: 57–78.

Eary, L. E., and D. Rai. 1989. Kinetics of chromate reduction by ferrous ions derived from hematite and biotite at 25°C. *American Journal of Science* 289:180–213.

Fuller C. C., J. R. Bargar, J. A. Davis, and M. J. Piana. 2002. Mechanisms of uranium interactions with hydroyapatite: Implications for groundwater remediation. *Environmental Science and Technology* 36 (2): 158–65.

Golab A. N., M. A. Peterson, and B. Indraratna. 2006. Selection of potential reactive materials for a permeable reactive barrier for remediating acidic groundwater in acid sulphate soil terrains. *Quarterly Journal of Engineering Geology and Hydrogeology* 39 (2): 209–23.

Gould, J. P. 1982. The kinetics of hexavalent chromium reduction by metallic iron. *Water Research* 16:871–77.

His, C. D., and D. Langmuirm. 1985. Adsorption of uranyl onto ferric oxyhydroxide: Application of the surface complexation site-binding model. *Geochimica Cosmochimica Acta* 49:1931–41.

Johnson, T. L., M. M. Scherer, and P. G. Tratnyek. 1996. Kinetics of halogenated organic compound degradation by iron metal. *Environmental Science & Technology* 30 (8): 2634–40.

Keely, J. F. 1989. Performance evaluations of pump-and-treat remediation. *U.S. Environmental Protection Agency, Superfund Ground Water Issue*. EPA/540/4-89/005. Robert S. Kerr Environmental Research Laboratory.

Kent, D. B., J. A. Davis, L. C. D. Anderson, B. A. Rea, and T. D. White. 1994. Transport of chromium and selenium in the suboxic zone of a shallow aquifer: Influence of redox and adsorption reactions. *Water Resources Research* 30 (4): 1099–1114.

Lee T., J.-W. Park, and J.-H. Lee. 2004. Waste green sands as reactive media for the removal of zinc from water. *Chemosphere* 56 (6): 571–81.

Longmire, P. A., D. G. Brookins, B. M. Thomson, and P. G. Eller. 1991. Application of sphagnum peat, calcium carbonate, and hydrated lime for immobilizing U tailings leachate, In *Scientific Basis for Nuclear Waste Management XIV*, vol. 212, ed. T. Abrajano Jr. and L. H. Johnson, 623–31. Pittsburgh: Materials Research Society.

Ma, Q. Y., T. J. Logan, and S. J. Traina. 1995. Lead immobilization from aqueous solutions and contaminated soils using phosphate rocks. *Environmental Science & Technology* 29:1118–26.

MacKenzie, P. D., S. S. Baghel, G. R. Eykholt, D. P. Horney, J. J. Salvo, and T. M. Sivavec. 1995. Pilot scale demonstration of chlorinated ethene reduction by iron metal: Factors affecting iron lifetime. Paper presented at Emerging Technologies in Hazardous Waste Management VII, Special Symposium of the American Chemical Society, American Chemical Society, Atlanta, September 17–20.

Mackenzie, P. D., T. M. Sivavec, and D. P. Horney. 1997. Extending hydraulic lifetime of iron walls. In *Proceedings of the International Containment Technology Conference and Exhibition*, St. Petersburg, FL, February 9–12, 781–87.

Marsh, T. L., N. M. Leon, and M. J. McInerney. 2000. Physiochemical factors affecting chromate reduction by aquifer materials. *Geomicrobiology Journal* 17 (4): 291–303.

Matheson, L. J., and P. G. Tratnyek. 1993. Processes affecting reductive dechlorination of chlorinated solvents by zero-valent iron. Paper presented at the 205th ACS National Meeting, American Chemical Society, Denver, March 28–April 2.

McRae, C. W., D. W. Blowes, and C. Ptacek. 1997. Laboratory-scale investigation of remediation of As and Se using iron oxides. Paper presented at the Sixth Symposium and Exhibition on Groundwater and Soil Remediation, Montreal, March 18–21.

Morrison, S. J., C. E. Carpenter, D. R. Metzler, T. R. Bartlett, and S. A. Morris. 2002a. Design and performance of a permeable reactive barrier for containment of uranium, arsenic, selenium, vanadium, molybdenum, and nitrate at Monticello, Utah. In *Handbook of Groundwater Remediation Using Permeable Reactive Barriers*, ed. D. L. Naftz, S. J. Morrison, C. C. Fuller, and J. A. Davis. New York: Academic Press.

Morrison, S. J., D. L. Naftz, J. A. Davis, and C. C. Fuller. 2002b. Introduction to groundwater remediation of metals, radionuclides, and nutrients with permeable reactive barriers. In *Handbook of Groundwater Remediation Using Permeable Reactive Barriers*, ed. D. L. Naftz, S. J. Morrison, C. C. Fuller, and J. A. Davis. New York: Academic Press.

Morrison, S. J., and R. R. Spangler. 1992. Extraction of uranium and molybdenum from aqueous solutions: A survey of industrial materials for use in chemical barriers for uranium mill tailings remediation. *Environmental Science & Technology* 26 (10): 1922–31.

——. 1993. Chemical barriers for controlling groundwater contamination. *Environmental Progress* 12 (3): 175–81.

Naftz, D. L., C. C. Fuller, J. A. Davis, S. J. Morrison, E. M. Feltcorn, G. W. Freethey, R. C. Rowland, C. Wilcowske, and M. Piana. 2002. Field demonstration of three permeable reactive barriers to control uranium contamination in groundwater, Fry Canyon, Utah. In *Handbook of Groundwater Remediation Using Permeable Reactive*

Barriers, ed. D. L. Naftz, S. J. Morrison, C. C. Fuller, and J. A. Davis. New York: Academic Press.

Naval Facilities Engineering Service Center. n.d. *Permeable Reactive Barrier Remediation of Chlorinated Solvents in Groundwater*. See: enviro.nfesc.navy.mil/erb/erb_a/restoration/ technologies/remed/phys_chem/PRBSuccess.pdf.

Orth, W. S., and R. W. Gillham. 1996. Dechlorination of trichloroethene in aqueous solution using Fe°. *Environmental Science & Technology* 30:66–71.

Palmer, C. D., and R. W. Puls. 1994. Natural attenuation of hexavalent chromium in ground water and soils. *U.S. Environmental Protection Agency, Ground Water Issue.* EPA/540/S-94/505.

Peld M., K. Tõnsuaadu, and V. Bender. 2004. Sorption and desorption of Cd^{2+} and Zn^{2+} ions in apatite-aqueous systems. *Environmental Science & Technology* 38 (21): 5626–31.

Powell, R. M., and R. W. Puls. 1997. *Permeable Reactive Subsurface Barriers for the Interception and Remediation of Chlorinated Hydrocarbon and Chromium (VI) Plumes in Ground Water. U.S. Environmental Protection Agency Remedial Technology Fact Sheet.* EPA/600/F-97/008.

Powell, R. M., R. W. Puls, S. K. Hightower, and D. A. Clark. 1995a. Corrosive and geochemical mechanisms influencing in situ chromate reduction by metallic iron. Paper presented at the 209th ACS National Meeting, American Chemical Society, Anaheim, CA, April 2–7.

Powell, R. M., R. W. Puls, S. K. Hightower, and D. A. Sabatini. 1995b. Coupled iron corrosion and chromate reduction: Mechanisms for subsurface remediation. *Environmental Science & Technology* 29 (8): 1913–22.

Powell, R. M., R. W. Puls, and C. J. Paul. 1994. Chromate reduction and remediation utilizing the thermodynamic instability of zero-valence state iron. In *Proceedings of the Water Environment Federation, Innovative Solutions for Contaminated Site Management. Water Environment Federation.* Miami, March 6–9.

Roberts, A. L., L. A. Totten, W. A. Arnold, D. R. Burris, and T. J. Campbell. 1996. Reductive elimination of chlorinated ethylenes by zero-valent metals. *Environmental Science & Technology* 30 (8): 2654–59.

Scott, M. J., F. B. Metting, J. S. Fruchter, and R. E. Wildung. 1998. Research investment pays off. *Soil Groundwater Cleanup.* October 6–13.

Simon F.-G., C. Segebade, and M. Hedrich. 2003. Behaviour of uranium in iron-bearing permeable reactive barriers: Investigation with [237]U as a radioindicator. *Science of the Total Environment* 307 (1–3): 231–38.

Sivavec, T. M., D. P. Horney, and S. S. Baghel. 1995. Reductive dechlorination of chlorinated ethenes by iron metal and iron sulfide minerals. Paper presented at Emerging Technologies in Hazardous Waste Management VII, Special Symposium of the American Chemical Society, Atlanta, September 17–20.

Skinner S. J. W., and C. F. Schutte. 2006. The feasibility of a permeable reactive barrier to treat acidic sulphate- and nitrate-contaminated groundwater. *Water SA* 32 (2): 129–35.

Sneddon I. R., P. F. Schofield, E. Valsami-Jones, M. Orueetxebarria, and M. E. Hoodson. 2006. Use of bone meal amendments to immobilize Pb, Zn and Cd in soil: A leaching column study. *Environmental Pollution* 144 (3): 816–25.

Thomson, B. M., S. P. Shelton, and E. Smith. 1991. Permeable barriers: A new alternative for treatment of contaminated groundwater. In *45th Purdue Industrial Waste Conference Proceedings*. Chelsea, MI: Lewis.

U.S. Environmental Protection Agency. 1998. *Permeable Reactive Barrier Technologies for Contaminant Remediation*. EPA/600/R-98/125. Washington, DC: Office of Solid Waste and Emergency Response, Office of Research and Development.

Waite, T. D., J. A. Davis, T. E. Payne, G. A. Waychunas, and N. Xu. 1994. Uranium (VI) adsorption to ferrihydrite: Application of a surface complexation model. *Geochimica Cosmochima Acta* 58:5465–78.

Waybrant, K. R., D. W. Blowes, and C. J. Ptacek. 1995. Selection of reactive mixtures for the prevention of acid mine drainage using in situ porous reactive walls. In *Sudbury '95, Mining and the Environment*. Ottawa, ON: CANMET.

White, A. F., and M. L. Peterson. 1998. The reduction of aqueous metal species on the surfaces of Fe(II)-containing oxides: The role of surface passivation. *American Chemical Society Symposium* 715:323–41.

CHAPTER 11

Microbial Remediation

I hear there's microbes in a kiss. This rumor is most rife. Come, lady dear, and make of me—An invalid for life.

—Anonymous

Support bacteria—they're the only culture some people have.

—Anonymous

11.1 INTRODUCTION

The process of bioremediation at a contaminated site involves the engineered use of active microbial biomass for the destruction, detoxification, and/or uptake of pollutants from soil, waste piles, groundwater, surface water, or other environmental media. Technologies are applicable to solids, slurries, and liquids, and, as with many of the technologies presented thus far, bioremediation can be performed either in situ or ex situ. Processes range from the simple, for example the application of inorganic nutrients and oxygen to the subsurface via wells, to complex, and include the addition of specialized cells to a soil slurry in aboveground reactor vessels with elaborate temperature, pH, and climate controls; effluent polishing; and wastewater treatment.

Bioremediation typically implies treatment of organic contamination, where the microbial cells utilize hydrocarbon molecules as a carbon source, thereby extracting energy for respiration and carbon for cellular growth. There are reported instances, however, in which metals or inorganics have been treated via bioremediation (Green-Ruiz 2006; Umrania 2006; Baxter and Cummings 2006; Krishna and Philip 2005).

Biological processes can be applied to a broad range of organic contaminants. Treatment is essentially a destruction process based on either oxidation or reduction reactions. Biological treatment is designed to accomplish: (1) transformation of organics into smaller and preferably less toxic molecules, and, where applicable, (2) dehalogenation of organic compounds. The overall process for the biologically mediated destruction of a hazardous organic molecule may be represented as:

$$(HC)_x + (N, P, S) + O_2 \rightarrow (\text{acid intermediates}) \rightarrow CO_{2(g)} + H_2O +$$
$$NO_3^- + SO_4^{2-} + \text{energy} + \text{microbial biomass} \qquad (11.1)$$

11.2. OVERVIEW OF RELEVANT MICROBIOLOGICAL PRINCIPLES

In most applications, bioremediation is carried out using communities of microbial species, rather than one or a few species. This is because most soils are already enriched with stable and complex microbial communities that have become adapted to the physical and chemical milieu specific to a site. Communities are also more efficient because different populations of organisms within a community will survive under different conditions (i.e., dry versus wet, cool versus warm soils, etc.). Finally, no single group will be capable of acting on all contaminant types; a range of organisms, and hence a range of physiological processes, will provide for more complete contaminant removal.

Bacteria, actinomycetes, fungi, algae, and protozoa are among the most numerous and important microorganisms in soil from the standpoint of both nutrient cycling and organic matter transformation. The first three groups listed comprise the microorganisms most responsible for the transformations of organic contaminants in soils. Most research in bioremediation has addressed bacteria, but fungi are also known to play an important role, especially with halogenated compounds (e.g., pentachlorophenol, a wood preservative).

11.2.1. Bacteria

Bacteria are essential to nutrient cycles of ecosystems including C, N, P, and S. Cells decompose plant and animal tissue, converting them via mineralization, immobilization, and humification reactions. Other microbial groups carry out many transformations similar to those of the bacteria; however, the bacteria stand out because of their ability to multiply rapidly and their vigorous decomposition of a wide range of substrates. Bacteria are the preeminent group of microorganisms in a bioremediation program because of their physiological diversity and furthermore because they are the most abundant group among all microbial populations in a soil. In a healthy—that is, noncontaminated and fertile soil—bacterial biomass can be substantial: one gram may contain several hundred million cells. Estimates of bacterial numbers vary according to the means of determination. Using estimates via plate counts, values range from several hundred thousand up to 10^7 bacteria per gram of dry soil. Estimates by direct microscopy provide values on the order of 10^8 to 10^{10} bacteria per gram (Alexander 1977). Thousands of bacterial species have been identified in soils throughout the world. The numbers of species and individual cells are a function of soil characteristics and environmental conditions such as soil moisture content, pH, and temperature.

Bacteria possess widely varying morphology as well as physiology. Among the major bacterial cell types are the bacilli (rod-shaped bacteria), which are the most numerous; cocci (spherical-shaped cells); and spirilla (spirals). The size of individual cells ranges from about 0.3 to 3.0 μm. Bacteria possess an outer layer known as the *capsule* or *slime* layer, which is composed mostly of polysaccharides or polypeptides. This capsule measures from 100 to 300 A° thick and may protect the cell from engulfment by protozoa (Cookson 1995). Beneath the capsule is a rigid cell wall, a cell membrane that encapsulates the cytoplasm, a nucleus, and numerous other organelles. Some of the bacilli persist in stressed environments by the formation of endospores, which endure because of their resistance to both desiccation and high temperatures. The endospore can persist in a dormant state long after the death of vegetative cells. When conditions are again adequate for vegetative growth, the spore will germinate. Spore-forming genera are present among both aerobic and anaerobic bacteria.

Bacteria are typically not free in the soil water because most cells adhere to clay particles, soil organic matter, and other colloidal surfaces. The environmental factors that influence soil bacterial numbers and activity include soil organic matter content, temperature, pH, nutrient supply, moisture, and aeration. Additional variables such as cultivation, season, and depth have also been documented.

Community size in mineral soils is in part a function of organic matter content. Thus, humus-rich locations have high bacterial numbers, a result of the greater root density and greater supply of organic matter available from the decomposition of roots and plant debris. The addition of carbonaceous materials also strongly influences bacterial numbers and activities; for example, the plowing-under of crop residues promotes a rapid response. This stimulation is most pronounced during the first months of decomposition and disappears after a season (Alexander 1977).

Bacterial growth is strongly influenced by temperature. Certain species develop best at temperatures below 20°C, and are termed *psychrophiles*. True psychrophilic bacteria are not common in soil, however. Thermophiles grow readily at temperatures of 45°C to 65°C. Most microorganisms, however, are mesophiles with optima in the range of 25°C to 35°C and a capacity to grow from about 15°C to 45°C. The majority of soil bacteria are mesophiles. Temperature regulates the rate of biochemical processes carried out by bacteria and increases the rate of reaction up to the point of optimum temperature for biochemical reactions.

The optimum pH regime for most bacterial species is near neutrality. Highly acid or alkaline conditions inhibit many common bacteria. There are exceptions, however. For example, *Thiobacillus ferrooxidans*, an autotrophic iron-oxidizing bacterium, catalyzes the oxidation of ferrous iron with the consequent production of sulfuric acid and can survive at pH 3.0 or lower. In most cases, however, the greater the hydrogen ion concentration, the smaller the size of the bacterial community. This may be a function of direct toxicity of the hydrogen (H^+) ion, the increased solubilization of metals in the growth medium, or a combination of the two. Liming of acid environments increases bacterial abundance.

Inorganic nutrients are required for optimal bacterial growth; therefore, flora are often affected by the application of inorganic fertilizers. Cultivation practices also exert direct and indirect biological effects. Plowing and tillage usually result in marked bacteriological fluctuations. Changes will vary with the type of operation (i.e., moldboard plowing versus harrowing), soil depth, and type of residues that are turned under. The effects occur from improving the soil structure and porosity, encouraging air movement, altering the moisture status, and exposing organic-bound nutrients to bacterial action (Alexander 1977).

11.2.2. Fungi

Fungi are unicellular or multicellular nonphotosynthetic higher protists. They possess cell walls, are nonmotile, and use organic material for both energy and carbon sources. Fungi produce a filamentous mycelial network composed of individual hyphal strands. In many cases, the mycelium is divided into individual cells by cross walls or septa. Individual hyphae may be vegetative or fertile, and the fertile filaments produce either sexual or asexual spores. The condia (asexual spores) are widespread and the sexual spores are relatively uncommon. Fungi can be differentiated into genera and species on the basis of morphology (Alexander 1977). Therefore, size, shape, structure, and cultural characteristics are important in taxonomy.

The filamentous fungi are almost exclusively strict aerobes. Fresh soil samples have been found to contain over 600 mg carbonaceous biomass per kg soil, representing 130 fungal species (Anderson 1984).

Fungi are heterotrophic; that is, their growth is dependent on the availability of oxidizable carbonaceous substrates. The primary environmental influences to fungi include the types and amounts of organic matter, pH, amount of moisture and aeration, temperature, and composition of native vegetation.

Fungal species grow over a wide pH range, although they tend to predominate in acidic pH regimes. In laboratory culture fungi can survive comfortably at pH values as low as 2.0, and some strains are active at pH 9.0 or above. Since bacteria and actinomycetes are intolerant of acid conditions, the microbial community in low-pH media is dominated by fungi.

Applications of inorganic fertilizers to soil modify the abundance of filamentous fungi. These changes are the result of acidification as well as of nutrient addition. For example, treatment with fertilizers containing ammonium salts increases numbers because microbial oxidation of the nitrogen leads to the formation of nitric acid, which favors the fungi and discourages the bacteria and actinomycetes (Alexander 1977). The general reaction is·

$$NH_4^+ \rightarrow \quad HONH_2 \rightarrow \quad HONNOH \rightarrow NO_2^- + H^+ \rightarrow NO_3^-$$

ammonium   hydroxylamine   hyponitrite   nitrite acid   nitrate

(11.2)

In terms of temperature requirements, most fungal species are mesophilic; a few thermophilic strains can be located in typical soil. Thermophiles are abundant only during the heating of compost piles. Thermophiles grow adequately between 50°C and 55°C but are inactivated at 65°C. Organisms actively growing at about 37°C are localized in the surface horizons, where heating is greatest during the summer months (Alexander 1977).

The overall metabolic processes of the fungi are less diverse than those of the bacteria. One fungus that has potential in the treatment of hazardous organics is *Phanerochaete chrysoporium*, a white rot fungus. This fungus produces an extracellular peroxidase enzyme that decomposes lignin, a complex polymer composed of phenylpropane units. The reaction of interest is relatively nonspecific and has been found to be effective in initiating the degradation of both PAHs and several chlorinated, recalcitrant compounds including pentachlorophenol (PCP) and chlorinated dibenzodioxins (Andersson et al. 2000; McGrath and Singleton 2000; Eweis et al. 1998).

11.2.3. Actinomycetes

The actinomycetes are often considered a middle group between the bacteria and the fungi. Like the latter group, most genera of actinomycetes produce slender, branched filaments that develop into a mycelium. The filament is typically long, and individual hyphae appear morphologically similar to fungal filaments. Actinomycetes are widely distributed in soil, compost piles, river sediments, and other environments. They are prevalent in surface soil and also in the lower horizons to great depths. They are second to bacteria in terms of abundance. Actinomycetes have been shown to decompose aromatics, chlorinated aromatics, steroids, and phenols (Eweis et al. 1998; Nnamchi et al. 2006; Das et al. 2005; U.S. EPA. 1983).

The primary environmental influences for actinomycetes include soil organic matter content, pH, moisture level, and temperature. The free-living forms of the actinomycetes are solely heterotrophic. Actinomycetes are strongly affected by the presence of oxidizable carbon, and their numbers are very high in organic-rich soils. Addition of organic wastes such as crop residues or animal manure to soil increases their abundance. The population may sometimes reach 10^8 per gram of soil with incorporation of crop residue, especially in high-temperature environments (Alexander 1977). Upon organic matter additions the bacterial and fungal flora usually proliferate, and the actinomycetes do not respond until later stages of decay. It is therefore possible that a microbial succession is taking place, that is, bacteria and fungi initiate the decomposition reactions due to their rapid growth and physiological diversity; subsequently, the actinomycetes appear when the readily available compounds have been metabolized and competition for substrates has decreased.

Actinomycetes thrive in neutral-pH environments and do not grow well under acidic conditions. In high-pH environments, a large proportion of the total microbial community may consist of the actinomycetes. Under conditions of waterlogging, for example at 85% to 100% water-holding capacity, the growth of actinomycetes is severely limited because they are strict aerobes (Alexander 1977). Actinomycetes are not as influenced by dry conditions as are the bacteria, and they are often favored by low moisture levels both in vegetative development and in formation of reproductive cells. Consequently, as a soil dries, the numbers of actinomycetes remain high while bacterial numbers decrease because of their intolerance to arid conditions.

11.3. MICROBIAL REQUIREMENTS FOR GROWTH AND REMEDIATION

The driving force of all microbial physiological reactions is the acquisition of energy for survival, that is, metabolic processes, reproduction, motility, etc. Microorganisms are often classified by the methods in which they obtain energy. For example, those that gain energy from the oxidation of chemical compounds are chemotrophs; those that gain energy from sunlight are phototrophs. Microbes can also be categorized based on carbon requirements. Organisms that use CO_2 as their main carbon source are labeled *autotrophs*. In contrast, those that feed on preformed organic materials are *heterotrophs*. There are, of course, numerous examples in which microorganisms will exist under more than one classification.

Microorganisms must experience vigorous growth (i.e., optimization of metabolic processes as well as reproduction) in order for bioremediation to be successful. The microbial populations essential to bioremediation are heterotrophic. Ideally, the hydrocarbon components of the contaminant plume will serve as an energy source. Additionally microbes will require the appropriate electron acceptors during oxidation-reduction processes, other nutrients, and an adequate physical and chemical environment.

11.3.1. Oxygen

Most microorganisms active in bioremediation processes are aerobic— that is, they require free oxygen in their metabolic processes. The aerobic heterotrophic group offers the greatest promise in bioremediation efforts, as hydrocarbon decomposition is most efficient (i.e., the greatest energy yield per mole of substrate is available). Some treatment processes make use of anaerobic microorganisms that do not require free oxygen; however, these processes are used only infrequently in environmental cleanup, for example, in the reductive dechlorination of a contaminant molecule such as tricholoroethyelene (Young et al. 2006; Aulenta et al. 2006; Sulfita and Sewell 1991). Microorganisms established in aqueous reactors, aquifers, or soil may be supplied with oxygen by pumping air or oxygen-supplying compounds (e.g., hydrogen peroxide) into the reaction zone. Cells growing in surface soil may be supplied with oxygen by tilling the soil to facilitate incorporation of air.

11.3.2. Moisture

Most microorganisms that are active in bioremediation live in water. Water may be free water, that is, occurring in soil pores, tank reactors, or aquifers, or it may occur as a film on the surface of a soil particle or oil droplet. Moisture affects microbial activity in several ways. Water is the major component of protoplasm; therefore, an adequate supply is necessary for vegetative development. Second, in order for a substrate molecule to be ingested, both it and the cell must be in contact with water. This will allow ready movement of the cell to substrate or vice versa. Additionally, exoenzymes, secreted by the cell in order to initiate substrate decomposition, require water for transport. Finally, when soil moisture becomes excessive, microbial growth is curbed. The effect is not a result of a direct toxic effect of water, but its excess limits gaseous exchange and lowers the available O_2 supply, thereby creating anaerobic conditions (Alexander 1977; Cookson 1995).

Microorganisms are strongly affected by the osmotic potential of the local environment. The osmotic potential affects the ability of the microbial cell to maintain an adequate amount of water. If the environment is too dry or if the water in the microbial environment contains excessive concentrations of solutes, the cell is unable to maintain the proper balance of protoplasmic water. This effect will interfere with bioremediation projects where, for example, contaminated soils contain high levels of dissolved salts. Changes in osmotic potential can inhibit microbial activity by upsetting normal metabolic processes and, in extreme cases, result in lysis, or the disintegration of cell walls.

11.3.3. pH

The pH range within which most bioremediation processes operate most efficiently is approximately 5.5 to 8. It is no coincidence that this is also the optimum pH range for many heterotrophic bacteria, the major microbial players in most bioremediation technologies. The optimum pH range for a particular situation, however, is site-specific. The pH is influenced by a complex relationship between organisms, contaminant chemistry, and physical and chemical properties of the local environment. Additionally, as biological processes proceed in the contaminated media, the pH may shift and therefore must be monitored regularly. The pH can be adjusted to the desired range by the addition of acidic or basic substances (i.e., mineral acids or limestone, respectively).

11.3.4. Nutrients

The heterotrophic bacteria, actinomycetes, and fungi possess fairly complex nutritional requirements. Nutrients serve three primary functions: supplying the needed energy for cell growth and biosynthetic reactions; providing the materials necessary for synthesis of protoplasmic components; and serving as electron acceptors for the energy-related reactions in the cell (Table 11.1). Energy sources for heterotrophs include sugars, starch, cellulose, hemicellulose, lignin, pectic substances, inulin, chitin, proteins, amino acids, and organic acids. Given the correct microbial populations and chemical and physical properties of an affected site, organic contaminant molecules will also serve as an energy source. The oxidation of these organics releases energy, a portion of which is used in the synthesis of protoplasm.

Table 11.1.   Nutrients required by microorganisms

Inorganics (minerals)	N, P, K, Ca, Mg, S, Fe, Mn, Cu, Zn, Co, Mo
Carbon sources	CO_2, HCO_3^- Organic compounds
Energy sources	Organic compounds (glucose, polysaccharides, cellulose, etc.) Inorganic compounds (Fe^{2+}) Light
Electron acceptors	O_2 NO_3^-, SO_4^{2-}, Fe^{3+}, CO_2 Organic compounds

Growth Factors
  a. Amino acids
  b. Vitamins
 	
  c. Other
	
	Alanine, cysteine, histidine, serine, tyrosine, etc.
	Nicotinic acid, riboflavin, pantothenic acid, biotin, PABA,
	     pyridoxine, thiamine, B_{12}, folic acid, etc.
	Purine bases, pyrimidine bases, peptides, etc.

Carbon dioxide, a product of both aerobic and anaerobic metabolism, is important not only because it completes the carbon cycle but also because of its direct influence on growth. In the classic terminology of microbiology, the chemoautotrophic and photoautotrophic microorganisms require CO_2 because it is their sole carbonaceous nutrient. However, the gas is stimulatory to and often required by many heterotrophs, and growth of many species will not proceed in the absence of CO_2. A portion of the CO_2 supplied, even to heterotrophs, is incorporated into the cell structure. The requirement for this gas rarely presents a problem in soil because of its continual evolution from decaying organic matter (Alexander 1977).

Nitrogen, P, K, Mg, S, Fe, Ca, Mn, Zn, Cu, Co, and Mo are integral parts of the cell's protoplasmic structure. These nutrients plus C, H, and O are needed for the synthesis of the microbial cell. Mineral nutrients are usually supplied as soluble salts in fertilizers. Carbon may be supplied in the form of animal manures (which will also supply many mineral nutrients), wood chips, or other materials. There must be a balance between the various mineral nutrients (N and P, for example) and the carbon source, or the microorganisms will not be able to make optimum use of the carbon source. For most bioremediation situations, biodegradation is optimal at C:N ratios in the range of 10 to 30 to 1, and N:P ratios of about 10 to 1, weight basis. These ratios may vary widely depending on the type of carbonaceous materials present (Cookson 1995).

The availability of nutrients to microorganisms is strongly influenced by pH. In the circumneutral pH range, trace metals (e.g., Cu, Co, Ni, Zn) are typically available in micro quantities. This degree of availability is generally adequate for most biota as excess quantities, for example under acid pH regimes, will prove toxic and inhibitory. Also at neutral pH, P is maximally available. A soil pH of 5.5 to 8 is therefore generally recommended during bioremediation.

Energy generation within a microbial cell is an oxidation process in which electrons are transported within the respiration pathway of the microbial cell. This electron flow generates energy through the electron transport chain, which consists of molecules that undergo repeated oxidation and reduction and transfer the electron from one molecule to another (Fig. 11.1). The electrons are transported in the system by several compounds, with one of the more significant being nicotinamide adenine dinucleotide phosphate, NADP (Fig. 11.2). The pyridine nucleotides and related compounds experience reversible oxidation and reduction, which results in the storage of energy within the microbial cell as energy-rich chemical bonds (Cookson 1995).

In order to be utilized, the substrate must penetrate into the organism. Often, the energy source enters with no difficulty, but microbial cells are impermeable to many complex molecules. These compounds must be first solubilized and simplified prior to their serving within the cell as energy sources. Here again is where exoenzymes are important in the initial dissociation of a complex substrate molecule, allowing for its eventual incorporation into the cell. Once inside the membrane, chemicals are catabolized (i.e., degraded) by microorganisms using one of three general pathways of metabolism:

1. In aerobic respiration, organic chemicals are oxidized to carbon dioxide and water or other end-products using molecular oxygen as the terminal electron acceptor. We would expect aerobic respiration to occur under highly oxygenated conditions. The generalized reaction for a glucose molecule is:

$$C_6H_{12}O_6 + 6O_2 \rightarrow 6CO_2 + 6H_2O + \text{energy} \qquad (11.3)$$

2. If the oxygen supply decreases, as may occur in a heavy soil with active microbial biomass, anaerobic respiration may be initiated. In this mode, microorganisms metabolize hydrocarbons in the absence or

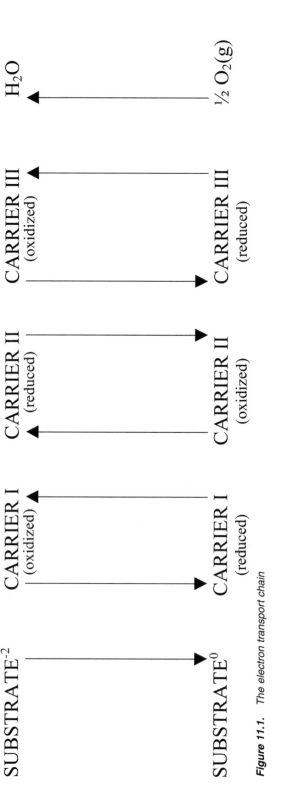

Figure 11.1. *The electron transport chain*

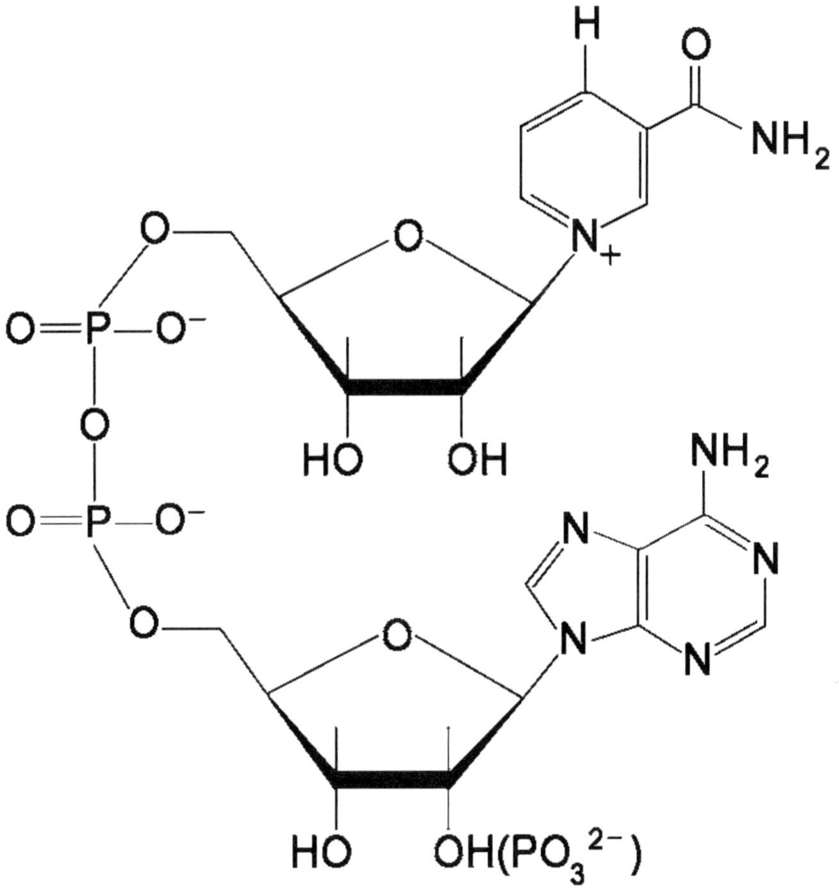

Figure 11.2. *Structure of nicotinamide adenine dinucleotide phosphate (NADP), a coenzyme critical to the electron transport chain*

near-absence of molecular oxygen, using inorganic substrates as terminal electron acceptors. Common substrates include nitrate, NO_3^-, sulfate, SO_4^{2-}, and Fe^{3+}. In anaerobic respiration, nitrate is reduced to nitrogen (N_2) or ammonium (NH_4^+), sulfate to sulfide (S^{2-}), ferrous iron (Fe^{2+}) to ferric iron (Fe^{3+}), and CO_2 to methane (CH_4)

3. Under highly reducing conditions and in the absence of inorganic electron acceptors, fermentation occurs. Hydrocarbons are degraded independent of oxygen, and organic compounds function as electron acceptors. Fermentation results in end-products including acetate, ethanol, propionate, and butyrate (Table 11.2).

Table 11.2.   Metabolism modes of microbial flora

Type	Electron Acceptor
Aerobic respiration	Oxygen (O_2)
Anaerobic respiration:	
Denitrification	Nitrate (NO_3^-)
Nitrate reduction	Nitrate (NO_3^-)
Sulfate reduction	Sulfate (SO_4^{2-})
Ferric iron reduction	Iron (Fe^{3+})
Sulfur reduction	Sulfur (S)
Fermentation	Organic compound
Methane fermentation	Carbon dioxide (CO_2)

11.3.5. Contaminant Properties

Microbial acclimation and growth, and bioremediation success, are affected in part by contaminant concentrations. A microbial consortium will maximize decomposition reactions within a range of contaminant concentrations. Below this range microbial activity may be minimal; above this range microbial activity will be inhibited. The concentrations at which microbial growth is supported or inhibited vary with the contaminant, medium (soil versus slurry versus groundwater), and distribution of individual species. Given long-term exposure, microbes have been known to acclimate to very high contaminant concentrations and other stressful conditions.

The bioavailability of a contaminant to microorganisms depends on several factors: (1) potential as a source of energy or nutrients, (2) solubility in water, (3) potential toxicity, and (4) tendency to adsorb to soil solids. Low-solubility contaminants—for example, long-chain aliphatics or condensed aromatics—are unlikely to occur in the aqueous phase and will be difficult to biodegrade. Low bioavailability can be due to adsorption of a contaminant molecule to soil solids, rather than insolubility. Hydrophobic contaminants partition from the soil water and concentrate in soil organic matter, resulting in nonavailability to microbes. Contaminant properties that affect sorption include molecular weight, structure, solubility, and polarity. Soil properties include the types and amounts of organic matter, types and amounts of clays, and presence of metal hydrous oxides.

Bioavailability is also a function of the utility of the molecule to the organism, that is, whether it acts as a substrate or cosubstrate. When the compound cannot serve as a metabolic substrate but is oxidized in the presence of a substrate already present or added to the system, the process is referred to as *co-oxidation* and the contaminant molecule is the *cosubstrate*. Co-oxidation is important for the biodegradation of high-molecular weight PAHs and some chlorinated solvents such as trichloroethene (TCE).

11.4. PATHWAYS OF HYDROCARBON METABOLISM

Biological processes can decompose and detoxify a broad range of biodegradable organic contaminants. Table 11.3 presents some common RCRA-regulated organic compounds that are susceptible to biodegradation. A commonly encountered soil and aquifer contaminant is gasoline,

Table 11.3. **Biodegradable RCRA-regulated organic compounds**

| Substrate | Respiration | | Fermentation | Oxidation | Co-oxidation |
	Aerobic	Anaerobic			
Straight chain alkanes	+	+	+	+	+
Branched alkanes	+	+	+	+	+
Saturated alkyl halides		+		+	+
Unsaturated alkyl halides		+		+	
Esters, glycols, epoxides	+	+	+	+	
Alcohols	+	+		+	
Aldehydes, ketones	+	+		+	
Carboxylic acids	+	+		+	
Amides	+	+			
Esters	+	+			
Nitriles	+	+			
Amines	+	+			
Phthalate esters	+	+		+	
Nitrosamines		+			
Thiols					
Cyclic alkanes	+		+	+	+
Unhalogenated aromatics	+	+		+	
Halogenated aromatics	+	+		+	+
Aromatic nitro cmpds	+	+			
Phenols	+	+	+	+	+
Halogenated side chain Aromatics	+		+	+	
Nitrophenols		+			
Halophenols	+			+	
2- & 3-ring PAHs	+			I	
Biphenyls	+				
Chlorinated biphenyls	+				
4-ring PAHs	+				
5-ring PAHs	+				
Organophosphates	+	+			
Pesticides and herbicides	+	+			

Source: U.S. Environmental Protection Agency 1985.

which is a mixture of hydrocarbons including alkanes, cycloalkanes, and aromatics. Soil microorganisms initiate aerobic degradation of the alkane components through attack of either the terminus of the molecule or at a point along the chain. The most common reactions are those in which one terminus of the molecule is oxidized. A typical degradative route involves the oxidation of the terminal methyl group to an alcohol (Fig. 11.3). The initial oxidation involves the incorporation of molecular oxygen. This alcohol probably undergoes a series of dehydrogenation steps to form the corresponding aldehyde and eventually a fatty acid. Once formed, the fatty acid is further metabolized by beta-oxidation, a process in which two

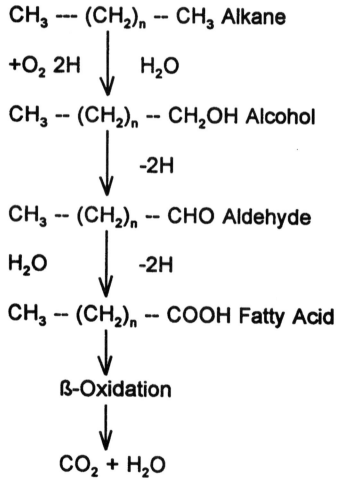

Figure 11.3.   *Oxidation of an alkane molecule by heterotrophic microorganisms*

carbons are removed from the chain and released as two moles of CO_2. The chain, containing two fewer carbons, has a new carboxylic acid group on the end, which is again available for beta-oxidation.

Microorganisms can also use cycloalkanes as a source of carbon and energy. For example, cyclohexane hydroxylation by a microbially produced monooxygenanse leads to the formation of an alicylic alcohol. Subsequent dehydrogenation of the alcohol forms a ketone, and further oxidation of the ketone results in the formation of lactone ring structure. The lactone is a substrate suitable for ring opening and is eventually converted to a dicarboxylic acid which, in turn, is subject to oxidation (Fig. 11.4) (Cookson 1995; U.S. EPA 1989).

Aromatic compounds also are subject to microbial attack by many different types of bacteria and fungi. In the case of benzene, a bacterial dioxygenase enzyme incorporates both atoms of molecular oxygen to form a *cis*-benzene dihydrodiol that is subsequently dehydrogenated, resulting in ring cleavage (Fig. 11.5). The intermediates produced by the above pathways eventually enter metabolic reaction sequences of the bacterial cell (Cookson 1995; U.S. EPA 1989).

All of the metabolic pathways discussed above require oxygen as coreactant. In addition, the organisms catalyzing these bioconversions use oxygen as a terminal electron acceptor. Hydrocarbon metabolism puts a large demand on oxygen resources; therefore, plans for biorestoration activities should consider how this oxygen demand will be supplied. Field technologies are discussed later in this chapter.

Some general rules of thumb regarding the biodegradation of alkanes, alkylaromatics, and aromatics are as follows (Cookson 1995; EPRI 1988; Bossert and Bartha 1984):

1. Gaseous *n*-alkanes (CH_4–C_4H_{10}) are removed by volatilization. Some are biodegradable but are used only by a narrow range of specialized hydrocarbon degraders, such as methanotrophs.
2. The *n*-alkanes, *n*-alkylaromatic, and aromatic compounds in the C_{10} to C_{22} range are the most readily biodegradable and the least toxic to microbes.
3. The *n*-alkanes, alkylaromatic, and aromatic hydrocarbons in the C_5 to C_9 range are readily volatilized due to their low molecular weights. These compounds are, however, biodegradable at low concentrations by some microorganisms (Cookson 1995).

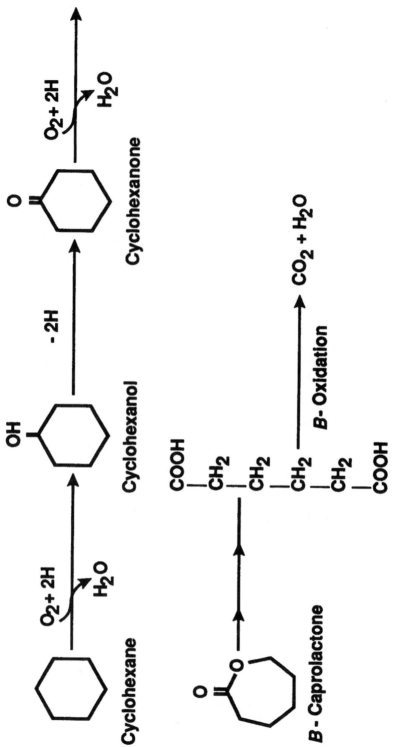

Figure 11.4. Oxidation of a cycloalkane molecule by heterotrophic microorganisms

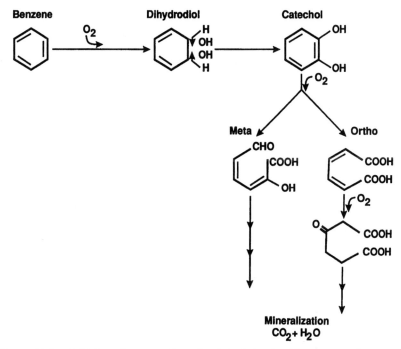

Figure 11.5. Oxidation of an aromatic molecule by heterotrophic microorganisms

4. Branched alkanes and cycloalkanes of the C_{10} to C_{22} range are less biodegradable than their *n*-alkane and aromatic counterparts. Branching interferes with beta-oxidation.

5. Highly condensed aromatic and cycloparaffinic systems, with four or more condensed rings, and the partially oxygenated and condensed components of tar, bitumen, and asphalt degrade slowly.

Depending on intended use, petroleum products contain a wide range of additives such as detergents, flow improvers, pour depressants, oxidation and corrosion inhibitors, octane improvers, anti-icing additives, combustion aids, biocides, and dyes. These additives possess a wide array of chemical structures; however, soil microorganisms possess the ability to transform many of these compounds.

11.5. INDIGENOUS VERSUS EXOGENOUS PARTICIPANTS

As part of the environmental site assessment, the contaminated soil should be assayed to determine whether the appropriate microbial consortia are present to carry out effective bioremediation. *Indigenous microorganisms* are defined as those that are native to the affected site. For remediation to be efficient and complete it may be necessary to stimulate the growth of these microbes; therefore, soil conditions such as pH, oxygen, and nutrient content may need to be adjusted. Once conditions are appropriate, indigenous microorganisms should utilize the hydrocarbon contaminants in the soil as a substrate. Under ideal circumstances, these contaminants will ultimately be converted to such nonhazardous substances as CO_2 and H_2O. The progress of the decomposition reactions must be assessed, so the levels of end-products such as CO_2 and H_2O are monitored for increases, and the levels of contaminants are measured for a decrease in concentration.

Indigenous microorganisms are typically employed at sites subjected to bioremediation. The contaminated soil should be sampled and brought to a laboratory, where the types of microorganisms present and their optimal growth conditions are measured. If the indigenous microorganisms successfully degrade the contaminant, field operations should be relatively straightforward. If the desired reactions do not occur, soil conditions may need to be modified. Furthermore, a different microbial population may be needed. If microbes needed for contaminant decomposition do not occur naturally, microbes collected from other areas (exogenous microorganisms), whose effectiveness has been documented for bioremediation, are incorporated into the contaminated soil. Soil conditions may need to be modified to ensure that the exogenous cells will survive and carry out necessary reactions (U.S. EPA 1992a).

Exogenous microorganisms are harvested from soil collected from other locations and cultured in the laboratory. The cells are placed in optimal living conditions (i.e., ideal temperature range, soil pH, concentration of nutrients, etc.). When their numbers are sufficiently high, the biomass is collected, treated and stored, transported to the site, and applied to the zone of operation. Once the degradation of the contaminants is complete, most of the exogenous microorganisms will die because they have depleted their food source and because the local environment will no longer be modified to suit their growth needs. The dead microbial cells should pose no contamination risk (U.S. EPA 1992a).

Relying on indigenous microorganisms is appropriate if useful strains are present and concentrated in the area of contamination. If indigenous organisms are already surviving in the original soil conditions, the process of optimizing the soil environment is not as complicated as it would be for exogenous microorganisms. Using indigenous microorganisms also tends to be less expensive than culturing and introducing exogenous cells into the soil. For all of these reasons, most bioremediation technologies make use of indigenous microorganisms whenever possible. However, exogenous microorganisms are needed when the appropriate suites of degrading microorganisms are not present in the soil.

11.6. FIELD TECHNOLOGIES

A bioremediation system must be designed in order to optimize and control all relevant microbial biochemical cycles. In order to support the microbial communities in survival in contaminated environments and in carrying out degradative reactions, numerous technologies have been developed. The specific technology employed is determined by the contaminants present, site conditions, types of microbes available, and cost.

11.6.1. In Situ Processes

Under the appropriate conditions, bioremediation can be successfully accomplished in situ; that is, soil microorganisms may be stimulated and/or added to treat low-to-moderate concentrations of organic contaminants in place, without excavating or otherwise disturbing contaminated soil. The reaction zone may be a soil horizon at or near the surface, or may occur in an aquifer many feet below the surface.

In some situations bioremediation can occur by the action of the indigenous microbial populations without the application of supplemental materials. This process, labeled *intrinsic bioremediation* or *passive degradation*, is normally extremely slow. For in situ bioremediation to be successful and reasonably rapid, it is necessary to stimulate the growth of microbes that react with and degrade contaminant molecules. Oxygen, nutrients, and other amendments are introduced as needed into the soil and groundwater. These additions correct many of the factors that limit microbial activity, and thus, the rate and extent of contaminant degradation. Depending on cleanup goals, in situ biodegradation can be used as the sole treatment technology or as one component of a treatment system involving other chemical and physical technologies.

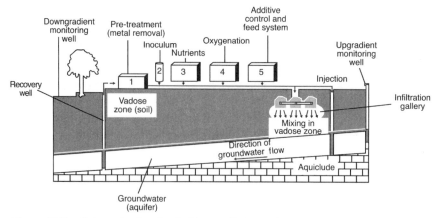

Figure 11.6.   *Schematic of an in situ bioremediation system*
U.S. Environmental Protection Agency 1984.

In situ systems commonly employ infiltration galleries together with groundwater pumping to introduce aerated, nutrient-enriched water into the contaminated zone through an array of injection wells, sprinklers, or trenches. Sufficient time is allowed for the reaction of microbial communities with the contaminants, and the treated water is eventually recovered downgradient (Fig. 11.6). The recovered water may be further treated (e.g., passage over granular activated carbon, or GAC) and reintroduced to the affected soil. Otherwise it may be discharged to a municipal wastewater treatment plant or to surface water.

In situ biodegradation is effective at degrading a range of organic compounds (Sui et al. 2006; Dettmers et al. 2006; Goi et al. 2006; U.S. EPA 1994, 1990b; Norris et al. 1993). As discussed earlier, water-soluble organic substrates possess a relative advantage in terms of biodegradability. However, relatively insoluble contaminants may be degraded if a suitable surfactant is supplied to the system, thereby increasing solubility. Compounds suitable for biodegradation include petroleum hydrocarbons (e.g., gasoline and diesel fuel), chlorinated and nonchlorinated pesticides, nonchlorinated solvents (e.g., ketones and alcohols), wood-treating wastes (e.g., creosote and pentachlorophenol), and some chlorinated aliphatics (e.g., trichloroethene). In situ biodegradation is typically not used to treat inorganics (e.g., acids and metals); however, it has been successful in the treatment of water contaminated with nitrate and phosphate (U.S. EPA 1994).

Several bacterial genera are known to be well suited for biodegradation and include *Pseudomonas, Arthrobacter, Alcaligenes, Corynebacterium, Flavobacterium, Achromobacter, Acinetobacter, Micrococcus, Nocardia,* and *Mycobacterium* (Norris et al. 1993). Others are listed in Table 11.4. The most suitable mixture for a particular contaminated site is a function of contaminant chemistry and properties of the recipient soil.

11.6.1.1. Removal of Free Product

Residual contamination, that is, that occurring as free product (NAPL) or adsorbed to soil colloids, commonly occurs at the time of discovery of the release and at the initiation of a remediation activity. An excess of NAPL compounds may be directly toxic to native microbial cells. Furthermore, immiscible compounds are not directly available to the cell. Microbes are capable of degrading only those contaminants that are directly available to the cell or its exoenzymes; in other words, compounds are

Table 11.4.   Bacteria and yeasts that oxidize aliphatic hydrocarbons

Bacteria	Yeasts
Achromobacter	Aspergillus
Acinetobacter	Candida
Actinomyces	Cladosporium
Aeromonas	Cryptococcus
Alcaligenes	Cunninghamella
Arthrobacter	Debaryomyces
Bacillus	Endomyces
Beneckea	Eupenicillum
Brevibacterium	Hansenula
Corynebacterium	Mycotorula
Desulfatibacillum	Pichia
Flavobacterium	Rhodotorula
Methylobacter	Saccharomyces
Methylobacterium	Selenotila
Methylococcus	Sporidiobolus
Methylocystis	Sporobolomyces
Methylomonas	Torulopis
Methylosinus	Trichosporon
Micromonospora	
Mycobacterium	
Nocardia	
Pseudomonas	
Spirillum	
Vibrio	

bioavailable when they are dissolved in water. Free liquids (NAPL) should therefore be removed before the bioremediation gallery is established. Pumping of free product may be required.

11.6.1.2. Water Treatment

An initial step in an in situ biodegradation system (Fig. 11.6) involves pretreating the infiltration water, if necessary, to remove metals. Groundwater, municipal drinking water, or trucked water may be used as infiltration water. The specific pretreatment steps are a function of site conditions (i.e., soil chemical properties, pH, etc.), water source, contaminant properties, chemistry of the metal(s) of concern, and treatment system used (U.S. EPA 1994). The relevant chemical properties of the water must be determined in advance in order to avoid adverse reactions. At a minimum pH, salinity level, total organic carbon, and dissolved Fe should be assessed.

If groundwater is used, excess dissolved Fe may bind applied phosphates, which are required for microbial growth. Soluble Fe will also deplete hydrogen peroxide or other oxidizing agents, which are often used as oxygen sources. The Fe can be complexed at this point in the treatment process by applying excess phosphate in the infiltration water. Likewise, addition of $CaCO_3$ or CaO will increase the pH of the water and result in the formation of iron oxides, carbonates, and other precipitates. Clogging of the system by metal precipitates must be considered during this phase (see "Clogging and Its Control," later in this chapter). Another consideration in using groundwater or recycled water is that toxic metals originally occurring in the contaminated soil may have to be removed from the recycled infiltration water so that the active microbial biomass is not inhibited.

Following pretreatment of the infiltration water, a microbial inoculum, containing either indigenous or exogenous microbial cells, can be added to augment the indigenous microbial community. An inoculum enriched from site samples may be injected at the site, or commercially available cultures known to degrade the contaminants can be supplied. The ability of exogenous microbes to survive in a foreign and toxic environment, as well as the ability to metabolize a range of substrates, should first be assessed in pilot tests (U.S. EPA 1994).

Nutrients essential to the activity of both indigenous and exogenous organisms are often applied to the in situ treatment train. Optimum nu-

Table 11.5.   Nutrients required for biological treatment

Major	C, H, O, N, P
Minor	Ca, Mg, S, Fe, K, Na, Cl
Micro	B, Co, Cu, Mn, Mo, Ni, Zn, V

trient levels are specific to the site and are best predicted via bench-scale testing. Nitrogen and phosphorus are commonly applied and should be included in such systems at a minimum. Trace elements may be added, but they typically occur at sufficient levels in soil and groundwater. Macro- and micronutrients important for microbial establishment and growth are listed in Table 11.5. Nitrogen application rates must be carefully determined to avoid excessive nitrate formation (U.S. EPA 1994, 1990b). Excessive quantities of nitrates in groundwater are linked with health problems in humans, especially infants. Similarly, P application rates must be calculated to prevent precipitation as calcium and iron phosphates.

Just before water is introduced to the contaminated site, the pH can be adjusted using simple additives. A neutral pH is recommended for most systems because this will favor the activity of common bacteria. Water can be acidified with simple inorganic acids; conversely, pH can be increased with pulverized lime, $Ca(OH)_2$. Limestone ($CaCO_3$) may also be used in pulverized form; however, it is less soluble than lime. High Ca concentrations may result in the precipitation of added phosphate, which will thus not be available to the microbial populations.

11.6.1.3. Hydraulics of the In Situ System

A major design function of the in situ reaction system is to control water movement through and out of the contaminated area. Such control is provided through installation of a series of injection wells, recovery wells, and barriers. The general principles and equipment for in situ bioremediation are relatively simple. However, achieving complete control is difficult in field applications due to the heterogeneity of a site (Cookson 1995). For example, the presence of impermeable layers, buried USTs, or drums will affect flow patterns, the ultimate degree of reaction, and effectiveness of capture of liquids.

The delivery system provides the necessary reagents to the contaminated zone in a manner that minimizes losses and clogging, and provides for uniform distribution of reagents within the zone. The system will vary based on the hydrological characteristics of the site and also the extent of the contaminant plume. Gravity delivery methods involve the direct application of treatment chemicals by sprinklers, irrigation, surface flooding, or trenches. Forced delivery methods inject the necessary additives through a perforated pressurized pipe.

11.6.1.4. Surface Application

Surface application of reagents via gravity application include flooding, spray irrigation, recharge basins, and trenches. Surface gravity delivery methods are applicable for soils contaminated to shallow depths (i.e., within several feet of the surface), sites of high permeability such as gravel and sand beds, and localized contamination (Sims et al. 1993).

Hydraulic conductivity usually decreases after start-up and then stabilizes. Continuous injection will result in reduced hydraulic conductivity. Infiltration is maximized when a cycle of injection and drying is used. One goal of the remedial program is to keep drying time to a minimum while maintaining hydraulic conductivity and microbial activity (Cookson 1995).

Although surface application systems are relatively low in cost, they limit the ability to maintain overall process control. Other drawbacks are flooding and the need for runoff controls and a collection system. Flooding is avoided by installation of berms, dikes, and drainage ditches, and by establishing cycling times between flooding and drying.

Surface application methods are not appropriate where impermeable layers exist between the surface and the contamination zone. Surface applications such as flooding and spray irrigation may not be appropriate in irregular terrain and significant slope. Slopes greater than 3% to 5% can result in runoff and reduced effectiveness of applied reagents (Cookson 1995). An additional consideration when evaluating the feasibility of gravity feed is the soil organic matter content. A high organic concentration may immobilize nutrients and decompose or adsorb electron acceptors. As a result, the progress of the bioremediation program may be hindered.

11.6.1.5. Subsurface Applications

Trenches and subsurface drains are common gravity-injection methods for bioremediation reagents. Subsurface drains are generally limited to shallow depths. An infiltration gallery consists of a gravel-filled pit or trench. The applied solution fills the pores in the gallery and is distributed to the surrounding soils vertically and horizontally. A trench drainage system can also be constructed by excavating a trench and installing perforated drainage pipe or bedding of gravel, which will serve as a distribution medium. The trench is then backfilled with gravel and covered with soil. Infiltration trenches have been placed as deep as 15 ft. It is typical to protect drains from clogging by using filter fabric. The perforated pipe can be wrapped or the filter fabric can be placed on the gravel backfill. Trench lengths have measured over 150 ft. The excavated area of a pulled underground storage tank also can be used as an infiltration gallery (Sims et al. 1993). If the above delivery systems are not sufficient to support the required level of biological activity, forced injection may be required (Cookson 1995).

Forced injection involves the delivery of remediation reagents under pressure into the contaminated zone. A series of injection wells is installed at the site based on the aerial extent of the plume and hydrologic factors. This system provides for flexibility in process control because the rate and location of delivery are controlled. Permeability, aquifer thickness, and depth to water table all affect the rate of travel of injected water into the contaminated zone (Cookson 1995). These systems are applicable to soils with hydraulic conductivities greater than 10^{-4} cm/s (fine sands, loams, silt loams) and high porosities (25%–50%). A maximum injection pressure must be set to prevent hydraulic fracturing and uplift in the subsurface, which would cause the liquids to travel upward, rather than through the contaminated zone (Sims et al. 1993).

Forced injection usually involves the use of vertical wells, but horizontal wells have been employed in some situations. The advantage of the horizontal well is that reagents can be delivered to portions of the subsurface that cannot be reached by vertical wells because of the presence of utilities or surface structures. Horizontal wells do not have to be drilled directly above a contaminant source to come into contact with and remove contaminants (Cookson 1995).

Oxygen is a key limiting factor for in situ bioremediation success. The zone of influence is often established by the distance that oxygen can be carried to concentrations of at least 1 mg/L. This will determine the necessary well spacing and overall costs for forced injection processes. Ideally, injection wells and recovery wells should be situated at a distance that allows added nutrients to reach the area of contamination less than six weeks from time of injection. The travel time and reaction rates for injected chemicals are estimated from treatability studies, and should be confirmed by field monitoring. A low oxygen supply rate relative to the contaminant load results in extended remediation times. An excessive rate of oxygen results in excessive costs for the project, and potential for soil gas binding (Cookson 1995).

11.6.1.6. Oxygen Sources

In the majority of applications, bioremediation is an oxidation process. During oxidation of the contaminants, microorganisms extract energy via electron transfer. Electrons are removed from the contaminant and transferred to a terminal electron acceptor which, during aerobic biodegradation, is oxygen. During decomposition of the organic substrate, oxygen concentrations in the subsurface may become depleted. Air, oxygen, or other oxygen sources (e.g., hydrogen peroxide, ozone) may need to be added to the infiltration water. If anaerobic degradation is being used, nitrate or sulfate may be added instead to serve as electron acceptors.

Oxygen can be added to the zone by pumping molecular oxygen or by allowing for chemical reaction with the release of O_2. Pure oxygen or air can be dissolved in water and applied to the contaminated zone. A common method of delivering oxygen is pumping oxygen-saturated water into the contaminated zone. The rate of oxygen supplied is a function of project goals, hydrocarbon concentration, injection rate, and the concentration of oxygen in the water. This method, however, provides only a low overall rate of oxygen delivery. The pumping of oxygenated water into the subsurface can result in biofouling, which will inhibit the flow of air outward into the well bore (Cookson 1995).

Water can contain dissolved oxygen, but only up to about 20 mg/L. Chemical oxygen supply involves the addition of a chemical such as hydrogen peroxide that can be converted to oxygen. With the addition of H_2O_2 to water, the O_2 content can be greatly increased. Hydrogen peroxide is highly soluble in water and decomposes to water and oxygen:

$$H_2O_2 \rightarrow H_2O + \tfrac{1}{2} O_2 \qquad (11.4)$$

H_2O_2 solutions from 100 to 500 mg/L have been beneficial to the microorganisms involved in hydrocarbon degradation. At 100 mg/L or above, hydrogen peroxide keeps the injection wells free of heavy biological growth. This prevents fouling, allowing more equal and more rapid transmission of oxygen to the treatment area. In a study in the Midwest, a solution of 1,000 mg/L was found to be suitable to the indigenous microbial populations during the decomposition of diesel fuel in a contaminated aquifer under a fleet facility.

A saturated subsurface is needed if hydrogen peroxide is employed, in order to prevent significant decomposition; that is, H_2O_2 is not practical for bioremediation of the unsaturated zone. Forced injection is usually necessary, since gravity feed will result in substantial losses due to reaction with surface soil constituents (Cookson 1995). Hydrogen peroxide decomposes readily because it is a nonselective oxidizing agent. Soil organic matter, ferrous iron (Fe^{2+}), nickel, and copper will catalyze its decomposition.

Adverse reactions sometimes occur with the use of hydrogen peroxide and ozone. For example, they may react violently with other compounds present in the soil, reduce the sorptive capacity of the soil (due primarily to organic matter decomposition), and produce oxygen gas bubbles that block soil pores. If the solution is too concentrated, it will oxidize bacterial cell membranes, thus killing the cells (U.S. EPA 1994, 1990b). Hydrogen peroxide at concentrations of approximately 1,500 to 2,000 mg/L has been found to be toxic to microorganisms. Hydrogen peroxide is relatively expensive to use, and commercial formulations (25%–30%) burn skin and are highly reactive with organic debris.

One method to alleviate some of the problems of oxygen delivery to the subsurface involves the addition of a solid oxygen supply material to the contamination zone (White et al. 1998; Koenigsberg 1997; Brubaker 1995; Bianchi-Mosquera et al. 1994; U.S. EPA. 1990a). For example, solid magnesium peroxide can be installed in a barrier wall through which a contaminated plume passes. The material can also be packed into replaceable filter socks or can be directly injected in slurry form. The material is insoluble and releases oxygen in a rate-controlled manner. These supplements can last from several months to a year depending on contaminant loading (Koenigsberg 1997).

Nitrate and sulfate have also been studied as electron acceptors in bioremediation projects. Microorganisms that use nitrate as an electron acceptor have been stimulated in situ by injecting acetate as a primary substrate and nitrate as the electron acceptor. Sulfate-reducing bacteria also are stimulated by acetate injections.

Situations with multiple contaminants, each having differing chemistries, may be treated by in situ technologies. Multiple metabolic modes, for example, a design that promotes a sequence of anaerobic and aerobic metabolic processes, can be devised for an in situ treatment program (Lee et al. 2002; Master et al. 2002). A two-zone in situ treatment approach was proposed for the treatment of multiple contaminants (Meade and D'Angelo 2005; Vira and Fogel 1991). Contaminants requiring anaerobic dehalogenation are first reduced in an anaerobic metabolic zone. The reduced products and other contaminants that are not treated by the anaerobic activity are then transferred to an aerobic metabolism zone for additional treatement.

11.6.1.7. Soil Treatment

The soil under treatment may need to be pretreated in order to render all process reagents effective. Soil pH adjustment using lime is dependent on several factors including soil texture, types and amounts of clay, and organic-matter content. Additionally, changes in soil pH will influence dissolution or precipitation of soil metals and may increase the mobility of hazardous materials. Therefore, the soil buffering capacity should be evaluated prior to application of amendments. A simple buffer test such as the Shoemaker-McLean-Pratt (SMP) test may be used (McLean 1982). As with most recommendations addressing optimization of the microbial community, liming or acidification requirements should be determined on a site-specific basis.

11.6.1.8. Transformation versus Decomposition; Residuals

Bioremediation technologies are intended to mineralize organic contaminants into innocuous by-products, that is, carbon dioxide, water, and inorganic salts. In many cases, however, only a partial degradation of a contaminant may occur with the consequent generation of intermediate products. It is important to determine the identity, toxicity, and mobility of these partially degraded compounds, since they may be nonbiodegradable in the current environment. Furthermore, these intermediates can be more toxic than the parent compound. Additional remedial actions may be necessary for their control.

Gaseous emissions will also be produced during in situ biodegradation. Off-gases will vary in terms of composition (including potential toxicity), concentration, volume, and, in some cases, on the microbial population active in the contaminated media. These emissions, which may consist of the original contaminant or any volatile degradation products, must be monitored and may require collection and treatment. Vapor treatment commonly includes passage over granular activated carbon, catalytic oxidation with metal powders, biofiltration, venting, or direct burning. Any by-products of emissions treatment will require appropriate disposal. It should be noted that activated charcoal is not well suited for the removal of halogenated aliphatic compounds and short chain aliphatics. It does, however, have an affinity for aromatics such as the BTEX compounds Cookson 1995).

11.6.1.9. Recovery Systems

Groundwater at an in situ treatment system will need to be intercepted and ultimately recovered for treatment and disposal. During passive (i.e., gravity) treatment, the process water is intercepted downgradient from the contamination zone. The treated water is typically collected by gravity flow in open ditches or buried drains. Active suction via standard well pumps is occasionally used; however, this will increase maintenance costs.

11.6.1.10. On-Site Concerns

A number of variables must be regularly monitored and controlled in order for in situ bioremediation processes to successfully decompose the organic plume. Microbial activity is reduced by deficiencies in nutrients, moisture, and oxygen levels. Extremes in soil pH and soil temperature limit microbial diversity and activity. Spatial variation of soil properties (e.g., moisture, oxygen, pH, nutrients) may result in inconsistent biodegradation due to variations in biological activity. Low hydraulic conductivity can restrict the movement of water, nutrients, and electron acceptors (e.g., oxygen and nitrate) through the contamination zone (Piotrowski 1989). Low percolation rates may cause amendments to be assimilated by soils immediately surrounding application points, preventing them from reaching remote areas. High metal concentrations can adversely affect the bioremediation of organics in soil or groundwater. Several metals can be transformed (i.e., oxidized, reduced, methylated, etc.) by organisms to produce new contaminants. The solubility, volatility, and sorption potential of the original soil contaminants can subsequently be altered (U.S. EPA 1984, 1994), leading to potential toxicological effects. Examples include the methylation of Hg and As (see chapter 2).

11.6.1.11. Clogging and Its Control

A common operating problem during in situ bioremediation is clogging of the injection wells and aquifer. This is commonly a result of the presence of suspended solids, metal precipitates, and biological growth (biofouling). When suspended solids clog aquifers, the hydraulic conductivity is significantly decreased. Suspended solids arise from clays from the recovery well, floc from poor surface treatment, or biological growth. Suspended solids should be reduced to levels less than 2 mg/L in the injected water (Cookson 1995).

Chemical precipitation results from the interactions of nutrients, substrate, oxygen, and biological activity with aquifer components. A common problem results from changes in redox potential of the soil and the addition of nutrients. Groundwater in an aquifer typically has a low redox potential because natural processes will have exhausted most of the native oxygen. This frequently results in high levels of dissolved minerals, especially Fe. When groundwater is recovered and treated, oxygen will inevitably be introduced even if an oxygen source is not added. Reintroduction of this oxygenated water can result in precipitation of Fe and other metals (Norris and Matthews 1994). Phosphate has caused aquifer clogging due to the formation of orthophosphate (Cookson 1995; Aggarwal et al. 1991). Phosphate should not be injected into calcareous soil because much added phosphate will be adsorbed and precipitated. Alternate phosphate sources have been used for in situ bioremediation and include sodium tripolyphosphate and other polyphosphates (Cookson 1995; Norris et al. 1993).

Microbial clogging of injection wells is another significant problem with in situ bioremediation. The addition of oxygen and nutrients stimulates biological growth at the well openings and the adjacent soils. To reduce clogging at the injection well, a pulse injection procedure can be utilized. The electron acceptors and nutrients are injected separately at alternating intervals. The separate injection of agents results in suboptimal conditions at the injection point, discouraging biological growth (Cookson 1995; Norris et al. 1993).

A common form of biofouling results from the growth of iron bacteria. Two species associated with well biofouling are *Gallionella ferruginea* and *Leptothrix* spp. (Tuhela et al. 1993). *Gallionella* is a major organism responsible for biofouling and is ubiquitous in the biosphere. The organism derives carbon from CO_2 or from organic compounds. The bacterium oxidizes ferrous iron to the ferric form (Cookson 1995; Tuhela et al. 1993):

$$4 \ Fe^{2+} + O_2 + 4H^+ \rightarrow 4 \ Fe^{3+} + 2 \ H_2O \qquad (11.5)$$

Ferric oxides with low solubilities such as ferrihydrite ($Fe_5HO_84H_2O$) subsequently form.

$$5 \ Fe^{3+} + 12 \ H_2O \rightarrow Fe_5HO_8 \cdot 4 \ H_2O + 15 \ H^+ \quad K_{sp} = 10^{-40} \qquad (11.6)$$

Precipitates will form on well screens and in the surrounding aquifer media. Such deposits can be controlled by periodically adding higher levels of H_2O_2. It may also be possible to use HCl to solubilize Fe precipitates.

11.6.1.12. Summary

In situ bioremediation, which avoids excavation and many emissions control costs, is generally cost-effective. This is attributed in part to low operation and maintenance requirements. During setup and operation, material handling requirements are minimal, resulting in lowered worker exposures and reduced health impacts. Although in situ technologies are generally slow and at times difficult to control closely, a large volume of soil may be treated.

Although in situ biodegradation may be successful in degrading and removing organic contaminants from one site, the identical treatment system may not be effective at other sites. Contaminant mixtures may be very complex and create a hostile environment for biota. Elevated concentrations of metals, pesticides, chlorinated organics, and inorganic salts may occur in the soil, which inhibit microbial activity and overall treatment performance. Additionally, variations in soil organic matter content, moisture regime, pH, and other factors will influence microbial activity. For these reasons, it is strongly recommended that treatability studies be conducted in order to assess the effectiveness of a particular in situ bio-remediation system at a site.

11.6.2. Slurry Biodegradation

In a slurry biodegradation system, contaminated soil or sludge is re-moved from the affected area and mixed with water to produce a slurry. This slurry is then continuously mixed and aerated within a reactor vessel or lined lagoon. Decomposition of organic contaminants takes place usually via aerobic processes. Slurry biodegradation has been shown to be capable of treating soils with contaminant concentrations up to 250,000 mg/kg. The method has been used to treat a range of organic contaminants such as coal tars, wood treating wastes, American Petroleum Institute (API) separator sludge, pesticides, fuels, and some halogenated organic compounds (Thomas et al. 2006; Kim and Weber 2005; Collina et al. 2005). It is espe-cially suited to the treatment of coal tars, refinery wastes, and organic and chlorinated organic sludges. The presence of heavy metals and other poten-tial toxins may inhibit microbial metabolism and require pretreatment. Listed Resource Conservation and Recovery Act (RCRA) wastes that have been treated are shown in Table 11.6 (U.S. EPA 1989). A schematic of a slurry bioremediation system is shown in Figure 11.7.

A significant benefit in the use of slurry biodegradation is the enhanced rate of contaminant degradation, a direct result of improved contact be-tween the microorganisms and hazardous compounds. The agitation of contaminants in the water phase provides for a high degree of solubiliza-tion of compounds and greater homogeneity.

Slurry-phase bioremediation is usually conducted as a batch process. Reactors include lagoons and open and closed systems (Fig. 11.8). The treatment train typically requires a settling tank or thickener and solids de-watering. Waste preparation includes excavation, screening to remove

Table 11.6.   RCRA-listed hazardous wastes treated by slurry biodegradation

K001	Wood treating wastes
K048	Dissolved air flotation (DAF) wastes
K049	Slop oil emulsion solids
K051	American Petroleum Institute (API) separator sludge

Source: U.S. Environmental Protection Agency 1990c.

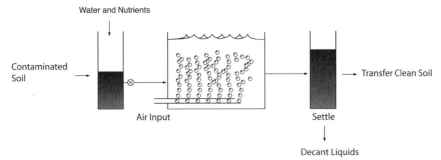

Figure 11.7. *Schematic of a slurry bioremediation system. (Reproduced with kind permission of the McGraw-Hill Companies, Inc.)*
U.S. Environmental Protection Agency 1989.

large debris, and transferring the soil material to the reactor area. Other preparation steps may include particle size reduction, water addition, nutrient and other microbial enhancer (e.g., surfactant) additions, and pH adjustment. Optimal feed characteristics for slurry biodegradation are (Cookson 1995; U.S. EPA 1990c; Richards 1965):

organic content:	0.25%–25% (w/w)
temperature:	15°–35°C
solids content:	10%–40% (w/w)
pH:	4.5–8.8
water:	60%–95% (w/w)
solids particle size:	< ¼"

Figure 11.8. *Slurry bioremediation taking place in an open lagoon. (Reprinted with kind permission of Slashbuster.com, Montesano, WA.)*

Figure 11.9.   *Aeration during slurry bioremediation taking place via mixing in an open lagoon. (Reprinted with kind permission of Slashbuster.com, Montesano, WA.)*

The soil is mixed with water, suspended in a slurry form, and mixed in a vessel to maximize contact between contaminants and the population of biodegrading microorganisms. The slurry phase can be 60% to 95% water by weight (Cookson 1995). Aeration is provided by floating or submerged aerators, compressors and spargers, or by dredging (Fig. 11.9). Aeration and mechanical agitation provide mixing. Nutrients are supplied to address chemical limitations to microbial activity; likewise, pH is adjusted as needed. Other materials such as surfactants can be used to increase substrate availability for biodegradation (Pope and Matthews 1993). Microorganisms may be added initially to seed the bioreactor or added continuously to maintain a preferred concentration of biomass.

It is necessary to monitor process control frequently in the use of slurry reactors. The high loading rates of organic-contaminated soil plus the effects of mixing and microbial processes can cause rapid changes in pH, microbial populations, nutrient needs, and electron acceptors. Once biodegradation of the contaminants is complete, the treated slurry is dewatered. A clarifier for gravity separation, hydrocyclones, or any standard dewatering equipment can be used to separate the solid phase and the aqueous phase of the slurry.

11.6.2.1. Reactors

The slurry reactor can be an engineered containment unit or a lagoon. Reactor designs are available that differ in the mechanics of oxygenation and mixing of the solid suspension. Floating direct-drive mixers with draft tubes, turbine mixers, and spargers provide aeration and mixing. Systems vary significantly in terms of energy requirements. Because retention times are often long, reactors that use less energy are the most cost-effective.

The use of open lagoons as holding ponds for hazardous and nonhazardous waste sludges had been common practice for decades. These may measure as large as several acres. Lagoons can be transformed to serve as a slurry bioremediation vessel and as the least costly treatment method. The relatively minimal materials handling reduces the risks to workers, nearby populations, and the local environment. However, engineering in situ lagoon bioremediation provides more difficult challenges than those for surface bioreactors. Unlike contaminated soil and groundwater, sludge lagoons can contain a broader chemical mixture. In addition, the chemical nature of sludges at one end or depth of a lagoon may be quite different at another location (Cookson 1995). Lagoon solids frequently require physical breaking and continuous dispersion for reasonable rates of biodegradation.

Mixing is an important process variable in slurry systems. Mixing must (Cookson 1995):

1. Maintain biomass, soil and other solid particles in a suspended state
2. Lift soils from the reactor base
3. Break up larger, insoluble particles into smaller ones that remain suspended
4. Emulsify oils and other NAPLs
5. Vary the degree of mixing to prevent an increase in toxicity, while maximizing degradation rates

Air sparging by itself has not been adequate in maintaining mixing for slurry reactors. Most soils and sludges are either too viscous or have settling velocities too great for suspension by sparging equipment. Air sparging also causes excessive volatile emissions.

A key engineering decision is selection of the microbial metabolism mode for degradation of the hazardous compounds. Because of the typical range of chemical properties, it is unlikely that one system will achieve complete treatment. If an aerobic system is selected, the stripping of volatile compounds is of concern to the operator. Volatile emissions have been a serious problem at some lagoon treatment facilities.

Oxygen supply can be augmented via the addition of pure oxygen and hydrogen peroxide. These will also minimize volatile emissions. Because air contains 20.9% O_2, large volumes of air must be injected for delivery of a given amount of oxygen. This excess gas is released from the lagoon with the transport of volatile emissions.

For soil contaminated with chlorinated hydrocarbons, an anaerobic metabolism mode can be provided, followed by an aerobic phase. This has the advantage of dehalogenating the chlorinated volatile compounds. In a subsequent phase, aeration can be provided for aerobic degradation of the remaining hydrocarbons. Disadvantages of anaerobic treatment would be the production of odors and the overall slower rate of degradation. Odor collection and treatment increase project costs. The application of an anaerobic metabolism mode followed by an aerobic phase has several advantages, however:

1. Anaerobic conditions can dehalogenate chlorinated volatile compounds.
2. There is greater detoxification of chlorinated aromatic compounds.
3. Air stripping of the chlorinated volatile compounds will not occur.
4. After anaerobic dehalogenation of volatile hydrocarbons, oxygen can be provided for aerobic degradation of the remaining hydrocarbons.
5. Operating cost is reduced because oxygen is not required during anaerobic treatment.

11.6.2.2. Residuals and Wastes

The primary waste streams generated in the slurry biodegradation system are treated solids (sludge or soil), process water, and off-gases. The solids are dewatered and may be further treated if they are still contaminated with organics. Inorganic and/or heavy metal contaminants can be treated in an on-site treatment system prior to discharge. Air emissions (e.g., BTEX) are possible during system operation. Air pollution control, for example passage over a bed of activated carbon, may be necessary.

11.6.2.3. Summary

Slurry biodegradation is not a feasible treatment method for all sites. A particular process may be capable of treating only a limited range of contaminants. Treatability tests should be conducted in order to determine the biodegradability of the contaminants and the solids/liquid separation that occurs at the end of the process.

Advantages of slurry phase bioremediation include greater and more uniform process control compared to other biological treatment technologies. The continuous mixing provides for increased contact between microorganisms and contaminants; improved distribution of nutrients, electron acceptors, or primary substrates; faster biodegradation rates; and breaking of soil-sludge particles. Furthermore, the addition of surfactants can enhance solubilities of contaminants. Slurry reactor systems experience higher degradation rates compared with those observed for solid systems.

Slurry phase systems have several disadvantages, which are related to additional process requirements and materials handling, causing higher costs. Slurry phase treatment is more costly than landfarming and composting (Cookson 1995; Hettiaratchi et al. 2001; Brox 1993). Significant quantities of wastewater can result from solids separation and dewatering after slurry treatment. This wastewater may require treatment before discharge. However, these disadvantages are often offset by the improved performance of slurry bioremediation over solid phase treatment.

11.6.3. Liquid Phase Bioremediation

There are situations in which it is advantageous to recover contaminated groundwater and treat it in an aboveground bioreactor. Microorganisms are encouraged to proliferate and are retained under optimized process conditions. Treated water is later returned to the site. The original principles of design originate from municipal and industrial wastewater treatment facilities. Several technologies are well adapted to the treatment of contaminated groundwater. However, some of the theory behind operations will differ.

In the treatment of domestic wastewater, reactor designs are based on the destruction and removal of a predictable range of contaminants, for example, dissolved organic matter. In the case of site remediation, however, the contaminants will vary from site to site and are often highly complex; therefore, designs of bioreactors are typically site-specific. Once again, treatability studies are usually necessary before designing field reactors.

Bioreactors usually fall into one of two categories: suspended growth and fixed film. In suspended growth reactors, the microbial populations are suspended as aggregates in the liquid. This biomass is termed *activated sludge*. In fixed-film reactors, biomass attaches to a solid support having very high surface area. This support layer is provided with a regular supply of oxygen while at the same time contacting the contaminated groundwater as a carbon source.

11.6.3.1. Activated Sludge

The activated sludge process is a suspended growth reactor, typically operated in a continuous mode. The major components of the process are an aeration tank and a sedimentation tank (Fig. 11.10). Biomass is reacted with the influent waste stream in an aeration tank. The solution is mixed thoroughly and aerated. Mixing is provided from physical mixers or air spargers fed by compressors. After the appropriate reaction time in the bioreactor, the biomass is transferred to a sedimentation tank. The quantity of suspended biomass accumulates quickly; therefore, sedimentation is necessary. The biomass is allowed to coagulate and settle. The clarified liquid is collected and is either discharged or treated further. The sludge is removed from the tank bottom. A portion of the biomass is recycled to the

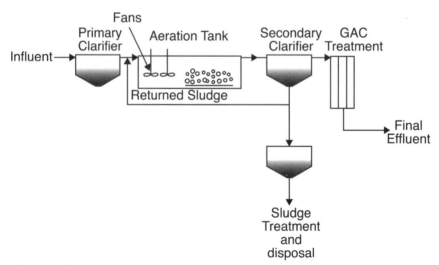

Figure 11.10.   *Schematic of an activated sludge process*

bioreactor, which allows for sustained microbial decomposition of the contaminants. The biomass is already acclimated to the waste stream constituents; there will therefore be no lag time for the microbes to act on the newly added wastes.

Activated sludge treatment systems are susceptible to shock loadings. Also, because of the difficulty in maintaining biomass, the activated sludge process is of only limited use for treating organic-contaminated groundwater (Cookson 1995). In limited cases, activated sludge treatment for groundwater has been coupled with industrial wastewater treatment at an industrial facility.

11.6.3.2. RBCs

Rotating biological contactors (RBCs) are an example of a fixed-film reactor for the treatment of contaminants in aqueous waste streams. An RBC is composed of a series of closely spaced corrugated plastic disks mounted on a horizontal shaft. The disks rotate through the aqueous wastes and approximately half of the RBC surface is immersed. The remainder of the surface area is exposed to the atmosphere, which provides oxygen to the attached microorganisms and promotes oxidation of the contaminants. Microbes become established on the surface of the disks and the organisms degrade the organics occurring in the waste. The substantial microbial population attached to the disks provides a high degree of waste treatment within a short time (U.S. EPA 1992b).

A typical RBC unit consists of 12-ft diameter plastic disks mounted along a 25-ft horizontal shaft. The total disk surface area is normally 100,000 ft^2 for a standard unit and 150,000 ft^2 for a high-density unit (Fig. 11.11) (U.S. EPA 1992b).

The overall RBC treatment process involves several steps (Fig. 11.12). Aqueous liquids are transferred from a storage tank to a mixing tank where reagents are added for pH adjustment, metal precipitation, and nutrient addition. The waste stream then enters a clarifier where floating debris, grease, metals, and suspended solids are separated from the raw influent by gravity (i.e., *primary treatment*). Clarifiers or screens remove materials that could settle in the RBC tank or plug the disks. The wastes collected from primary clarification may contain metallic and organic contaminants and may require additional treatment.

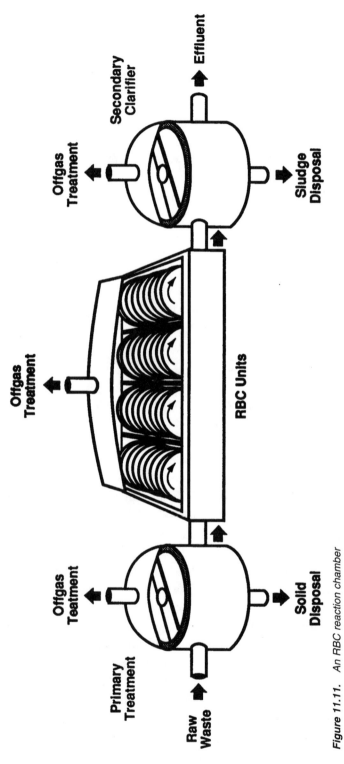

Figure 11.11. *An RBC reaction chamber*
U.S. Environmental Protection Agency 1992b.

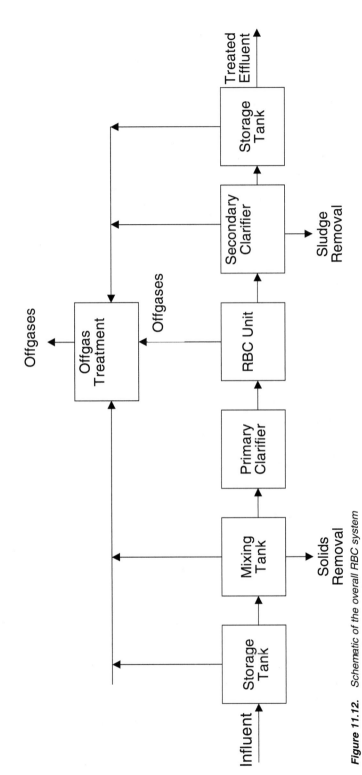

Figure 11.12. Schematic of the overall RBC system
U.S. Environmental Protection Agency 1992b.

The effluent from the clarifier enters the RBC. The disks rotate through the liquid at a rate of about 1.5 rpm. A microbial slime forms on the disks, which degrade the organic and nitrogenous contaminants present in the waste stream. The rotating motion of the disks through the aqueous waste causes excess biomass to regularly shear off. After RBC treatment, the treated effluent goes through a secondary clarification stage to separate the suspended biomass solids from the treated effluent. Additional treatment of the solids and effluent may be required. Clarified secondary effluents may be discharged to a surface stream while residual solids must be disposed of appropriately.

Biological systems can degrade only the soluble fraction of organic contamination. Thus the applicability of RBC treatment is ultimately dependent on the solubility of the contaminant. RBCs are generally applicable to influents containing organic concentrations of up to 1% organics, or between 40 and 10,000 mg/L of SBOD (soluble biochemical oxygen demand). RBCs can be designed to reduce influent biochemical oxygen demand (BOD) concentrations below 5 mg/L SBOD, and ammonia-nitrogen (NH_3-N) levels below 1 mg/L (Walker; Opatken and Bond 1988). RBCs are effective for treating solvents, halogenated organics, acetone, alcohols, phenols, cyanides, ammonia, and petroleum products (U.S. EPA 1989, 1992b, 1987).

Staging, which employs a number of RBCs in series, establishes biological cultures acclimated to successively decreasing organic loadings. As the waste stream passes from stage to stage, progressively increasing levels of treatment occur (U.S. EPA 1992b; Envirex, Inc.). Staging can also improve the system's ability to handle shock loads by absorbing the impact of a load in the initial stages. RBCs can be compartmentalized with baffles or separate tanks to provide for separate microbial communities (Cookson 1995).

Removal efficiency of RBC systems is affected by the type and concentration of organics present, liquid residence time, rotational speed, media surface area exposed, and pre- and post treatment. Issues to be addressed in RBC design include the organic hydraulic load rates, design of the disk system, rotational velocity, tank volume, media area exposed, retention time, primary treatment and secondary clarifier capacity, and sludge storage and treatment (U.S. EPA 1992b, 1987). Storage should be provided to hold the aqueous treated product until it has been tested to determine its acceptability for disposal or reuse.

During the entire treatment process, gases may be produced as a result of aeration by mixing and sparging processes, or by volatilization of hydrocarbon contaminants. The gases must be collected for treatment.

As is the case of the bioremediation systems discussed thus far, RBCs are not effective at removing inorganics or nonbiodegradable organics. Water containing high concentrations of metals and certain pesticides, herbicides, or highly chlorinated organics can resist RBC treatment by inhibiting microbial activity. It may be necessary to pretreat waste streams to remove toxic compounds prior to RBC treatment (O'Shaughnessy 1982). RBCs are susceptible to excessive biomass growth, particularly when organic loadings are high. If the biomass fails to slough off and an excessively thick (approximately > 90–125 mil) biomass layer forms, the shaft and disks may be damaged.

All bioremediation systems, including RBCs, are sensitive to temperature changes. Biological activity will decrease at temperatures higher than 55°C. Covers should be employed to protect the units from colder climates. Covers should also be used to inhibit algal growth and to control the release of volatiles (U.S. EPA 1992b).

11.6.3.3. Trickling Filter

A trickling filter (packed media) consists of a bed of coarse materials such as stones, slats, or plastic media, over which wastewater is slowly applied. Trickling filters have been a popular biological treatment process and are common for treating municipal wastewater for BOD removal. Trickling filters do not actually filter, as the name implies. The rocks in a filter measure 25 to 100 mm in diameter and hence the openings are too large to strain out solids.

A common design consists of a packed bed of stones placed from 1 to 3 m deep in a large diameter basin through which the wastewater passes (Fig. 11.13). The bed of stones serves to provide large amounts of surface area where the microorganisms attach and grow in a slime on the rocks as they feed on the organic matter. The wastewater is typically distributed over the surface of the rocks by a rotating arm. Basin diameters may be as much as 60 m. As the wastewater trickles through the bed, a microbial growth establishes itself on the surface of the support material in a fixed film. The wastewater passes over the attached microbial layer, providing contact between cells and substrate.

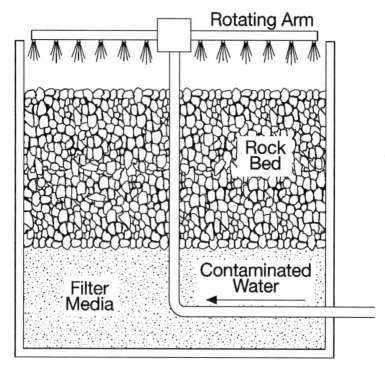

Figure 11.13. *A trickling filter system for treatment of groundwater contaminated with hydrocarbons*

Excess growth of cells washes from the rock media regularly and will cause excessive levels of suspended solids in the effluent if not removed. The flow from the filter is passed through a sedimentation basin (secondary clarifier or final clarifier) to allow these solids to settle out.

Under high organic loadings, the slime growths can be so heavy that they plug the void spaces between the rocks, causing flooding and failure of the system. The volume of void spaces is limited in a rock filter, restricting air circulation and available O_2, and hence the amount of organic waste that can be treated.

The residuals produced in a fixed-film reactor are normally small when compared to the residuals produced in a suspended growth system. The residuals, depending on site-specific requirements, may require additional treatment prior to disposal. Residuals must be disposed of appropriately (e.g., land disposal, incineration, solidification, etc.).

11.6.4. Land Treatment

Land treatment techniques for bioremediation (landfarming, bioreclamation, biopiles) are commonly used for treatment of contaminated soil but certain chemical plant sludges, industrial wastes, and petroleum waste sludges have also been added to soil for treatment. Contaminants most commonly treated are petroleum compounds including fuel, lubricating oil, and organic wood preservatives. Other applications include soil contaminated with coal tar wastes, pesticides, and explosives. Until passage of the Land Disposal Restrictions (40 CFR 2004), petroleum refineries used land treatment to dispose of a wide range of hazardous wastes. Landfarming can be regarded as a combination of biodegradation and soil venting; microbial oxidation reactions occur in combination with volatilization.

A common field installation calls for the affected soil to be excavated and moved to a prepared location (a land treatment unit, LTU, or cell) which is better suited for control of the process. Treatment involves the installation of layers (lifts) of contaminated soil to a cell. The cell is usually graded at the base to provide for drainage and lined with clay and/or plastic liners to contain all runoff within the LTU. It may also be provided with sprinklers or irrigation, drainage, and soil water monitoring systems. Because of the high water application rates, LTUs are often bordered by berms (Fig. 11.14) (Cookson 1995).

The hydrocarbon contamination levels suitable for land treatment will vary with contaminant type and site conditions. In some cases, soils with higher levels of contaminants than are recommended for land treatment can be mixed with less contaminated soil to achieve desired starting levels. Petroleum contamination as high as 25% by weight of soil has been reported as treatable, although 5% to 8% by weight or less is more readily treated (EPRI 1988; Pope and Matthews 1993).

A major benefit of the land treatment technique is that it allows for very close monitoring of process variables that control the decomposition of hydrocarbons. A typical landfarming field system is designed and implemented as follows:

1. Cell Preparation

The LTU is constructed by preparing the base. Large debris is removed to protect liners placed on it, and grading is necessary in order to control

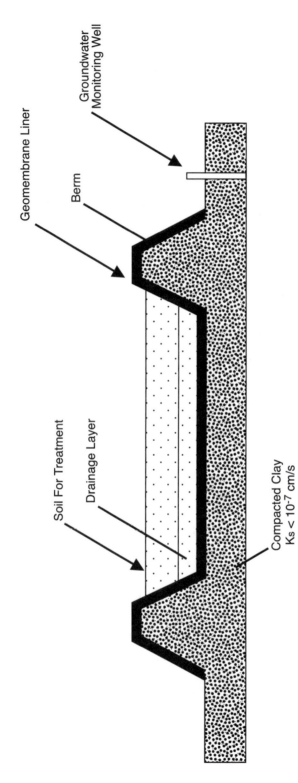

Figure 11.14. Cross-section of a land treatment unit

runoff from the LTU. The first layer installed is a liner of compacted clay. A second, optional layer may be a geomembrane liner, for example chemically resistant PVC or HDPE. A drainage system is then installed above the liners for leachate collection. This may consist of a network of perforated PVC piping situated within a highly permeable bedding, for example pea gravel. A sand or soil layer, ranging from 2 to 4 ft thick, is placed above the liner(s) and drainage system to protect them from heavy equipment (Fig. 11.15) (Cookson 1995). Ditches or berms are installed at the periphery of the cell in order to prevent run-on and to capture runoff. Requirements for the site will vary depending on local regulatory authorities.

2. Soil Preparation

The contaminated soil is excavated and screened to remove debris (greater than about 1 in. diameter), and placed on top of the porous sand or soil subbase. Most tractor-mounted tilling devices can till only to a

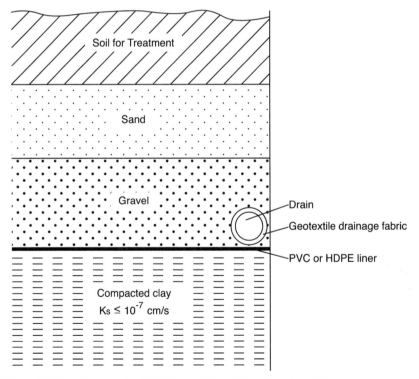

Figure 11.15.   *Close-up of an LTU liner and leachate collection system*

depth of about 12 in. Large tractors with specialized equipment that can till to depths of 3 ft or more have been used for in situ land treatment. Large augers are now available that can move soil from 50 to 100 ft depths to the surface. Any debris (for example, wood shavings) occurring in the contaminated soil that may adsorb the contaminants should be removed if possible and treated separately (Pope and Matthews 1993).

3. Addition of Nutrients

As with the other bioremediation systems described, microorganisms will require carbon sources and nutrients, both for adequate growth and for efficiently carrying out degradation reactions. Simple agricultural fertilizers containing N, P, and K can supply the required macronutrients. Soil nitrogen can be applied as fertilizer-grade ammonium nitrate or urea, and phosphorus as triple superphosphate. Inorganic nutrients are generally added in mass ratios of approximately 100:10:1 hydrocarbon:N:P. Trace K is sometimes also added. Single-dose applications should not exceed 3 lb nutrient per cubic yard of soil to prevent osmotic effects (Cookson 1995; EPRI 1988). Ammonium fertilizers are known to decrease soil pH due to nitrification processes. Agricultural fertilizer is often supplied in pellet form, which is suitable for application over large areas. It will furthermore serve as a slow-release nutrient supply. Water-soluble fertilizers can be applied through irrigation systems, allowing application rates need to be closely controlled. This will also allow for immediate availability to the microorganisms.

Wood chips, sawdust, or straw are low-cost sources of carbon. Animal manures are often used to supply both carbon and nutrients. These can be broadcast and tilled in to the soil surface. The high organic levels in these amendments increase sorptive properties of soil, thereby decreasing mobility of organic contaminants. Organic amendments also increase the soil water-holding capacity, which is beneficial in sandy soils but causes difficulty in clayey soils and in LTUs having poor drainage. An additional benefit of manure application is that it will provide an enormous and diverse biomass of heterotrophic microorganisms. Manure should be applied to each lift at the rate of about 3% to 4% by weight of soil. The manure should first be sieved and then thoroughly tilled into the soil (Pope and Matthews 1993).

The manure additive should be analyzed for total N and P content. The operator should also be aware that fresh manure may contain excessive quantities of soluble salts and may also release significant amounts of ammonia, both of which inhibit microbial growth. If salt levels, as indicated by electrical conductivity (EC) readings, are high, it may be necessary to leach the soil with water to remove excess salts before biodegradation can occur. High levels of sodium may be detrimental to soil structure. Applying calcium supplements such as gypsum, $CaSO_4$, followed by leaching may reduce sodium levels. Leaching of contaminants may also occur at the same time and must be monitored.

Sometimes inorganic micronutrients may be needed to enhance microbial activity in sterile environments (e.g., contaminated subsoils and other geologic strata). Animal manures are a low-cost material that will supply a range of micronutrients.

As a result of mineralization reactions, soil pH may need to be adjusted. Liming agents include CaO and $CaCO_3$, among others. Acidification can be carried out with simple inorganic acids (sulfuric, phosphoric), elemental sulfur, or aluminum sulfate.

4. Inoculation

Exogenous microbial cultures are becoming increasingly popular for addition to bioremediation units; however, exogenous microorganisms rarely compete well enough with indigenous populations to sustain useful population levels. Additionally, most soils that have been exposed to biodegradable wastes over the long term already contain adequate numbers of indigenous microorganisms that are effective degraders.

5. Tillage and Mixing

After placement of soil in the LTU and after the addition of nutrients, each lift should be tilled, disked, or plowed. This will enhance oxygen infiltration, mixing of additives, contaminant contact with microorganisms, and produce a more homogeneous growth media. Tillage generally will require several passes with a disk harrow or similar equipment. The soil is then watered and allowed to incubate. Effective land treatment is limited to the top 12 to 24 in. of soil. At depths below 12 in. the oxygen supply is generally insufficient for land treatment. Tilling mixes the soil and increases the oxygen levels, but is usually limited to 12 in. or less (Cookson 1995; Pope and Matthews 1993).

The land treatment process is often limited in clayey soils, especially if soils remain relatively moist. This limitation is related to difficulties in oxygen transfer. Clayey soils should be applied in shallower lifts than sandy soils. Permeability, oxygen incorporation, and tilth can be improved by adding organic matter or other bulking agents to the soil. A cover may be placed over the LTU to limit rainfall infiltration.

6. Moisture Control

Soil moisture content should be near the lower end of the recommended range before tilling. Tilling saturated soil may destroy soil structure, reduce oxygen and water incorporation, and reduce microbial activity. Tilling should not occur until at least 24 hours after irrigation. Tilling more than is necessary for enhanced oxygen incorporation and contaminant mixing may destroy soil structure and compact soil below the tilling zone (Pope and Matthews 1993).

Regular maintenance of soil moisture is critical to optimizing bioremediation in LTUs. Monitoring soil moisture and scheduling irrigation is essential. For optimal degradation rates, the soil should receive periodic moisture to maintain a fairly constant moisture level. The soil should be tilled at intervals between six weeks and three months (EPRI 1988). The appropriate moisture level for the soil to be treated can be determined in the field or laboratory using simple tests. A range of 70% to 80% field capacity is suggested as an optimum level of soil moisture. A soil is at field capacity when applied water no longer drains by the action of gravity — that is, micropores are filled with water and macropores are filled with air. This condition allows for adequate amounts of both air and water to soil microorganisms. If soils are allowed to become excessively dry, cells may lyse and microbial activity will cease. Too much soil moisture will limit microbial activity by excluding oxygen and favoring anaerobic conditions. Furthermore, since these soils are nonvegetated, excess water may result in erosion of soil plus contaminants.

The addition of a bulking agent such as wood chips, sand, or sawdust can increase porosity of the soil and improve drainage.

Surface drainage of the LTU can be critical in the event of excessive irrigation or high rainfall. If soil is saturated for more than a few hours, aerobic microbial actvity may be reduced. The LTU drainage system, often a sand layer or a geotextile/drainage net layer under the LTU, is installed so that soil water in excess of field capacity will be quickly drained away so microbial activity will not be inhibited. The contaminated soil layer will take up water from irrigation or rain until the soil nears saturation, at which point excess water will be discharged into the drainage system.

7. Leachate Treatment

Hydrocarbon degradation can be a slow process, relying on a succession of microbial communities. During the relevant microbially-catalyzed reactions, leachates produced can be recycled back to the soil in the LTU. Depending on local climate, it may be useful to install a roof or other cover to limit the amount of precipitation contacting the cells. This will limit the quantity of leachate generated for treatment. Liquid storage capacity should be provided so that runoff and leachate water can be recycled onto the LTU. In many cases leachate and runoff water cannot be discharged without treatment. Monitoring of groundwater and soil may be performed for large operations to ensure that the hydrocarbons are within the treatment area, and to assess total hydrocarbon, nutrient, and pH levels.

In some situations, soils that contain petroleum compounds can be applied to the site at regular intervals. Reapplication will replenish the carbon supply and maintain biological activity at the desired level.

11.6.4.1. Completion of the Project

Measurements of the success of degradation reactions can be conducted using simple field tools, for example a photoionization detector for the nonspecific measurement of gaseous hydrocarbons, to gas chromotographic analysis of soil and soil water for specific contaminants and their products of decomposition. Some methods for hydrocarbon analysis are listed in chapter 5, "Environmental Site Assessments." Once the desired goals are realized the soil can be returned to the excavated site or applied to other uses.

11.6.4.2. Overview of Landfarming

The landfarming technique is a relatively inexpensive and low-technology practice, and is not highly labor-intensive. The method requires large amounts of land. It also may result in the release of contaminants to the air and possibly to noncontaminated soil and water. As with other bioremediation applications, pesticides, halogentated hydrocarbons, metals, and inorganic salts will inhibit microbial activity, especially at low pH. Used motor oil may not be appropriate for landfarming due to its relatively high metal and PAH content (see chapter 3).

Many gasoline components possess a high vapor pressure (i.e., are of significant volatility); therefore, land treatment of gasoline-contaminated soil will result in releases by volatilization. A permit for hydrocarbon emissions may therefore be needed. Diesel and kerosene fuels possess some volatiles but weathered forms that are low in volatile components may be appropriate for land treatment. Most of the heavier petroleum products (fuel oils, lubricating oils, waste sludges, and oils) are also suitable for land treatment. Petroleum products that consist mostly of long chain hydrocarbons (20+ carbons) and other high-molecular weight compounds (asphalts, tars, 5–6 ring PAHs) are not suitable for land treatment because of the biorefractory nature of such compounds and the difficulty of mixing them with soil. Commercial bacterial preparations may be suitable to degrade such compounds (Cole 1994; Pope and Matthews 1993).

11.7. BIOREMEDIATION: AN OVERVIEW

Bioremediation has the advantage of being less costly than conventional cleanup methods such as incineration or excavation and landfilling of toxic soil material. Additionally, this technology will degrade and detoxify the contaminant rather than simply transfer it, as in the case of soil washing or soil vapor extraction. Bioremediation is also a relatively simple technology. It can be carried out with minimal disruption to the affected site, few emissions of volatile organics, and minimal health risks to workers on-site. There are disadvantages, however, to its utilization. Much of the experience in this technology has been gained in the laboratory. Little is known regarding the products of decomposition of the contaminants. It is also difficult to experience in the field the same successes of the laboratory, where conditions are controlled and relatively uniform. Success of the entire process is related to the control of several environmental factors including moisture and oxygen content, nutrient levels, and adequate pH and temperature range. Cleanup goals may not be achieved because some contaminants may be only partly biodegradable. Furthermore, as bioremediation proceeds, degradation reactions will slow and the cells may switch to other substrates or stop growing (Eweis et al. 1998).

11.8. CASE HISTORY 1

The French Limited Superfund Site in Crosby, Texas, is a former industrial waste storage and disposal facility measuring 22.5 acres. Between 1966 and 1971, approximately 70 million gal of industrial wastes from local petrochemical companies were disposed at the site. Wastes included tank bottoms, pickling acids, and off-specification product from petroleum refineries and petrochemical plants. Most of the waste was deposited in an unlined, 7.3-acre lagoon. Wastes were also processed in tanks and burned (U.S. EPA 1995b).

The lagoon had been established in an abandoned sand pit that filled with water to a 20 to 25 ft depth. The primary contaminants identified in the lagoon included PAHs, halogenated semivolatiles, halogenated volatiles, nonhalogenated volatiles, metals, and nonmetallic elements. The wastes were concentrated in a 4 ft-thick layer of tarlike sludge at the base of the lagoon and a 5- to 6-ft layer of subsoil (U.S. EPA 1989, 1995b; Hasbach 1993). Specific constituents included PCBs at concentrations up to 616 mg/kg; volatile organics up to 400 mg/kg for an individual contaminant; pentachlorophenol up to 750 mg/kg; semivolatiles up to 5,000 mg/kg for an individual contaminant; and metals up to 5,000 mg/kg for an individual metal. The thick, viscous, oily, black layer of sludge consisted of a mixture of petrochemical sludges, kiln dust, and tars (primarily styrene and soils). Subsoil material varied from fine-grained silts to coarse sand (U.S. EPA 1995b).

The U.S. EPA identified approximately 90 companies as PRPs for site cleanup, and in 1983 the PRPs formed a task group that agreed to perform the cleanup. The following remedial alternatives were considered for the French Ltd. Site (U.S. EPA 1995b, 1988):

- no action
- encapsulation of contaminants by slurry walls and a multilayered cap
- on-site incineration of sludge and contaminated subsoil
- on-site incineration of sludge and chemical fixation of contaminated subsoil in place
- biological treatment of sludge and contaminated subsoil

The EPA proposed incineration as the remedial technology for the sludge and contaminated soil at an estimated cost of $75 to $125 million. The PRP task group then investigated other more cost-effective alternatives. A pilot-scale bioremediation treatability study was conducted in a 0.6-acre section of the lagoon. As a result of the study, the Record of Decision (ROD) replaced incineration with in situ biodegradation for remediation of the site (U.S. EPA 1995b, 1988; DEVO 1992). Biological treatment was selected because it was considered capable of meeting cleanup goals within a reasonable period of time and at a lower cost than incineration. However, if bioremediation was found to not be successful in the lagoon, the ROD called for the use of incineration.

The slurry phase bioremediation system used at French Ltd. was designed to stimulate indigenous microorganisms to oxidize the organic wastes with aeration, pH control, and nutrient addition. The tar-like sludge was sheared and introduced into a mixed liquor using centrifugal pumps. The subsoil was sheared and introduced into the liquor using subsoil mixers. Controlled shearing was a major factor in controlling the growth of biomass. Controlling the level of dissolved oxygen and pH (U.S. EPA 1995b, 1988; Hasbach 1993) also regulated biomass growth. Four sludge mixers provided the shear mixing of sludges, and four hydraulic subsoil mixers provided the shear mixing of lagoon bottom subsoils. The mixed liquor contained about 5% to 10% solids during operation (U.S. EPA 1995b, 1988). The sludge and subsoils were treated separately; this process kept the sludge from coating the soil particles and maximized the surface area available for treatment, thereby enhancing treatment effectiveness.

The lagoon was divided into two treatment cells of approximately equal volume. The cells were created by installing a sheet piling wall across the lagoon to provide for equal treatment media volume in each cell, allowing for sequential remediation. Additional benefits of sequential remediation were the limiting of air emissions during the operation, reducing the amount of capital equipment to purchase, and allowing for process improvements during the remediation operation.

The treatment cells were designed to hold a total mixed liquor volume of 34 million gal (17 million gal in each cell), and to maintain a minimum dissolved oxygen concentration of 2.0 mg/L. Based on treatability studies, an oxygen uptake rate of 0.30 mg/L/min. was chosen for the aeration supply. Oxygen requirements for each cell were calculated to be about 2,500 lb/hr (U.S. EPA 1995b, 1988).

The main components of the bioremediation process included a MixFlo aeration system, a liquid oxygen supply system, a chemical feed system, and dredging and mixing equipment (Fig. 11.16). A pure oxygen aeration system was selected over an air-based system in order to lower organic emissions during the remediation activity. Greater amounts of organic vapors are released from air-based aeration systems because greater amounts of air are needed to generate the required dissolved oxygen content. The MixFlo system has higher transfer efficiencies than air-based aeration systems (90% as opposed to 30%) and uses high-purity oxygen. The combination of higher transfer efficiency and high-purity oxygen reduces the amount of organic off-gases from the treatment process (Hasbach 1993).

The MixFlo aeration system dissolves oxygen in a two-stage process. First, water is pumped from the treatment area and pressurized. Pure oxygen is then injected into the water. The resulting two-phase mixture passes through a pipeline contractor where 60% of the injected oxygen dissolves. In the second stage, the oxygen/water mixture is reinjected into the treatment area.

At the French Ltd. site, oxygen was injected in eight pipeline contractors into the mixed liquor. Furthermore, raft-mounted self-powered circulation mixers were utilized (U.S. EPA 1995b, 1988).

Batch systems for chemical addition were used to control pH and nutrient chemistry of the mixed liquor during treatment. Hydrated lime was diluted on-site to 15% concentration. To offset nutrient losses, N was added as hydrated urea (46% N by weight) and P was added as liquid ammonium phosphate. The system was designed to add batches of up to 1,500 gal of chemicals to the lagoon at several locations.

Treatment performance was monitored using subsoil and sludge samples and mixed liquor samples. Five indicator compounds were reduced in concentration over the course of treatment. Benzene, for example, was reduced from 608.0 mg/kg to 4.4 mg/kg in one cell and from 393.3 mg/kg to 5.2 mg/kg in the second cell (U.S. EPA 1995b, 1988).

Cleanup criteria were achieved within ten months of treatment for the first cell and eleven months for the second cell. For individual constituents, cleanup goals were met soonest for vinyl chloride (four

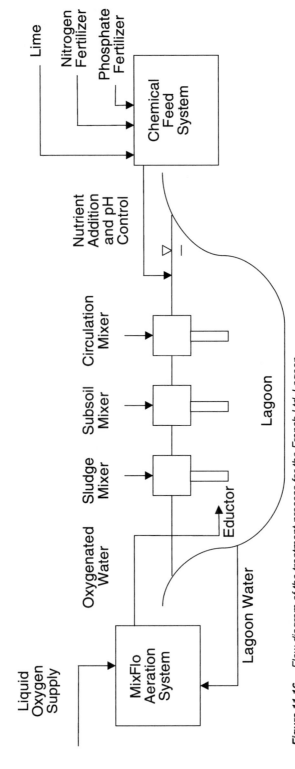

Figure 11.16. *Flow diagram of the treatment process for the French Ltd. Lagoon*
U.S. Environmental Protection Agency 1995b.

months in the first cell, one month in the second cell) and total PCBs (four months in the first cell, one month in the second cell). Benzo[a]-pyrene required the longest treatment time to meet cleanup goals. Concentrations of vinyl chloride were reduced to below detection limits in the first cell and 6.6 mg/kg in the second; benzene was reduced to 4.4 mg/kg in the first cell and 5.2 mg/kg in the second; and benzo[a]pyrene to 6.0 mg/kg in the first cell and 6.8 mg/kg in the second. PCBs were biodegraded in the slurry phase system to concentrations below the action levels established for the site (Table 11.7). Apparently the arsenic and metals had no deleterious effects on growth of hydrocarbon-degrading organisms.

An air monitoring program was established to monitor potential releases of VOCs from the bioremediation operation. Automated instrumentation was placed around the treatment cell. The data showed no excesses over the established criteria for releases of VOCs; total VOC concentrations ranged from 0.3 to 1.6 ppm, well below the action level

Table 11.7.   Concentration of contaminant compounds over time, first treatment cell

Day	Vinyl Chloride	Benzene	Benzo[a] pyrene	Total PCBs	Arsenic
			mg/kg		
Cleanup Criteria	43.0	14.0	9.0	23.0	7.0
96	314.8	608.0	BDL	77.0	9.2
110	29.4	162.3	BDL	6.4	20.3
124	32.5	119.8	BDL	N/A	121.2
145	0.5	10.8	BDL	11.4	125.4
166	0.8	25.6	BDL	15.8	N/A
187	1.2	41.9	14.4	13.4	17.9
201	BDL	18.8	27.4	10.3	84.7
215	BDL	16.3	BDL	13.2	61.8
229	BDL	10.9	28.0	3.1	10.2
239	1.2	7.3	33.7	8.7	1.2
253	4.8	12.1	26.3	14.7	1.4
272	4.3	7.6	3.1	7.4	BDL
275	BDL	7.3	8.7	6.8	BDL
289	BDL	6.0	7.4	4.6	BDL
293	BDL	5.8	4.8	6.0	1.1
295	BDL	4.4	6.0	7.9	NR

BDL = below detection limit
NR = not reported

Source: U.S. Environmental Protection Agency 1995b.

of 11 ppm specified in the ROD. These data, in combination with the operating data, indicate that organic compounds including vinyl chloride, benzene, and benzo[a]pyrene were removed from the lagoon via biodegradation.

After soil and sludge cleanup objectives had been achieved, reverse osmosis was used to treat the surface water in the lagoon. Forty million gallons of surface water were processed through the system and discharged to the San Jacinto River. As the lagoon was dewatered, it was backfilled with clean soil. The site was then planted with grass and native vegetation and contoured to drain away from the lagoon (Collins and Miller 1994).

The total cost of remediating the soil and sludge in the lagoon at French Ltd. was $49 million, including costs for pilot studies, technology development, project management, EPA oversight, and backfill of the lagoon (Table 11.8). About 55% of the project costs ($26,900,000) were for activities directly associated with treatment, such as solids/liquids/vapor/gas preparation and handling, pads/foundations/spill control, mobilization/setup, start-up/testing/permits, training, and operation (three years). About 34% of project costs were for before-treatment activities and 11% for after-treatment activities. The $26,900,000 in costs for activities directly associated with treatment converts to $90/ton of sludge and soil treated (300,000 tons treated) (U.S. EPA 1995b, 1988).

Table 11.8.   Breakdown of project costs for the French Ltd. cleanup activity

Project Clement	Cost ($)
Development and pilot-scale work	12,200,000
Floodwall	2,300,000
Operation, maintenance, analytical	22,900,000
Dewatering	1,000,000
Fixation	400,000
Technical support	2,900,000
Administrative	3,100,000
Demobilization	1,900,000
EPA oversight	2,300,000
TOTAL	49,000,000

Source: U.S. Environmental Protection Agency 1995b.

11.9. CASE HISTORY 2

The Burlington Northern Superfund site, located in Baxter and Brainerd, Minnesota, operated a railroad tie treating plant between 1907 and 1985. The preserving process involved pressure-treating wood using a heated creosote/coal tar or creosote/fuel oil mixture. Wastewater generated from the process was disposed into two shallow, unlined surface impoundments. The first impoundment measured approximately 60,000 ft^2 and was filled with sludge and buried under clean fill in the 1930s. A second impoundment was used from the 1930s until 1982. Soil and groundwater beneath these impoundments became contaminated as a result of waste leaching. Soil at three additional areas at Burlington Northern was also determined to be contaminated (Remediation Technologies, Inc. 1995a, 1995b; U.S. EPA 1995a).

The site was found to be contaminated with PAHs and other nonhalogenated semivolatile organic compounds including naphthalene, acenaphthylene, acenapthene, fluorene, phenanthrene, anthracene, fluoranthene, pyrene, benzo[a]anthracene, chrysene, benzo[b and k]fluoranthenes, benzo[a]pyrene, benzo[ghi]perylene, dibenzo[a,h]anthracene, indeno-[1,2,3]pyrene, and phenols. Total PAH concentrations for so-called visibly contaminated soils in the surface impoundments were as high as 70,633 mg/kg, with individual PAHs measuring up to 21,319 mg/kg (acenapthene), 7,902 mg/kg (phenanthrene), and 10,053 mg/kg (fluoranthene) (Table 11.9) (U.S. EPA 1995a).

As part of the mandated remediation activity, Burlington Northern was required to excavate and treat soils and sludges that were visibly contaminated and that contained free oils that could migrate to groundwater.

Table 11.9.   **Average PAH concentrations for visibly contaminated soils in the surface impoundments, Burlington Northern Superfund Site**

Compound	Impoundment 1	Impoundment 2
Total 2-ring PAHs	15,565	31,464
Total 3-ring PAHs	5,895	11,839
Total 4- and 5-ring PAHs	12,522	27,330
Total PAHs	33,982	70,633
Benzene extractables	66,100	112,500
Total phenols	16	65

Source: Remediation Technologies, Inc. 1995b.

Three alternatives for treatment of contaminated soils and sludges were considered for the site (U.S. EPA 1995a):

- land treatment of contaminated soils and sludges
- incineration of contaminated soils and sludges
- land treatment of contaminated soils, and incineration of sludges

On-site land treatment of contaminated soils and sludges was selected because it was considered to be protective of public health and the environment, and was the lowest-cost alternative. Additionally, tests consisting of six pilot-scale test plots and six bench-scale reactors demonstrated the feasibility of using land treatment for the contaminated soils and sludges (U.S. EPA 1995a; Environmental Research & Technology 1985).

A land treatment unit (LTU) was constructed at the site. The unit was constructed over one former surface impoundment after the visibly contaminated soils and sludges were removed. The area available for treatment measured approximately 255 × 450 ft (about 115,000 ft^2). The following layers were installed at the base of the LTU:

- 100-mm thick high-density polyethylene membrane liner (for the bottom and the side slopes of the LTU)
- 18 in. of silty sand
- 6 in. of gravel
- 24 in. of clean, silty sand

The bottom of the LTU sloped 0.5%. The LTU was enclosed by containment berms to control the flow of run-on and runoff. The gravel layer served as a leachate collection system during treatment. Two-ft wide leachate collection drains were placed in the gravel layer. The drains were lined with gravel, and perforated pipe wrapped with filter fabric was installed to collect leachate. This plumbing carried leachate to a sump (Remediation Technologies, Inc. 1995b; U.S. EPA 1993).

Soil and sludge excavated from the surface impoundments and other contaminated areas at the site were stockpiled adjacent to the LTU. Initially, approximately 1,100 to 1,500 yd^3 of soil and sludge were spread over the LTU to a depth of 6 to 8 in. each year. Dump trucks transported the contaminated materials from the stockpile to the LTU.

Land treatment was conducted annually from May through October, and the system was operated for nine seasons. The treatment area was tilled weekly to 12 in. with a tractor-mounted rototiller. A major purpose of mixing was to increase the microbial population in the current year's lift. This was accomplished via introduction of air, volatilization of low-molecular weight organics, and improving overall permeability for air and water movement. A 24-in. ripper was used on limited occasions to break up the compacted soil layer beneath the tillage zone. The LTU was irrigated to maintain a soil moisture content of approximately 10% by weight. Soil pH was maintained between 6.2 and 7.0 with the addition of liming materials, and the C:N:P ratio was maintained near 100:2:1 with application of cattle manure (Remediation Technologies, Inc. 1995b; U.S. EPA 1993).

Leachate from the LTU, collected in the sump, was discharged to an on-site storage tank. Some of the leachate was applied to the LTU as irrigation water while the remainder was discharged to a local sewer system. Upon completion of the land treatment operation a cover was placed over the LTU.

To assess LTU treatment performance, each lift of contaminated soil and sludge was sampled immediately after application and then monthly through the end of the treatment season. Samples were analyzed for methylene chloride-extractable (MCE) hydrocarbons and PAHs. At the end of the last treatment season, samples were collected at four depths in the LTU to assess residual concentrations of MCE hydrocarbons and PAHs.

The cleanup goal for total PAHs in soils and sludge was 8,632 mg/kg for all nine treatment seasons, which was achieved. Total PAHs in soil before treatment ranged from 626 to 17,871 mg/kg, and from 564 to 4,326 mg/kg after treatment. The average value for total soil PAHs after treatment was 1,854 mg/kg, well below the cleanup goal (Table 11.10).

The cleanup goal for MCE hydrocarbons (21,000 mg/kg) was not met in any treatment season. Concentrations of soil MCE hydrocarbons before treatment ranged from 26,000 to 89,000 mg/kg, and from 22,000 to 48,000 mg/kg after treatment, all of which exceed the cleanup goal. The average value after treatment was 33,000 mg/kg. Because the cleanup goal for MCE hydrocarbons was not met at the end of the treatment period, Burlington Northern was required to carry out a contingency procedure of

Table 11.10. Total PAH concentrations in the LTU at
start and end of each treatment season

Season	Before Treatment	After Treatment
	mg/kg	
1	16,160	1,895
2	17,871	4,326
3	12,931	3,145
4	10,887	2,518
5	6,008	1,275
6	6,097	948
7	626	564
8	13,471	1,220
9	3,544	795
Average	9,733	1,854

Source: Remediation Technologies, Inc. 1995b.

placing a cover over the treatment area to prevent infiltration of liquid through the treatment zone.

Residual concentrations of MCE hydrocarbons and PAHs did not vary substantially with depth in the LTU among the treatment seasons. Through the top 56 in. of the unit, concentrations of MCE hydrocarbons varied less than 10% with depth, and concentrations of total PAHs varied about 26% with depth. Additionally, contaminants in the LTU soils did not migrate to the uncontaminated layers below the unit. After treatment, the concentrations of MCE hydrocarbons and total PAHs in the uncontaminated soil below the contaminated material were substantially lower than in the treated soil.

PAH treatment efficiency, measured as a percent reduction in average concentration before and after treatment, decreased with increasing number of ring structures in the PAH molecule. Two-ring PAHs were reduced by an average of 96%, three-ring PAHs by 92%, and four- and five-ring PAHs by 60% (Table 11.11). Two-ring PAHs were reduced to concentrations below analytical detection limits for two of the nine treatment seasons (U.S. EPA 1995a).

With the exception of naphthalene and 2-methylphenol, the range of concentrations measured in the leachate were below groundwater action levels. Naphthalene measured as high as 590 μg/L (action level = 30 μg/L) and 2-methylphenol measured as high as 87 μg/L (action level = 30 μg/L) (U.S. EPA 1995a).

Table 11.11.   Residual concentrations of MCE hydrocarbons and PAHs in the LTU at completion of land treatment activity

Compounds	0–8 in.	8–32 in.	32–56 in.	56–66 in.
MCE hydrocarbons	26,900	24,800	25,300	450
Total 2-ring PAHs	65.13	45.95	49.5	0.02
Total 3-ring PAHs	225	128	199	0.15
Total 4-ring PAHs	382	276	256	0.17
Total 5-ring PAHs	123.5	154.8	226.7	0.225
Total PAHs	795.63	608.35	731.2	0.565

Source: Remediation Technologies, Inc. 1995b.

QUESTIONS

1. List the electron acceptor(s) required in the metabolism of an organic compound during aerobic respiration; during anaerobic respiration.

2. Choose the correct answer: All other factors being equal, in situ bioremediation would be most effective for a site contaminated with: (a) Cd^{2+}; (b) DDT; (c) Cr^{6+}; (d) PAHs; (e) gasoline; (f) $> C_{100}$ alkanes.

3. Choose the correct answer: A biorefractory molecule: (a) is not amenable to bioremediation; (b) may be a heavily chlorinated hydrocarbon; (c) is recalcitrant; (d) includes PCBs and PAHs; (e) all of the above.

4. During in situ bioremediation, well water may be used for introducing nutrients. For which specific compounds/elements may this water require treatment?

5. In order to increase the DO content of infiltrating water during ISB, H_2O_2 at levels of ____ can be added.

6. List and discuss the common limitations to bioremediation for site remediation.

7. Complete the chemical reaction showing the oxidative decomposition of hexadecane to CO_2 and H_2O.

$$CH_3(CH_2)_{14}CH_3 \rightarrow \underline{\hspace{1cm}} \rightarrow \underline{\hspace{1cm}} \rightarrow \underline{\hspace{1cm}} \rightarrow CO_2 + H_2O$$

a. RCOH b. RCH$_4$ c. RCOR d. RCHO e. RCH$_3$ f. RC=CH$_2$ g. RCOOH

8. Branched alkanes biodegrade more quickly in soils compared to straight chain alkanes. True or false? Explain your answer.

9. For what specific purpose(s) do soil bacteria carry out oxidative degradation of organic materials?

10. During slurry bioremediation, high loading rates of organic-contaminated soil plus the effects of mixing and microbial processes can cause rapid changes in slurry pH and N levels. Explain the mechanisms for these phenomena.

11. During in situ bioremediation, it is important to remove free product; such molecules may become toxic to microbes if allowed to accumulate. Explain.

12. Oxygen availability is a key limiting factor during in situ bioremediation. True or false?

13. Of the organic molecules listed below, determine which: have low water solubility; are most toxic to microorganisms; will experience slowed beta oxidation; are removed more rapidly by volatilization rather than biodegradation.

- n-alkanes, C_5–C_9
- n-alkanes above C_{22}
- cycloalkanes $< C_{10}$
- highly condensed aromatics
- branched alkanes
- PCBs

REFERENCES

Aggarwal, P. K., J. L. Means, and R. E. Hinchee. 1991. Formulation of nutrient solutions for in-situ bioremediation. In *In-Situ Bioremediation, Applications and Investigations for Hydrocarbon and Contaminated Site Remediation*, ed. R. E. Hinchee and R. F. Olfenbuttel. Boston: Butterworth-Heinemann.

Alexander, M. 1977. *Introduction to Soil Microbiology*. 2nd ed. New York: John Wiley and Sons.

Anderson, J. P. E. 1984. Herbicide degradation in soil: Influence of microbial biomass. *Soil Biology and Biochemistry* 16:483–89.

Andersson, B. E., S. Olsson, T. Hentry, L. Welinder, and P. A. Olsson. 2000. Growth of inoculated white-rot fungi and their interactions with the bacterial community in soil contaminated with polycyclic aromatic hydrocarbons, as measured by phospholipids fatty acids. *Bioresource Technology* 73 (1): 29–36.

Aulenta, F., V. Tandoi, M. Potalivo, M. Majone, and M. P. Papini. 2006. Anaerobic bioremediation of groundwater containing a mixture of 1,1,2,2-tetrachloroethane and choloroethenes. *Biodegradation* 17 (3): 193–206.

Baxter, J, and S. P. Cummings. 2006. The impact of bioaugmentation on metal cyanide degradation and soil bacteria community structure. *Biodegradation* 17 (3): 207–17.

Bianchi-Mosquera, G. C., R. M. N. Allen-King, and D. M. Mackay. 1994. Enhanced degradation of dissolved benzene and toluene using a solid oxygen-releasing compound. *Groundwater Monitoring and Remediation* 9 (1): 120–28.

Bossert, I., and R. Bartha. 1984. The fate of petroleum in soil ecosystems. In. R.M. Atlas ed. Petroleum Microbiology. Macmillan, New York, NY.

Brox, G. 1993. Bioslurry treatment. Proceedings Applied Bioremediation. Fairfield, N.J.

Brubaker G. R. 1995. The boom in in situ bioremediation. *Civil Engineering-ASCE* 65 (10): 38–41.

Cole, G. M. 1994. Assessment and Remediation of Petroleum Contaminated Sites. Boca Raton, FL: CRC Press.

Collina, E., A. Franzetti, F. Gugliersi, M. Lasagni, D. Pitea, G. Bestetti, and P. Di Gennaro. 2005. Napthalene biodegradiation kinetics in an aerobic slurry-phase bioreactor. *Environment International* 31 (2): 167–71.

Collins, M., and K. Miller. 1994. Reverse osmosis reverses conventional wisdom with Superfund cleanup success. *Environmental Solutions* (September).

Cookson, J. T. 1995. *Bioremediation Engineering. Design and Application*. New York: McGraw-Hill.

Das, A. C., P. Sukul, D. Mukherjee, A. Chakravarty, and G. Sen. 2005. A comparative study on the dissipation and microbial metabolism of organophosphate and carbamate insecticides in orchaqualf and fluvaquent soils of West Bengal. *Chemosphere* 58 (5): 579–84.

Dettmers, D. L., K. L. Harris, L. N. Petersen, G. D. Mecham, J. S. Rothermel, T. W. Macbeth, K. S. Sorenson Jr., and L. O. Nelson. 2006. Remediation of a TCE plume using a three-component strategy. *Practice Periodical of Hazardous, Toxic and Radioactive Waste Management* 10 (2): 116–25.

DEVO Enterprises, Inc. 1992. *French Limited: A Successful Approach to Bioremediation.* Washington, DC.

Electric Power Research Institute. 1988. *Remedial Technologies for Leaking Underground Storage Tanks*. Chelsea, MI: Lewis.

Envirex, Inc. *Rex Biological Contactors: For Proven, Cost-Effective Options in Secondary Treatment*. Bulletin 315-13A-51/90-3M.

Environmental Research & Technology. 1985. *Treatment Demonstration Report. Creosote Contaminated Soils. Prepared for Burlington Northern Railroad. Prepared by Environmental Research & Technology, Inc*. Document D245.

Eweis, J. B., S. J. Ergas, D. P. Y. Chang, and E. D. Schroeder. 1998. *Bioremediation Principles*. Boston: McGraw-Hill.

40 CFR. 2004. *Part 268. Land Disposal Restrictions*. Washington, DC: U.S. Government Printing Office.

Goi, A., N. Kulik, and M. Trapido. 2006. Combined chemical and biological treatment of oil contaminated soil. *Chemosphere* 63 (10): 1754–63.

Green-Ruiz, C. 2006. Mercury(II) removal from aqueous solutions by nonviable *Bacillus* sp. from a tropical estuary. *Bioresource Technology* 97 (15): 1907–11.

Hasbach, A. 1993. Biotreatment of PCB sludges cuts cleanup costs. *Pollution Engineering*, May 15.

Hettiaratchi, J. P. A., P. L. Amaatya, E. A. Jordan, and R. C. Joshi. 2001. Slurry phase experiments as screen protocol for bioremediation of complex hydrocarbon waste. *Practice Periodical of Hazardous, Toxic, and Radioactive Waste Management* 5 (2): 88–97.

Kim, H. S., and W. J. Weber Jr. 2005. Polycyclic aromatic hydrocarbon behavior in bioactive soil slurry reactors amended with a nonionic surfactant. *Environmental Toxicology and Chemistry* 24 (2): 268–76.

Koenigsberg, S. 1997. Enhancing bioremediation: New magnesium peroxygen compounds accelerates natural attenuation. *Environmental Protection*.

Krishna, K. R., and L. Philip. 2005. Bioremediation of Cr(VI) in contaminated soils. *Journal of Hazardous Materials* 121 (1–3): 109–17.

Lee, T. H., M. Ike, and M. Fujita. 2002. A reactor system combining reductive dechlorination with cometabolic oxidation for complete degradation of tetrachloroethylene. *Journal of Environmental Sciences* 14 (4): 445–50.

Master, E. R., W. W. Mohn, V. W.-M. Lai, B. Kuipers, and W. R. Cullen. 2002. Sequential anaerobic-aerobic treatment of soil contaminated with weathered aroclor 1260. *Environmental Science and Technology* 36 (1): 100–103.

McGrath, R., and I. Singleton. 2000. Pentachlorophenol transformation in soil: A toxicological assessment. *Soil Biology and Biochemistry* 32 (8–9): 1311–14.

McLean, E. O. 1982. Soil pH and lime requirement. In *Methods of Soil Analysis*, 2nd ed., ed. A. L. Page, R. H. Miller, and D. R. Keeney. Madison, WI: American Society of Agronomy.

Meade, T., and E. M. D'Angelo. 2005. [^{14}C]Pentacholorphenol mineralization in the rice rhizosphere with established oxidized and reduced soil layers. *Chemosphere* 61 (1): 48–55.

Nnamchi, C. I., J. A. N. Obeta, and L. I. Ezeogu. 2006. Isolation and characterization of some polycyclic aromatic hydrocarbon degrading bacteria from Nsukka soils in Nigeria. *International Journal of Environmental Science and Technology* 3 (2): 181–90.

Norris, R. D., K. Dowd, and C. Maudin. 1993. The use of multiple oxygen sources and nutrient delivery systems to effect in situ bioremediation of saturated and unsaturated soils. In *Symposium on Bioremediation of Hazardous Wastes: Research, Development, and Field Evaluations*. EPA/600/R-93/054. Cincinnati: U.S. Environmental Protection Agency.

Norris, R. D., and J. E. Matthews. 1994. *Handbook of Bioremediation*. Boca Raton, FL: CRC Press.

Opatken, E. J., and H. K. Bond. 1988. Stringfellow leachate treatment with RBC. *Environmental Progress* 7:23–31.

O'Shaughnessy. 1982. Treatment of oil shale retort wastewater using rotating biological contactors. Water Pollution Control Federation, 55th Annual Conference, St. Louis.

Piotrowski, M. R. 1989. Bioremediation: Testing the waters. *Civil Engineering*.

Pope, D. F., and J. E. Matthews. 1993. *Bioremediation Using the Land Treatment Concept*. EPA/600/R-93/164. Washington, DC: U.S. Environmental Protection Agency, Office of Research and Development.

Remediation Technologies, Inc. 1995a. *Remedial Action Report for the BNSF Former Tie Treating Plant, Brainerd, Minnesota. Prepared for Burlington Northern Santa Fe Railroad. November.*

———. 1995b. *Treatment Completion Report for the BNRR Former Tie Treating Plant Brainerd, Minnesota. Prepared for Burlington Northern Railroad, Overland Park, Kansas. Fort Collins, Colorado. May.*

Richards, L. A. 1965. Physical condition of water in soil. In *Methods of Soil Analysis*, ed. C. A. Black. Madison, WI: American Society of Agronomy.

Sims, J. L., R. C. Sims, R. R. Dupont, J. E. Matthews, and H. H. Russell. 1993. In situ bioremediation of contaminated unsaturated subsurface soils. EPA/540/S-93/501. Washington, DC: U.S. Environmental Protection Agency, Office of Solid Waste and Emergency Response.

Sui, H., X. Li, G. Huang, and B. Jiang. 2006. A study on cometabolic bioventing for the in situ remediation of trichloroethylene. *Environmental Geochemistry and Health* 28 (1–2): 147–52.

Sulfita, J. M., and G. W. Sewell. 1991. *Anaerobic Biotransformation of Contaminants in the Subsurface. Environmental Research Brief.* EPA/600/M-90/024. Ada, OK: U.S. Environmental Protection Agency, Robert S. Kerr Environmental Research Laboratory.

Thomas, R. A. P., D. E. Hughes, and P. Daily. 2006. The use of slurry phase bioreactor technology for the remediation of coal tars. *Land Contamination and Reclamation* 14 (2): 235–40.

Tuhela, L., S. A. Smith, and O. H. Tuovinen. 1993. Microbiological analysis of iron-related biofouling in water wells and a flow-cell apparatus for field and laboratory investigations. *Groundwater* 31:982–88.

Umrania, V. V. 2006. Bioremediation of toxic heavy metals using acidothermophilic autotrophes. *Bioresource Technology* 97(10): 1237–42.

U.S. Environmental Protection Agency. 1983. *EPA Guide for Identifying Cleanup Alternatives at Hazardous Waste Sites and Spills: Biological Treatment.* EPA/600/3-83/063.

———. 1984. *Review of In-Place Treatment Techniques for Contaminated Surface Soils.* Vol. 2, *Background Information for In Situ Treatment.* EPA/540/2-84/003b. Cincinnati.

———. 1985. *Handbook: Remedial Actions at Waste Disposal Sites.* Rev. ed. EPA/625/6-85/006. Cincinnati.

———. 1987. *Data Requirements for Selecting Remedial Action Technology.* EPA/600/2-87/001. Washington, DC: Office of Emergency and Remedial Response.

———. 1988. *Superfund Record of Decision, French Limited, Texas. March.*

———. 1989. *Superfund LDR Guide #6A: Obtaining a Soil and Debris Treatability Variance for Remedial Actions.* OSWER Directive 9347.3-06FS.

———. 1990a. *Enhanced Bioremediated Utilizing Hydrogen Peroxide as a Supplemental Source of Oxygen.* EPA/600/2-90/006. Ada, OK: U.S. Environmental Protection Agency, Robert S. Kerr Environmental Research Laboratory.

———. 1990b. *Handbook on In Situ Treatment of Hazardous Waste-Contaminated Soils.* EPA/540/2-90/002. Cincinnati, OH.

———. 1990c. *Slurry Biodegradation.* EPA/540/2-90/016. Washington, DC: Office of Emergency and Remedial Response.

———. 1992a. *A Citizen's Guide to Using Indigenous and Exogenous Microorganisms in Bioremediation.* EPA/542/F-92/009. Washington, DC: Office of Solid Waste Emergency Response.

———. 1992b. *Rotating Biological Contactors*. EPA/540/S-92/007. Washington, DC: Office of Emergency and Remedial Response.

———. 1993. *Five-Year Review Report. Burlington Northern Brainerd/Baxter Minnesota. U.S. EPA, Region V, Chicago, IL. January 27, 1993*.

———. 1994. *In Situ Biodegradation Treatment*. EPA/540/S-94/502. Washington, DC: Office of Emergency and Remedial Response.

———. 1995a. *Land Treatment at the Burlington Northern Superfund Site, Brainerd/Baxter, Minnesota. Cost and Performance Report*. Washington, DC: Office of Solid Waste and Emergency Response, Technology Innovation Office.

———. 1995b. *Slurry-Phase Bioremediation at the French Limited Superfund Site Crosby, Texas. Cost and Performance Report*. Washington, DC: Office of Solid Waste and Emergency Response, Technology Innovation Office.

Vira, A. and S. Fogel. 1991. Bioremediation: The treatment for tough chlorinated hydrocarbons. *Biotreatment News* 1:8.

Walker Process Corporation. *EnviroDisc Rotating Biological Contactor*. Bulletin 11-S-88. See: www.walker-process.com.

White, D. M., R. L. Irvine, and C. R. Woolard. 1998. The use of solid peroxides to stimulate growth of aerobic microbes in tundra. *Journal of Hazardous Materials* 57 (1–3): 71–78.

Young, T. S. M, M. C. Morley, and D. D. Snow. 2006. Anaerobic biodegradation of RDX and TCE: Single- and dual-contaminant batch tests. *Practice Periodical of Hazardous, Toxic, and Radioactive Waste Management* 10 (2): 94–101.

CHAPTER 12

Phytoremediation

Until man duplicates a blade of grass, nature can laugh at his so-called scientific knowledge. . . . It's obvious that we don't know one millionth of one percent about anything.

—Thomas A. Edison

What is a weed? A plant whose virtues have not yet been discovered.

—Ralph Waldo Emerson, *Fortune of the Republic* 1878

12.1. INTRODUCTION

Plant-based remediation systems can serve as a cost-effective treatment system for soils having properties that impede the success of conventional technologies (e.g., low permeability, saturation, dense structure, mixtures of contaminants). Phytoremediation is a low-cost, low-technology process defined as the engineered use of green plants to extract, accumulate, and/or detoxify environmental contaminants. Phytoremediation employs common plants including trees, vegetable crops, grasses, and even annual weeds to treat heavy metals, inorganic ions, radioactives, and organic compounds. When the appropriate plants are cultivated in contaminated soils, the root system functions as a dispersed uptake system. Contaminants are taken up with soil water and degraded, metabolized, and/or sequestered in the plant, while evapotranspiration from aerial parts maximizes the movement of soil water through the plant.

Certain plants have been identified that can take up and concentrate metals and other inorganics from soil into leaves, stalks, seeds, and roots.

Organic compounds can be degraded or immobilized in the root zone or incorporated into shoot tissues and metabolized. Relevant mechanisms involve the biological, chemical, and physical processes involved in the uptake, storage, and metabolism of substrates by the plant and/or the microorganisms that occur in the root zone (Fig. 12.1) (Hinchman et al. 1997). An example of a simple phytoremediation system in use for years is the constructed wetland, in which aquatic plants such as water hyacinths are cultivated to remove contaminants (metals, nitrate, etc.) from municipal or industrial wastewater.

Phytoremediation is useful for soils contaminated with relatively immobile contaminants to shallow depths. This technology can work well in low-permeability soils, where most technologies have a low success rate. It can also be used in combination with conventional cleanup technologies

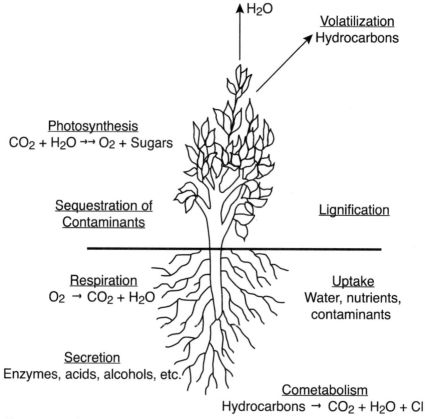

Figure 12.1.   *Oxygen, water, and chemical cycling through a green plant*

(e.g., pump-and-treat). Phytoremediation can be an alternative to harsher remediation technologies such as solidification/stabilization, incineration, and soil washing, which destroy the biological portion of the soil, alter its chemical and physical properties, and create a relatively inert material. Phytoremediation can benefit the soil, leaving an improved, self-sustaining soil ecosystem at a fraction of the cost of current technologies. As a result of using green plants over the long term, there are obvious improvements to the aesthetics of the affected area.

Certain plants possess a remarkable capability to survive and even flourish in soils designated hazardous. In many cases, common agronomic practices can be utilized to provide for a productive environment in which plants serve as a feasible treatment mechanism for contaminants.

12.2. PHYTOEXTRACTION OF METALS

Most metals that pose environmental hazards typically occur naturally in soils and plants in trace quantities, that is, a few mg/kg (see chapter 2). Trace metals considered essential for plant growth include cobalt (Co), chromium (Cr), copper (Cu), iron (Fe), manganese (Mn), molybdenum (Mo), nickel (Ni), vanadium (V), and zinc (Zn). Many metals are toxic above "micro" concentration levels; therefore, plants have developed mechanisms to regulate cellular concentrations of metals, primarily by regulating metal uptake from soil and translocation within the plant. For most metals, uptake occurs primarily through the roots, where the majority of mechanisms to prevent metal toxicity are found. For example, plants possess transport systems that can take up ions selectively from soil.

The specific mechanisms that enable certain plants to incorporate and tolerate high amounts of toxic elements are not yet clear. In one classification system proposed by Baker (1981), categories of plant uptake mechanisms include accumulators, indicators, and excluders. *Accumulators* survive in metal-rich soils by concentrating metals in aboveground tissues. The accumulation is often in organs or as metabolized forms so they are less harmful to the plant. Accumulators concentrate high levels of toxic elements independently of the soil concentration. *Indicator plants* control the translocation of toxic elements from roots to shoots, so that the concentration in the soil is reflected as a proportional concentration in the aboveground biomass. *Geobotanical indicators* are plants whose composition reflects the composition of the parent soil/rock formation so well that they can be used to locate mineral deposits. *Excluders* restrict the amount of toxic element that is transferred to the aboveground biomass until a concentration is reached at which the mechanism breaks down, with subsequent uncontrolled translocation (Baker 1981; Negri and Hinchman 1996).

More than one definition of a *hyperaccumulator* is in use; however, the basic meaning is consistent. *Hyperaccumulators* are plants that take up toxic elements and accumulate them in aboveground biomass at levels many times the usual concentrations, with little or no adverse affect to the plant (Table 12.1) (Baker and Brooks 1989). Some hyperaccumulators of Ni and Zn may contain as much as 5% each on a dry-weight basis (Blaylock et al. 1997; Brown et al. 1995). An outstanding example of hyperaccumulation is found in the latex of the New Caledonian tree *Sebertia acuminata*, which accumulates more than 20% Ni. Other accumulators include greater than 10% Zn accumulation by penny cress (*Thlaspi calaminare*), 10% Ni accumulation by alyssum (*Alyssum bertolonii*), up to 3% Cr concentration in *Pimela suteri* and broom tea tree (*Leptospermum scoparium*), and up to 3% uranium by *Uncinia leptostachya* and *Coprosma arborea*. The Indian mustard plant, *Brassica juncea*, can accumulate 3.5% dry weight of leaves with Pb (Kabata-Pendias 2001). Hemp dogbane (*Apocynum* sp.) and common ragweed (*Ambrosia artemisiifolia*) also accumulate significant amounts of Pb (Sutherson 1997). The Zairean hyper-

Table 12.1. Selected species of metal hyperaccumulators

Metal	Plant Species	Percentage of Metal in Dry Weight of Leaves (%)	Native Location
Cd	Thlaspi caerulescens	< 1	Europe
Co	Haumaniastrum robertii	1	Zaire
Cr	Brassica juncea	< 1	India
Cu	Aeolanthus biformifolius	1	Zaire
Ni	Phyllanthus serpentinus	3.8	New Caledonia
	Alyssum bertoloni and 50 other species of alyssum	> 3	Southern Europe and Turkey
	Sebertia acuminata	25 (in latex)	New Caledonia
	Stackhousia tryonii	4.1	Australia
Pb	Brassica juncea	< 3.5	India
	Ambrosia artemisiifolia	< 1	North America, Europe
Zn	Arabidopsis halleri	< 1	Eurasia and Northern Africa
	Thlaspi species	< 3	Europe
	Viola species	1	Europe

accumulator *Haumaniastrum katangense* has been cropped on soil contaminated with radioactive Co (Baker and Brooks 1989). Several researchers (Arapis 2006; Fesenko et al. 2003; Dushenkov et al. 1999; Lasat et al. 1998; Entry et al. 1996; Salt and Kay 1999) have isolated higher plants that remove ^{137}Cs from soil. An accumulation of up to 1% Hg has been reported for white birch (*Betula papyrifera*) (Negri and Hinchman 1996). Baker and Brooks (1989) identified 145 hyperaccumulators of Ni, 26 of Co, 24 of Cu, and 8 of Mn.

Almost all metal-hyperaccumulating species in use today were discovered on metal-rich mineral outcroppings. Such plants are endemic to these soils, indicating that hyperaccumulation is a physiologic adaptation to metal stress (Baker and Brooks 1989). The majority of hyperaccumulating species discovered so far are restricted to a few limited geographical locations.

A simple and common application of phytoremediation is *phytoextraction*, which involves the use of hyperaccumulating plants to transport metals from the soil to concentrate them into roots and aboveground shoots. In certain cases, contaminants can be concentrated thousands of times higher in the plant than in the soil. Following harvest of the extracting crop, the metal-rich plant biomass can be digested (for example, composted) or ashed to reduce its volume, and the resulting material can be processed as an "ore" to recover the contaminant (e.g., valuable heavy metals, radionuclides). If recycling the metal is not economically feasible, the small amount of ash (compared to the original plant biomass or the large volume of contaminated soil) can be disposed of appropriately.

Phytoextraction is based on the ability of plants and their associated rhizospheres to solubilize, absorb, and concentrate dilute contaminants. Critical components of the rhizosphere, in addition to a diverse range of free-living microorganisms, include root exudates. These secretions provide substrate for soil microorganisms by containing sugars and carbohydrates, and also chelating agents (e.g., citric and acetic acid) that make the ions of both nutrients and contaminants more mobile in the soil.

Numerous plants, both woody and nonwoody, have been identified with the capacity to translocate and accumulate metals into aboveground biomass (Fig. 12.2). Some grasses accumulate high levels of metals in their shoots without exhibiting toxic effects (Fowler et al. 2004; Pang et al. 2003; García et al. 2004; Pichtel and Salt 1988). However, their low biomass production results in relatively low yield of metals. The breeding of

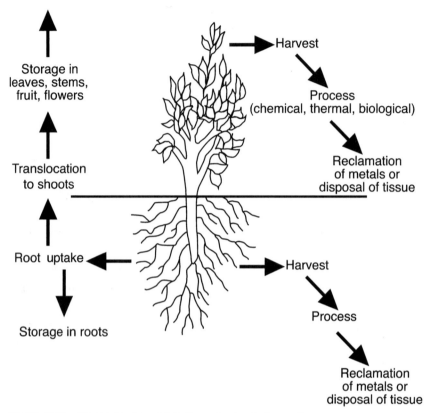

Figure 12.2. *Phytoextraction of metallic contaminants from soil*

hyperaccumulating plants that produce large amounts of biomass would make metal extraction more effective. Many crop plants accumulate metals in roots and aboveground shoots. This is particularly true for certain leafy vegetables (e.g., cabbage, lettuce, spinach) and root crops (potato, carrot) (Channon et al. 2005; Tandi et al. 2004; Mantovi et al. 2003; U.S. EPA 1983), although other crops such as corn (*Zea mays* L.) and soybean (*Glycine max*) have shown to be effective (Blaylock et al. 1997; Muchuweti et al. 2006; Liu et al. 2005; Huang et al. 1997). Using crop plants to extract metals from the soil is practical because of the plants' high biomass production and relatively fast rate of growth. Another benefit is that they are relatively easy to cultivate with commonly used equipment. While extraction by crops has advantages from a remediation standpoint, there exists a potential threat to the food chain. Regulations established under RCRA for hazardous waste (40 CFR 1996) include limits on the amounts of Cd, Pb, and other metals that can be applied to soils grown for crops.

The use of trees can result in extraction of significant amounts of metals because of their high biomass production. Researchers in the United Kingdom (Salt C. A. et al 1995) have established alder, birch, and pine trees on metal-enriched soils from an abandoned steelworks. In addition to removing soil metals, trees serve to establish green belts in brownfields and/or urban areas. The use of trees in phytoremediation may create concerns about falling leaves, however. When metal-laden leaves fall and disperse, recirculation of metals back to the site and migration off-site by wind can occur.

It is strongly preferred that metal accumulation occurs in shoot rather than root tissue in order to simplify tissue harvest (Fig. 12.3). In most plants the roots sequester the majority of the contaminant that is removed. Techniques and equipment for harvesting roots, including young tree roots, are being evaluated for use with hyperaccumulating plants. Sequestration of heavy metals in roots as opposed to translocation to aboveground plant parts reduces the possibility of dispersion of the contaminants via food chains by wildlife, domestic animals, or birds. However, root harvest is energy intensive and slow compared to shoot harvest. Furthermore, there is an increased exposure hazard to workers involved in root harvest.

Figure 12.3. *Poplar trees planted for the extraction of zinc, copper, and nickel from a former industrial waste site*

12.2.1. Technical Feasibility

The success of phytoextraction of soil metals is variable, and depends on:

1. Concentration of contaminant(s). Phytoremediation is best used at sites with low to moderate metal content. Excess quantities of soil metals will impair normal plant physiologic processes. What is considered "excessive" is a function of individual plant factors and soil conditions. Plants may experience slowed vegetative growth, impaired maturation, or death on exposure to excessive concentrations. Specific examples of damage by metals include root blockage by the formation of metal precipitates, interference in the uptake of metals required for plant growth (e.g., Cd^{2+} can substitute for Zn^{2+} in some situations), or enzyme dysfunction from metal saturation. Heavily contaminated soils may not permit normal plant growth without the addition of soil amendments.

2. Depth of contamination. Rooting depth for many non-woody species can be up to 24 in., depending on the plant and soil type. Certain deep-rooted trees (for example, poplars) can extend roots up to 10 ft.

3. Chemical forms of the metal. The capability of a plant to accumulate metals is dependent in large part on the chemistry of the soil system in which the plants are established. Soil metals occur in numerous forms, with varying degrees of "bioavailability" to plants (see chapter 2). Metals that have aged in place for many years tend to crystallize into nonreactive or partly reactive forms. In certain situations, elemental metal may occur at a site. For example, sites have been assessed in which Pb ingots and metallic Pb from automobile batteries are clearly visible in the soil (Pichtel et al. 2000). Metal in this form is obviously unavailable to plants except over extremely long periods.

   Of paramount importance to uptake is the actual chemical *species*, or fraction, of that metal. Soil fractionation procedures in combination with plant uptake bioassays may serve to assess metal bioavailability (Pichtel and Salt 1988; Tessier et al. 1979; Sims and Kline 1991; Petruzzelli 1989; Sposito et al. 1982). Attempts have been made to partition metals into chemically distinct forms through the use of sequential extraction with selective reagents. For example, soils have been extracted sequentially with H_2O, KNO_3, NaOH,

Na_2EDTA, and hot HNO_3. These reagents are expected to remove the soluble, exchangeable, organic-bound, carbonate-bound, and residual soil metals, respectively. The order of plant-available metals is:

$$soluble = exchangeable > organic\text{-}bound =$$
$$carbonate\text{-}bound >> residual$$

Such bench-scale analyses of soil metals may provide very useful indices of phytoremediation success.

4. The presence of potentially interfering contaminants. Types and amounts of soil organic matter will affect the availability of metals. Some may strongly chelate and immobilize metals, rendering them only slowly extractable by the plant root. The presence of NAPL in the soil will slow plant growth by interfering with availability of soil water. NAPL may also be directly toxic to the plant by acting as a surfactant/dispersant.

5. Soil chemical and physical properties. The general soil chemical milieu can strongly influence metal uptake by the plant. The amount of biomass that can be produced is one of the limiting factors affecting phytoremediation; therefore, optimal fertility, with fertilization of the site, should be considered for increased productivity of the selected plant species. Amendment of soils to change pH, nutrient composition, or microbial activity can be selected in treatability studies to assess the efficiency of phytoremediation. Likewise, soil moisture status must be considered. Soil texture and structure will influence infiltration rate, available moisture, and potential for leaching and runoff.

6. Plant factors. Total contaminant removal is determined by many plant attributes. These include tolerance to the contaminant; tolerance to soil conditions (pH, salinity, structure, permeability); tolerance to the local climate; rate of uptake; transpiration rate; plant biomass production; root type, fibrosity, rooting depth, and harvestability; duration of growth (annual, biennial, perennial); dormancy; and resistance to pests and disease (Salt D. E. et al. 1995; Shimp et al. 1993).

7. Degree of site preparation. Many contaminated sites have served as waste dumps and may contain unconsolidated and large wastes.

Debris should be removed from the site prior to tillage and planting. Tillage, surface drainage, irrigation, and controls of run-on and runoff may be needed at the site.

Many hyperaccumulator species are not suitable for phytoremediation in the field due to low biomass production and slow growth. It has therefore been suggested to use high biomass species such as maize (*Zea mays* L.), pea (*Pisum sativum* L.), oat (*Avena sativa* L.), canola (*Brassica napus* L.), and barley (*Hordeum vulgare* L.), while optimizing plant- and soil-management practices to enhance metal uptake (Blaylock et al. 1997; Sposito et al. 1982; Shen et al. 2002; Ajwa, Banuelos, and Mayland 1999; Ebbs and Kochian 1998; Banuelos et al. 1997). Greenhouse-scale studies have shown that certain crop plants are capable of promising rates of phytoextraction. Maize, alfalfa, sorghum, and sunflower (*Helianthus annuus*) were found to be effective due to their rapid growth rate and substantial biomass production (Sposito et al. 1982; U.S. EPA 2000). The highest bioaccumulation of lead among crop plants is reported for leafy vegetables (especially lettuce) grown near nonferrous metal smelters where plants are exposed to lead sources in both soil and air. In these locations, lettuce has been found to contain up to 0.15% Pb (dry weight) (Smith et al. 1995). Lead has also been found to accumulate in certain crops such as oats grown on biosolids-amended soils (Pichtel and Anderson 1997).

12.2.2 Agronomic Practices for Enhancing Phytoextraction

As with production of any crop plant, metal-accumulating plants respond favorably to establishment of optimum soil chemical and physical characteristics and plant husbandry. For example, application of the appropriate fertilizer materials increases biomass production. Some precautions are worth noting, however. For example, the addition of phosphorus fertilizer during phytoextraction can inhibit Pb uptake due to precipitation as pyromorphite and chloro-pyromorphite (Chaney et al. 2000). Foliar application of P is one means to circumvent this problem.

Planting practices also affect success of metal uptake from soil. The degree of metal extraction depends markedly on the total quantity of biomass produced. Plant density (number of plants/m^2) affects biomass production as it affects both yield per plant and yield per hectare. In general, a higher planting density tends to minimize yield per plant and maximize yield per hectare. Density may also affect the pattern of plant growth and development. For example, at higher stand density, plants will compete more aggressively for light. As a result, more nutrients and energy may be allocated for plant growth as opposed to developmental processes (e.g., flowering and reproduction). Additionally, the distance between plants may affect the structure of the root system with subsequent effects on metal uptake (Lasat 2000).

Growth of weeds and proliferation of diseases may decrease yields; therefore, crops cultivated for soil remediation must be rotated. If phytoremediation is anticipated to last for only a short period (e.g., two to three years) monoculture may be acceptable. However, for longer-term applications (as is the case for most metal phytoextraction projects), successful metal cleanup probably will not be achieved with only one species. Plant rotation is even more important when multiple crops per year are to be grown (Lasat 2000).

12.2.3. Treatment of Biomass

The total amount of contaminant that a plant can remove in a growing season depends on the plant's contaminant concentration in the harvested biomass multiplied by its total biomass (Negri and Hinchman 1996). Metal-enriched plant residues can be treated as hazardous waste or recycled as metal ore (Sas-Nowosielska et al. 2004). In the latter case, reclamation as "biological ores" is usually accomplished by smelting or acid extraction of the dried or ashed tissue. Even if the plant ashes do not contain sufficient metal concentration to be useful in smelting, phytoextraction remains beneficial because it reduces by as much as 95% the amount of hazardous waste to be landfilled (U.S. EPA 1997). The "bio-ore" product contains both metal and the fuel for its own smelting (Fig. 12.2) (Cunningham and Berti 1993). Keller and others (2005) investigated whether thermal treatment could be a feasible option for evaporatively separating metals from plant residues. Gasification (i.e., pyrolysis) was found to be a better method than incineration to increase volatilization and, subsequently, recovery, of Cd and Zn from plants.

12.2.4. Benefits of Phytoextraction

Some of the major benefits of phytoextraction include:

1. Potential for the production of green belts. This is especially valuable in urban brownfield areas.
    There are cases in which woodlots are being cultivated on urban metal-rich sites. These can provide the additional benefit of serving as wildlife habitat.
2. A low-cost practice. Operators are needed for soil tillage, fertilizing, and seeding. There is no specialized field equipment needed; standard plows, planters, and harvesters work effectively. The plant tissue is harvested and processed as needed.
3. Versatility. Plants may be successful at sites that are not suited to heavy equipment or vehicles (for example, highly saturated soils).

12.2.5. Disadvantages of Phytoextraction

Some significant disadvantages of phytoextraction include (Sutherson 1997):

1. Longer times are required for remediation compared with other technologies. Phytoextraction is not suitable for sites in which there is an immediate health or environmental threat.
2. There is the potential for the release of biomass via wind dispersal of leaves or transport through the food chain.
3. Careful screening and pilot-scale tests are recommended in order to ensure the compatibility of plants to the soil material.
4. There is no single plant that will successfully remove all metals from soil. Since many hazardous sites are heterogeneous (i.e., many metals may occur), several species or genera may be needed in order for all target metals to be treated.

12.3. ORGANIC CONTAMINATION

Phytoremediation of organic (e.g., hydrocarbon) contaminated soils involves: (1) uptake of the contaminant by the plant followed by storage or metabolism, and/or (2) degradation in the plant rhizosphere (Fig. 12.4).

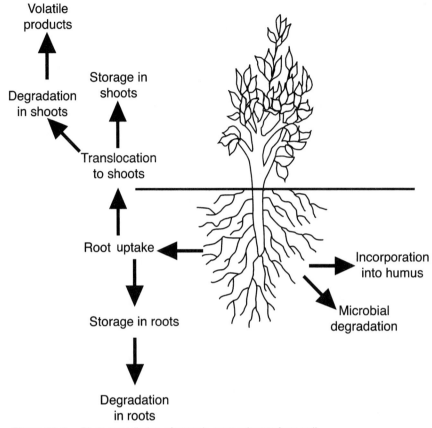

Figure 12.4.   *Phytoremediation of organic contaminants from soil*

The two mechanisms may occur simultaneously. The following chemical balance indicates microbial growth in the plant root zone on the hydrocarbon substrate (Shimp et al. 1993):

$$Ch_mO_l + aNH_3 + bO_2 \rightarrow \qquad (12.1)$$
$$y_cCH_pO_nN_q + zCH_rO_sN_t + cH_2O + dCO_2$$

For *phytodegradation* of organics to be successful, the contaminants must be available for uptake and metabolism by the plant or by its associated microbial populations. Bioavailability is a function of the solubility of the compound in water versus in hydrocarbons, soil type (e.g., organic matter content, types and amounts of clay minerals) and the age of the contaminant.

The study of soil-applied pesticides over the past several decades provides useful data regarding the feasibility of phytoremediation of organics (Lunney et al. 2004). A common parameter used to predict plant uptake from soil is the octanol-water partitioning coefficient (K_{ow}). This coefficient is measured by mixing a test compound with a solution of octanol (a C_8 hydrocarbon) and water, and the mixture is allowed to settle. An aliquot each of the octanol and of the water is removed and the concentration of the contaminant in each liquid is measured. The coefficient is calculated as:

$$K_{ow} = [\text{contaminant in octanol}] / [\text{contaminant in water}] \qquad (12.2)$$

Contaminants with a log $K_{ow} < 1$ are considered highly water-soluble, can accumulate in plants and are typically mobile in both plant xylem and phloem. Pollutants with log K_{ow} values of approximately 1 to 4 are taken up by roots and are considered xylem-mobile. Compounds in this range, many of which are environmental pollutants, should be amenable to phytoremediation (Cunningham and Berti 1993). Compounds with log K_{ow} values > 4 are strongly adsorbed to roots and are only minimally translocated to the shoot. Remediation technologies that either harvest roots or rely on degradation reactions at root surfaces may be applicable for treatment of these compounds (Banks and Schwab 1993).

Once absorbed inside the plant, compounds are either sequestered, bound to plant structural constituents, metabolized, or passed through the plant and volatilized through the stomata. The pesticide industry has studied the metabolism of organics within plants. The selective herbicide market exploits the differences between the metabolic capacities of crop and weed plants (Cunningham and Berti 1993). Desirable (i.e., crop) plants metabolize the selective herbicide into a nontoxic compound; however, the weeds do not and are consequently killed. These metabolic capacities of plants may be adapted for the remediation of contaminated soils; in other words, plants absorb pollutants from the soil and metabolize them into nontoxic materials or incorporate them into stable cellular constituents (e.g., lignin). In efforts to broaden the uses of currently registered herbicides, researchers are extending this degradative capacity by incorporating microbial or mammalian genes into the plant genome (Cunningham and Berti 1993; Inui 2005; Schäffner et al. 2002).

12.3.1. The Rhizosphere and Associated Microbial Consortia

Not all phytodegradation processes occur within the plant. For example, plant enzymes released into the soil may produce catalytic effects and thus be useful. The metabolic capacity, and consequently remediation success of plant-associated microbial systems, is also being studied, including those within the rhizosphere, and plant-leaf microflora and endophytic (within the plant) organisms. In the rhizosphere, accelerated rates of degradation for many pesticides as well as trichloroethylene and petroleum hydrocarbons, have been observed (Menon et al. 2004; Xia et al. 2003; Costa et al. 2000; Schnoor et al. 1995).

Some plants are known to metabolize certain hydrocarbon compounds within a specific portion of the biomass; however, microorganisms act on a wider range of substrates, carry out more complex and difficult degradative steps, and generally transform the contaminant molecule to a simpler end structure than do plants alone. Some microbial populations that are known to carry out significant reactions occur in the plant rhizosphere. The rhizosphere is a metabolically active zone directly adjacent to the plant root. It possesses a high density of heterotrophic microbial populations, and it is enriched in plant exudates including simple sugars, carbohydrates, alcohols, acids, and enzymes. As a result of the rich microbial diversity and nutrient content, this is also a zone where organic contaminants that are normally poor microbial substrates can be microbially degraded by *co-metabolism*. Co-metabolism is the process by which a compound that cannot support the growth of microorganisms is degraded when another, more readily metabolized substrate is present. The root zone, where up to 25% of all the crop biomass can be sloughed off, is an ideal environment for this to occur.

Microbial growth is typically substrate- or energy-limited. On occasion it is limited by the availability of N, P, or trace elements. Plant-aided biodegradation depends on: (1) the composition of the microbial consortia in the rhizosphere; (2) root exudates that may act as supplemental substrates; (3) N supplied in soil water or via decaying organic matter or fixation of atmospheric N_2; (4) oxygen transfer to the soil; and (5) kinetics of the microbial degradation (Shimp et al. 1993).

Research in rhizosphere-induced phytoremediation of organics is addressing the appropriate choice of plant host, rooting patterns, and associated microflora (Cunningham and Berti 1993; Xia et al. 2003;

Dominguez-Rosado et al. 2004; Anderson and Walton 1992). Research is investigating the composition of root exudates, exudation of specific compounds to induce microbial reactions, inoculation of the rhizosphere with microbes that are efficient degraders, and alternative ways of sequestering the metabolically more active microbes into the plant tissue and structure. The potential of ectomycorrhizal associations to facilitate cleanup of soil contaminated with persistent organic pollutants has also been considered (Meharg and Cairney 2000).

12.4. PHYTOSTABILIZATION

Contaminants that are tightly adsorbed to soil particles and resist uptake by microbes or plants are not suitable for phytoextraction or phytodegradation. If contaminants are also inert to other organisms (e.g., soil arthropods), *phytostabilization* may be considered. Phytostabilization uses plants to limit the mobility and bioavailability of metals in soils. Ideally, phytostabilizing plants should tolerate high levels of soil metals and should be able to immobilize them in the soil by sorption, precipitation, complexation, or oxidation-reduction reactions. Additional stabilization can occur by raising the soil pH. Phytostabilizing plants also should exhibit low accumulation of metals in shoots to eliminate the possibility that residues in harvested shoots might become hazardous wastes. In addition to stabilizing soil metals, phytostabilizing plants can also stabilize the soil surface to minimize erosion.

Since many sites contaminated with metals lack established vegetation, metal-tolerant plants are used for revegetation to prevent soil erosion and leaching. This approach, however, is technically defined as a containment rather than a remediation technology. Some scientists and engineers consider phytostabilization to be an interim measure to be utilized until a suitable remediation technology is determined to be feasible or cost-effective. Others, however, are developing phytostabilization as a standard protocol of metal remediation technology, especially for sites at which metal removal is not economically feasible.

After field applications conducted by a group in the United Kingdom, three grasses were made commercially available for phytostabilization: *Agrostis tenuis*, cv Parys for Cu wastes, *Agrostis tenuis*, cv Coginan for acid Pb and Zn wastes, and *Festuca rubra*, cv Merlin for calcareous Pb and Zn wastes (Smith and Bradshaw 1979). Pichtel and Salt (1988) found *Agrostis capillaris* L. var. 'Heriot,' *Festuca ovina* L., *F. rubra* L. var 'Boreal,' *Lolium perenne* L., and *Phleum pratense* L. var. 'Scots' to be suitable in phytostabilizing several contaminated UK sites including an abandoned Pb mine, an abandoned metalworks facility, and a Cr-contaminated dyeworks facility.

12.5. FUTURE DEVELOPMENT

Increased rates of metal uptake, increased translocation to aboveground biomass, and higher yields of harvested plant biomass are under consideration and study via selective breeding and genetic engineering. Recent testing has revealed that genetically altered species of both rice and mustard can take up mercuric ions from the soil and convert them to metallic mercury, which is transpired through the leaves (U.S. EPA 1997; Heaton et al. 2003; Rugh 1996). Testing of plants and microorganisms may lead to the identification of plants that have metal accumulation qualities that exceed those now documented.

A U.S. Department of Energy report entitled *Summary Report of a Workshop on Phytoremediation Research Needs* noted three key areas of research and development for plant-based treatment of soil contaminated with metals:

1. Mechanisms of uptake, transport, and accumulation of metals: Research is needed to develop better understanding of the use of physiological, biochemical, and genetic processes in plants that relate to tolerance of contaminant-enriched sites, decomposition, and translocation of contaminants.
2. Genetic evaluation of hyperaccumulators: Research is being conducted to collect plants growing in soils that contain high levels of metals and screen them for specific traits useful in phytoremediation.
3. Field evaluation and validation: Research is needed in field testing to accelerate implementation of phytoremediation technologies. Standardization of field-test protocols and subsequent application of test results to real-world situations also are needed.

12.6. SUMMARY

There are several distinct advantages (for example, legal, economic, aesthetic) to remediating a contaminated site while at the same time minimizing disturbance to the surface (Table 12.2). Research in applying and enhancing phytoremediation continues to expand (Table 12.3), as many current engineering technologies for treating contaminated surface soils are costly, energy-intensive, and disruptive to a site. Phytoremediation, when fully developed, could result in marked cost savings and in the restoration of sites by a non-invasive, solar-driven, in situ method that actually benefits a soil and, in many cases, can be aesthetically pleasing.

Table 12.2. Advantages and disadvantages of phytoremediation technology

Type of Phytoremediation	Advantages	Disadvantages
Phytoextraction by trees	High biomass production	Potential for off-site migration and leaf transportation of metals to surface
		Metals are concentrated in plant biomass and must eventually be disposed
Phytoextraction by grasses	High accumulation growth rate	Low biomass production; slow process
		Metals are concentrated in plant biomass and must eventually be disposed
Phytoextraction by crops	High biomass and increased growth rate	Potential threat to food chain through ingestion by herbivores
		Metals are concentrated in plant biomass and must eventually be disposed
Phytostabilization	No disposal of contaminated biomass required	Remaining liability issues, including maintenance for indefinite period of time
Phytodegradation in the rhizosphere	No disposal of contaminated soil	Limited to hydrocarbons only
Phytovolatilization	Limited application (As, Hg)	Possibility of releasing toxins to the atmosphere. Permit may be required

Source: United States Environmental Protection Agency 1997.

Table 12.3. Phytotechnology use at Superfund sites contaminated with chlorinated solvents, metals, explosives, and pesticides

Site Name	Site Location	ROD Date	Contaminants	Phytotechnology Status
Aberdeen Pesticides Dumps	NC	06/04/99	Dieldrin, hexachlorobenzene, hexachlorahexane	Ongoing (1999–)
Aberdeen Proving Ground	MD	09/27/01	1,1,2,2-tetrachlorothane; 1,1,2-trichloroethane; 1,1-DCE; 1,2-dichloroethane, 1,2-DCE; PCE; TCE; VC	Ongoing (1996–)
Argonne National Laboratory West 1	ID	09/29/98	Cesium-137, silver, mercury, chromium	Completed (1999–2002)
AT & SF Albuquerque	NM	06/27/02	2-methylnapthalene, benzo(a)anthracene, benzo(b)fluoranthene, benzo(k)fluoranthene, dibenzo(a,h)anthracene, dibenzofuran, ideno(1,2,3-cd)pyrene, napthalene, zinc	Predesign
Atlas Tack Corporation	MA	03/10/00	Benzene, chromium, copper, cyanide, mercury, nickel, zinc	Design (2003–)
Boarhead Farm	PA	11/18/98	Benzene, cadmium, nickel TCE	Designed/not installed (2003)
Bofors-Nobel Inc.	MI	ROD amendment: 07/16/99	3,3-dichlorobenzidine; acetone; arsenic; VC; PCE; aniline; benzene; toluene; xylene; zinc	Pilot completed (1999–2002); design phase (2005–)

(continued)

Table 12.3. *(continued)*

Site Name	Site Location	ROD Date	Contaminants	Phytotechnology Status
Carswell Naval Air Station	TX	08/96	TCE, DCE	Ongoing (1996–2006)
Combustion, Inc.	LA	05/28/04	DCA, PCB, benzene, lead mercury, nickel, silver, toluene, toluene diisocynate, toluene diamine	Ongoing (2002–)
Del Monte Corp.	HI	09/25/03	Ethylene dibromide; 1,2-dibromo-3-chloropropane; 1,2-dichloropropane; 1,2,3-trichloropropane (pesticides)	Ongoing (1998–)
East Palo Alto	CA	RCRA drop site	Arsenic, sodium	Ongoing (1981–)
Fort Dix	NJ	Field demonstration	Lead	Completed (1997–2002)
Fort Wainwright	AK	06/27/97	Aldrin, DDD, DDT, dieldrin	Completed (1997–2001)
Naval Undersea Warfare Station	WA	09/28/98	TCA, halogenated volatiles	Ongoing (1999–2009)
Sangamo Electric Dump/ Crab Orchard National Wildlife Refuge	IL	ROD amendment: expected in 2005	1,1-DCE; PCE; VC	Planned (2006–)
Tibbetts Road	NH	09/28/98	TCE	Ongoing (1998–2015)

Source: U.S. Environmental Protection Agency 2005.

12.7. CASE HISTORY

The Aberdeen Proving Grounds (Edgewood, MD) was established as a U.S. Army weapons-testing facility in 1918. Weapons testing and munitions disposal have resulted in extensive soil and groundwater contamination at the Proving Grounds.

The installation is divided into two sections, the Edgewood and the Aberdeen areas. Within the former, the J. Fields Toxic Pits Site had been used for years as an open burning facility for munitions and chemical agents. Large volumes of chlorinated solvents were disposed there as well. As a result, a plume of chlorinated solvents has formed in the aquifer below the pits. Concentrations of total VOCs in the groundwater range from less than 20,000 μg/L to over 220,000 μg/L (Table 12.4) (Chappell 1997).

Due to the contamination present, the Edgewood area was placed on the Superfund National Priorities List. Several technologies were considered for cleaning the soil and groundwater at the site. Soil washing, vapor extraction, and capping were considered for the soils, and pump-and-treat and air sparging for the groundwater. All were eliminated from consideration because technologies involving a rigid installation design would experience difficulties with perched water tables and the potential for encountering unexploded bombs buried on-site. Pumping and treating the water would be difficult because of the high concentrations of contaminants and strict discharge regulations. Soil excavation was not considered feasible due to cost. The site was eventually considered for a pilot-scale phytoremediation system (Chappell 1997; Tobia and Compton 1997).

The Department of Defense and the U.S. EPA jointly funded pilot-scale applications of phytoremediation. At the Fields site, hybrid poplars were

Table 12.4.   Primary contaminants at Aberdeen Proving Grounds' J. Fields phytoremediation site

Contaminant	Concentration (μg/L)
1,1,2,2-tetrachloroethane	170,000
Trichloroethene (TCE)	61,000
cis-1,2-dichloroethene (c-DCE)	13,000
Tetrachloroethene (PCE)	9,000
Trans-1,2-dichloroethene (t-DCE)	3,900
1,1,2-trichloroethane (TCA)	930

Sources: Chappell 1997; Tobia and Compton 1997.

planted over a shallow plume of chlorinated solvents in order to hydraulically contain the contaminants and to treat groundwater.

The phytoremediation strategy employed at the Fields site began with an
assessment for phytotoxicity of on-site pollutants and to determine any nutrient deficiencies that would affect tree growth. A total of 183 hybrid
poplars (*P. trichocarpa x deltoides* [HP-510]) were planted over the areas of
highest pollutant concentration around the leading edge of the plume. In order to promote root growth into the saturated zone, each tree was planted
with a plastic pipe around its upper roots. A drainage system was installed
to remove rainwater and promote root tropism to groundwater.

Extensive monitoring has taken place to determine the fates of the pollutants, tree transpiration rates, and the best methods for monitoring phytoremediation sites (Table 12.5). The sampling design at the site involves
collecting soils, transpiration gases, and tissue from tree roots, shoots,
stems, and leaves. Results will be used to determine concentrations of
contaminants and their metabolites along the translocation pathway
(Chappell 1997).

Eight monitoring wells were in place at the time of tree planting and
five additional wells were installed. Two pairs of lysimeters were installed.
Tree sap flow rates are being monitored in order to determine the pumping rates of the trees. An on-site weather monitor was used during sampling to correlate tree evapotranspiration rates with weather fluctuations.

Groundwater monitoring data indicate that the trees are pumping large
amounts of groundwater—there is a 2 ft depression in the water table beneath the trees in comparison to earlier data (Chappell 1997). Tree tissue
samples indicate the presence of trichloroacetic acid (TCAA), a breakdown
product of TCE. Chlorinated solvents (TCE and 1,1,2,2-tetrachloroethane)

Table 12.5.   Monitoring methods at Aberdeen Proving Grounds' J. Fields site

Type of analysis	Parameters tested
Plant growth measurements and visual observations	Diameter, height, health, pruning, replacement
Groundwater and vadose zone sampling and analysis	14 wells and 4 lysimeters to sample for VOCs, metals, and nutrients
Soil sampling and analysis	Biodegradation activity, VOCs, metals
Tissue sampling and analysis	Degradation products, VOCs
Plant sap flow measurements	Correlate sap flow data to meteorological data
Transpirational gas sampling and analysis	Various methods

Sources: Chappell 1997; Tobia and Compton 1997.

are also being transpired by the trees. Other researchers (Newman et al. 1997) have also detected TCAA in plant tissues in hybrid poplar tissue in a greenhouse study. The J. Fields site experienced about 10% tree loss during the first year. Some loss was due to the transplant process, and deer damaged many. The cost for installation of 183 trees was $15,000. Costs of monitoring varied due to experimenting with numerous monitoring techniques at the site (Chappell 1997).

QUESTIONS

1. Explain why the rhizosphere (as compared to nonvegetated soil) is critical to enhanced hydrocarbon decomposition by plants.
2. What are the appropriate classes of plants (e.g., trees, weeds) to use for phytoremediation? Is one class better suited for phytoextraction than another? For rhizosphere-enhanced degradation?
3. Discuss the method(s) to treat metal-enriched plant tissue once a hyperaccumulator plant has been harvested.
4. Most plants are unsuitable for phytoremediation if the contaminant occurs beyond 2 to 4 ft or more below the surface. True or false? Explain your answer.
5. The chemical form of a metal in the soil (e.g., soluble, bound to organic matter, bound to carbonates) significantly affects uptake by plants. Explain and provide an example.
6. All other factors being equal, Pb is much easier for plants to take up compared to Cd. True or false? Explain.
7. How could the presence of oily wastes interfere with plant uptake of Cd, Zn, and Cr?
8. Discuss one major disadvantage of phytoremediation technology for the cleanup of soil heavily contaminated with plutonium-239.
9. Phytoremediation is typically not well suited for low-permeability soils. True or false? Discuss.
10. In order to promote plant uptake of soil Pb, how can the soil be amended or otherwise managed? Be specific.

REFERENCES

Ajwa, H. A., G. S. Banuelos, and H. F. Mayland. 1999. Selenium uptake by plants from soils amended with inorganic materials. *Journal of Environmental Quality* 27:1218–27.

Anderson, T. A., and B. T. Walton. 1992. *Comparative Plant Uptake and Microbial Degradation of Trichlorethylene in the Rhizospheres of Five Plant Species—Implications for Bioremediation of contaminated surface Soils.* Oak Ridge, TX: Oak Ridge National Laboratory. Environmental Science Division, Pub. 3809. ORNL/TM-12017.

Arapis, G.D. 2006. Root and foliar uptake of [134]Cs by three tobacco plant varieties. *Revue d'écologie (la terre et la vie)* 60 (4): 333–40.

Baker, A. J. M. 1981. Accumulators and excluders—strategies in the response of plants to heavy metals. *Journal of Plant Nutrition* 3:643–54.

Baker, A. J. M., and R. R. Brooks. 1989. Terrestrial higher plants which hyperaccumulate metallic elements—a review of their distribution, ecology and phytochemistry. *Biorecovery* 1:81–126.

Banks, K. M., and A. P. Schwab. 1993. Dissipation of polycyclic aromatic hydrocarbons in the rhizosphere. In *Symposium on Bioremediation of Hazardous Wastes: Research, Development and Field Evaluations.* EPA/600/R-93/054. Washington, DC: U.S. Environmental Protection Agency.

Banuelos, G. S., H. A. Ajwa, B. Mackey, L. Wu, C. Cook, S. Akohoue, and S. Zambruzuski. 1997. Evaluation of different plant species used for phytoremediation of high soil selenium. *Journal of Environmental Quality* 26:639–46.

Blaylock, M. J., D. E. Salt, S. Dushenkov, O. Zakharova, C. Gussman, Y. Kapulnik, B. D. Ensley, and I. Raskin. 1997. Enhanced accumulation of Pb in Indian mustard by soil-applied chelating agents. *Environmental Science & Technology* 31:860–65.

Brown, S. L., R. L. Chaney, J. S. Angle, and A. J. M. Baker. 1995. Zinc and cadmium uptake by hyperaccumulator *Thlaspi caerulescens* grown in nutrient solution. *Soil Sci. Soc. Am. J.* 59:125–31.

Chamon, A. S., M. Rahman, W. E. H. Blum, M. H. Gerzabek, M. N. Mondol, and S. M. Ullah. 2005. Influence of soil amendments on heavy metal accumulation in crops on polluted soils of Bangladesh. *Communications in Soil Science and Plant Analysis* 36 (7–8): 907–24.

Chaney, R. L., Y. M. Li, S. L. Brown, F. A. Homer, M. Malik, J. S. Angle, A. J. M. Baker, R. D. Reeves, and M. Chin. 2000. Improving metal hyperaccumulator wild plants to develop commercial phytoextraction systems: Approaches and progress. In *Phytoremediation of Contaminated Soil and Water*, ed. N. Terry and G. Bañuelos, 129–58. Boca Raton, FL: CRC Press.

Chappell, J. 1997. *Phytoremediation of TCE Using* Populus. Status report prepared for the U.S. EPA Technology Innovation Office. Washington, D.C. See: clu-in.com/phytoTCE.htm.

Costa, R. M., Camper N. D., Riley M. B. 2000. Atrazine degradation in a containerized rhizosphere system. *Journal of Environmental Science and Health.* Part B, *Pesticides, Food Contaminants, and Agricultural Wastes* 35 (6): 677–87.

Cunningham, S. D. and W. R. Berti. 1993. Remediation of contaminated soils with green plants: An overview. *In Vitro Cell. Dev. Biol.* 29:207–12.

Dominguez-Rosado, E., J. Pichtel, and M. Coughlin. 2004. Phytoremediation of soil contaminated with used motor oil: I. Laboratory and growth chamber studies. *Environmental Engineering Science* 21:157–68.

Dushenkov, S., B. Sorochinsky, A. Mikheev, A. Prokhnevsky, and M. Ruchko. 1999. Phytoremediation of radiocesium-contaminated soil in the vicinity of Chernobyl, Ukraine. *Environmental Science & Technology* 33 (3): 469–75.

Ebbs, S. D., and L. V. Kochian. 1998. Phytoextraction of zinc by oat (*Avena sativa*), barley (*Hordeum vulgare*) and Indian mustard (*Brassica juncea*). *Environmental Science & Technology* 32:802–6.

Entry, J. A., N. C. Vance, M. A. Hamilton, D. Zabowsky, L. S. Watrud, and D. C. Adriano. 1996. Phytoremediation of soil contaminated with low concentrations of radionuclides. *Water, Air, and Soil Pollution* 88:167–76.

Fesenko, S. V., R. Avila, D. Klein, E. Lukaus, N. V. Sukhova, N. I. Sanzharova, and S. I. Spirdonov. 2003. Analysis of factors determining accumulation of ^{137}Cs by woody plants. *Russian Journal of Ecology* 34 (5): 309–13.

40 CFR. 1996. *Part 264. Standards for Owners and Operators of Hazardous Waste Treatment, Storage and Disposal Facilities*. Washington, DC: U.S. Government Printing Office.

Fowler, D., D. Branford, R. Donovan, P. Rowland, U. Skiba, E. Nemitz, and F. Choubedar. 2004. Measuring aerosol and heavy metal deposition on urban woodland and grass using inventories of ^{210}Pb and metal concentrations in soil. *Water, Air, and Soil Pollution: Focus* 4 (2–3): 483–99.

García, G., Å Faz, and M. Cunha. 2004. Performance of *Piptatherum miliaceum* (Smilo grass) in edaphic Pb and Zn phytoremediation over a short growth period. *International Biodeterioration and Biodegradation* 54 (2–3): 245–50.

Heaton, A. C. O., R. B. Meagher, C. L. Rugh, T. Kim, and N. J. Wang. 2003. Toward detoxifying mercury-polluted aquatic sediments with rice genetically engineered for mercury resistance. *Environmental Toxicology and Chemistry* 22 (12): 2940–47.

Hinchman, R. R, M. C. Negri, and E. G. Gatliff. 1997. Phytoremediation: Using green plants to clean up contaminated soil, groundwater, and wastewater. 12th Annual Conference on Contaminated Soils. University of Massachusetts. Amherst, MA, October 18–23.

Huang, J. W., J. Chen, W. R. Berti, and S. C. Cunningham. 1997. Phytoremediation of lead-contaminated soils: Role of synthetic chelates in lead phytoextraction. *Environmental Science & Technology* 31:800–805.

Inui, H., and H. Ohkawa. 2005. Herbicide resistance in transgenic plants with mammalian p450 monooxygenase genes. *Pest Management Science* 61 (3): 286–91.

Kabata-Pendias, A. 2001. *Trace Elements in Soils and Plants*. 3rd ed. Boca Raton, FL: CRC Press.

Keller, C., C. Ludwig, F. Davoli, and J. Wochele. 2005. Thermal treatment of metal-enriched biomass produced from heavy metal phytoextraction. *Environmental Science and Technology* 39 (9): 3359–67.

Lasat, M. M. 2000. *The Use of Plants for the Removal of Toxic Metals from Contaminated Soil*. Prepared for The U.S. Environmental Protection Agency. See: clu-in.org/download/remed/lasat.pdf.

Lasat, M. M., M. Fuhrmann, S. D. Ebbs, J. E. Cornish, and L.V. Kochian. 1998. Phytoremediation of a radiocesium-contaminated soil: Evaluation of cesium-137 bioaccumulation in the shoots of three plant species. *Journal of Environmental Quality* 27: 165–69.

Liu H., A. Probst, and B. Liao. 2005. Metal contamination of soils and crops affected by the Chenzhou lead/zinc mine spill (Hunan, China). *Science of the Total Environment* 339 (1–3): 153–66.

Lunney, A. I., B. A. Zeeb, and K. J. Reimer. 2004. Uptake of weathered DDT in vascular plants: Potential for phytoremediation. *Environmental Science & Technology* 38 (22): 6147–54.

Mantovi, P., G. Bonazzi, E. Maestri, and N. Mamiroli. 2003. Accumulation of copper and zinc from liquid manure in agricultural soils and crop plants. *Plant and Soil* 250 (2):249–57.

Meharg, A. A., and J. W. G. Cairney. 2000. Ectomycorrhizas—extending the capabilities of rhizosphere remediation? *Soil Biology and Biochemistry* 32 (11–12): 1475–84.

Menon, P., M. Gopal, and R. Prasad. 2004. Dissipation of chlorpyrifos in two soil environments of semi-arid India. *Journal of Environmental Science and Health*. Part B, *Pesticides, Food Contaminants, and Agricultural Wastes* 39 (4): 517–31.

Muchuweti, M., R. Zvauya, M. D. Scrimshaw, J. N. Lester, J. W. Birkett, and E. Chinyanga. 2006. Heavy metal content of vegetable irrigated with mixtures of wastewater and sewage sludge in Zimbabwe: Implications for human health. *Agriculture, Ecosystems and Environment* 112 (1): 41–48.

Negri, M. C., and R. R. Hinchman. 1996. Plants that remove contaminants from the environment. *Laboratory Medicine* 27:36–40.

Newman, L., S. Strand, J. Duffy, G. Ekuan, M. Raszaj, B. Shurtleff, J. Wilmoth, P. Heilman, and M. Gordon. 1997. Uptake and biotransformation of trichloroethylene by hybrid poplars. *Environmental Science & Technology* 31:1062–67.

Pang, J., M. H. Wong, G. S. Y. Chan, J. Zhang, and J. Liang. 2003. Physiological aspects of vetiver grass for rehabilitation in abandoned metalliferous mine wastes. *Chemosphere* 52 (9): 2003.

Petruzzelli, G. 1989. Recycling wastes in agriculture: Heavy metal bioavailability. *Agric. Ecosyst. Environ*. 27:493–503.

Pichtel, J., and M. Anderson. 1997. Trace metal bioavailability in municipal solid waste and sewage sludge composts. *Bioresource Technology* 60:223–29.

Pichtel, J., K. Kuroiwa, and H. T. Sawyerr. 2000. Distribution of Pb, Cd and Ba in soils and plants of two contaminated sites. *Environmental Pollution* 110:171–78.

Pichtel, J., and C. A. Salt. 1998. Vegetative growth and trace metal accumulation on metalliferous wastes. *Journal of Environmental Quality* 27:618–24.

Rugh, C. 1996. Mercuric ion reduction and resistance in transgenic *Arabidopsis thaliana* plants expressing a modified bacterial MerA gene. *Proceedings of the National Academy of Sciences* 93:3182–87.

Salt, C. A., and J. W. Kay. 1999. The seasonal pattern of radiocaesium partitioning within swards of *Agrostis capillaris* at two defoliation intensities. *Journal of Environmental Radioactivity* 45 (3): 219–34.

Salt, C. A., K. A. S. Pathiratne, J. A. Hipkin, and P. Hiley. 1995. Metal contamination of soil materials and trees on a reclaimed steelworks site. *Science of the Total Environment*.

Salt, D. E., M. Blaylock, N. P. B. A. Kumar, V. Dushenkov, B. D. Ensley, I. Chet, and I. Raskin. 1995. Phytoremediation: A novel strategy for the removal of toxic metals from the environment using plants. *BioTechnology* 13:468–74.

Sas-Nowosielska, A., J. M. Kuperberg, K. Krynski, R. Kucharski., E. Malstrokkowski, and M. Pogrzeba. 2004. Phytoextraction crop disposal—an unsolved problem. *Environmental Pollution* 128 (3): 373–79.

Schäffner, A., B. Messner, C. Langebartels, and H. Sandermann. 2002. Genes and enzymes for in-planta phytoremediation of air, water and soil. *Acta Biotechnologica* 22 (1–2): 141–52.

Schnoor, J. L., L. A. Licht, S. C. McCutcheon, N. L. Wolfe, and L. H. Carreira. 1995. Phytoremediation of organic and nutrient contaminants. *Environmental Science & Technology* 29:318–23.

Shen, Z.-G., X.-D. Li, C.-C. Wang, H.-M. Chen, and H. Chua. 2002. Lead phytoextraction from contaminated soil with high-biomass plant species. *Journal of Environmental Quality* 31:1893–1900.

Shimp, J. F., J. C. Tracy, L. C. Davis, E. Lee, W. Huang, and L. E. Erickson. 1993. Beneficial effects of plants in the remediation of soil and groundwater contaminated with organic materials. *Environmental Science & Technology* 23:41–77.

Sims, J. T., and J. S. Kline. 1991. Chemical fractionation and plant uptake of heavy metals in soils amended with co-composted sewage sludge. *Journal of Environmental Quality* 20:387–95.

Smith, L. A., J. L. Means, A. Chen, B. Alleman, C. C. Chapman, J. S. Tixier, S. E. Brauning, A. R. Gavaskar, and M. D. Royer. 1995. *Remedial Options for Metals—Contaminated Soils.* Boca Raton, FL: CRC Press.

Smith, R. A. H., and A. D. Bradshaw. 1979. The use of metal tolerant plant populations for the reclamation of metalliferous wastes. *Journal of Applied Ecology* 16:595–612.

Solhi, M., H. Shareatmadari, and M. A. Hajabbasi. 2005 Lead and zinc extraction potential of two common crop plants, *Helianthus annuus* and *Brassica napus. Water, Air, and Soil Pollution* 167 (1–4): 59–71.

Sposito, G., L. J. Lund, and A. C. Chang. 1982. Trace metal chemistry in arid-zone field soils amended with sewage sludge: I. Fractionation of Ni, Cu, Zn, Cd and Pd in solid phases. *Soil Sci. Soc. Am. J.* 46:260–64.

Sutherson, S. S. 1997. *Remediation Engineering: Design Concepts.* Boca Raton, FL: CRC Press.

Tandi N. K., J. Nyamangara, and C. Bangira. 2004. Environmental and potential health effects of growing leafy vegetables on soil irrigated using sewage sludge and effluent: A case of Zn and Cu. *Journal of Environmental Science and Health.* Part B, *Pesticides, Food, Contaminants and Agricultural Wastes* 39 (3): 461–71.

Tessier, A., P. G. C. Campbell, and M. Bisson. 1979. Sequential extraction procedure for the speciation of particulate trace metals. *Anal. Chem.* 51:844–51.

Tobia, R., and H. Compton. 1997. *Phytoremediation of TCE in Groundwater Using Populus.* Status report prepared for the U.S. EPA Technology Innovation Office. Washington, DC.

U.S. Environmental Protection Agency. 1983. *Process Design Manual for Land Application of Municipal Sludge.* EPA/625/1-83-016. Cincinnati.

United States Environmental Protection Agency. 1997. Recent Developments for In Situ Treatment of Metal Contaminated Soils. EPA-542-R-97-004. Office of Solid Waste and Emergency Response.

———. 2000. *An Overview of the Phytoremediation of Lead and Mercury.* Washington, DC: Office of Solid Waste and Emergency Response Technology Innovation Office. See: clu-in.org

———. 2005. *Use of Field-Scale Phytotechnology for Chlorinated Solvents, Metals, Explosives and Propellants, and Pesticides.* EPA 542-R-05-002. Washington, DC: Office of Solid Waste and Emergency Response. See: www.clu-in.org.

Xia, H., L. Wu, and Q. Tao. 2003. A review on phytoremediation of organic contaminants. *Chinese Journal of Applied Ecology* 14 (3): 457–60.

CHAPTER 13

Innovative Technologies

Learning and innovation go hand in hand. The arrogance of success is to think that what you did yesterday will be sufficient for tomorrow.

—William Pollard

Every great advance in science has issued from a new audacity of imagination.

—John Dewey

Ideas are like rabbits.

—John Steinbeck

13.1 INTRODUCTION

More rapid and more sophisticated technologies to address remediation of contaminated soil, substrata, and water are continually coming available worldwide. There is a broad range of applicability, feasibility, and cost concerns for each technology. Applications address many contaminant types, sites, and levels of sophistication. This chapter will provide only a brief view of some promising methods.

13.2. ELECTROKINETIC REMEDIATION

Electrokinetic remediation, also referred to as *electrokinetic soil processing*, *electromigration*, *electrochemical decontamination*, or *electroreclamation*, involves the application of low-density direct current between electrodes placed in the soil to mobilize contaminants that occur as charged species. This is therefore a separation and removal technique for radionuclides, metals, and some organic contaminants from saturated or unsaturated soils, slurries, and sediments.

Electrodes can be installed horizontally or vertically (depending on the location and shape of the contaminant plume) in deep, directionally drilled tunnels or in trenches around sites contaminated by leaking USTs; by spillage from industrial processes; by leachate from agricultural fields, landfills, and mine tailings; and by deposition from the air and subsequent leaching into the soil and groundwater (Lageman 1993).

The principle of electrokinetic remediation relies on application of a low-intensity direct current through the soil between two or more electrodes. Most soils contain water in the pores between particles, and this water has an electrical conductivity due to the presence of salts in the soil. The applied current is in the range of mA/cm^2 of cross-sectional area between the electrodes or an electric potential difference on the order of a few volts/cm across the electrodes placed into the ground. The current mobilizes charged species, particles, and ions in the soil by the following processes: electromigration (transport of charged chemical species under an electric gradient), electro-osmosis (transport of pore fluid under an electric gradient), electrophoresis (movement of charged particles under an electric gradient), and electrolysis (chemical reactions influenced by the electric field) (Rodsand and Acar 1995).

As depicted in Figure 13.1, groundwater and/or a processing fluid (supplied externally through the boreholes that contain the electrodes) serves as the conductive medium. The additives in the processing fluid, the products of electrolysis reactions at the electrodes, and the dissolved contaminant species in the soil are transported through the soil by conduction under electric fields. This transport, when coupled with a removal phase of sorption, precipitation/dissolution, and volatilization/complexation, provides the mechanism for the electrokinetic remediation process.

Electrolysis reactions dominate at each electrode. Solution pH will vary at the electrodes as a result of the electrolysis of water. Oxidation occurs at the anode, where an acid front is generated if water is the primary pore fluid present. Reduction occurs at the cathode and produces a base front. The solution becomes acidic at the anode because hydrogen ions are produced and oxygen gas is released, and the solution be-

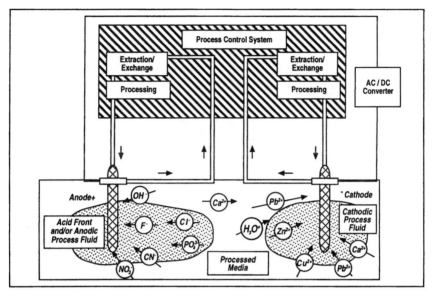

Figure 13.1. *Schematic of single electrode configuration and geometry used in electroki-netic remediation*
U.S. Environmental Protection Agency 1995a.

comes basic at the cathode, where hydroxyl ions are generated and hy-drogen gas is released (Eqs. 13.1 and 13.2). At the anode, the pH could decrease to < 2.0, and it could increase at the cathode to > 12 depend-ing on the current applied (U.S. EPA 1997; Jacobs et al. 1994; Acar and Alshawabkeh. 1993).

Anode
$$2H_2O - 4e^- \rightarrow O_{2\,(g)} + 4H^+ \qquad (13.1)$$

Cathode
$$2H_2O + 2e^- \rightarrow H_{2\,(g)} + 2OH^- \qquad (13.2)$$

The acid front eventually migrates from the anode to the cathode. Movement of the acid front by advective forces results in the desorption of contaminants from the soil. This migration also results in temporary soil acidification. In some cases metallic electrodes may dissolve as a re-sult of electrolysis and introduce corrosion products into the soil mass. However, if inert electrodes, such as carbon, graphite, or platinum are used, no residue will be introduced in the treated soil mass as a result of the electrokinetic process. Water or some other suitable salt solution may be added to the system to enhance the mobility of the contaminant and increase the effectiveness of the technology. For example, buffer solutions may change or stabilize pore fluid pH.

Contaminants arriving at the electrode(s) can be removed by any of several methods, either at the electrodes or in a treatment unit that pumps the processing fluid from the soil. For example, ions may be electroplated, precipitated, or coprecipitated at the electrode. Additionally, the ion-enriched soil water may be removed by wells installed upgradient of the electrode. The water may be treated by evaporation/condensation, passage through ion exchange columns, or via electrochemical techniques or simple chemical precipitation (e.g., a calcium hydroxide solution will precipitate metals from the process fluid).

Several environmental variables affect the overall migration of ions, particles, and/or fluids between electrodes. These include soil mineralogy, pore fluid composition and conductivity, electrochemical properties of the species in the pore fluid, and the porosity and tortuosity of the porous medium (Acar and Alshawabkeh 1993).

Before electrokinetic remediation is undertaken at a site, field and laboratory screening tests must be conducted to determine whether the particular site is amenable to the treatment technique.

- Field conductivity. Spatial variability of geologic layers should be delineated because buried metallic or insulating material can cause variations in the electrical conductivity of the soil. This will affect the overall ability of the system to mobilize contaminants. In addition, the presence of deposits that exhibit very high electrical conductivity, which may render the technique ineffective, should be assessed.
- Chemical analysis of water. Pore water should be analyzed for dissolved anions and cations as well as for the concentration of the contaminant(s). In addition, electrical conductivity and pH should be measured.
- Chemical analysis of soil. The buffering capacity and geochemistry of the soil should be determined at the affected site. Soil pH should be determined because this affects the valence, and hence the solubility and sorption of contaminant ions.
- Bench-scale tests. Because many physical and chemical reactions of soil are interrelated, it may be useful to conduct bench-scale tests to predict the performance of electrokinetic remediation at the field scale. Transport, removal rates, and amounts of contamination remaining can be examined for different removal scenarios.

A pilot test of the electrokinetic process was conducted at the site of a former paint factory in Groningen, the Netherlands. Pollution consisted of heavy metals such as Pb and Cu, which had leached into the soil from sludge that had been dredged and dumped onto fields. The sludge was heavily polluted with metals in the form of paint residues (solid particles). The Pb concentration range was 300 to $> 5,000$ mg/kg, and Cu concentrations ranged from 500 to 1,000 mg/kg (Lageman 1993).

The test area was 70 m long and 3 m wide. Electrode setup consisted of one horizontal cathode at 0.5 m below ground surface and a row of vertical anodes installed at a depth of up to 1 m and spaced 1 m apart. Current was applied 10 hours per day for 43 days after which Pb was reduced by up to 70%, while Cu concentrations were reduced by 80%. In the layer just beneath the sludge, metal concentrations increased as a result of additional dissolution of the paint particles. The already acidic soil was acidified further through electrokinetic generation of H^+, resulting in the dissolution of paint particles, which then acted as new sources of pollution.

Recent experiments show that electrokinetic remediaton can be used in combination with other remediation techniques such as pump-and-treat, biodegradation, and vacuum extraction (Table 13.1). When combined with electrical heating, the electrokinetic technique can also be used to remove polar and nonpolar organic chemicals from soil and groundwater (Lageman 1993).

Table 13.1.   Performance of electrokinetic remediation at five field sites in Europe

Site Description	Volume (ft³)	Contaminants	Initial Concentration (mg/kg)	Final Concentration (mg/kg)
Former paint factory	8,100 peat/ clay soil	Cu	1,220	< 200
		Pb	> 3,780	< 280
Operational galvanizing plant	1,350 clay soil	Zn	> 1,400	600
Former timber plant	6,750 heavy clay soil	As	> 250	< 30
Temporary landfill	194,400 sand	Cd	> 180	< 40
Military air base	68,000 clay	Cd	660	47
		Cr	7,300	755
		Cu	770	98
		Ni	860	80
		Pb	730	108
		Zn	2,600	289

Source: United States Environmental Protection Agency 1997.

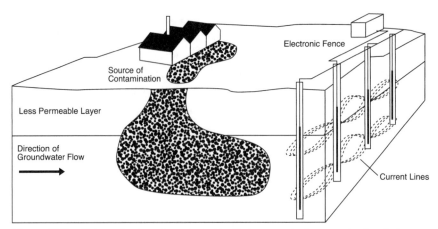

Figure 13.2. *Schematic view of an electrokinetic fence enclosing a contaminant plume*
U.S. Environmental Protection Agency 1997.

A variation of the electrokinetic process involves the installation of electrokinetic fences. The electrokinetic phenomena that occur when soil is electrically charged can be used to fence off hazardous sites. Electrokinetic fencing combines containment and remediation. With an electrokinetic fence it is possible to capture electrically charged (polar) contaminants while treated water passes through the fence. The fence can also increase soil temperatures in the area inside the fence to accelerate biodegradation processes. Electrokinetic fences can be installed both horizontally and vertically and at any depth (Fig. 13.2).

13.4. IN SITU VITRIFICATION

The in situ vitrification (ISV) process is designed to treat soil, sludges, sediments, and mine tailings contaminated with a wide variety of organic and inorganic contaminants. The technology uses joule heating to melt the waste matrix, destroying organic compounds in the process and encapsulating the inorganic constituents in a monolithic and leach-resistant form. In joule heating, electric current flows through the material and transfers heat energy to the material (U.S. EPA 1995b).

The typical ISV arrangement involves the use of a square array of four graphite electrodes spaced up to 18 to 20 ft part. This allows formation of a maximum melt width of about 35 to 40 ft and a maximum melt depth of

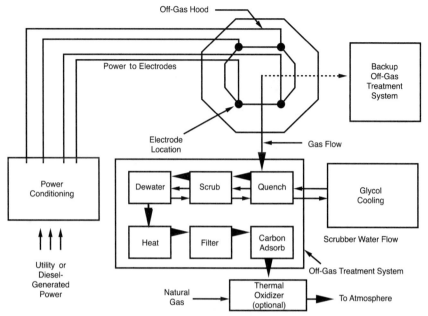

Figure 13.3.   Components of in situ vitrification technology
U.S. Environmental Protection Agency 1995b.

approximately 20 ft. The electrode spacing is partly dependent on soil characteristics, and the electrodes are lowered gradually as the melt progresses. Figure 13.3 shows a typical ISV equipment layout and figure 13.4 a side view of a system designed by Geosafe (U.S. EPA 1995b).

A conductive mixture of flaked graphite and glass frit is placed just below the soil surface between the electrodes to act as a starter path, since dry soil is usually not electrically conductive. A layer of insulation then covers the soil surface. The starter path facilitates the flow of current between the electrodes until the ground matrix reaches a temperature and viscosity sufficient to conduct the current and produce melting. At this point the soil warms to approximately 2,900°F to 3,600°F (1,600°C to 2,000°C), well above the melting (fusion) temperature of soils (2,000°F to 2,500°F or 1,100°C to 1,400°C). Temperatures at an individual electrode can reach as high as 3,300°F (1,800°C). The graphite and glass starter path is eventually consumed by oxidation. Upon melting, most soils become electrically conductive; thus, the molten mass becomes the primary conductor and heat transfer medium. As a result of the joule heating, the

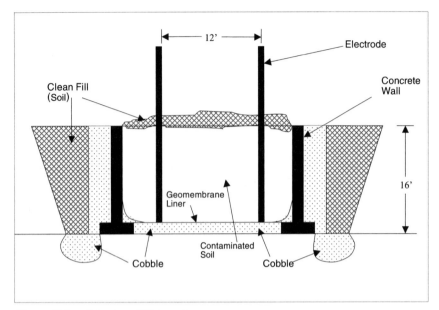

Figure 13.4.   *Side view of ISV reaction zone*
U.S. Environmental Protection Agency 1995b.

soil viscosity is lowered. At this point the melt begins to grow within the soil matrix, extending laterally as well as downward. Power is maintained at levels sufficient to overcome heat losses from the surface and to the surrounding soil. Convection currents within the melt aid heating of the melt. Heat is transferred to the adjacent soil by conduction from the melt. The melt grows outward to a width approximately 50% wider than the electrode spacing. The molten zone becomes roughly a cube with slightly rounded corners on the bottom and sides; this shape reflects the higher power density around the electrodes (U.S. EPA 1995b).

During processing, ISV eliminates the void volume of soils, resulting in volume reduction. Further volume reduction also occurs since soil components such as humus and organic contaminants are removed as gases and vapors. The overall volume reduction (typically 20% to 50%) creates a subsidence volume above the melt (Weston 1988).

The possible dispositions of contaminants resulting from ISV processing include chemical and thermal destruction, removal to the off-gas treatment system, chemical and physical incorporation within the residual product, lateral migration ahead of the advancing melt, and escape to the environment (U.S. EPA 1995b). As the thermal gradient advances on organic materials, they are either drawn into the melt or laterally migrate into the dry zone where they are vaporized and ultimately pyrolyzed. Only a small fraction of vapor passes through the melt itself. Organic pyrolysis products are typically gaseous; because of the high viscosity of the molten material, these gases move slowly through the melt, usually on a path adjacent to the electrodes, toward the upper melt surface. While some of these gases may dissolve into the molten mass, the remainder move to the surface where those that are combustible react in the presence of air. Pyrolysis and combustion products are collected in an off-gas collection hood and are subsequently treated in the off-gas treatment system (Fig. 13.5). Because of the high temperature of the melt, no residual organic contaminants are expected to remain in their original form within the vitrified product (U.S. EPA 1995b).

The behavior of inorganic materials upon exposure to the advancing thermal gradient is similar to that of the organics. Inorganic compounds may thermally decompose or otherwise enter into reactions with the melt. Typically, the metals present are incorporated into the vitrified residual. Immobilization may occur when the contaminants are incorporated into the glass network or encapsulated (surrounded) by the glass. If large

Figure 13.5.   *Off-gas treatment system. (Reproduced with kind permission of AMEC Corp., Washington, DC.)*

amounts of nonvolatile metals are present, they may sink to the bottom of the melt and concentrate.

An off-gas collection hood covers the processing area. Flow of air through the hood is controlled to maintain a vacuum, which prevents escape of fugitive emissions from the hood and ground surface interface. Air provides oxygen for combustion of pyrolysis products and organic vapors. An induced draft blower draws the off-gases, pyrolysis products, and air from the hood into the off-gas treatment system. The off-gas is treated by quenching, pH-controlled scrubbing, mist elimination, particulate filtration, and activated carbon adsorption.

Once power to the electrodes is shut off, the melt begins to cool. In most cases no attempts are made to force cooling of the melt; slow cooling is expected to produce a vitreous (amorphous) and microcrystalline structure (Fig. 13.6). Removal of the hood is normally accomplished within 24 hours after power to the electrodes is discontinued. The used graphite electrodes are severed near the melt surface and are left within the treated monolith. After the off-gas hood is removed and the electrodes are severed, the subsidence volume is filled to the desired depth with clean backfill.

13.5. PLASMA CENTRIFUGAL FURNACE

The plasma centrifugal furnace (PCF) is an ex situ technology that uses heat generated from a plasma torch to melt and vitrify solid feed material. Organic contaminants are vaporized and decomposed by the intense heat of the plasma and are oxidized by the air used as the plasma gas before passing to the off-gas treatment system. Metal-containing solids are vitrified into a monolithic nonleachable mass (U.S. EPA 1992).

Figure 13.6.   *Vitreous material occurring after ISV treatment*
U.S. Department of Energy.

The PCF system is composed of a thermal treatment unit and an exhaust gas treatment unit (Fig. 13.7). The thermal treatment unit consists of a feeder, a primary chamber, a plasma torch, an afterburner, a secondary chamber, and a collection chamber. Contaminated soil and hazardous waste are loaded manually from sealed containers into a spiral feeder. The waste is fed uniformly and continuously into the centrifugal reactor through a chute connecting the feeder to the primary chamber, which is a rotating tub with a copper throat. The copper throat, at the bottom of the primary chamber, is used to strike the arc of the plasma torch. The torch is then moved slowly up and down the side of the primary chamber during heatup. Feeding of the waste material begins once the primary chamber temperature is greater than 2,000°F and the secondary chamber temperature is greater than 1,800°F. Solid material is retained in the tub by centrifugal force.

The plasma torch uses electrical discharges to add energy to plasma torch gases in order to increase the gas temperature beyond that normally attainable by chemical reaction. The plasma torch produces an arc that directly contacts a conducting portion (copper throat) of the centrifugal reactor. The heat generated by the plasma torch brings the waste material to temperatures sufficient to melt soil (typically on the order of 3,000°F). This intense heat melts contaminated soil, incorporating any inorganic and metal components into a stable material. Organic components are volatilized by the heat of the plasma and oxidized by the air used as the plasma gas. Oxygen may also be added in the primary chamber to enhance combustion of organics.

The afterburner, located immediately downstream of the primary chamber, provides an additional heat input beyond that supplied by the plasma torch to combust products of incomplete combustion (PICs). The afterburner operates on a natural gas flame. The organics that are volatilized and oxidized are drawn off to the gas treatment system.

A typical gas treatment system may consist of a quench tank, a jet scrubber, a packed-bed scrubber, a demister, and a stack blower. A mildly caustic scrubber solution (pH 8.5) is used in the quench tank, jet scrubber, and packed-bed scrubber. The scrubber sump is equipped with a chiller to cool the scrubber water circulating through the exhaust gas treatment equipment so that all the moisture can be removed from the exhaust gases. The chilled scrubber water proceeds first to the quench tank where it cools the exhaust gas stream from approximately 1,000°F to 40°F. From the

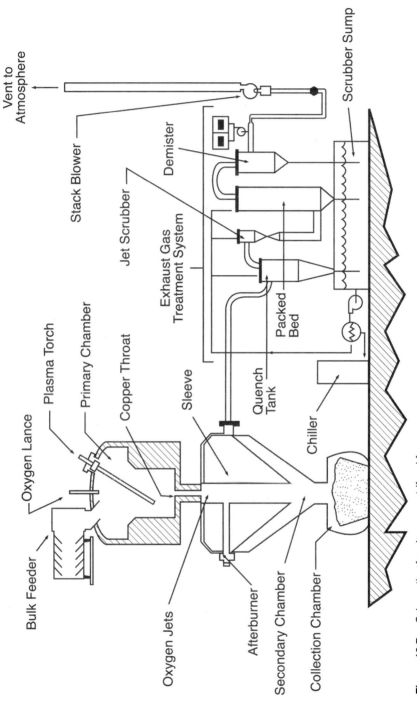

Figure 13.7. *Schematic of a plasma centrifugal furnace*
U.S. Environmental Protection Agency 1992.

Vent to Atmosphere

Stack Blower

Demister

Jet Scrubber

Exhaust Gas Treatment System

Scrubber Sump

Packed Bed

Quench Tank

Chiller

Oxygen Lance

Plasma Torch

Primary Chamber

Copper Throat

Sleeve

Bulk Feeder

Oxygen Jets

Afterburner

Secondary Chamber

Collection Chamber

quench tank, the scrubber water passes to a jet scrubber that is designed to remove particulates and acid gases. A counterflow packed-bed scrubber provides additional removal of acid gases. A demister then removes moisture droplets entrained in the flow. The clean gases are exhausted through a stack. A blower at the exhaust stack maintains a negative pressure in the system and prevents any leakage (U.S. EPA 1992).

13.6. PNEUMATIC FRACTURING AND HOT GAS INJECTION

As discussed in chapter 9, soil vapor extraction (SVE) has been a popular method for the removal of volatile hydrocarbons from the vadose zone. A primary limitation to SVE technology, however, is that the vadose zone formation must be sufficiently permeable for air to flow and mobilize the volatile contaminants into the airstream. A method has been devised to facilitate the cleanup of soil and rock formations with poor air permeability, for example, shales and clay. The method involves injecting short bursts ($<$ 1 min) of compressed air into the formation, causing it to fracture at weak points. These fractures, which occur mostly in the horizontal direction in clay and shale formations, enlarge and extend existing fissures and/or create new fissures. Where these fractures connect an extraction well with an air injection well or other source of air, they allow increased flow through the formation and increase the permeability of the formation. The increased airflow then allows increased quantities of trapped and adsorbed organics to be removed by volatilization. An additional benefit of this technique is that the creation and extension of fractures provides access to areas of the formation that were not previously accessible to treatment (U.S. EPA 1993a).

Fracturing is conducted over narrow depth intervals using a proprietary lance equipped with rubber packers that are expanded by pressurization with air (Fig. 13.8). The effect of the pressure pulse is concentrated, and the design minimizes the propagation of vertical fractures by providing resistance above and below. Once fracturing has been successfully achieved in several intervals, the permeability of the formation is significantly increased. Wells are installed as with conventional SVE technology; for example, vacuum extraction from a central well with surrounding wells that are either air injected or open to the atmosphere, or air injection into a central well with vacuum extraction from surrounding wells. After pneumatic

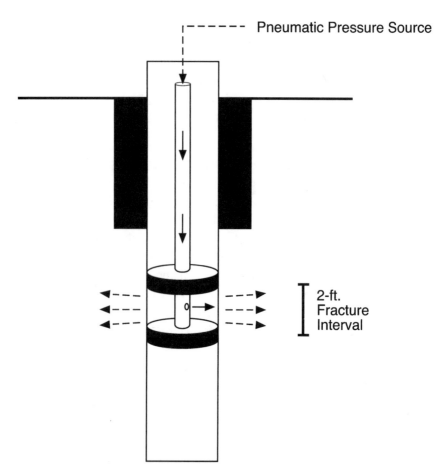

Figure 13.8.   *A pressure injector used to fracture subsurface strata*
U.S. Environmental Protection Agency 1993a.

fracturing, the radius of influence for vapor extraction is expanded, and in situ removal of VOCs can be accomplished. Hot gas injection into bedrock can accelerate VOC removal by vapor extraction, particularly when used simultaneously with pneumatic fracturing. Hot gas can be produced by the catalytic oxidation of VOCs removed from the site and can attain temperatures of approximately 1,000°F.

In a system devised by Accutech and the Hazardous Substance Management Research Center at the New Jersey Institute of Technology, a vacuum extraction system was developed consisting of a single trailer that housed compressors, a manifold, a water knock-out vessel, and compressor/vacuum blowers. Two granular activated carbon adsorption drums (55 gal) were installed in series to remove VOCs from the ex-tracted air before it was exhausted to the atmosphere. Alternate means for gas removal such as catalytic oxidation may be cost effective at higher concentrations (> 50 ppmv).

Additional practical concerns with this technology include the neces-sity of employing high-temperature grouts when installing well casings that will be exposed to extreme heat during the hot gas injection phase. Furthermore, if hot exhaust gases from catalytic oxidation of VOCs are di-rectly injected into the formation, it must be demonstrated that the gases are not contaminated (for example, with HCl from destruction of chlori-nated VOCs) and will not adversely affect groundwater or the formation (U.S. EPA 1993a).

13.7. LOW TEMPERATURE THERMAL AERATION

The low temperature thermal aeration (LTTA) system is a thermal treat-ment technology that desorbs organic compounds from soil at tempera-tures of 300°F to 800°F. The major components of the system include a material dryer, a pug mill mixer, two cyclone separators, a baghouse, a venturi scrubber and carbon filter, and two vapor-phase activated carbon beds (Fig. 13.9) (U.S. EPA 1995d).

Contaminated soil is fed into the system from feed hoppers by convey-ors. A screening system may be used, if necessary, prior to feeding soil into the hoppers. Other pretreatment procedures such as soil dewatering are employed as needed. The conveyors supply soil to the elevated end of a rotating materials dryer that heats the soil to approximately 800°F by a flow of hot air. A propane or fuel oil burner heats the airstream. Organic contaminants in the soil are desorbed and vaporized in the dryer. Vapor-ized organic compounds and airborne soil particles are then directed to cy-clone separators. The dry, hot soils are discharged at the lower end of the materials dryer into an enclosed pug mill mixer. Water is introduced to the pug mill to control dust generation during handling.

A pair of cyclone separators performs the next treatment step. The di-rection and flow rate of the exhaust gas from the materials dryer is estab-lished so that large particles drop out of the airstream. The particles are collected at the base of the conical section of the separators and trans-ferred by screw auger to the pug mill. In the pug mill, the particles are quenched along with the treated soils. The exhaust gas stream from the

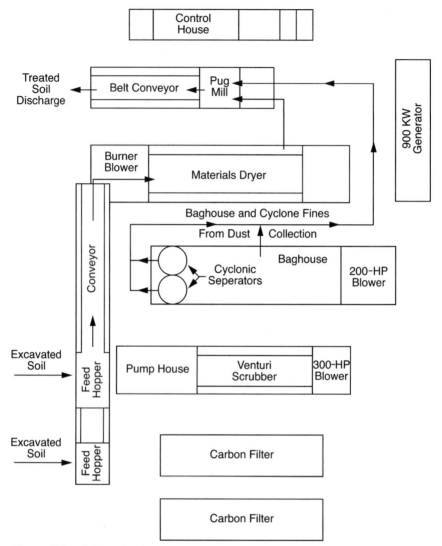

Figure 13.9.   *Schematic of soil processing used for a low temperature thermal aeration system*
U.S. Environmental Protection Agency 1995d.

cyclone separators is directed to the baghouse for additional particulate removal. Gases released from the baghouse are then directed to the venturi scrubber. The venturi scrubber, which can use a fine spray of water or alkali, removes about 95% of the particles > 0.2 m in size, neutralizes acid gases, and removes water-soluble components from the airstream. The scrubber water is filtered and then passed through a carbon filter. The gas stream exiting the venturi scrubber receives final treatment in two vapor-phase granular activated carbon (GAC) beds connected in parallel. Gas is directed into the bottom of each GAC bed. An induced draft fan draws gas through the GAC and exhausts it through a 40-ft stack (U.S. EPA 1995d).

Any treatment water and makeup water from the LTTA system is transferred to the pug mill for soil quenching. No wastewater is generated in the process.

The full-scale transportable system consists of six major components assembled on nine flatbed trailers. Additional components include soil conveyors, a power generator, a control trailer, and additional support facilities. The entire system and support areas require approximately 10,000 sq ft of operating space.

The developer of the LTTA system, Canonie Environmental Services Corporation, reports that the LTTA system can process a wide variety of soils with differing moisture and contaminant concentrations. However, the technology is best suited for soils with a moisture content of less than 20%. Wastes with a moisture content greater than 20% may require dewatering. Pretreatment screening or crushing of oversized material (> 2 in.) or clay shredding may also be required for some applications (U.S. EPA 1995d).

13.8. EVAPORATION-CATALYTIC OXIDATION

The POWWER technology (U.S. EPA 1993b) reduces the volume of an aqueous waste and catalytically oxidizes volatile contaminants. It has been successfully applied to VOCs, semivolatile organic compounds (sVOCs), cyanides, ammonia, and other constituents. The system consists of an evaporator to reduce influent water volume, a catalytic oxidizer to oxidize the volatile contaminants in the vapor stream from the evaporator, a scrubber to remove acid gases produced during oxidation, and a condenser to treat the vapor stream leaving the scrubber (Fig. 13.10).

Water to be treated is delivered into a 500-gal stainless steel feed tank. The feed pump, which is gravity fed from the tank, pumps the feed to the evaporator. The feed tank is equipped with an agitator mounted on the top of the tank to mix additives into the water (feed waste). To control foaming in the vapor body, an antifoaming agent can either be added to the water in the feed tank or injected directly into the vapor body. The

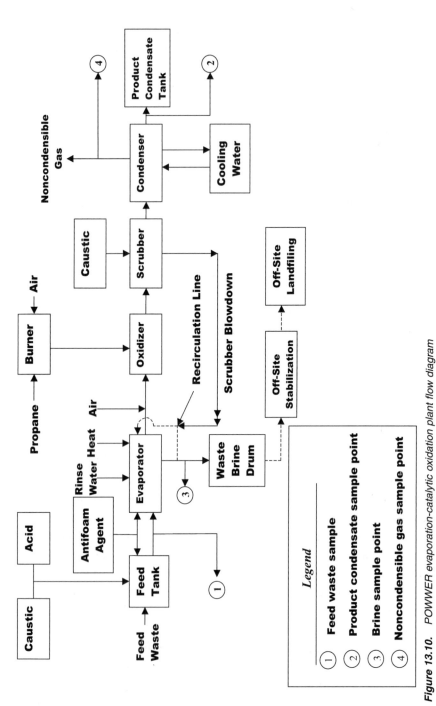

Figure 13.10. POWWER evaporation-catalytic oxidation plant flow diagram
U.S. Environmental Protection Agency 1993b.

feed waste pH is monitored and adjusted in the feed tank before being treated in the evaporator. The feed rate depends on the type of waste to be treated.

The first step in the process is volume reduction, which is achieved through evaporation. All volatile compounds are vaporized depending on the relative volatility of each compound and the composition of the feed waste. The technology utilizes this lack of specificity to treat complex wastewater mixtures. The evaporator consists of three main pieces of equipment: the heat exchanger, the vapor body, and the entrainment separator. As feed waste is pumped to the evaporator it combines with heated process liquor. The liquid waste is then further heated in a vertical shell-and-tube heat exchanger. Heat is supplied by steam generated in a boiler. Liquid waste flows through the tube side of the heat exchanger and steam passes through on the shell side. After passing through the heat exchanger, the liquid waste enters the vapor body, where boiling occurs and vapor is released. The vapor consists mostly of water and volatile contaminants, both organic and inorganic.

The second step in the process is oxidation of volatile organics and in-organics in the vapor stream from the evaporator. The process is designed to operate with a catalyst in either a fluidized or static bed mode. The fluidized bed mode ensures sufficient contact between the catalyst and the vapor. The oxidizer consists of three main pieces of equipment: the recuperative heat exchanger, the oxidizer heater, and the catalytic oxidizer. The inlet vapor is preheated along with oxidation air in a heat exchanger, with vapor exiting the catalytic oxidizer. The preheated vapor from the evaporator is further heated to oxidation temperature by the oxidizer heater, a direct-fired propane burner. The heated vapor then enters the catalytic oxidizer and passes through the catalyst bed where oxidation takes place. The pressure drop across the catalyst bed is monitored at all times for clogs in the catalyst bed. Possible oxidation products include carbon dioxide, water, hydrochloric acid, sulphur dioxide, nitrogen oxides, and products of incomplete combustion.

The third step involves scrubbing the vapor stream to neutralize the acid gases produced in the oxidizer. The scrubber consists of a packed bed in which the vapor passes countercurrently through a caustic solution. The scrubber neutralizes and removes the acid gases produced by oxidation. Vapor exiting the scrubber is cooled and condensed in a shell-and-tube condenser. Vapor is cooled on the shell side by noncontact cooling water passing through the tube side. The temperature of the product condensate is about 125°F (U.S. EPA 1993b).

The catalyst used in the system oxidizer is the main innovative feature of the system. The catalyst is a proprietary nonprecious metal oxide contained in a specific support medium. The catalyst is not as expensive or limited in versatility as a precious metal catalyst. The catalyst has been designed to withstand problems common to precious metal catalysts such as fouling, activity suppression, and poisoning. Due to the nature of the catalyst, periodic makeup is required to replace attrition losses (U.S. EPA 1993b).

13.9. STEAM ENHANCED RECOVERY

The steam enhanced recovery process (SERP) is an in situ process designed to remove volatile and semivolatile organic contamination using steam to provide heat and pressure to the affected material. The process is applicable to the treatment of contaminated soils and groundwater. The process works by injecting steam through injection wells constructed to a depth at or below the contaminant plume. Extraction wells are operated under vacuum to create a pressure gradient in the soil to draw the liquids, vapor, and contaminants through the soil. Liquid and vapor streams removed by the extraction wells are directed to an aboveground liquid and vapor treatment system (Fig. 13.11) (U.S. EPA 1995c).

Site geology is important in determining whether SERP will be applicable. Site requirements for effective operation include:

1. The contamination must consist of volatile and/or semivolatile compounds such as those found during spilled fuel events.
2. The soil must have moderate to high permeability.
3. There must be a confining layer below the depth of contamination. This layer can take the form of a continuous low-permeability layer such as a bedrock aquiclude, or a water table (for LNAPL compounds).
4. A low-permeability surface layer may be needed to prevent steam breakthrough for shallow treatment applications (U.S. EPA 1995c).

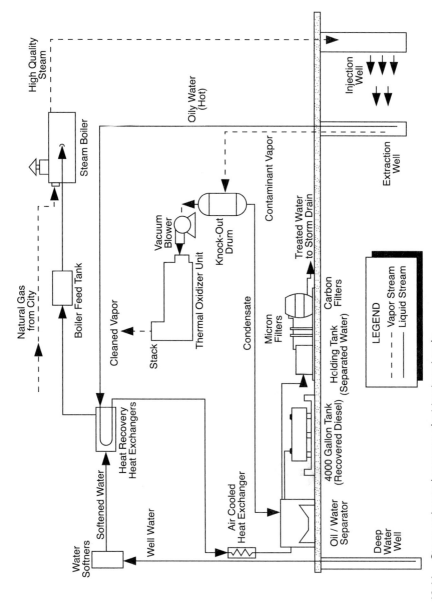

Figure 13.11. *Steam enhanced recovery plant treatment prain*
U.S. Environmental Protection Agency 1995c.

The removal of volatile and semivolatile contamination from the soil by SERP occurs via several mechanisms. High-temperature steam (approximately 250°F) heats the soil to the steam temperature in a pattern radiating from the injection wells toward the extraction wells, following pressure gradients. As the soil heats, contaminants that have boiling points lower than that of water will vaporize. The vapor will then be pushed ahead of the steam front. This results in a band of liquid contaminant that is formed just ahead of the advancing steam. When the steam front reaches an extraction well the vapor, liquid, and contaminants are removed.

The Rainbow Disposal site in Huntington Beach, California, was contaminated by a spill of diesel fuel, which is composed primarily of longer-chain hydrocarbon compounds (C_8 or heavier). Diesel compounds, although less dense than water, are heavier than those in most other petroleum-based fuels (e.g., gasoline or jet fuel) and are less volatile and more viscous. These properties make diesel a more difficult contaminant to remove from soil than most other petroleum-based fuels.

SERP was applied at the Rainbow Disposal site covering an area of 2.3 acres. The system of process wells was designed to treat the entire area concurrently. Thirty-five steam injection wells and 38 vapor/liquid extraction wells were constructed in the treatment area. The wells were placed in a repeating pattern of four injection wells surrounding each extraction well. The distance between adjacent injection well/extraction well pairs on this site was approximately 45 ft; between adjacent wells of the same type, the spacing was approximately 60 ft. Well spacing for a site is determined based on the permeability of the soil in the treatment area, the size of the area, and the depth and concentration of the contaminants. It was found that about 700 gal of diesel fuel were collected in liquid form, and approximately 15,400 gal were oxidized in the vapor treatment system (U.S. EPA 1995c). However, significant quantities of fuel could not be recovered from this site.

In a similar study, a dynamic underground stripping process was developed to recover gasoline contamination from a subsurface plume. The process uses steam injection, vacuum extraction, and electrical heating to effect contaminant removal from soil and groundwater. This system was found to be more successful than SERP because gasoline contains more volatile contaminants, the electric heating enhanced volatilization, and the latter system used more effective monitoring of the steam zone for operational control (U.S. EPA 1995c).

QUESTION

1. Describe the process and mechanism of electrokinetic remediation. Can it be effectively combined with phytoextraction? With phytostabilization? Explain.

REFERENCES

Acar, Y. B., and A. N. Alshawabkeh. 1993. Principles of electrokinetic remediation. *Environmental Science & Technology* 27:2638–47.

Jacobs, R. A., M. Z. Sengun, R. E. Hicks, and R. F. Probstein. 1994. Model and experiments on soil remediation by electric fields. *Journal of Environmental Science and Health*. Part A, *Environmental Science and Engineering* 29:1933–39.

Lageman, R. 1993. Electroreclamation: Applications in the Netherlands. *Environmental Science & Technology* 27:2648–50.

Rodsand, T., and Y. B. Acar. 1995. Electrokinetic extraction of lead from spiked Norwegian marine clay. *Geoenvironment 2000* 2:1518–34.

U.S. Environmental Protection Agency. 1992. *Retech, Inc., Plasma Centrifugal Furnace*. EPA/540/A5-91/007. Washington, DC: Office of Research and Development.

———. 1993a. *Accutech Pneumatic Fracturing Extraction and Hot Gas Injection, Phase I*. EPA/540/AR-93/509. Washington, DC: Office of Research and Development.

———. 1993b. *CWM PO*WW*ER Evaporation-Catalytic Oxidation Technology*. EPA/540/AR-93/506. Washington, DC: Office of Research and Development. .

———. 1995a. *Emerging Technology Bulletin: Electrokinetic Soil Processing. Electrokinetics, Inc*. EPA/540/F-95/504. Washington, DC: Office of Solid Waste and Emergency Response.

———. 1995b. *Geosafe Corporation In Situ Vitrification. Innovative Technology Evaluation Report*. EPA/540/R-94/520. Washington, DC: Office of Research and Development.

———. 1995c. *In Situ Steam Enhanced Recovery Process Hughes Environmental Systems, Inc*. EPA/540/R-94/510. Washington, DC: Office of Research and Development. Washington, D.C.

———. 1995d. *Low Temperature Thermal Aeration (LTTA) Process Canonie Environmental Services, Inc*. EPA/540/AR-93/504. Washington, DC: Office of Research and Development.

———. 1997. *Recent Development for In Situ Treatment of Metal Contaminated Soils*. EPA/542/R-97/004. Washington, DC: Office of Solid Waste and Emergency Response.

Weston, Roy F., Inc. 1988. *Remedial Technologies for Leaking Underground Storage Tanks*. Chelsea, MI: Lewis.

CHAPTER 14

Technology Selection

My will shall shape the future. Whether I fail or succeed shall be no
man's doing but my own. I am the force; I can clear any obstacle before me or I can be lost in the maze. My choice; my responsibility; win
or lose, only I hold the key to my destiny.

—Elaine Maxwell

I believe that we are solely responsible for our choices, and we have
to accept the consequences of every deed, word, and thought throughout our lifetime.

—Elisabeth Kubler-Ross

When choosing between two evils, I always like to try the one I've
never tried before.

—Mae West

BACKGROUND

As discussed in chapter 1, the number of contaminated sites in the United
States alone may number in the hundreds of thousands. The range of con
tamination includes crude and refined petroleum products, metallic
wastes, inorganics, and radioactives. In addition to public health and environmental concerns related to soil and groundwater contamination,
cleanups are notoriously expensive. The costs of remediating sites with
soil contamination, for example from leaking USTs, may range from

$10,000 up. Costs for remediating sites with groundwater contamination can range from $100,000 to over $1 million depending on the extent of contamination.

According to the U.S. Environmental Protection Agency (EPA), a key factor in the high cost of site cleanups is the use of remediation technologies that are either inappropriately selected or not optimally designed and operated given the specific conditions of the site. Excavation and landfilling, still a commonly used method for managing contaminated soils, does not truly remediate soils; rather, this activity simply transfers the hazard from one location to another. In addition to being costly, transporting contaminated soil off-site increases the risk of harming human health and the environment by the dispersal of soil particles and vapors. Pump-and-treat continues to be the most popular method for remediating groundwater; however, the success of this method is often limited because either the source of contamination is not adequately addressed, or the system is not optimized. Even when properly operated, pump-and-treat systems have inherent limitations: they may not work well in complex geologic settings or heterogeneous aquifers; They often stop reducing contamination long before reaching intended cleanup levels; and in some situations they can make sites more difficult to remediate by smearing contamination across the subsurface (U.S. EPA 2004).

With so many sites requiring remediation at such substantial costs, state and federal agencies are encouraging the use of faster, more effective, and less costly alternatives to conventional cleanup methods. The EPA continues to encourage state and local governments to promote the use of the most appropriate cleanup technology for each affected site.

The purpose of this chapter is to focus on appropriate technology use for site cleanup, taking into consideration site-specific conditions and the nature and extent of contamination.

As stated in the preface, there is no standardized list of procedures for treatment or removal of hydrocarbon and metallic contaminants from surface soil, subsoil, and/or groundwater. The choice of a technology is based on a constellation of factors, technical and otherwise, such as the characteristics of the affected site, specific properties of the contaminant, characteristics specific to the release itself, and capabilities specific to the technology. Beyond these technical criteria, issues such as cost, and even political considerations, must be addressed in choosing the appropriate remediation technology for a site.

This chapter focuses on engineering-related considerations for evaluating the technologies presented in this book. This chapter should be used alongside published technical sources, information from professional-training courses, and scientific journals.

To help in the review process, the discussion of each technology contains a brief review of the technology and checklists that list the most important factors to evaluate for the successful implementation of each technology.

ISOLATION (CONTAINMENT) (CHAPTER 6)

Isolation involves the physical segregation of subsurface contaminants from noncontaminated soil and groundwater. A number of systems are available to isolate the affected area so that contaminants are contained, either for permanent isolation or for removal or treatment at a later date. Specific systems that can effectively limit the spread of the contaminant include: diverting the flow of groundwater; subsurface barriers placed in the direction of flow to control lateral spread; and placement of an impermeable cap on the land surface to reduce infiltration of precipitation and run-on. These techniques have the common purpose of isolating the contaminant; they do not remove or destroy the contaminant.

Table 14.1.   Soil and site properties

Parameter or Issue	Optimal	Not Preferred or Detrimental	Comments
Presence of sensitive environmental receptors (e.g., wetlands, wildlife refuges)	None occurring within a large radius	In proximity to affected site	If water table is drawn down, may affect hydrology of wetlands. May need to install buffers to protect sensitive sites. Regulatory concerns about excavation near sensitive sites
Presence of subsurface structures	None	Fiber-optic cables, electric, sewer, water, steam, etc., susceptible to damage by excavation	May need to protect drinking-water wells, utility lines, etc. Document all buried structures in advance

(*continued*)

Table 14.1. (*continued*)

Parameter or Issue	Optimal	Not Preferred or Detrimental	Comments
Depth to groundwater	Deep aquifer	Shallow aquifer	High water table makes containment difficult
Soil particle size analysis	Soils high in clay	Soils high in sand and gravel (high porosity) may require containment	Dense (clayey) soils may be self-containing (i.e., limit contaminant migration)
K_s	$< 10^{-5}$ cm/sec	$> 10^{-3}$ cm/sec	Soils with high K_s may require containment
Soil surface area	< 0.1 m²/g	> 1 m²/g	Higher adsorption hinders groundwater diversion
Precipitation	Low to moderate with good infiltration	High precipitation and consequent runoff will make containment difficult	Additional engineering measures may be required, e.g., berms, diversion ditches

Table 14.2. Contaminant properties

Parameter or Issue	Optimal	Not Desired or Detrimental	Comments
Contaminant types	VOCs, gasoline, other mobile compounds; soluble metals and inorganics	Technology not useful or necessary for heavy oils and some metals (e.g., lead)	
Contaminant phase (hydrocarbons only)	Liquid (free liquid or dissolved)	Vapor	
Contaminant viscosity	High (> 20 cPoise)	Low (< 2 cPoise)	
DNAPL contamination	Shallow depth to confining layer	Deep to aquiclude	Keyed-in wall necessary
Time since release	Recent	Long (> 1 year)	If too old (and plume too extensive), difficult to divert groundwater

Table 14.3.   System parameters

Parameter or Issue	Optimal	Not Desired or Detrimental	Comments
Managing the contaminant	Subsurface hydrology well-defined		The technology can be combined with pump-and-treat
Runoff controls	If precipitation is moderate to heavy, install system for controlling runoff	Inadequate runoff controls make containment difficult	
Caps	Multilayers beneficial as they divert runoff. Also, vegetative layer protects	Cap exposed to rainfall, sunlight, wind, etc., may be damaged	Caps especially important when highly soluble contaminants present—prevents excess surface layers dispersion of plume

EXTRACTION PROCESSES (SOIL FLUSHING) (CHAPTER 7)

Soil extraction is an in situ technology that removes single or multiple contaminants from the subsurface. An appropriate extracting solution is either surface-applied or injected below grade to solubilize contaminants. Extracted liquids are treated and collected for disposal, or reinjected to the subsurface.

Table 14.4.   Soil and site properties

Parameter or Issue	Optimal	Not Desired or Detrimental	Comments
Depth to groundwater	< 40 ft to contaminated aquifer	Deep and/or confined aquifers	The technology can be combined with pump-and-treat
Soil particle size analysis	Sandy, gravelly, loamy soils	Dense, compacted clays	Rapid flow will enhance treatment and removal
Hydraulic conductivity	Faster than 1×10^{-3} cm/sec	Slower than 1×10^{-5} cm/sec	Rapid flow will enhance treatment and removal
Soil chemical properties	Acidic or near-neutral pH (for metals removal),	High concentrations of Ca, Fe, or other metals	Cationic soil metals (Ca^{2+}, Mg^{2+}, Fe^{2+}) will

(*continued*)

Table 14.4. (*continued*)

Parameter or Issue	Optimal	Not Desired or Detrimental	Comments
Soil chemical properties (*continued*)	low organic-matter content	(when using chelating agents and acids); high organic matter content	saturate chelating agents; organic matter may immobilize chelating agent
Extent of plume	Small, confined contamination	Large, diffuse site (> 1 ha)	
Presence of subsurface structures	None	Fiber-optic cables, electric, sewer, water, steam, other, susceptible to damage by excavation	Document all buried structures in advance
Rock fractures	None	Present	
Precipitation	Low to moderate	High	If high precipitation, may need to install berms and other run-on and runoff controls
Location	Rural/industrial/suburban	Urban	NPDES permit may be required for disposal into storm drainage

Table 14.5. Contaminant properties

Parameter or Issue	Optimal	Not Desired or Detrimental	Comments
Number of contaminants	One	Multiple	Multiple contaminants may require several extracting solutions; technology may not work optimally
Hydrocarbon contaminants	More soluble hydrocarbons, low molecular weight	Heavy hydrocarbons (asphaltics, tars, etc.)	If nonaqueous (nonpolar) contaminants occur, may be necessary to obtain large

(*continued*)

Table 14.5. (*continued*)

Parameter or Issue	Optimal	Not Desired or Detrimental	Comments
			volumes of surfactants; heavy hydrocarbons (e.g., coal tars) may be impossible to mobilize
Contaminant phase	Dissolved	Vapor	
Aqueous contaminants	Aqueous-based extracting solutions (acids, chelating agents, other)	Oily hydrocarbons	Hydrocarbons and other nonpolar contaminants will hinder water movement

Table 14.6.   System parameters

Parameter or Issue	Optimal	Not Desired or Detrimental	Comments
Nature of the extracting solution	Effectively solubilizes contaminant; must not itself be a hazardous compound	May itself become a groundwater contaminant	Some acids and surfactants may destroy soil structure; some may be toxic; acids will kill native microbes
Extraction well installation	Wells installed within the radius of influence	Wells too far apart; plume outside range of influence	Radius of influence must be sufficiently large to recover all solubilized contaminant

IN SITU SOLIDIFICATION/STABILIZATION (CHAPTER 8)

Solidification and stabilization (S/S) technologies are conducted by mixing contaminated soil with a binding agent to form a crystalline matrix that incorporates the contaminated materials. Inorganic binders include cement, cement kiln dust, fly ash, and blast furnace slag. Certain organic wastes can be immobilized using organic binders such as bitumen (asphalt). During solidification, contaminants are immobilized within a solid matrix in the form of a monolithic block. Stabilization converts contaminants to a less- or a nonreactive form, typically by chemical processes.

Table 14.7. Soil and site properties

Parameter or Issue	Optimal	Not Desired or Detrimental	Comments
Location	Remote (rural)	Urban, suburban	Regulatory approval may be easier in rural areas (Cole 1994)
Depth to groundwater	Deep aquifer	Shallow potable aquifer	High groundwater levels make containment difficult
Precipitation	Low to moderate with little runoff	High with excessive runoff	High precipitation will increase contaminant leaching
Soil types	Mineral soils	High organic matter	Organic matter interferes with cement-based S/S fixative process
Presence of subsurface structures	None	Fiber-optic cables, electric, sewer, water, steam, etc., susceptible to damage by excavation	Document subsurface structures in advance

Table 14.8. Contaminant properties

Parameter or Issue	Optimal	Not Desired or Detrimental	Comments
Metallic contaminants	Similar chemistry of contaminants	Varying chemistry (e.g., Cr and As)	Varying chemistry may stabilize one contaminant while solubilizing a second. If Cr and As are the contaminants of concern, their valence states should be known.
Metals, radioactives are the primary inorganic contaminants	Aqueous chemistry	Oily nonpolar hydrocarbons	Presence of hydrocarbons interferes with cement-based S/S fixative process

Table 14.9.   System Parameters

Parameter or Issue	Optimal	Not Preferred or Detrimental	Comments
Portland cement or pozzolanic-based treatment	Metals, inorganic contaminants	Oily, nonpolar contaminants	Binder must be compatible with contaminant
Thermoplastic-based treatment	Oily wastes	Aqueous wastes	

SOIL VAPOR EXTRACTION (CHAPTER 9)

Soil vapor extraction (SVE) is an in situ remedial technology that reduces concentrations of volatile constituents occurring in soil pores or adsorbed to soils in the vadose zone. A vacuum is applied to the soil to create a negative pressure gradient that causes movement of vapors toward extraction wells. Volatile constituents are readily removed from the subsurface through the extraction wells. The extracted vapors are then treated, as necessary, and discharged to the atmosphere.

SVE technology has been proven effective in reducing concentrations of volatile organic compounds (VOCs) and certain semivolatile organic compounds (SVOCs) found in petroleum products at UST sites. SVE is generally more successful when applied to the more volatile petroleum products such as gasoline. Diesel fuel, heating oils, lubricating oils, and kerosene, which are less volatile than gasoline, are not readily treated by SVE.

Table 14.10.   Soil and site properties

Parameter or Issue	Optimal	Not Preferred or Detrimental	Comments
Depth to groundwater	At least 15–20 ft	High water table	If high water table is encountered, sparging may be used
Soil moisture content	Generally dry or moist. Working in the vadose zone.	Saturated. Water table fluctuates markedly within the affected zone during the year	Consider biosparging when working below the water table
Soil temperature	Warm soils (> 20°C)	Cool soils (< 20°C) limit volatilization of vapors	Warm soils (> 20°C) favor SVE
Soil particle size analysis	Sands and gravels may impart high	Dense, clayey soils	Dense soils will require many

(continued)

Table 14.10. (*continued*)

Parameter or Issue	Optimal	Not Preferred or Detrimental	Comments
	K_s and therefore promote vapor extraction		more extraction wells as they restrict the radius of influence. If soils are dense, install a surface seal. Install air injection or passive inlet wells
Soil air conductivity	High ($> 10^{-4}$ cm/sec)	Low ($< 10^{-6}$ cm/sec)	
Site geology	Homogeneous	Heterogeneous	Undocumented layers of dense material will affect removal rate
Precipitation	Low to moderate precipitation will promote the presence of air (and vapors) in pore spaces	Heavy precipitation (and wet soils) will exclude vapors from soil voids	Capping may be necessary to prevent excess water infiltration
Presence of subsurface structures	None	Fiber-optic cables, electric, sewer, water, steam, etc., are susceptible to damage by excavation	Document all subsurface structures in advance
Presence of surface structures	None	Many	If many structures, consider horizontal well installation

Table 14.11. **Contaminant properties**

Parameter or Issue	Optimal	Not Preferred or Detrimental	Comments
Contaminant types	Light (low molecular weight) hydrocarbons (e.g., gasoline, jet fuel) are more amenable to SVE	Heavy, high-molecular weight hydrocarbons (heavy oils)	
Vapor pressure	> 100 mm Hg	< 10 mm Hg	If contaminant vapor pressure is < 0.5 mm Hg some type of enhancement (e.g.,

(*continued*)

Table 14.11.   (*continued*)

Parameter or Issue	Optimal	Not Preferred or Detrimental	Comments
			heated air injection) may be needed to increase volatility
Boiling points of the contaminant constituents	< 300°C	> 300°C	A higher boiling point indicates higher molecular weight and hence less volatility
Henry's Law constant	> 100 atm	< 100 atm	
Water solubility	< 100 mg/L	> 1,000 mg/L	Low solubility implies greater concentration of hydrocarbons

Table 14.12.   **System parameters**

Parameter or Issue	Optimal	Not Preferred or Detrimental	Comments
Water table	Deep (below base of extraction wells)	Shallow	May be necessary to lower water table via pumping. Alternatively, use air sparging
Properties of extracted vapors	Relatively innocuous	Excessive vapor concentrations emitted, or concentrations of hazardous vapors above acceptable limits	Install vapor treatment system. Many choices available depending on site factors and regulatory requirements

REACTIVE BARRIER WALLS (CHAPTER 10)

Permeable reactive barriers (PRBs) are subsurface structures installed downgradient of a contaminant plume to allow the passage of groundwater while promoting the degradation or removal of contaminants by specific chemical and physical reactions. PRBs have been used to successfully treat or remove metallic, radioactive, nonmetallic, and hydrocarbon contaminants from groundwater. Several variations of PRB configurations are available.

The PRB is installed across the flow path of a contaminant plume. The reactive media is installed in order to be in intimate contact with the surrounding aquifer material. The reactive treatment zone inhibits contaminant movement via employing reactants and agents including zero-valent iron or other metals, zeolites, humic materials, chelating agents, sorbents, and active microbial cells.

Table 14.13. Soil and site properties

Parameter or Issue	Optimal	Not Preferred or Detrimental	Comments
Location	Remote (rural)	Urban, suburban	Regulatory approval may be easier in rural areas
Depth to groundwater	< 40 ft to contaminated aquifer	Excessively deep to contaminated aquifer	
Extent of plume	Small, confined contamination	Large, diffuse site (> 1 ha)	
Soil particle size analysis	Sandy, gravelly	Dense, heavy clays	
Hydraulic conductivity	Faster than 1×10^{-3} cm/sec	Slower than 1×10^{-5} cm/sec	Rapid flow will enhance treatment and removal
Precipitation	Low to moderate	High	Run-on and runoff controls may be necessary
Presence of subsurface structures	None	Fiber optics, water, sewer, steam, etc. may interfere with installation of PRB	Determine the location of all structures in advance
Presence of surface structures	None	May interfere with installation of PRB	

Table 14.14. Contaminant properties

Parameter or Issue	Optimal	Not Preferred or Detrimental	Comments
Hydrocarbon contaminant	ZVI, reduced iron barrier		
Heavy metal contaminant	ZVI, reduced iron, limestone, apatite, microbial barrier		
Redox-sensitive elements (e.g., chromate, arsenate)	ZVI, reduced iron, limestone, apatite, microbial barrier		
Liquid viscosity	Low (< 2 cPoise)	High (> 20 cPoise)	
Time since release	Recent (< 1 month)	Long (> 12 months)	

Table 14.15.   System parameters

Parameter or Issue	Optimal	Not Preferred or Detrimental	Comments
Runoff controls	If precipitation is moderate to heavy, install controls for controlling runoff		Inadequate runoff controls will make containment difficult

IN SITU MICROBIAL REMEDIATION (CHAPTER 11)

In situ bioremediation encourages growth of indigenous microorganisms to enhance biodegradation of organic contaminants in the saturated zone. In situ bioremediation degrades hydrocarbons that are dissolved in groundwater and adsorbed onto the aquifer matrix.

Bioremediation requires a delivery system for providing an electron acceptor, nutrients, and an energy source (carbon). In a typical in situ bioremediation system, groundwater is extracted using wells and, if necessary, treated to remove residual dissolved constituents. The treated groundwater is then mixed with an electron acceptor and nutrients, and reinjected upgradient of the contaminant source. Infiltration galleries or injection wells may be used to reinject treated water. Extracted water that is not reinjected must be discharged, typically to surface water or to publicly owned treatment works. In situ bioremediation can be implemented in a number of treatment modes, including aerobic, anaerobic, and co-metabolic.

Table 14.16.   Soil and site properties

Parameter or Issue	Optimal	Not Preferred or Detrimental	Comments
Hydraulic conductivity	$> 10^{-3}$ cm/sec	$< 10^{-5}$ cm/sec	
Impermeable layers	Present	Absent	
Groundwater chemistry	Dissolved Fe < 10 mg/L	Dissolved Fe > 10 mg/L	High Fe concentrations will cause clogging of well screens
Soil moisture content	$> 30\%$ by vol.	$< 10\%$ by vol.	
Soil pH	6–8	< 5.5 or > 8.0	Extremes in pH will denature microbial enzymes
Soil and groundwater temperature	10°C–45°C	$< 10°C$ or $> 45°C$	Extremes in temperatures will denature

(continued)

Table 14.16. (*continued*)

Parameter or Issue	Optimal	Not Preferred or Detrimental	Comments
			microbial enzymes and inactivate microbial populations
Total heterotrophic bacteria count	> 1,000 CFU/g dry soil		
C:N:P ratio	Between 100:10:1 and 100:1:0.5	< 100:10:1 or > 100:1:0.5	Low N will inhibit microbial reproduction
Soil moisture	40%–85%	< 40% or > 85%	

Table 14.17. Contaminant properties

Parameter or Issue	Optimal	Not Preferred or Detrimental	Comments
Degradability of constituents	Biorefractory index > 0.1	Biorefractory index < 0.01	
Dominant phase	Dissolved	Free liquid (NAPL)	
Contaminant solubility	High (> 1000 mg/L)	Low (< 100 mg/L)	
Total petroleum constituent concentrations	< 50,000 ppm		Excessively high hydrocarbon concentrations, even of a biodegradable contaminant, can be toxic
Total heavy metals	< 2,500 ppm		Excessive metals will inactivate microbial enzymes
Time since release	Long (> 12 months)	Short (< 1 month)	Longer times will allow more time for hydrocarbon transformation to dissolved forms

Table 14.18. System parameters

Parameter or Issue	Optimal	Not Preferred or Detrimental	Comments
Presence of free product	Free-product recovery system needed		
Determination of area of influence	Appropriate well placement, given		

(continued)

Table 14.18. (*continued*)

Parameter or Issue	Optimal	Not Preferred or Detrimental	Comments
	total area to be cleaned up and area of influence of each injection/ extraction well		
Subsurface soil and groundwater sampling for tracking constituent reduction and biodegradation conditions	Set up schedule for tracking constituent reduction. Control nutrient addition on a periodic or continuous basis.		Install appropriate nutrient delivery systems

LANDFARMING

Landfarming, also known as land application, is an aboveground remediation technology for soils that reduces concentrations of petroleum constituents through biodegradation and aeration (venting). This technology involves spreading excavated contaminated soils in a thin layer on the ground surface and stimulating aerobic microbial activity within the soils through aeration and/or the addition of minerals, nutrients, and moisture. The enhanced microbial activity results in degradation of adsorbed petroleum product constituents through microbial respiration. If contaminated soils are shallow (i.e., < 3 ft below ground surface), it may be possible to effectively stimulate microbial activity without excavating the soils. If petroleum-contaminated soil is deeper than 5 ft, the soils should be excavated and placed on to the ground surface.

Table 14.19. Soil and site properties

Parameter or Issue	Optimal	Not Preferred or Detrimental	Comments
Total heterotrophic bacteria count	> 10^6 CFU/g dry soil	< 1,000 CFU/g dry soil	
Soil pH	6.0–8.0	< 5.5 or > 8.0	
Soil moisture content	40%–85% (vol/vol)		
Soil temperature	10°C–45°C	< 10°C or > 45°C	
C:N:P ratio	100:10:1 to 100–1:0.5		
Precipitation rate	30–45 in./yr	Soil too wet will impair aerobic microorganisms	Irrigation may be needed for excessively dry soils

Table 14.20. Contaminant properties

Parameter or Issue	Optimal	Not Preferred or Detrimental	Comments
Contaminants to be treated	Lightweight hydrocarbons (gasoline, jet fuel, diesel fuel, kerosene)	Heavy (high MW) hydrocarbons; PAHs; heavy metals	Air emissions may need to be monitored and, if necessary, controlled
Degradability of constituents	Biorefractory index > 0.1	Biorefractory index < 0.01	
Concentration of total petroleum constituents	< 50,000 mg/kg		Excessively high hydrocarbon concentrations, even of a biodegradable contaminant, can be toxic
Total heavy metals	< 2,500 mg/kg	> 3,000 mg/kg	

Table 14.21. System parameters

Parameter or Issue	Optimal	Not Preferred or Detrimental	Comments
Technical feasibility	A treatability study has been conducted; biodegradation has been demonstrated, nutrient application defined, and potential toxic conditions checked		
Available land area	Large (> 10 acres)	Small (< 1 acre)	Consider landfarm depth and additional space for berms and access
Treatment of heavy hydrocarbons	Frequent mixing of soil material		
Daily operations	Run-on and runoff controlled; erosion control measures specified; frequency of application and composition of nutrients and pH adjustment materials specified; moisture addition; other suboptimal natural site		

(*continued*)

Table 14.21. (*continued*)

Parameter or Issue	Optimal	Not Preferred or Detrimental	Comments
	conditions addressed in landfarm design		
Operation plan	Anticipate frequency of aeration, nutrient addition, moisture addition		
Monitoring progress of bioremediation	Conduct quarterly monitoring for soil pH, moisture content, bacterial populations, nutrient levels, contaminant concentrations. Monitor contaminant reduction and biodegradation conditions in LTU soils		

PHYTOREMEDIATION (CHAPTER 12); PHYTOEXTRACTION OF METALS

Phytoextraction involves the use of hyperaccumulating plants to transport metals from the soil to concentrate them into roots and aboveground shoots. Following harvest of the extracting crop, the metal-rich plant biomass can be processed to recover the contaminant (e.g., valuable heavy metals, radionuclides). If recycling the metal is not economically feasible, the small amount of ash (compared to the original plant biomass or the large volume of contaminated soil) can be disposed of appropriately.

Table 14.22. Soil and site properties

Parameter or Issue	Optimal	Not Preferred or Detrimental	Comments
Location	Brownfield, urban		Phytoremediation zones can provide "green belts"
Depth of contamination	Well within rooting zone of plants	Beyond root zone	If beyond rooting zone, affected soil can be excavated and placed in layers on surface for plant treatment

(*continued*)

Table 14.22. (*continued*)

Parameter or Issue	Optimal	Not Preferred or Detrimental	Comments
Soil fertility status	Low N, P, K, micronutrients	Moderate concentrations of N, P, K, micronutrients	Commercial and organic fertilizer materials are usually readily available
Soil organic matter	Low ($< 0.1\%$)	Moderate to high ($> 1\%$)	Organic matter can be added in the form of manures, composts, etc.
Soil pH	5.5–7.5	Strongly acidic or alkaline	
Soil salinity	Low (< 1 dS/m)	High (> 4 dS/m)	
Presence of toxins	None	Presence of excess heavy metals, salts, etc.	

Table 14.23. Contaminant properties

Parameter or Issue	Optimal	Not Preferred or Detrimental	Comments
Contaminants	One	Multiple	Multiple contaminants may create toxicity issues, more frequent crop rotation
Contaminant types	Aqueous	Hydrophobic compounds (e.g., oily wastes, hydrocarbon solvents)	Hydrophobic materials will inhibit water movement and may cause plant toxicity
Contaminant form (metals)	Soluble, exchangeable	Crystalline, insoluble	Site-specific metal chemistry must be determined

Table 14.24. System parameters

Parameter or Issue	Optimal	Not Preferred or Detrimental	Comments
Soil management	Removal of weeds (tillage, herbicides); adequate moisture		Plant growth must be optimized to achieve both maximal root and shoot growth, and

(*continued*)

Table 14.24. (*continued*)

Parameter or Issue	Optimal	Not Preferred or Detrimental	Comments
			thus maximum access to soil metals and extraction
Crop management	Optimal planting density	Plants excessively crowded together, or spaced too far apart	Maximize soil material covered by healthy extracting plants
Chelate application	Chelate not toxic, readily biodegradable	Potentially toxic chelating agent applied in single large dose	May be beneficial to apply at multiple intervals instead of as one large dose

REFERENCES

Cole, G. M. 1994. *Assessment and Remediation of Petroleum Contaminated Sites*. Boca Raton, FL: CRC Press.

U.S. Environmental Protection Agency. 2004. *How to Evaluate Alternative Cleanup Technologies for Underground Storage Tank Sites: A Guide for Corrective Action Plan Reviewers*. EPA 510-B-94-003, EPA 510-B-95-007, and EPA 510-R-04-002. See: www.epa.gov/OUST/pubs/tums.htm.

APPENDIX TO CHAPTER 14

Technology Selection for Contaminated Site

Refer to the phase 2 ESA exercise (appendix to chapter 5) and to the website http://www.govinstpress.com/books/Pichtel/ for the site plan and complete well logs.

Based on site and contaminant characteristics, what technology or technologies would you recommend to clean this site? Consider soil and groundwater properties, plume direction, proximity to buried structures, and other relevant data.

Cost Analysis of Remediation Projects

Based on the technical information presented in the previous chapters, it should be obvious that the cost of bringing a remediation project to completion will vary over a wide spectrum. Important factors that potentially affect project costs include concentration of contaminants in the affected media; required cleanup levels, hydrogeologic conditions, completion schedules, and permit fees (for example, for treatment of a specific media, treatment of off-gases, disposal of treated soil, etc.). As a result, projects may range in cost from several thousand dollars to tens of millions of dollars.

Cost data for 51 selected remediation projects are presented in Table A.1. Data are provided as either total project costs or a division into capital costs and operations and maintenance. In some cases there are cost categories embracing pre-treatment, during treatment, and posttreatment activities. Where applicable, a cost per cubic yard of soil, per 1,000 gallons of water, or per pound of contaminant is given. Information is also provided on the quantity of media (soil or groundwater) treated and on the amount of actual contaminant(s) removed from the media.

It is difficult to compare costs for different projects because of differences in site-specific factors. Cost data in Table A.1 have not been adjusted for inflation to a common-year basis.

Ex situ Bioremediation (Soil):

Site Name, Location	Quantity Treated	Quantity of Contaminant Removed	Project Costs ($)	Treatment Costs	Contaminant Type(s), Sources Primary, Secondary Treatment
Bonneville Power Administration Superfund Site, WA	1048 yd^3	-	1,280,000	$1220/yd^3	PAHs and other SVOCs; Included extensive technology demonstration activities
Brown Wood Preserving Superfund Site, FL	8100 yd^3	-	635,000	$78.4/yd^3	PAHs; Constructed lined treatment system; Moderate initial contaminant concentrations
Dubose Oil Products Co. Superfund Site, FL	13,137 yd^3	-	4,990,000	$380/yd^3	BTEX, cVOCs, Other SVOCs, other VOCs; Treatment system constructed in building, including leachate collection, inoculate generation, vacuum extractions, and wastewater treatment
Fort Greely UST Soil Piles, AK	9800 yd^3	-	749,000	$76.4/yd^3	BTEX, PHC; Operation and maintenance only in summer months; no liner
Fort Wainwright, North Post Site Soil Remediation, AK	4240 yd^3	-	433,000	$102/yd^3	BTEX; Remediation technology costs only activities included liner construction, drainage, tilling, and addition of nutrients
Glasgow Air Force Base UST Removal, MT	4800 yd^3	-	60,000	$12.5/yd^3	PHC; Application primarily consisted of soil tilling
Havre Air Force Station, Remove Abandoned USTs, MT	1786 yd^3	-	48,700	$27.3/yd^3	BTEX; Application primarily consisted of soil plowing and tilling
Lowry AFB, CO	5400 yd^3	-	130,000	$24.1/yd^3	BTEX, PHC; Conducted on plastic sheeting, nutrients added once and aerated; interim costs

Site Name, Location	Quantity Treated	Quantity of Contaminant Removed	Project Costs ($)	Treatment Costs	Contaminant Type(s), Sources Primary, Secondary Treatment
Matagora Island Air Force Base, TX	500 yd^3	-	77,600	\$155/yd^3	BTEX; Costs of entire project including excavation, treatment, and monitoring
Umatilla Army Depoit Activity (FS), OR	10,969 yd^3	-	5,260,000	\$479/yd^3	Other SVOCs; Composting conducted in building; One of the first biotreatment projects for soil contaminated with explosives; Maintained high moisture content

In situ Bioremediation (Soil):

Site Name, Location	Quantity Treated	Quantity of Contaminant Removed	Project Costs ($)	Treatment Costs	Contaminant Type(s), Sources Primary, Secondary Treatment
Dover AFB, Area 6, DE	1667 yd^3	-	551,000	\$331/yd^3	Not full scale complete; cVOCs, Heavy metals; Direct injection of air and propane; cometabolic aerobic; pilot test
Hill AFB, Site 914, UT	5000 yd^3	-	863,000	\$173/yd^3	BTEX, PHC; Early bioventing application, combined with soil vapor extraction
Lowry AFB (in situ), CO	Not reported	-	75,300	Not calculated	BTEX, PHC; High initial contaminant concentrations; Used horizontal trenches

Site Name, Location	Quantity Treated	Quantity of Contaminant Removed	Project Costs ($)	Treatment Costs	Contaminant Type(s), Sources Primary, Secondary Treatment
Edwards AFB, CA	1517 yd^3	-	445,000	$293/yd^3	Not full scale complete; cVOCs; Recirculation between two aquifer systems; aerobic
Pinella Northeast Site, Anaerobic Bioremediation, FL	1238 yd^3	-	359,000	$290/yd^3	Not full scale complete; cVOCs; Recirculation with addition of benzoate, lactate, and methanol; Anaerobic; Intended to supplement active pump-and-treat system
Texas Gulf Coast Aite, TX	Not reported	-	630,000	Not calculated	cVOCs; Recirculation with addition of methanol; Anaerobic; Intended as a precursor to monitored natural attenuation
Departmenf of Energy, Savannah River Site, M Area Process Sewer/Integrated Demonstration Site, SC	Not reported	-	729,000	Not calculated	Not full scale complete; cVOCs; Direct injection of cometabolites; aerobic; Soil vapor extraction employing horizontal wells
Confidential Site, Maryland	~ 405,000 gallons	Not provided	161,400	$0.02/gallon treated	Permeable reactive barrier; Use of a permeable reactive barrier to treat groundwater contaminated with halogenated volatiles
Multiple (3) Naval Facilities	Hunters Point: 10,518 ft^2 Jacksonville: Not provided Lakehurst: 12,820 ft^2	Not provided	Hunters Point: 1,679,300 Jacksonville: 259,000 Lakehurst: 255,500	Not provided	In situ chemical reduction-nanoscale zero-valent ion; Use of in situ chemical reduction to treat groundwater contaminated with halogenated volatiles at three Naval facilities

Site Name, Location	Quantity Treated	Quantity of Contaminant Removed	Project Costs ($)	Treatment Costs	Contaminant Type(s), Sources Primary, Secondary Treatment
Thermal Desorption:					
Waldick Aerospace Devices Superfund Site, NJ	5,175 tons	-	2,890,000	$558/ton	PHC, Metal, VOC; Emission control used wet scrubber and thermal treatment for gas phase
Re-Solve, Inc. Superfund Site, MA	44,000 tons	-	24,100,000	$548/ton	PHC, SVOC, PCB; Emission control with wet scrubber for gas phase, granular activated carbon for gas and liquid phases, oxidative treatment for liquid phase
Port Moller Radio Relay Station, AK	14,250 tons	-	7,070,000	$496/ton	PHC, VOC; Emission control with thermal treatment for gas phase
Wide Beach Development Superfund Site, NY	42,000 tons	-	19,300,000	$459/ton	SVOC, PCB; Emission control with granular activated carbon and wet scrubber for gas phase, plus granular activated carbon and oxidative treatment for liquid phase
Outboard Marine Corporation Superfund Site, IL	12,755 tons	-	4,720,000	$370/ton	SVOC, PCB; Emission control with granular activated carbon and wet scrubber for gas phase, plus granular activated carbon and oxidative treatment for liquid phase

Soil Vapor Extraction:

Site Name, Location	Quantity Treated	Quantity of Contaminant Removed	Project Costs ($)	Treatment Costs	Contaminant Type(s), Sources Primary, Secondary Treatment
Amcor Precast, UT	7500 yd^3	-	240,610	$32.08/yd^3	Ongoing; PHC, BTEX
Camp LeJeune Military Reservation Superfund Site, Site 82, Area A, NC	17,500	-	591,305	$35.79/yd^3	Completed; cVOCs, BTEX; Off-gas treatment with granular activated carbon
Commencement Bay, South Tacoma Channel Well 12A Superfund Site, WA	41,720	-	4,477,689	$107.33/yd^3	Completed; cVOCs
Davis-Monthan AFB, Site ST-35, AZ	63,000	585,700 pounds	225,909	$3.59/yd^3	Completed; cVOCs; Off-gas treatment with thermal oxidizer
Defense Supply Center Richmond Superfund Site, VA	1000	-	97,745	$102.64/yd^3	Completed; cVOCs; Off-gas treatment with granular activated carbon
Fairchild Semiconductor Corporation Superfund Site, CA	42,000	16,000 pounds	4,442,609	$105.78/yd^3	Completed; cVOCs, BTEX; Off-gas treatment with granular activated carbon

Site Name, Location	Quantity Treated	Quantity of Contaminant Removed	Project Costs ($)	Treatment Costs	Contaminant Type(s), Sources Primary, Secondary Treatment
Garden State Cleaners, NJ	600	-	197,009	$328.35/yd^3	Completed; cVOCs; Off-gas treatment with granular activated carbon
Hastings Groundwater Contamination Superfund Site, CA	185,000	600 pounds	456,862	$2.47/yd^3	Completed; cVOCs; Off-gas treatment with granular activated carbon
Intersil/Siemens Superfund site, CA	280,000	3000 pounds	801,299	$2.86/yd^3	Completed; cVOCs; Off-gas treatment with granular activated carbon
Rocky Moutain Arsenal Superfund Site, Motor Pool Area OU 18, CO	70	34,000 pounds	212,399	$6.25/yd^3	Completed; cVOCs; Off-gas treatment with granular activated carbon

On-Site Incineration:

Site Name, Location	Quantity Treated	Quantity of Contaminant Removed	Project Costs ($)	Treatment Costs	Contaminant Type(s), Sources Primary, Secondary Treatment
Bayou Bonfouca, LA	250,000 tons	-	74,000,000	$300/ton	Contaminants: PAHs; Medium: sediment; Design: Rotary kiln, secondary combustion chamber, gas conditioner, scrubber, and mist eliminator
Celanese Corpoation Shelby Fiber Opeartions, NC	4660 tons	-	2,000,000	$440/ton	Contaminants: ethylene glycol, VOCs, PAHs, phenol; Medium: soil and sludge; Design: Rotary kiln, secondary combustion chamber, quench duct, baghouse, and packed-bed scrubber

On-Site Incineration:

Site Name, Location	Quantity Treated	Quantity of Contaminant Removed	Project Costs ($)	Treatment Costs	Contaminant Type(s), Sources Primary, Secondary Treatment
Former Nebraska Ordnance Plant, NE	16,449 tons	-	7,000,000	$430/ton	Contaminants: explosvies and propellants; Medium: soil and debris; Design: Rotary kiln, secondary combustion chamber; water quench, and mist eliminator
MOTCO, TX	23,021 tons	-	33,000,000	$1400/ton	Contaminants: Styrene tars and VOCs; Medium: Soil, sludge, organic liquids, aqueous wastes; Design: Rotary kiln, secondary combustion chamber, second incinerator with single liquid injection chamber, both has quench system, gas conditioner, wet scrubber, and mist eliminator
Petro Processors, LA	213,376 gallons (as of June 1997)	-	4,800,000	$22/gallon	Contaminants: chlorinated hydrocarbons, PAHs, Oils; Medium: organic liquids and fumes; Design: Horizontal liquid injection incinerator, quench tank, wet scrubber, particulate scrubber, entrainment separator
Sikes Disposal Pits, TX	496,000 tons (soil and debris)	-	81,000,000	$160/ton	Contaminants: Organic phenolic compounds; Medium: soil and debris; Design: Rotary kiln, secondary combustion chamber, quench section, and two-stage scrubber

Pump-and-Treat:

Site Name, Location	Quantity Treated	Quantity of Contaminant Removed	Project Costs ($)	Treatment Costs	Contaminant Type(s), Sources Primary, Secondary Treatment
French Ltd., TX	78,000 gallons	-	16,000,000	$200/1000 gallons	Benzene, toluene, chloroform, 1,2-dichloroethane, vinyl chloride; Ex situ treatment: biological treatment, granular activated carbon adsorption, physical/chemical removal of metal
TCAAP, MN	1,400,000 gallons	-	12,000,000	$8.4/1000 gallons	1,2-dichloroethene, 1,1,1-tetrachloroethane, tetrachloroethene (TCE, PCE); Ex situ treatment: air stripping
McClellan AFB, OU B/C, CA	96,000 gallons	-	5,600,000	$58/1000 gallons	Tetrachloroethene (TCE, PCE), cis-1,20dichloroethene, 1,2-dichloroethane; Ex situ treatment: air stripping
DOE, Savannah River, SC	240,000 gallons	-	5,200,000	$21/1000 gallons	Tetrachloroethene (TCE, PCE), 1,1,1-tetrachloroethane; Ex situ treatment: air stripping
Des Moines, IA	550,000 gallons	-	2,200,000	$3.9/1000 gallons	Tetrachloroethene (TCE); Ex situ treatment: air stripping
Old Mill, OH	1700 gallons	-	2,100,000	$1300/1000 gallons	Tetrachloroethene (TCE, PCE), 1,2-dichloroethene, ethylbenzene; Ex situ treatment: granular activated carbon adsorption, air stripping

Site Name, Location	Quantity Treated	Quantity of Contaminant Removed	Project Costs ($)	Treatment Costs	Contaminant Type(s), Sources Primary, Secondary Treatment
U.S. Aviex, MI	96,000 gallons	-	1,900,000	$20/1000 gallons	1,1,1-tetrachloroethane, 1,2-dichloroethane, diethyl ether, 1,1-dichloroethene, tetrachloroethene (TCE, PCE), BTEX; Ex situ treatment: air stripping
DOE, Kansas City, MO	11,000 gal	-	1,900,000	$170/1,000 gal	Tetrachloroethene (PCE, TCE), cis-1,2-dichloroethene, trans-1,2-dichloroethene, vinyl chloride; ex situ treatment: oxidation
Keefe, NH	11,000 gal	-	1,900,000	$170/1,000 gal	Tetrachloroethene (PCE, TCE), 1,2-dichloroethene, benzene, 1,2-dichloroethene; ex situ treatment: physical/chemical removal of metal, air stripping
SCRDI Dixiana, SC	4500 gal	-	1,900,000	$420/1,000 gal	Tetrachloroethene (PCE, TCE), 1,1,1-tetrachloroethene, 1,1-dichloroethene, 1,1,2-tetrachloroethane, 1,1,2,2-tetrachloroethane, chloroform, carbon tetrachloride, benzene, dichloromethane; ex situ treatment: air stripping
King of Prussia, PA	57,000 gal	-	1,800,000	$32/1,000 gal	1,1-dichloroethane, trans-1,2-dichlrorethene, 1,1,1-trichloroethane, tetrachloroethene (PCE, TCE), tetrachloroethane, benzene, toluene, ethylbenzene, beryllium, chromium, copper, nickel, cadmium, mercury, zinc; ex situ treatment: granular activated carbon adsorption, physical/chemical removal of metal, air stripping

References

U.S. Environmental Protection Agency. August 2006. *Abstracts of Remediation Case Studies*. Vol. 10. EPA542-R-06-002. Washington, DC: Federal Remediation Technologies Roundtable. Washington, D.C.

U.S. Environmental Protection Agency. September 2001. *Remediation Technology Cost Compendium–Year 2000*. EPA-542-R-01-009. Washington, DC: Solid and Solid Hazardous Waste Emergency Response.

Glossary of Terms

Accumulator   Plant that absorbs high concentrations of an element or compound into tissue with no apparent detrimental effect.

Acid   A liquid or solid that donates a proton (H^+) to another substance. A substance that causes destruction to skin tissue at the site of contact or that corrodes steel. Liquids possess a pH of less than 7.0.

Actinomycetes   A group of heterotrophic, mostly filamentous aerobic microorganisms.

Activated carbon   Pyrolyzed carbonaceous material used to remove potentially toxic substances from gaseous or aqueous media.

Activated sludge   A process of removing BOD from wastewater. Microbial cells are introduced into a reaction vessel and allowed to decompose organic compounds. Newly produced microbial biomass is collected and reintroduced into the process.

Acute effect   An adverse effect on an organism, generally after a single exposure, with severe symptoms developing rapidly.

Acute toxicity   Detrimental effects of a chemical that occur within a relatively short time frame (hours to months).

Adsorption   Attraction of solid, liquid, or gas molecules, ions, or atoms to particle surfaces by physiochemical forces.

Advection   Unidirectional bulk movement, such as water or a dissolved ion under the influence of a hydraulic gradient.

Aerobic   System or process in which oxygen, O_2, is required or is present. The biological state of living in the presence of oxygen.

Aliphatic hydrocarbon   Class of hydrocarbons that contain no aromatic rings. The class includes alkanes, alkenes, alkynes, and cyclic hydrocarbons.

Alkali   A liquid or solid substance that is caustic. Strong alkalis in solution are corrosive to the skin and mucous membranes. Substances with a pH greater than 7.0.

Alkalinity   A solution having a pH value greater than 7.0. A measure of the capacity of liquids to neutralize strong acids. Alkalinity results from the presence of bicarbonates, carbonates, hydroxides, silicates, phosphates, and some other substances.

Alkylaromatic   Aromatic compounds containing alkyl substituents.

Alkynes   Hydrocarbons composed of molecules that contain one or more carbon-carbon triple bonds.

Alkene   Hydrocarbons composed of molecules that contain one or more carbon-carbon double bonds. Also known as *olefins*.

Anaerobic   System or process in which oxygen is not required or is absent.

Anhydrous   Free from water.

Anion   An ion that is negatively charged.

Anoxic   Conditions lacking molecular oxygen.

Anthropogenic   Man-made.

Aquiclude   An impermeable layer of geologic strata occurring beneath the surface. Will not permit groundwater to flow through.

Aquifer   Underground formation of porous geologic strata such as sand, rock, gravel, etc., that can store and supply groundwater to wells or springs.

Aquifer, confined   Aquifer possessing a confining layer between the zone of saturation and the surface.

Aquifer, unconfined   Aquifer that has no confining layers between the zone of saturation and the surface.

Aquitard   See *aquiclude*.

Aromatic hydrocarbons   Hydrocarbons composed of six-membered rings, with alternating double and single carbon-carbon bonds.

Artesian   An aquifer situated between two impermeable layers and under greater than atmospheric pressure.

Asphalt   A black, bituminous material composed of hydrocarbons having a high boiling point. It is found in nature or can be prepared by the pyrolysis of coal, tar, petroleum, and lignite tar. It melts on heating and is insoluble in water.

AST   Aboveground storage tank.

ASTM   American Society for Testing and Materials.

Bacteria   Single-celled microscopic organisms. Aerobic, anaerobic, facultative anaerobes exist.

Bacteria, aerobic   Bacteria that require the presence of dissolved or molecular oxygen for their metabolic processes.

Bacteria, anaerobic   Bacteria that do not require oxygen for metabolism; growth may be hindered by the presence of oxygen.

Bacteria, facultative   Bacteria that can exist under either aerobic or anaerobic conditions.

Bentonite   A 2:1 aluminosilicate clay formed from weathering of feldspars and composed mainly of montmorillonite and beidellite. Characterized by high swelling upon wetting. Bentonite is commonly used as a landfill liner and to fill around well casings.

Benzene C_6H_6. An aromatic hydrocarbon characterized by a six-carbon ring, with alternating double and single bonds.

Berm   A constructed ridge of soil.

Binder   A cement-like material or resin used to hold particles together.

Bioaccumulation   The increase in concentration of certain substances up a food chain. An important mechanism in concentrating pesticides and heavy metals in animals at the top of a food chain.

Biocide   A substance that, when absorbed, ingested, inhaled, or otherwise consumed in small quantities, causes illness or death, or retardation of growth.

Biodegradability   Degree to which a substance may be decomposed by the enzymatic activities of microorganisms.

Biodegradation   Decomposition of a substance into simpler compounds by the action of microorganisms.

Biohazard   Biological hazard. Infectious agents presenting a risk to the well-being of humans or other biota.

Biological treatment   A process by which hazardous waste is rendered nonhazardous or is reduced in volume by the action of microorganisms.

Biomass   Living plant, animal, or microbial tissue.

Bioremediation   The use of biological processes to degrade organic contaminants in soil, sediments, strata, or water.

Biosolids   Solids derived from the treatment of municipal wastewaters. Also known as *sewage sludges*.

Biosphere   The thin sphere of life surrounding the Earth. Embraces parts of the atmosphere, the lithosphere, and the hydrosphere.

Bitumen   Naturally occurring or pyrolytically obtained dark, tarry hydrocarbons consisting almost entirely of carbon and hydrogen, with little oxygen, nitrogen, or sulfur. These hydrocarbons possess a very high boiling point.

Brownfield   An abandoned or underutilized industrial site within a city limits. Has the potential to contain a hazardous condition from wastes and other effluents.

BTEX   Benzene, toluene, ethylbenzene, and xylene. Added to automotive gasoline to improve combustibility. All are hazardous per RCRA.

Buffer   A solution that resists changes in pH.

Capping system   An impermeable system designed to reduce surface water infiltration, control gas and odor emissions, improve aesthetics, and provide a stable surface over a site.

Carcinogen   A substance capable of causing cancer.

Cation   A positively charged ion.

Cation exchange capacity   A measure of the number of equivalents of negative charge on a colloidal surface such as clay or organic matter. Often measured in units of millequivalents per 100 grams solids, or cmol/kg.

CEC   Cation exchange capacity.

Cement   A mixture of calcium aluminates and silicates made by combining lime and clay while heating.

Centigrade (Celsius)   A scale for measuring temperature, in which 100° is the boiling point of water at sea level (one atmosphere) and 0° is the freezing point.

CERCLA   Comprehensive Environmental Response, Compensation and Liability Act of 1980. CERCLA sets liability standards for environmental impairment and authorizes identification and remediation of abandoned waste sites.

CFR   Code of Federal Regulations. The U.S. government document in which all federal regulations are published. Each Title of Chapter is concerned with a different federal department agency.

Chalcophile   Minerals that crystallized in a reducing environment to form sulfide minerals.

Chelate   The bonding of a multidentate organic molecule with a metal via more than one bond. Typically a very strong association.

Chemical reduction   A process that decreases the oxidation state of an atom through the acquisition of electrons.

Chemical oxidation   A process that increases the oxidation state of an atom through loss of electrons.

Chemical precipitation   The use of chemicals to precipitate dissolved and suspended matter.

Chlorinated dibenzodioxins   A group of polychlorinated compounds characterized by two benzene rings linked by two oxygen bridges.

Chlorinated dibenzofurans   A group of polychlorinated compounds characterized by two benzene rings linked by one oxygen bridge.

Chronic effect   Adverse effects resulting from repeated doses of, or exposures to, a substance over a prolonged period of time.

Clay   Finest-grained portion of soil. Particles that exhibit plasticity within a range of water contents and that exhibit considerable strength when air-dry. The USDA definition includes all particles less than 2 μm in diameter.

Colloid   A particle measuring less than 1 μm across. Colloids tend to remain suspended in water due to Brownian movement.

Comprehensive Environmental Response, Compensation and Liability Act   Also known as the Superfund Law. Provides a mechanism for the cleanup of the most dangerous, abandoned, and uncontrolled hazardous waste sites in the United States.

Confined aquifer   Aquifer bounded above and below by impermeable strata; an aquifer containing confined groundwater.

Containment   Technologies that reduce the mobility of a contaminant plume in the subsurface via construction of physical barriers. Also utilized to reduce the flow of water through contaminated media.

Contaminant   An undesirable minor constituent that renders another substance impure.

Diffusion   Movement of molecules toward an equilibrium driven by concentration gradients (i.e., mass transfer).

Dioxins   See *chlorinated dibenzodioxins*.

Disposal drum   Drum used to overpack damaged or leaking containers of hazardous materials for shipment.

DNAPL   Dense nonaqueous phase liquid. A nonpolar (i.e., hydrophobic) liquid that is denser than water and will sink to the bottom of an aquifer if released to the subsurface.

Electrokinetics   A technology that removes metals and other contaminants from soil and groundwater by applying an electric field in the subsurface.

Endophytic   Within a green plant.

EPA   See *United States Environmental Protection Agency*.

Evapotranspiration   Return of water to the atmosphere by the combined action of evaporation and release by vegetation.

Excluder   Green plant that survives on contaminated soil by excluding particular toxins from entering the root.

Explosive limits   The minimum and maximum concentration of a substance in air which can be detonated by spark, shock, fire, etc. See *flammable limits*.

Exothermic reaction   Chemical reaction that releases energy.

Exposure   Subjection to a toxic substance or harmful chemical or physical agent through inhalation, ingestion, puncture, or absorption.

Ex situ   External to the system. For example, the excavation of soil from a site followed by treatment.

FID   Flame ionization detector.

Fermentation   Microbial process in which organic compounds serve as both electron donors and electron acceptors.

Flammable limits   The minimum and maximum concentration of flammable hydrocarbon vapors in air that will support combustion. The lowest concentration is the lower flammable limit (LFL) and the highest concentration is the upper flammable limit (UFL).

Flashpoint   The lowest temperature at which a liquid gives off enough vapor to form an ignitable mixture with air and support a flame when a source of ignition is present. Tests used to determine flashpoint are open-cup and closed-cup.

Fly ash   The finely divided residue from the combustion of coal or other solids (e.g., MSW), and which is transported from the firebox by flue gas.

Fume   Cloud of fine solid particles arising from the heating of a solid material such as lead.

Fungi   Nonphotosynthetic unicellular and multicellular microorganisms that require organic compounds for growth.

Furans   See *chlorinated dibenzofurans*.

Gas   A state of matter in which a material has very low density, can expand and contract greatly in response to changes in temperature and pressure, easily diffuses into other gases, and uniformly distributes itself throughout a container.

GC/MS   Gas chromatography/mass spectrometry. Analytical method and apparatus used for determination and quantification of organic compounds.

Groundwater   Water occurring beneath the earth's surface that fills the pores between solids such as sand, soil, or gravel.

Grout   Material injected into a soil or rock formation to change the physical characteristics of the formation. In solidification/stabilization applications, *grout* is a synonym for *binder*.

Grout curtains   Containment barrier formed by grout injection.

Halogenated organic compounds   Organic compounds that contain halogens such as chlorine, bromine, or fluorine within their structure.

Hazardous and Solid Waste Amendments   Enacted in 1984, a set of sweeping amendments to RCRA that include specifications for hazardous waste incineration systems, hazardous waste landfills, and bans on land disposal of hazardous wastes.

Hazardous material   Any substance or mixture having properties capable of producing adverse effects on public health or the environment if improperly managed.

Hazardous waste   Any material listed as such in Title 40 CFR 261, or that possesses any of the characteristics of corrosivity, ignitability, reactivity, or toxicity as defined in Title 40 CFR 261, or that is contaminated by or mixed with any of the previously mentioned materials (40 CFR 261.3).

Heavy metals   Metals of high atomic weight and density, such as lead and cadmium, that are toxic to living organisms.

HSWA   Hazardous and Solid Waste Amendments.

Humus   The stabilized organic material that remains after microbial degradation of plant and animal matter.

Hydraulic conductivity   The amount of water that can move through a cross-section of material per unit time.

Hydrophobic   Literally, *water fearing*. A compound that is insoluble in water and soluble in hydrocarbons.

Hydrophilic   Literally, *water loving*. A compound that is soluble in water and insoluble in hydrocarbons.

Hygroscopic   Property of adsorbing moisture from the air.

Hyperaccumulator   Plants that take up toxic elements and accumulate them in aboveground biomass at levels many times the usual concentrations, with little or no adverse affect to the plant

Immobilization   The reduced ability of contaminants to move through or escape from soil or waste.

Impermeability   The degree to which fluids, particularly water, cannot penetrate in significant quantities through soil or other media.

Incineration   An engineered process using controlled combustion to thermally degrade hazardous wastes. Devices commonly used for incineration include rotary kilns and liquid injectors. Incineration is used primarily for the destruction of organic wastes.

Inert (*v*)   The displacement of oxygen from a confined space such as an underground storage tank. Inerting often utilizes gases such as nitrogen or carbon dioxide.

Infiltration   The flow of fluid into a substance through porous or small openings. Commonly used to denote the flow of water into soil material.

Inorganic compounds   Chemical compounds that do not contain carbon.

Ion   An atom or molecule that has acquired a net electric charge by the loss or gain of electrons.

In situ   In place. For example, within the intact soil at a site.

Kaolinite   A common 1:1-type clay mineral having the general formula $Al_2(Si_2O_5)(OH_4)$.

Kiln dust   Fine particulate by-product of cement production or lime calcination.

Land treatment facility   A facility where hazardous waste is applied or incorporated into the soil surface. Such facilities are disposal facilities if the waste remains after closure.

Landfill   An engineered waste disposal facility. Used for disposal of MSW, hazardous wastes, or special wastes, such as fly ash. Modern landfills are required per the HSWA to possess impermeable liners and systems for leachate collection and removal.

Leachate   Any liquid, including any suspended components in the liquid, that has percolated through or drained from material during leaching.

LEL   Lower explosive limit. See *LFL*.

LFL   Lower flammable limit. The lowest concentration of a hydrocarbon vapor in air that can support ignition from a spark or flame.

Light nonaqueous phase liquid   Contaminant that is not soluble in water and is less dense than water. LNAPLs float on groundwater.

Liner   A protective layer, manufactured of natural or synthetic materials, installed along the bottom or sides of a landfill. The purpose of a liner is to reduce migration of leachate into groundwater beneath the site or laterally away from the site.

Lipophilic   Literally, *fat loving*. A nonpolar molecule that dissolves readily in hydrocarbons.

LNAPL   See *light nonaqueous phase liquid*.

LTU   Land treatment unit, or treatment cell in landfarming of contaminated soil.

LUST   Leaking underground storage tank.

Maximum contaminant level   The maximum amount of a contaminant in water detectable by standard analytical methods. The Safe Drinking Water Act requires the U.S. EPA to set MCLs in water delivered to users of public water systems.

MCL   See *maximum contaminant level.*

Metalliferous   Metal-enriched.

Metalloid   An element possessing properties of both metals and nonmetals. A semimetal; for example, arsenic or seleniuim.

Microorganisms   Microscopic organisms including bacteria, actinomycetes, fungi, some algae, slime molds, protozoa, and some multicellular organisms.

Miscible   Soluble in water.

Monolith   A freestanding solid.

Montmorillonite   A group of 2:1 aluminosilicate clay minerals characterized by a sheetlike internal molecular structure. These clays swell on wetting, shrink on drying, and possess a high cation exchange capacity.

MSW   See *municipal solid waste.*

Municipal solid waste (MSW)   Solid waste generated at residences, commercial establishments, and institutions. Also known as *domestic solid waste.*

Mutagen   An agent that permanently damages genetic material.

NAPL   Nonaqueous phase liquid.

National Priorities List (NPL)   List of CERCLA sites (40 CFR Part 300 Appendix B). Sites that pose the highest overall hazard to public health and the environment, and are given highest priority for funding for cleanup.

Neutralization   The process by which the acid or alkaline properties of a solution are reduced by addition of reagents to bring hydrogen and hydroxide concentrations to an equal value.

Nonaqueous-phase liquids (NAPLs)   Organic fluids that will partition to a separate organic phase, that is, will not dissolve into water.

Nonpolar   An uncharged molecule. A compound that is lipophilic and hydrophobic.

NPL   See *National Priorities List.*

Organic   Compounds that contain carbon in combination with one or more elements, typically derived from living organisms.

OSHA   Occupational Safety and Health Administration. Federal agency established by the Occupational Safety and Health Act of 1970.

Oxidation   Chemical reaction that involves the removal of electron(s) from an atom, thus resulting in an increase in the atom's oxidation state.

Oxidation/reduction   The change in oxidation state of an element resulting from the transfer of electrons.

Oxidizer   A chemical that initiates or promotes combustion of other materials, thereby causing fire either of itself or through the release of oxygen or other gases.

Ozone O_3, a highly reactive form of oxygen.

PAH   Polycyclic aromatic hydrocarbons. Petroleum hydrocarbons containing multiple, fused benzene rings. Several PAHs are hazardous to health and the environment.

Paraffin hydrocarbons   Hydrocarbon chains that contain no carbon-carbon multiple bonds. Paraffin hydrocarbons are also known as *saturated hydrocarbons* or *alkanes*.

Partitioning   Distribution of a solute between two or more phases.

Pathogen   Any microorganism capable of causing disease.

PCBs   See Polychlorinated biphenyls.

PCB transformer   Any transformer that contains 500 ppm PCBs or greater (40 CFR 761.3).

PCDF   Polychlorinated dibenzofurans. A class of toxic chemical compounds occurring as a thermal degradation product of PCBs.

PCP   Pentachlorophenol, a chlorinated phenol used as a wood preservative intelephone poles.

Percolation   Movement of water under hydrostatic pressure or gravity through the interstices of rock, soil, or wastes. Typically a deep movement into subsurface aquifers.

Permeability   A measure of flow of a liquid through the pore structure of a soil, strata, or waste. A function of both the fluid and solid media. If the permeating fluid is water, the permeability is termed *hydraulic conductivity*.

Petroleum   A naturally occurring mixture of several hundred hydrocarbons. Crude petroleum is refined to produce gasoline, diesel, jet fuel, and other products.

pH   A measure of the hydrogen ion concentration of an aqueous solution. A pH of 7.0 is neutral. Higher values indicate alkalinity and lower values indicate acidity.

PID   Photoionization detector.

Plume   Extent of contaminant migration in soil or groundwater.

Polar   A charged molecule; hydrophilic.

Polychlorinated biphenyls (PCBs)   Any of 209 compounds or isomers of the biphenyl molecule that have been chlorinated to various degrees. Regulated under 40 CFR 761.3.

Polymerization   Chemical reaction in which a large number of simple molecules combine to form a chainlike macromolecule. This reaction can occur with the release of heat.

Pore   A cavity or void in a solid.

Pore size distribution   The total range of pore sizes in solids. Each material has a unique pore size distribution and associated permeability

Porosity   The ratio of the volume of voids in rock, soil, etc., to the total volume of the medium.

Portland cement   A cement produced by pulverizing clinker consisting of calcium silicates and usually containing calcium sulfate.

Potentially responsible party   PRP, the individual or organization that is potentially liable for the contamination and cleanup costs of CERCLA sites.

POTW   Publicly owned treatment works. A municipal wastewater treatment plant or a sewage treatment plant.

Pozzolan   A siliceous or aluminous material, which possesses little or no cementitious value but will, in finely divided form and in the presence of moisture, chemically react with calcium hydroxide to form cementitious compounds.

ppb   Parts per billion. A unit for measuring concentration. Also $\mu g/kg$ on a solids basis, or $\mu g/L$ on a liquid basis.

ppm   Parts per million. A unit for measuring concentration. Also mg/kg on a solids basis, or mg/L on a liquid basis.

Precipitation   Process in which dissolved or suspended matter in water aggregates to form solids that separate from the liquid phase by gravity.

Purge   Displacement and removal of hydrocarbon vapors from a confined space such as an underground storage tank. Purging often utilizes gases such as nitrogen or carbon dioxide.

Pyrophoric   A chemical that will ignite spontaneously in air.

RCRA   See *Resource Conservation and Recovery Act*.

Recalcitrant   Difficult to degrade, whether in the context of chemical or biological degradation.

Redox   Oxidation-reduction.

Reduction   Chemical reaction in which an atom gains electrons, thereby decreasing its oxidation state. Opposite of an oxidation reaction.

Resource Conservation and Recovery Act (RCRA)   A comprehensive set of regulations, enacted in 1976, that address the proper management of solid and hazardous wastes.

Rhizosphere   Zone directly adjacent to the plant root. An area active biologically and chemically due to the release of compounds from the root, and the presence of microbial biomass.

Rotating biological contactor   Mechanical unit in which contaminated water is treated aerobically, via promoting the formation of microbial films on thin plastic disks that are continuously rotated through a waste stream and air.

Semimetal.   See *metalloid*.

Sheet piles   Vertical groundwater barriers constructed by driving piling, often steel or concrete, into the subsurface.

Sludge   A solid, semisolid, or liquid waste generated from a municipal, commercial, or industrial wastewater-treatment plant, water-supply treatment plant, or air-pollution control facility with the exception of specific exclusions such as the treated effluent from a wastewater-treatment plant (40 CFR 260.10)

Slurry   Fluid mixture of water and fine insoluble particles.

Slurry wall   A vertical barrier constructed in a trench and composed of a slurry material.

Smoke   An air suspension (aerosol) of particles, often originating from combustion. Smoke generally contains droplets and dry particles.

Soil flushing   Involves extraction and injection of aqueous solutions to remove contaminants from the subsurface in-situ, that is, without excavation of the contaminated materials.

Soil permeability   Ease with which water can pass through a soil.

Soil washing   A system of reacting a contaminated soil with a selected extraction solution in order to remove the contaminant. A physical or chemical separation, often carried out in a reactor vessel, that is, ex situ.

Solidification   A process in which materials are added to contaminated soil or hazardous waste to convert the soil or waste to a solid or to improve its handling and physical properties. The process may or may not involve a chemical bonding between the soil, its contaminants, and the binder.

Solidification/stabilization (S/S)   A treatment process that inhibits mobility or interaction in the environment through chemical reactions and/or physical interactions to retain or stabilize the contaminants.

Solubility   The maximum concentration of a substance dissolved in a solvent at a given temperature.

Solubility product   An equilibrium constant defined for equilibria between solids and their respective ions in solution.

Sorption   The processes by which an element, ion, or compound attaches to the surface of a particle by physicochemical processes.

S/S-treated waste   A waste liquid, slurry, or sludge that has been converted to a stable solid (granular or monolithic) by an S/S treatment process.

Stabilization   A process by which a waste is converted to a more chemically stable form. The term may include solidification, but also includes chemical changes to reduce contaminant mobility.

Storage tank   Any manufactured, nonportable, covered device used for containing pumpable hazardous wastes.

Superfund   The Comprehensive Environmental Response, Compensation and Liability Act (CERCLA). Also refers to sites listed on the National Priorities list (NPL) to respond to releases of hazardous substances and cleaning up hazardous waste sites.

Surface impoundment   Any natural depression or excavated and/or diked area built into or on the land, which is fixed, uncovered, and lined with soil or synthetic material, and is used for treating, storing, or disposing of wastes. Examples include holding ponds and aeration ponds.

Surfactant   Surface-active agent; a soluble compound that reduces the surface tension of liquids or reduces interfacial tension between two liquids or a liquid and a solid.

SW-846   Test Methods for Evaluating Solid Waste, Physical/Chemical Methods. SW-846 is a compendium of approved test methods, sampling, and monitoring guidance for use in solid waste analyses.

Synthetic liner   Landfill or lagoon liner manufactured of polymeric materials, for example, polyvinyl chloride.

TCLP   See *Toxicity Characteristics Leaching Procedure.*

Teratogen   A physical or chemical agent that causes nonhereditary birth defects.

Toxicity   Capacity of a substance to produce injury or illness through ingestion, inhalation, or absorption through any body surface.

Toxicity Characteristics Leaching Procedure (TCLP)   An analytical extraction and test to determine the leaching potential of landfilled hazardous contaminants in solid waste.

TPH   Total Petroleum Hydrocarbons. Refers to U.S. EPA Method 418.1 or 8015, which describe the procedures for quantifying the petroleum hydrocarbon content of a sample.

TSCA   See *Toxic Substances Control Act.*

Transpiration   The release of water and gases from a green plant, for eventual return to the atmosphere.

UEL   Upper explosive limit. See *UFL.*

UFL   Upper flammable limit. The highest concentration of a hydrocarbon vapor in air that will support combustion.

Underground storage tank   A tank regulated under RCRA Subtitle I to store petroleum products or hazardous materials.

UST   See *underground storage tank.*

United States Environmental Protection Agency   The main federal agency charged with setting regulations to protect the environment.

Vapor   The dispersion of liquid or solid molecules to the air at standard temperature and pressure.

Vapor density   The ratio of the vapor weight of a substance compared to that of air. If the ratio is greater than 1, the vapors are heavier and may settle to the ground. If lower than 1, the vapors will rise.

Vapor pressure   The pressure of a vapor in equilibrium with its liquid at a specified temperature. High vapor pressure indicates high volatility.

Vegetative cover   Plant growth occurring on soil, spoils, landfill covers, etc.

Vegetative uptake   Elements are taken up through the root systems of plants and, in some cases, translocated.

Vertical barrier   A rigid structure placed at the perimeter of a contaminated site. Reduces the movement of contaminated groundwater offsite or limits the flow of uncontaminated groundwater through the site.

Virus   Small particle typically composed of a strand of ribonucleic acid in a protein coat.

Viscosity   The resistance of a material to flow.

Vitrification   A technology that utilizes high-temperature treatment for reducing the mobility of metals and other contaminants in soil by incorporation in a vitreous (glasslike) monolith.

Volatile organic compound (VOC)   An organic compound with a low boiling point. Converts readily from the liquid phase to the gaseous phase at ambient conditions.

Volatile matter   Material capable of being vaporized or evaporated quickly.

Wastewater   Contaminated process water from the treatment of wastewater, soils, sediments, and sludges.

Xenobiotic   An anthropogenic compound considered foreign to the environment. From the Greek *xenos* (strange). Often recalcitrant and hazardous.

List of Acronyms and Abbreviations

ASTM	American Society for Testing Materials
BDL	below detection limit
BOD	biochemical oxygen demand
BTEX	benzene, toluene, ethylbenzene, and xylene
Btu	British thermal unit
C	carbon
°C	degrees Celsius
CCl_4	carbon tetrachloride
CERCLA	Comprehensive Environmental Response, Compensation, and Liability Act of 1980
CESQG	conditionally exempt small-quantity generator
CFR	Code of Federal Regulations
CO	carbon monoxide
CO_2	carbon dioxide
DNAPL	dense nonaqueous phase liquid
DoD	U.S. Department of Defense
DOE	U.S. Department of Energy
DOT	U.S. Department of Transportation
DRE	destruction and removal efficiency
EPA	U. S. Environmental Protection Agency
°F	degrees Fahrenheit
Fe^{o}	zero-valent iron
FID	flame ionization detector
GAC	granular activated carbon
HCl	hydrochloric acid (or hydrogen chloride)
HDPE	high-density polyethylene

H_2O_2	hydrogen peroxide
ICP	inductively coupled plasma
kg	kilogram
KPa	kilopascal
L	liter
LBP	lead-based paint
LDPE	low-density polyethylene
LDR	Land Disposal Restrictions
LEL	lower explosive limit
LNAPL	light nonaqueous phase liquid
MCL	maximum contaminant level
MSW	municipal solid waste
MTBE	methyl tert-butyl ether
NAD	nicotinamide adenine dinucleotide
NAPL	nonaqueous phase liquid
NIMBY	not in my backyard
NEPA	National Environmental Policy Act
ng	nanogram (1 gram $\times$ 10^{-9})
NO_x	nitrogen oxides
NPL	National Priorities List
OSHA	Occupational Safety and Health Administration
PAH	polycyclic aromatic hydrocarbons
PCB	polychlorinated biphenyls
PCDD	polychlorinated debenzodioxins
PCDF	polychlorinated dibenzofurans
PCE	perchloroethylene (tetrachloroethene)
PCP	pentachlorophenol
PID	photoionization detector
POTW	publicly owned treatment works
ppb	parts per billion
ppm	parts per million
PRB	permeable reactive barrier
PRP	potentially responsible parties
psi	pounds per square inch
PVC	polyvinyl chloride
RCRA	Resource Conservation Recovery Act
SG	specific gravity
SOx	sulfur oxides

SVE	soil vapor extraction
TCE	trichloroethylene
TCLP	toxicity characteristics leaching procedure
TDS	total dissolved solids
TOC	total organic carbon
TPH	total petroleum hydrocarbons
TSCA	Toxic Substances Control Act
UEL	upper explosive limit
μg	microgram
μm	micrometer
UST	underground storage tank
VC	vinyl chloride
VOC	volatile organic compound

Index

About the Author

John Pichtel is a professor of natural resources and environmental management at Ball State University in Muncie, Indiana. He is a certified hazardous materials manager. Dr. Pichtel holds memberships in the Institute of Hazardous Materials Managers, the Sigma Xi Scientific Society, the American Society of Agronomy, and the Indiana Academy of Science.

Dr. Pichtel received a PhD in environmental quality/agronomy from the Ohio State University in 1987. He joined the faculty of Ball State University, where he has conducted research in remediation of contaminated sites, environmental chemistry, and hazardous waste management. Dr. Pichtel was twice awarded a Fulbright Fellowship. He was appointed docent in remediation science at the Tampere University of Technology in Finland. He has served as a consultant in field remediation projects, and has conducted environmental assessments and remediation research in the United States, the United Kingdom, Ireland, Finland, and Poland.

Dr. Pichtel enjoys painting, sculpture, gardening, and the study of world history. He lives in Indiana with his wife, son, and daughter.